DATE DUE

AP 29 '98			
MY '04			

DEMCO 38-296

PEOPLE, POWER, AND POLITICS

PEOPLE, POWER, AND POLITICS

An Introduction to Political Science

THIRD EDITION

John C. Donovan
Richard E. Morgan
Christian P. Potholm
Marcia A. Weigle
of
Bowdoin College

Littlefield Adams Quality Paperbacks

LITTLEFIELD ADAMS QUALITY PAPERBACKS

a division of Rowman & Littlefield Publishers, Inc.
4720 Boston Way, Lanham, Maryland 20706

British Cataloging in Publication Information Available

Library of Congress Cataloging-in-Publication Data

People, power, and politics / by John C. Donovan,
Richard E. Morgan, Christian P. Potholm, Marcia A.
Weigle. — 3rd ed.
    p.   cm.
Rev. ed. of: People, power, and politics / John C.
Donovan, Richard E. Morgan, Christian P. Potholm. 2nd
ed. © 1986.
Includes bibliographical references and index.
1. Political science.   I. Donovan, John C.
JA66.D66   1993
320—dc20   92–36210 CIP

ISBN 0–8226–3025–7 (pbk. : alk. paper)

Printed in the United States of America

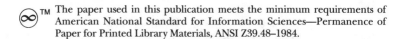 The paper used in this publication meets the minimum requirements of
American National Standard for Information Sciences—Permanence of
Paper for Printed Library Materials, ANSI Z39.48–1984.

Contents

Preface   xi

PART I   THE LANGUAGE OF POLITICS

1   Coming to Grips with Politics   3
People, Power, and Politics   3
At the Top of the 1990s   4
The Varieties of Conflict   8
Politics as the Father of Lies   10
The Fog of Rhetoric   12
The Challenge of Analysis   13
The Plan for What Follows   14
Notes   15
Suggested Readings   16

2   The Evolution of Political Thought   19
The Concept of the State   19
Basic Terminology   22
Classical Political Theory   24
The Middle Ages   30
The Rise of Liberalism   32
*Box 2-1. The Protestant Reformation and the Rise of
    Liberalism*   34
The Marxist Challenge to Liberalism   36
Box 2-2. Karl Marx   37
Summary   39
Notes   40
Suggested Readings   41

3   Classifying Political Systems   43
A World of Differences   43
Primitive Political Systems   43
Classifying Modern Political Systems   45
Constitutionalism   50
Box 3-1. Aspects of Law   51

Democracy   52
Further Refinements   53
Those Blockbuster Words   57
Summary   61
Notes   62
Suggested Readings   63

PART II   POLITICS AND SOCIETY

4   **Public Opinion, Polling, and Political Culture**   67
Who Is the Public?   67
Rejuvenational Capability   68
National Character   72
Public Opinion   75
Box 4-1. Soviet Opinion   77
Box 4-2. The Poll Gorbachev Hated, from Argumenty i Fakty
   80
*Box 4-3. Voices from Moscow: What They Say about Their
   System*   82
Box 4-4. Perestroika in the USSR   83
Box 4-5. RU-486: The Answer?   85
Summary   88
Notes   88
Suggested Readings   89

5   **Interest Groups and Political Parties**   91
Politics as Process   91
Linkage Mechanisms: Interest Groups and Political Parties
   93
Political Linkages—The United Kingdom   96
Political Linkages—France   102
Box 5-1. 1988 French Presidential Elections   109
Box 5-2. 1988 French Legislative Elections   110
Political Linkages—The USSR   111
Summary   118
Notes   119
Suggested Readings   120

6   **Elections, Campaigns, and Voting**   123
The Universality of Elections?   123
Elections   124

Box 6-1. Affirmative Action and Abigail Thernstrom 127
Campaigns 128
Ballot Measures 131
Box 6-2. Ballot Measures 132
Voting 133
Summary 138
Notes 138
Suggested Readings 139

PART III STRUCTURES OF GOVERNMENT

7 The Age of the Executive? 143
Leadership in a World of Change and Conflict 143
Transactional and Transformational Leaderships 145
Conditions Conducive to Executive Leadership 145
Constraints on Executive Leadership 150
Box 7-1. Taming the Prince 152
Ronald Reagan—Case Study in Executive Leadership 154
Reexamining Presidential Leadership: The Prime-Time
    Presidency 155
Iron Triangles and Issue Networks 157
The Iron Lady and Her Civil Servants—Case Study 158
Box 7-2. The Long Career of Margaret Thatcher 160
Summary 162
Notes 163
Suggested Readings 164

8 Legislative Assemblies 167
Why Study Legislatures? 167
Basic Functions of Legislatures 168
The British Parliament 170
The Congress of the United States 173
What National Legislatures Really Do 178
Summary 183
Notes 184
Suggested Readings 186

9 Bureaucracies and Politics 189
The Bureaucracy Problem 189
Bureaucracy as Organization 191
Bureaucratic Politics 192
Box 9-1. FDR's View of Bureaucracies 194

Bureaucracy in the United Kingdom   198
Box 9-2. Whitehall: A Village   201
Political Style and Bureaucratic Environment   204
Growth of Bureaucracies   208
Summary   214
Notes   215
Suggested Readings   217

10 The Roles of Courts and Judges   219
Courts and Rights   219
The Evolution of Courts   220
Courts as Mechanisms for Settling Disputes   221
Courts as Definers of Law   223
Courts as Intragovernmental Arbiters   224
Courts as Mechanisms of Social Control   226
Courts as Mechanisms of Political Control   228
Courts as Policymakers   230
Summary   237
Notes   237
Suggested Readings   239

PART IV   PROBLEMS OF POLITICAL CHANGE

11 International Relations and the Cold War Arms Race   243
Goals and Goal Formation   243
The Judgment of Goals   252
The Cold War Arms Race   253
Summary: Ending the Arms Race   261
*Box 11-1. The START Treaty: New Limits for Strategic
    Forces*   262
Notes   263
Suggested Readings   264

12 Superpower Relations   265
The Politics of Nations   266
The Postwar World: Differing Views   267
U.S. Policies Toward the Soviet Union   270
Soviet Policies Toward the United States   272
Box 12-1. The Lithuanian Dilemma   273
Détente   275
Gorbachev: The Great Change   278

Box 12-2. New Political Thinking: Gorbachev's Foreign Policy Agenda 279
The New Special Relationship 279
Box 12-3. Domestic Incentives for Gorbachev's New Political Thinking 280
The Breakup of the Soviet Empire—Regional Impact 282
The Breakup of the Soviet Empire—International Impact 286
Summary 289
Notes 290
Suggested Readings 291

13 **Stability and Change**   293
The Forces of Change 293
Stages of Societal Development 295
Political Leadership and the Forces of Change 301
Box 13-1. Capabilities Analysis 307
Political Devolution 308
Summary 309
Notes 309
Suggested Readings 311

14 **Change in a Communist Political System: The USSR**   313
The Nature of Change in Political Systems 314
The Case of the Soviet Union 314
The Period of Stagnation and Pressures for Change 316
The Gorbachev Era I: Reform from Above 321
The Gorbachev Era II: Revolution from Below 328
A Failed Coup and the End of Empire 334
A New Russian Democracy? 336
Summary 338
Notes 339
Suggested Readings 340

15 **Conclusion: Seeing Politics Whole**   341
Notes 343

Index   345

About the Authors   357

Preface

People, Power, and Politics has shown a lot of staying power, or "legs" in the parlance of the media. Professors and students all across the country have called and written to indicate how refreshing and substantial they found the previous editions. The authors are most grateful for this ongoing support and for the confidence shown in the work, especially by our editor, Bert Lummis. He has helped us immeasurably in ensuring a smooth transition following the death of John Donovan, who was the inspiration for the original project. John's passing left a tremendous hole in the book and in our lives, and we are only now beginning to fill both.

In addition, the third edition has been delayed by the onrush of events in the former Soviet Union and Eastern Europe. More than anything else, we tried to design a book that did not "chase after headlines," and we have been gratified by the extent to which the concepts of the first edition have stood the test of time. Nevertheless, it seemed prudent to let events in what had been the Soviet sphere of influence unfold and to see what amendments, if any, they ultimately offered for developmental and revolutionary theory.

Both remaining authors felt some distance from those momentous changes and saw a need to add a Soviet expert's contribution to those chapters that focus on explaining them. We are fortunate, therefore, to be joined now by our colleague Professor Marcia A. Weigle, one of the best younger experts on the countries of the former Soviet system and other postcommunist regimes. Her contribution of chapters dealing with these matters, and her suggestions and criticisms and additions throughout, have strengthened the book immensely.

We would also like to thank others who put in long and productive hours making this the best of the three editions. Mary Inman, Jennifer James, Curt Perrin, and especially Jessie Lynn Guptill did outstanding research work and helped to make sure we did not overlook important ongoing dimensions of a political nature.

Once again, kudos to Mrs. Virginia Linkovich, whose excellent typing, essential proofreading, and sunny disposition made our jobs so much easier. A special thanks as well to Carrie Ciaccio who worked so long and hard on the copyediting process. She has a great future in publishing.

Richard E. Morgan
Christian P. Potholm
Marcia A. Weigle
Brunswick, Maine
September 1992

Part I

The Language of Politics

1

Coming to Grips with Politics

One of the most treasured insights of the modern poll is: ideas have no consequences, nor do words. The successful poll chooses words not for their denotation, but for their connotation. In modern political discourse words have only flavor and aroma—no colonies and no consequences.

—R. Emmett Tyrrell

The politician is an honest man,
He tells his lies by rote.
The journalist makes up his lies,
And takes you by the throat.

—W. B. Yeats

PEOPLE, POWER, AND POLITICS

As our title suggests, politics involves the exercise of power by some people over other people. "Power" is one of the most important and one of the most elusive concepts in the vocabulary of social science. Everybody uses the word frequently, but usually without considering precisely what they mean by it. Is the American president the "most powerful" chief executive in the world because the president commands the military establishment with the greatest destructive force backed by the world's largest and most highly developed economy? Or is the American president among the weakest of chief executives because of the constitutional system of separation of powers and checks and balances that often results in majorities in Congress being unresponsive to the president's leadership?

In this book, *power* is understood to mean the capacity of a person to move other persons by persuasion, fear, respect for authority, or other inducements to behave in accordance with his or her priorities and objectives.[1] This can be accomplished by means as diverse as reason, physical coercion, inspired rhetoric, and the promise of material reward—the time-honored "campaign contribution" or "something for expenses." And power is characteristically exercised to achieve desired ends or goals. *Policy* consists of the objectives in the service of which those who possess power are prepared to exert it. Policymakers are those who define the goals and objectives for which power is to be exercised.

It is a basic reality of human existence that, from the simplest level of the clan or village to the more advanced level of the nation-state and, indeed, to the international arena, persons and groups and countries do not agree on policy. In fact, they bitterly disagree (usually with utter self-righteousness) over the objectives for which power should be wielded. Furthermore—human societies being what they are—different persons and groups and countries possess different and fractional sorts of power. Thus, power is pitted against power in the struggle over outcomes or policy. People desire mutually exclusive ends and seek to subordinate the ends that others favor to their own favored ends by securing and then wielding power. Seeking to exercise power in the pursuit of policy objectives is what we mean by *politics*. And the essence of politics is conflict.

There is nothing sinister or threatening about this, although many varieties of politics observed in the world today are both threatening and sinister. All that is implied by this view of politics as conflict is that it is an inevitable feature of the human condition and inevitably problematic. Conflict can be managed in reasonable, bloodless, and participatory ways as well as by the sword and the bribe. And although following a coherent line of policy (whether in a city council or at the international negotiating table) requires choosing the ends favored by some people over the ends favored by other people, the ways of doing this vary from the highly civilized to the purely barbaric.

AT THE TOP OF THE 1990s

Political change rarely organizes itself into neat chronological packages. Nonetheless, it is natural for us, looking backward, to attempt to organize and make sense of our political experience by identifying certain major changes with the decades in which they took place. Thus, in America, we have thought of the 1930s as a period of dramatic institutional change at the national level and the launching of a limited welfare state. Similarly, the 1960s have gone down as a decade of political dislocation and protest, and the 1980s as a time in which more conservative impulses surfaced in the American polity: we learned the word *yuppie* and bandied jokes about 23-year-old stockbrokers and BMWs.

But it is a good bet that the decade of the 1990s will be identified with even more dramatic change. For as the 1990s opened, it was clear that political patterns that had existed not just for the preceding decade, but since the middle of the twentieth century, were being swept away. What was unclear was the precise shape of the new things to come. The changes that opened the 1990s were immensely hopeful. Things that in 1980 had been taken as almost immutable political realities, such as the Berlin Wall and the subjugation of Eastern Europe by the power of the Soviet Union, were simply gone. And change within the Soviet successor state— Russia—began to move, at least incrementally, in the direction of pluralism and greater respect for basic human rights.

But promising—even inspiring—as the changes of 1990 were, they did not usher in a brave new world of tranquility and cooperation. Indeed, while superpower tensions (between the United States–NATO and the Soviet Union–Warsaw Pact) abated, (indeed, the Warsaw Pact and NATO were already being deemphasized as military alliances), new patterns of conflict were emerging that, while perhaps not as cataclysmically threatening as the old, were very serious indeed.

In a very real sense, what was happening as the 1990s began was the decline of certain major conflicts and their replacement by other newer conflicts that analysts were forced to rush to get in focus and understand. Politics, as we have suggested, is about conflict; and neither the rise of Mikhail Gorbachev nor the opening of the Berlin Wall nor the accession of noncommunist governments in Eastern Europe meant the end of conflict or the end of politics or, as one observer prematurely suggested, the end of "history."

This last suggestion came from Francis Fukuyama, a political scientist working for the State Department.[2] By "history" Fukuyama meant the struggle between popularly based democratic governments and authoritarian governments that had been the central conflict of world political history since the seventeenth century. Authoritarianism is finished; this was Fukuyama's message in a nutshell. Fukuyama recognized that, while particular authoritarian regimes continue to exist (and may for some time), democratization is triumphant and the future will see a kind of protracted mopping-up operation in which retrograde authoritarian systems are sooner or later dismantled. Certainly the events in Europe, and the transition of a number of Latin American nations from military to elected civilian rule as the 1990s opened, gave plausibility to Fukuyama's argument. But even if one accepts that the decline of authoritarianism is irreversible, that does not mean the end of political conflict—indeed, of bitter political conflict erupting into war. Here we shall be concerned precisely with the new patterns of conflict and politics that are emerging as the old, post–World War II, twentieth-century political order comes to an end and a new one painfully, and by fits and starts, emerges.

If anyone doubts the persistence of politics as conflict, she or he should consider the events of the first week of January 1990, when we began writing this chapter. In Romania—so recently swept by a popular revolution that had toppled the 20-year dictatorship of Nikolai Ceausescu— officials of the old Communist party scrambled to sever their ties and to announce that the party was dissolving itself. A special election, they announced, would be held in April. Reformers, however, were wary that elements of the old ruling elite would simply reconsolidate under a new name and with "new management." The demand in the streets was for all former communists to be out of government, if not imprisoned. And indeed these fears seemed to take on plausibility when viewed against the background of events in East Germany. There, after a popular revolution that was virtually bloodless, a reconstituted Communist party under the leadership of Gregor Gysi appeared to be rallying in an effort to maintain its hold on power. The prime minister, Hans Modrow, had proposed creating a new domestic security force to replace the one that had been disbanded in disgrace after the popular uprising; and the Liberal Democratic, Christian Democratic, and National Democratic parties, which were linked with the communists in the coalition government that was only two months old, threatened to withdraw from that government. (Widespread outrage, including the sacking of the old security police headquarters by a mob, forced the abandonment of the plan for a new force; but communist spokespersons referred darkly to the rise of "neo-Nazi" forces, and division increased within reform factions.)

In Latin America there was widespread adverse reaction to the U.S. military intervention in Panama that had resulted in the deposition and arrest of General Manuel Noriega. Although there was little sympathy for Noriega, there was resentment at what was perceived as "Yankee interventionism"; the carefully crafted cooperation between the United States and the South American countries in combating the international drug trade seemed in danger of collapse.

On the second day of the year 1990, David N. Dinkins was sworn in as mayor of New York City, and Vaclav Havel assumed the presidency of a newly noncommunist Czechoslovakia. Despite the fact that the one—Mayor Dinkins—was a politician of long experience and the other—President Havel—a playwright and intellectual who found himself at the center of a popular political convulsion, both gave the strong impression of persons of great decency faced with awesome, perhaps impossible, jobs. Mayor Dinkins was forced to begin his administration by announcing a delay in the hiring of new police officers, after he had campaigned on the necessity of adding to the force. And President Havel, after a few weeks in office, commented that his time in jail—he had been imprisoned by the former communist government—had been excellent preparation for serving as president.

In the Soviet Union, the stresses of emerging nationalism cast a shadow not only over President Gorbachev's program of *perestroika* (economic, social, and governmental restructuring), but over the very existence of the Union of Soviet Socialist Republics. Moscow announced that troops were being rushed to the border between Soviet Azerbaijan and Iran, where crowds of Moslem Azerbaijani nationalists had been conducting sustained demonstrations for an open border. (For months before, Azerbaijanis had been slipping into a state of virtual civil war with their Armenian Christian neighbors.) With large Moslem populations in several of its member republics, the Soviet leadership could not have been attracted to the idea of an open border with the militant Islamic republic in Iran. Meanwhile, Gorbachev was preparing to leave for a three-day trip to Lithuania in an attempt to persuade that member republic to abandon, or at least postpone, its demands for complete independence from the Soviet Union. Nor was it only the other Baltic republics of Latvia and Estonia that were poised to break away if Lithuania succeeded; the Ukraine—perhaps the most important of the member republics after the Russian Republic itself—was expected to make a strong bid for independence if any of the smaller units were let go.

So many things in what was then the Soviet Union were unsettled, and the pace of change so great ("out of control," some said), that the ultimate success and political survival of Gorbachev himself were already in doubt during that first week of 1990. *Daedalus,* the respected quarterly published by the American Academy of Arts and Sciences, appeared with an article—attributed only to "Mr. Z"—predicting that Gorbachev could not succeed in reforming the Soviet economy while at the same time preserving the Communist party as an institution.[3] The nom de plume *Mr. Z* recalled the famous "Mr. X" article in which George Kennan, then an official of the U.S. State Department, outlined the argument for the "containment doctrine" that became the basis of American foreign policy for the next four decades. And Mr. Z had a clear message for Western policymakers: heroic measures to help Gorbachev would only be counterproductive. For as long as the preservation of the CPSU (Communist Party of the Soviet Union) was central to Gorbachev's effort he could not succeed—since party rule was the very thing responsible for Soviet economic backwardness. Aid to Gorbachev would only prop up the rule of the party and postpone the possibility of real change for the Russian people.

Nor were national divisions troubling only in the Soviet Union. The newly emancipated nations of Eastern Europe—notably Bulgaria with a significant Turkish (Moslem) population, and Czechoslovakia and Hungary riven by ancient ethnic hostilities—were beginning to understand that, however distasteful communism rule had been, it had kept the lid on conflict between nationalities. Now, regimes seeking to establish themselves as democratic and pluralist would have to cope with these forces, newly unleashed. Observers in the West worried and remembered how it was that the word *balkanization* had entered the language of political analysis to denote fragmentation and intractable ethnic strife.

From Panama came the news that Captain Linda Bray, commander of a military policy company, had become the first woman to lead U.S. troops in a combat operation—against a kennel holding guard dogs used by the Panamanian Defense Forces of General Manuel Noriega. The original report had it that the kennel was "heavily defended" and "three PDF [Panamanian Defense Force] men were killed." Opponents of the U.S. prohibition against women in the armed forces being assigned to combat roles were heartened, and Representative Patricia Schroeder announced that she would introduce legislation to suspend the "combat exclusion" for a trial period of four years. The *New York Times* published several editorials, one with the title "Onward, Women Soldiers." By the end of the week, however, the Pentagon had scaled back the story. Captain Bray, by radio, had ordered her troops at the scene to fire a warning shot and demand the surrender of the PDF soldiers holding the kennel. These U.S. troops were then fired upon and a Spanish-speaking U.S. soldier, with a bullhorn, threatened to call in artillery. At that point the Panamanians apparently fled into the woods, and Captain Bray later arrived on the scene to take possession of the kennel. There was no confirmation that anyone had been killed, but the controversies produced by the story were bruising enough.

On Thursday, General Manuel Noriega, who had been holed up in the Vatican Embassy in Panama City for 11 days, surrendered to U.S. soldiers and was immediately arrested and flown to Miami to face a criminal indictment for drug dealing. But while this resolved a conflict in one sense (since the capture of Noriega had been a prime objective of the U.S. intervention in Panama), it opened another. The new conflict was legal, with experts arguing about the propriety of the general's arrest and its possible impact on a future trial, and political commentators speculating about the possibility that Noriega would stonewall prosecution by demanding highly classified CIA and other U.S. documents as part of his defense and by threatening to reveal information he gleaned from U.S. and other Western intelligence services with whom he collaborated in the 1970s and early 1980s.

The week ended with more tensions developing between the United States and Latin America when Colombia withdrew its support from a plan—already, apparently, under way—for U.S. Naval Forces to patrol its coast for drug runners. And there was more bad news from Argentina—one of the South American countries that had recently emerged from military dictatorship—where President Carlos Saul Menem struggled desperately with runaway inflation that threatened not only the economy, but the future of the fragile democracy.

But while politics is conflict (and *war* is the pursuit of political conflict by violent means), the patterns of political conflict are constantly changing. And very occasionally, these pattern changes are so swift and dramatic that observers have to struggle desperately not to be trapped in old ways of thinking and to improvise new ways.

THE VARIETIES OF CONFLICT

It is important to note that the political conflicts that surfaced in the news in the first week of 1990 were of different but interrelated kinds. In

Romania, the struggle was *factional,* between those who were part of the former ruling caste (the Communist party) and multiple reform factions propelled into prominence by events leading to the collapse of the Ceausescu regime. The former group (the old communists) was struggling to cling to some part of its rapidly passing power. The insurgent factions sought to paint the "survivors" in the darkest colors, and to call for purges and a return to the death penalty for those implicated in last-ditch attempts to perpetuate the Ceausescu regime by force. The insurgents themselves sought to gain undisputed control over the country and to exclude altogether the remnant of their former oppressors. But the reformers were divided; the surviving former communists were not. The reformers lacked knowledge and experience of running the country; the survivors of the former elite knew how.

The conflict between the United States and many of its Latin American neighbors over the intervention in Panama was obviously a case of *international* conflict. And it was not at all a simple one. The Latin nations were reacting out of an accumulated sense of grievance against the United States as the "Colossus to the North," insensitive to the sovereignty of its American neighbors and ready to disregard that sovereignty callously in its own national interest. This was complicated by the fact that some Latin nations—notably Mexico, Colombia, and Peru—were under great pressure from Washington to act effectively against drug producers and traffickers within their borders. Indeed, at the very time the U.S. intervention in Panama was being mounted, there were far-ranging joint operations in preparation between the United States and Latin countries for dealing with drugs. This U.S. pressure to join in antidrug operations was also a source of tension. Some Latin American political leaders saw their countries as being dragooned into elaborate antidrug effort when the U.S. drug crises really resulted from the existence within the United States of a lucrative market. "Why should the Yankees come to us to reduce supply when they do so little to reduce demand?" And just beneath the surface of this dispute was the festering problem of the huge debt owed by Latin American countries to U.S. banks. This fueled both an economic resentment and a hunger to refinance the debt so as to preserve access to U.S. capital markets. And on the "Yankee" side, there was also—just beneath the surface—a profound unhappiness with the Latin American nations that accumulated during the Reagan administration, for not being willing to take sufficiently vigorous action to ensure collective security in the hemisphere, especially with reference to the former Sandinista regime in Nicaragua.

In the Soviet Union, the conflicts unleashed by Mikhail Gorbachev's loosening of state and party controls were ethnic or *communal*—ancient hatreds, with roots running back many centuries. The claims of Lithuanians and Azerbaijanis and Armenians and Ukranians might be framed in the modern rhetoric of national self-determination, but no one could doubt that more fundamental cultural and religious factors were actually fueling the conflicts. And to make matters worse, early 1990 saw an upsurge of Great Russian nationalism, with attendant anti-Semitism.

By contrast, the comparatively minor flap in the United States over the exploits of Captain Bray in Panama reflects a more subtle kind of conflict: conflict between *interest groups*. The law excluding women from combat is one of the few remaining important legal distinctions between men and women in the United States. Feminist interest groups and their allies want it eliminated—not because of eagerness to volunteer for front-line duty, but because of its symbolic significance in assuming that there are some things women cannot or should not do. Critics of feminism want the combat exclusion kept, for the same symbolic reasons. And the American military establishment is divided: the Pentagon wants to be able to utilize women soldiers freely to ease its job of keeping units up to strength in the context of an all-volunteer force; traditionalists fear that women in combat or near combat positions will make it harder to develop the warrior spirit and small-unit cohesion necessary for success in battle. This is why on editorial pages, in journals of opinion, and around seminar tables there will be debate over what did or did not happen at that Panamanian dog kennel—with the contending sides seeking to impose their respective verbal imprints as the reality of the case. (The issue was to resurface with a vengeance later in the year with the major U.S. military deployment in Saudi Arabia.)

Finally, the conflict over whether and how General Noriega can receive a fair trial in the United States reflects deep-seated *philosophical* or *ideological* differences between people. What are the demands of law and justice? Is departure from regular, familiar procedures always to be reprobated? Or do the demands of justice from time to time require a legal system to show flexibility in procedure? These are not American questions unique to the United States, but questions that arise in all systems that attempt to take the rule of law seriously.[4]

POLITICS AS THE FATHER OF LIES

When people or groups are involved in conflict, words become weapons. This is not because the people involved are dishonest or are striving to deceive the public. It is simply that the object of the political actor is to win (or at least to survive), and this is a very different enterprise from dispassionate analysis that seeks to perceive and present issues with all of their subtleties and "shades of grey" intact.

Conflict—the stuff of politics—takes place not only among self-interested groups and nations, but also among alternative visions of what is "good." An issue that illustrates this use of words as weapons in such a conflict involves the American debate over the generation of nuclear power.

No one would deny that ensuring people's safety against the radiation hazards resulting from a serious accident in a nuclear power plant is good. The risk of such an accident is very small, but the potential for injury is very high.

Yet the country needs power. As the 1990s began, American dependence on foreign oil was once again on the rise. The combination of conservation, solar energy, and synthetic fuels cannot take up the slack for many years. And in any case, the reduction in living standards, economic growth, and military strength that would result from this approach may make it unacceptable. With the high cost and finite supply of oil, the only economically viable alternative to nuclear power is coal-fired generation. The risk factor for coal power is the reverse of that for nuclear power. The risk is certain, but the numbers of dead and injured will be hundreds per year rather than the thousands per occurrence conceivable in a nuclear mishap.

Different persons and groups assess the risks differently. Intellectually honest proponents of "conservation–solar–synfuels" admit the depressing economic consequences that would flow from adoption of their alternative. (They may even rejoice in the prospect of more austere lifestyles imposed on Americans after a half-century of living "too high.") Similarly, honest proponents of nuclear power recognize the risk of accident and admit that the dangers of low-level radiation are not completely understood. These proponents, however, reluctantly prefer the immediately cheaper electricity and physically cleaner environment that nuclear power offers. Candid proponents of coal power emphasize the terrible consequences of a serious nuclear accident, stress the unknown hazards of low-level radiation, and reluctantly prefer the certain annual deaths and environmental degradation that the choice of coal power inflicts.[5]

There is no clear right and wrong in this matter. It is a conflict among persons with differing temperaments and perceptions of reality and among groups with economic stakes to defend—the power companies on the one hand, and the growing numbers of small but ambitious alternative-energy firms on the other.

But in the real-life political arena, none of the participants in the conflict behaves in an intellectually honest fashion. After all, who will go before a large audience or a TV camera to say, "In this lousy world, my unattractive option is only slightly preferable to the depressing option favored by my opponent"? Instead, the participants exaggerate the advantages of their own positions and the disadvantages of their opponents' positions. They shade the truth—first, for their audiences, and then, in many cases, for themselves.

So, the level of verbal pollution rises. The strident "No Nukes" folk denounce nuclear power as the work of the devil, and the technocrats reassure us in soothing tones that the risks of nuclear power are really trivial and that anyone who cannot see this is a superstitious fool. Meanwhile, the politicians carefully weave their way through the conflict. In the best style of democratic politics, they bend one way on Monday, another way on Tuesday, and claim to be leading boldly on Wednesday.

THE FOG OF RHETORIC

The political landscape, like all battlefields, is perpetually obscured by a fog of rhetoric. This results in the sometimes systematic—but sometimes quite unconscious—distortion of reality; it confuses us about what is actually going on. The candidate, the prime minister, and the interest-group lobbyist are all using language to evoke in their audience the feelings and reactions that will work to their particular advantages. Furthermore, journalists covering politics often compound the distortion of reality that their subjects engage in. This is because journalists are partially trapped by the words they must report and are often emotional participants in the political process, with their own biases to advance. Journalists can easily end up compounding the distortions of their subjects by distortions of their own.[6]

The result is that the public discussion of politics—whether carried on by elected officials, government bureaucrats, or journalists—tends to take place in a highly stylized form. It is often "against the rules" for anyone to say precisely what is on his or her mind. Verbal conventions of varying degrees of rigidity must be observed. One extreme occurred in the former Soviet Union and still occurs in the People's Republic of China, where certain key phrases are manipulated to communicate things that are not stated explicitly.[7]

To be involved in political conflict is to use words as weapons. Today we speak of media consultants' being "spin doctors," as if there were something new about the phenomenon; but there is not. To act politically is to try to put your verbal stamp—the interpretation that will advance your policy goals—on what is always an ambiguous reality. What may be new today, at least in America, is the brazenness and novelty of the euphemisms and neologisms (new words, often made up for political purposes) that are now being pressed into service along all parts of the political spectrum. In the Reagan years we had "revenue enhancement" for taxes; and "affirmative action" for racial and sexual preferences goes back to Lyndon Johnson's administration. Applicants are not rejected, but "deselected"; things are not reduced, but "downsized." While it may be tempting to write this off as harmless silliness (which some of it certainly is), that would be a mistake. For, as William Lutz, a professor of English at Rutgers University, reminds us, it is language designed to alter our perception of reality. The inventing of new words and terms often is a way of seeking to direct our thinking by encouraging us to forget the baggage of familiar accumulated meaning and nuance attached to common words and terms that have a signifying history—a track record of use and serviceability within our literary culture. They should instantly arouse the suspicion of the serious analyst of politics.[8]

Often, the words and metaphors and catch phrases that betray us are part of our popular culture. They are uncritically transmitted from generation to generation as shopworn clichés of war and peace. The word *war* seems to denote the worst of all human situations—terrible and undesirable in the extreme. *Peace,* on the other hand, denotes the best—the ultimately desirable state of affairs. But we know that, for particular groups and nations at particular times, there may be outcomes less desirable than war. Slavery and genocide are realities that must also enter into our judgments. We also know that war is sometimes better avoided by preparing to wage it than by "seeking peace." In the late twentieth century, the sharp eighteenth-century distinction between being at war and being at peace has broken down. But our simplistic use of the terms continues, especially in sloganeering. Therefore, the Strategic Air Command, whose stock-in-trade was massive airborne violence, chose its motto *Peace Is Our Profession* because it *sounded* so nice.

THE CHALLENGE OF ANALYSIS

What has been said thus far does not overstate the difficulties facing the student in beginning the study of politics. Be assured, however, that the enterprise is possible and eminently worth pursuing. It is certainly true that a reasonable person is well advised to believe nothing and no one concerning politics until he or she has looked at the problem from a variety of perspectives and in a calm and reflective fashion. But the profoundly cynical view—that everyone is an interested participant so there can be no evenhanded analysis—is not justified.

Certainly all who comment on politics have an interest and a stake in the ongoing conflicts. No analysis is ever completely neutral. But it is possible for one who is determined to *observe* politics to describe reality and not to have that description completely driven by political bias. What is important in such analysis is a commitment of overriding moral significance: the commitment to use language to portray reality—in all of its complicated crosscurrents and variations—rather than to simplify it into an appealing picture that will promote one's own conception of the good. Philosophers throughout the ages, scholars with a primary commitment to careful description and accurate explanation of reality, along with the best of political journalists, have left a rich heritage of vocabulary and concept to enable you to penetrate the confusions and distortions that cloud perceptions of contemporary public affairs.[9]

It is often mistakenly assumed that political sophistication lies in adopting certain fashionable positions on public issues. This is nonsense. A politically sophisticated person is precisely one who is not imprisoned by the jargon used unreflectingly in contemporary politics. That is, such a person possesses his or her own intellectual resources—a political vocabulary and a stock of concepts for political analysis—to use in describing reality independently of the self-interested and ritualized distortions that fill the air.

Another common misconception about political sophistication is that it involves knowing huge quantities of factual information. Now it is certainly true that, no matter how good someone's general education, no one is worth listening to if he or she knows *nothing* of what he or she is talking about at the moment. Hence the intellectually interesting analyst-commentator must have control of some factual information. But in most cases these threshold levels of information are not terribly high. It is not necessary, for example, to understand the physics of multiple-targeted reentry vehicles (MIRVs) in order to understand the significance of such weapons in the strategic balance of power between the former Soviet Union and the United States. It is not necessary to know the speed of a cruise missile to know that it is a very slow-moving, low-level weapon. General factual knowledge is usually the more important sort for political analysis; but if one lacks the mental apparatus for political analysis, no amount of factual information in any degree of detail can produce more than miserable confusion.

THE PLAN FOR WHAT FOLLOWS

The goal of this book is to provide you with the "mental apparatus," the intellectual equipment for penetrating the verbal confusions and distortions of contemporary politics. We hope to help you make your own assessments of political reality and of the significance of the roles that actors play on the political stage—to move with you, the reader, beyond the simplicities of the TV and newspaper commentators. As already suggested, two sorts of resources are necessary to develop skill in political analysis: first, a vocabulary that provides more subtle and reliable terminology for political analysis than is available in the political marketplace; and second, the ability to use this vocabulary to develop concepts of political analysis that move us beyond the oversimplifications of today's news.

To accomplish this, the rest of Part I (Chapters 2 and 3) is devoted to what might be called the building blocks of political sophistication: vocabulary and concepts. We shall survey the history of political thought and the development of the discipline of political science, touching on major figures and ideas. We shall then examine different types of political systems and develop a vocabulary for identifying and discussing the various components of those systems. We shall also explore the pitfalls involved in using such emotionally powerful but ambiguous terms as "freedom," "equality," and "justice."

Part II (Chapters 4, 5, and 6) deals with what might be called the "communicative" dimensions of political systems. In all political systems, processes operate by which political allegiances and expectations are passed from one generation to the next. Mechanisms exist to allow the expression of public opinion and to communicate citizens' desires and needs to the decision-making apparatus of the regime. And in political systems characterized by electoral competition for governmental office, methods must exist to organize the electoral process. In these chapters we will look at interest groups, political parties, the mechanics of political socialization, and the formation of public opinion. We shall also touch on electoral politics and the organization of elections.

In Part III of the book (Chapters 7–10), our concern shifts to the structures of government that are common to modern political systems. Although these structures exhibit many subtle and sometimes misleading differences in terminology and function in different political systems, it is useful to consider the ways in which executive leadership, legislative assemblies, bureaucracy, and court systems operate.

Finally, in Part IV (Chapters 11–15), we turn to political problems that arise in the international arena and to the issue of political change within nation-states. This section is necessarily selective. The international political problems of today are so many and varied that it would take a dozen volumes to address them all, and change is moving at a staggering pace. Nonetheless, the issues that we address here seem to us sufficiently pressing and sufficiently common to contemporary experience to merit analysis in detail.

It is important to remember that this book unfolds progressively. The discussions of linkage mechanisms, governmental structures, and contemporary political problems build on the vocabulary and the store of concepts that are developed in Part I. The discussions of institutions in Part III assume that you are familiar with linkage mechanisms treated in Part II, and the exploration of political problems in Part IV will be of greater value and interest to you if you have read both Parts II and III.

NOTES

1. This is derived from a number of famous formulations in the literature of political science. Richard E. Neustadt characterized the power of the American president as the power to persuade rather than command. "The essence of a

President's persuasive task is to convince (his targets) that what the White House
wants of them is what they ought to do for their sake and on their own authority.''
See Richard E. Neustadt, *Presidential Power* (New York: Wiley, 1960), p. 34. By
this approach, influence is a special case of power, rather than the other way
around as some writers have it: see Harold D. Lasswell and Abraham Kaplan,
Power and Society (New Haven, Conn.: Yale University Press, 1950).

    2. Francis Fukuyama, "The End of History," *National Interest* (Summer
1989): 3–35.

    3. Z, "To the Stalin Mausoleum," *Daedalus* (Winter 1990): 295–344.

    4. See Lea Brilmayer, *Justifying International Acts* (Ithaca, N.Y.: Cornell
University Press, 1989).

    5. Compare, for instance, Amory Lovins, "Energy Strategy: The Road Not
Taken," *Foreign Affairs* (October 1976); and Samuel McCracken, *The War
against the Atom* (New York: Basic Books, 1982).

    6. Particularly good on this in the British context is Ian Robertson, *The Survival
of English* (London: Cambridge University Press, 1973).

    7. See, for instance, the many examples of language codes in Robin Edmonds,
Soviet Foreign Policy: The Brezhnev Years (New York: Oxford University Press,
1983).

    8. William Lutz, *Doublespeak: From Revenue Enhancement to Terminal Living*
(New York: Harper and Row, 1989).

    9. See, for instance, Geoffrey Perret, *A Country Made by War* (New York:
Random House, 1989).

SUGGESTED READINGS

Adas, Michael. *Machines as the Measure of Men: Science, Technology, and
Ideologies of Western Dominance.* Ithaca, N.Y.: Cornell University Press, 1989.

Alt, James E. *Political Science.* Berkeley: University of California Press, 1983. A
fresh look at a supposedly maturing discipline.

Barzun, Jacques. *The Culture We Deserve.* Middletown, Conn.: Wesleyan University Press, 1989. A rich source of observations on the ways language is used
politically.

Charlesworth, James C. *Contemporary Political Analysis.* New York: Free Press,
1967. A still valuable collection of essays by distinguished political scientists
stressing various approaches to political analysis.

Dahl, Robert A. *Modern Political Analysis.* Englewood Cliffs, N.J.: Prentice-
Hall, 1963. A short but very rigorous and influential introduction to thinking
systematically about politics.

Gerth, H. H., and C. Wright Mills. *From Max Weber.* New York: Oxford
University Press, 1946. An accessible presentation of Weber's thought on
politics.

Johnson, Paul. *Modern Times*. New York: Harper and Row, 1983.

Mackenzie, W. J. M. *Politics and Social Science*. Baltimore, Md.: Penguin, 1967. A sustained and wide-ranging exploration of the development of political science.

Minogue, Kenneth. *Alien Powers: The Pure Theory of Ideology*. New York: St. Martin's Press, 1985. A very subtle exploration of the dangers of ideological thinking.

2

The Evolution of Political Thought

For the Lawes of Nature (as *Justice, Equity, Modesty, Mercy* and . . . *doing to others, as we would be done to,*) of themselves, without the terrour of some power, to cause them to be observed, are contrary to our Naturall Passions, that carry us to Partiality, Pride, Revenge, and the like. And Covenants, without the Sword, are but Words, and of no strength to secure a man at all.

—THOMAS HOBBES

The more prevalent philosophical view of the past few centuries has been the charitable conviction that men and nations are essentially good, and that once they are liberated from the fetters of superstition, tradition, and oppressive political order, men will unite into one happy family governed by the popular will. In one form or another, it was the dream of Robespierre and Napoleon, of Marx and Lenin, and of Adolph Hitler, who once confided to Hermann Rauschning that national states had outlived their usefulness. The time had come, he said, for world government.

—THOMAS FLEMING

THE CONCEPT OF THE STATE

It is a maxim of rhetoric that more than half of any speaker's real argument consists of the way the key terms are defined. Knowing how words are being used, and therefore being able to decide whether we agree or disagree with these usages, is the prime requisite of productive discussion of any subject. At its simplest level, the *state* is nothing more than formally organized government as we know it in the modern world. A state is a legally formalized entity having accepted jurisdiction over a territory and a population and the capacity, within that territory, to make rules binding on the whole population and to enforce those rules through generally accepted legal procedures and applications of force. The state is an entity in which *sovereignty*—the authoritative capacity to govern within a country—rests. In this capacity, the state defends and speaks for its citizens in the international arena and in relationships with other states.

Is it possible for a society to manage its business without a state? The answer, clearly, is yes. In Chapter 3 we will discuss the characteristics of primitive (premodern) governmental arrangements. Here certain kinds of public or general decisions are made for the community as a whole in ways that do not involve any formal, continuing, specialized mechanism of government that operates in accordance with customary or written rules to achieve its objectives. A state, then, is an outgrowth of a developed or modernized political system.

Perhaps the most serious confusion surrounding the term *state* for an American student results from our use of the word to characterize the multiple regional subgovernments within the American union, such as the State of Mississippi, the State of New York, and the State of Alaska. This use is a vestige of the immediate post–Revolutionary War situation when, in the 1780s, the 13 former British colonies found themselves newly independent nations scattered along the eastern seaboard of North America. In the American federal system, the "state" governments continue to possess some of the attributes of independent nationhood. However, other crucial attributes of "the state" inhere in the national government of the United States. This entity *and* the 50 regional governmental entities properly make up the American state.[1]

The Covenant and the Sword

Leon Trotsky, leader of the Bolshevik Revolution in Russia in 1917 along with V. I. Lenin, once remarked that "every state is founded on force."[2] The great German political and social theorist Max Weber (1864–1920) used this observation as the basis for his development of the most widely employed definition of a state. Weber argued that, although force is certainly not the common everyday means by which a state orders the doings of its population, the relationship between the state and force "is an especially intimate one."[3] What Weber meant is that in modern society the state is the agency that, if it is to survive and be successful, claims "the monopoly of the legitimate use of physical force within a given territory." Thus the state has force available as an ultimate recourse in dealing with lawbreakers; this distinguishes the state from other social institutions. Other institutions—for example, the Roman Catholic Church, the DuPont Company, the Trade Unions Council of Great Britain, and a tribal council in Kenya—all do have power; they can influence purposefully the behavior of persons. But they do not possess the special power of the state: the capacity to make decisions that are binding on all of the population within a given territory and are ultimately underwritten by the forces of the police and army.

But if states ultimately rest on the capacity to employ force to direct and order certain public matters for a population, why do we have them at all? And why do the people accept their authority? Weber outlines a umber of ways in which particular states could acquire acceptance (what e calls "legitimacy") in the eyes of their citizens.

The first source of legitimacy that Weber identifies is *tradition,* "the ternal yesterday." In the premodern political setting, for example, when he state was only beginning to emerge as an identifiable institution, the radition of patriarchy (rule by the father, or the father of a leading family) night operate to confirm the authority of a new chieftain.

Weber also wrote of the legitimizing power of personal grace—what he alled *charisma.* Here the mechanism of the state acquires authority ecause of the personal qualities of the leader and the special bond of onfidence between the citizens and the leader: "The elected war lord, he plebicitarian ruler, or even the great demagogue."[4]

Finally, Weber suggested that the legitimacy of a state (its authority in he eyes of its citizens) might rest on *legality.* That is, the validity of the egal structure of the state draws its support from rationally created rules, vhich are themselves regarded as authoritative.

Weber made it clear that these three sources of legitimacy are "pure ypes" and that, in the actual world of states and statecraft, these three nechanisms of legitimization might operate in various combinations. His rucial point, however, was that the state, if it is to survive, must be able o generate a response to itself as legitimate—if not from all the people, t least from some politically important sectors of the population.

Weber's observations provide insight into how states come to be ccepted by their populations, but he leaves unanswered the nagging uestion "Why?" Why, indeed, should individuals subordinate them-elves to an institution that reserves the ultimate right to discipline them y force? They may respond to an established regime because of ancient radition, for love of a leader, or because they respect the rational nature f the constitutional arrangement of the state. But why should such a nechanism have evolved at all?

The Anarchist Alternative

There have been dissenters from the conclusion that the state is esirable or even necessary. To anarchists, formal government is part of he human problem, not part of its solution. At the core of this tradition re two somewhat dissimilar thinkers: the French philosopher Pierre-oseph Proudhon (1809–65) and a Russian, Mikhail Bakunin (1814–76). roudhon's *anarchism* was essentially romantic and philosophical. Opti-istic about human nature, Proudhon was convinced that humans' ra-onal and altruistic capacities are sufficient for people to live in decent armony with their neighbors without the central control exercised over em by the state. Decisions, when necessary, would be taken by consen-us of the small face-to-face committees that make up the polity. Bakunin dded a distinctly more sinister note to anarchist theory: the purgative

and purifying function of violence. By the very process of destroying th
state (along with the church and other important social institutions
humans would be freed and perfected to find their new way, free c
external oppression.

Anarchism continues to have great appeal to the imagination. All tha
is required is that one accept two premises: that humans are naturall
good, and that no formal public system of social control is needed to kee
them from aggressing against one another. But the fact remains that th
weak of any society need to be protected from the predatory and stronɡ
The state can contain conflicts between groups of its citizens and repres
the violence that would otherwise prevail. But this primary utility of th
state to the human species carries with it an equally important risk
Suppose the state itself becomes the bully. Suppose its machinery come
under the control of an unscrupulous leader or acquisitive gang. Th
engine of social control and the keeper of social peace then quickl
become the engine of tyranny and exploitation. The monopoly of forc
that was necessary to contain violence becomes nothing more than
form of violence itself. Thus we come to the question that has trouble
political philosophers throughout the ages. When does the exercise c
power by the state become tyrannical, and how can the degeneration of
state into tyranny be avoided?

In our survey of the major epochs in the development of politic;
thought, we shall see various answers given to this question. Befor
turning to this survey, however, we need to define a few more key terms

BASIC TERMINOLOGY

We began with the observation that politics is about conflict. But ther
are many sorts of conflicts running through our lives, and we would nc
call all of them political. We may thoroughly dislike our next-doc
neighbors, with their noisy children and vicious dog, and other people o
the block may feel the same way. But this conflict does not becom
political until government gets involved. Once we (the good neighbors
band together to secure passage of a zoning ordinance that will prever
our obnoxious neighbors from putting up a prefabricated aluminum bar
in order to raise pigs, we have entered into the realm of politics.

What is a *political system?* The term describes the ongoing proces
whereby the government in a particular country controls the citizens an
the wants and fears of the citizens are made known to the governmen
Thus the political system of France, for example, includes not only th
governmental institutions, but also political parties, interest groups, an
the news media.

People place demands on government: they clamor for various public
policy outcomes. These demands are then articulated and brought to bea

ɔn government (the formal apparatus of the state) in a variety of ways. *Public policy* is the set of authoritative choices that make its role distinct. But the state's action, once resources have been allocated or people's ɔehavior regulated, gives rise to a new set of fears and wants, and these ɪn turn find expression and are brought to bear on the government. In a ɪever-ending cycle, demands arise and are articulated through social ȿtructures, structures compete, government responds, and the cycle ɔegins again. This process and the institutions through which it operates ɔonstitute a political system.

Perhaps the most lucid presentation of this basic model comes from a ɔontemporary student of politics, David Easton of the University of Ɔhicago.⁵ Easton conceives of a political system in which demands are ɪrticulated and brought to bear on government by mediating structures, ȝovernmental decisions are implemented in the form of public policy, and ɪhese decisions then affect the citizenry, creating new demands, and so ɔn. This simple yet very useful idea is visually represented in Figure 2-1.

Demands are the things we want from government (lower taxes, free ɪnedical care, and so on) as expressed in voting, through party and ɪnterest-group activity, and even through public opinion polls. *Support* is ɪhe sum of our positive feelings ("affects," as the psychologists say) ɪoward the regime. Without some substantial bases of support, a government would have to rule with violence alone; and this—as it appears to ɔe from history—is a short-term expedient at best. Demands and support ɪre the "inputs" into the political system from the larger society (the 'environment" in the diagram). The institutions and processes of the political system then operate to produce "outputs" in the form of ɪecisions and actions—what we call "public policy." These decisions

Figure 2-1   A Simplified Model of a Political System

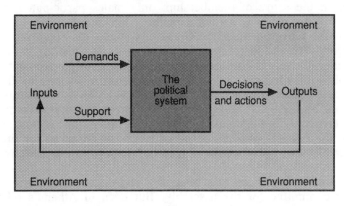

Ȿource: David Easton, *A Systems Analysis of Political Life* (Chicago: University of Chicago Press, 1979). Reprinted by permission.

and actions, in turn, affect the society (the environment) in ways tha●
create new demands and perhaps new bases of support for the system.

With this basic terminology in mind, let us turn to the historica●
evolution of political analysis.

CLASSICAL POLITICAL THEORY

The splendid civilization that was classical Greece developed in the las●
thousand years before Christ, in the hilly terrain of the Anatolian penin●
sula along the Aegean Sea. In this mountain-divided land, the Greek●
developed a number of independent city-states, the most important o●
which were Athens, Sparta, Thebes, and Corinth. Athens in particula●
enjoyed prosperity and a cultural flowering in the third and fourth centu●
ries before Christ. The Athenian legacy of reflection about human nature●
society, and behavior stimulated and provided base points for all politica●
analysis thereafter. Much of our terminology—concepts such as justice●
liberty, constitutional government, and law—was first systematically
developed by Greek, and especially Athenian, thinkers.

In considering the contribution of the Greeks, however, it is importan●
to note that the ancient city-state (the political unit in terms of which a●
Greek reflection about politics is cast) was an exceedingly small place by
modern standards; in the fifth century B.C., Athens had about 40,00●
adult male citizens. (Plato would have limited its population to 5,040, anc
Aristotle thought its area would be too large if a person could not se●
across it.) The population was separated into three political classes
slaves, noncitizens (foreigners traveling through or staying to trade), anc
citizens. Citizenship was a privilege of birth, and a Greek remained ●
citizen of the city to which his parents belonged. Although women wer●
citizens in the sense of membership, only males participated in civi●
business. Citizenship was thus something like membership in a goo●
men's club.[6] Government of the Greek city-states was organized aroun●
an assembly of the male citizenry. Except during periods in which ●
tyrant illegally seized control of the mechanisms of government, these
assemblies afforded citizens some participation in overseeing the per●
formance of those who actually ruled within the city—magistrates, ta●
collectors, and so on. In addition to the assembly, the city-state (or *polis*●
characteristically had a council. In the more aristocratic states, such a●
Sparta, the council was composed of elders who served for life, anc
membership was a prerogative of certain families born to the governin●
class.

The council at Athens was popularly chosen and was, in effect, ●
steering committee for the assembly. But even in Athens's relatively
democratic arrangement, the council (numbering 500) was too awkward ●
mechanism to oversee the continuing business of government. The coun●

cil was reduced to a working size by a system of rotation in office; each member was active for one-tenth of the yearly term. This committee of about 60 members was in actual control and oversaw government in the name of the entire council. It appears that the council formulated measures for consideration by the assembly and directly supervised the multipurpose public officials called "magistrates." The council also controlled the military and other commissions and administrative bodies that performed governmental functions within Athens.

At least this was so when Athenian democracy was operating at its best. But this was not always the case. Politics in the Greek city-states, and even in Athens, shifted back and forth between the more democratic and the more aristocratic oligarchical. There were also periods of complete breakdown, when tyrants—sometimes demagogues—succeeded in operating outside the constitution. It was against this background of political turbulence that Greek political thought evolved. Athenians took citizenship and participation in the affairs of government very seriously indeed, as reflected in the famous funeral oration of the statesman Pericles (c. 495–29 B.C.), who, while extolling the honor of the Athenian soldiers who had fallen in a war with Sparta, reminded his fellow citizens that their participation in civic life was their highest social duty. But even this level of commitment by a small and, by the standards of the time, highly sophisticated citizenry was not sufficient to guarantee that things always went well and that potential tyrants had no opportunities.

Athens eventually lost the war with Sparta (the Peloponnesian War). This shock, combined with the effects of a disastrous plague, destabilized Athenian democracy. Pericles fell from power, and Athens's power declined.

Plato

The inherent weakness of democracy was the central theme of Plato, the first great Athenian political writer. Born into the Athenian aristocracy, Plato was dismayed by the decline in Athenian power and economic well-being following its wars with Sparta. The democracy of the Periclean period had proved vulnerable to internal confusion, and a leadership capable of sustaining Athenian economic and military power had not emerged. Plato had high hopes for the Revolt of the Thirty in 404 B.C., which substituted an artistocratic oligarchy for the democratic regime that had failed so badly. But far from justifying Plato's hopes, the performance of the oligarchy was even worse than that of the democratic system it replaced. And when the democratic regime was restored, one of its major acts was to execute Socrates, who had been democracy's consistent critic.

Thus, in Plato's eyes the case was amply made. The political arrangements of the Greek city-state were inherently unstable and incapable of providing a satisfactory form of government. This rejection of "politics as usual" is crucial to understanding Plato's great work, his *Republic*. The fluctuations of politics in the city-states between inefficient democracy and unresponsive oligarchy had convinced Plato that a whole new approach was necessary.

Plato's *Republic* is one of the most remarkable political writings of all time. This is not because its prescriptions are correct or desirable. In fact, much of it proves unrealistic and even potentially mischievous. Rather, it represents the effort of a first-rate mind to imagine a kind of political system that would avoid all of the perceived weaknesses and evils of existing politics. The *Republic* demonstrates that we are, in large part, stuck with the difficulties of ordinary politics because the alternatives are either impossible or too distasteful to accept.

The construction of Plato's ideal state begins with the idea that virtue is knowledge—the basic teaching of Plato's master, Socrates. From this, Plato generalized that the nature of perfect government is knowable. Therefore the good state, the virtuous state, would be one ruled by a knowledge of what is precisely correct public policy in every situation. Such knowledge is not easily achieved, and those few who are capable of attaining it must, obviously, be the rulers of the ideal state. This is the basis of Plato's conception of the philosopher-kings—the group of superbly intelligent and educated leaders who, by the exercise of their reason, would be able to discern the correct course for the polity in every aspect of its life. Education was to be of prime importance within Plato's republic, not only because of the need to rear a group of philosopher-kings, but also so that the rest of the citizens (the nonrulers) would understand thoroughly their function within the community.

Both democracy and politicians (in the ordinary sense of those who represent the ideas of the people and traffic in those ideas) were scorned by Plato. Truth, and therefore virtue, did not lie in the opinions of people, but rather were to be divined by the reasoning of the most highly trained and best qualified. Thus, in the *Republic* there was no need for law in the ordinary sense; law was only a crude substitute for the knowledge that the philosopher-kings would possess and on the basis of which they could direct affairs. One did not need law for the community if there was someone on the scene who always knew what was right.

In the *Republic,* justice consisted of everyone performing his or her proper function. Injustice occurred when someone did not understand the nature of his or her role and therefore was not capable of performing in a virtuous fashion.

Plato was convinced that certain institutions of Greek society (what leftist social critics today might call "bourgeois" institutions) would interfere with the possibility of a rational ordering of the community. Marriage, the rearing of children by their own parents, and the private ownership of property (which gives rise to differences in wealth within he community) were all considered undesirable. They were ways in which people expressed their individual wants and opinions, rather than ending their wills to the public good as divined by the philosopher-kings. Therefore, in the ideal republic, there were no marriages; children would e reared in common, with their education strictly supervised by the philosopher-kings; and property would be held in common, with especially strict restraints on the economic position of the philosopher-kings since luxurious living might blunt their perceptions of virtue).

The *Republic* has often been criticized as an argument for an authoritarian system. Plato did not conceive it as such, because the philosopher-ings would simply be directing people to do what is right; and surely, Plato would have said, there is no real coercion in being directed to the ight. It is only when one doubts whether there is a single right answer to very governmental question and whether the answer may be known through the application of reason that the authoritarianism of the *Republic* becomes apparent. If there isn't a single right way, or if reasonable people erceive the right way in different terms, then to put a single elite in the osition of directing the affairs of the community becomes naked authorarianism.

Later in his life Plato became more and more conscious of this difficulty. Although he never abandoned his vision of the republic as the ultimately desirable arrangement of the state, he did, in the *Statesman* and the *Laws,* recognize that in the real world it would be necessary to rely on a sound constitution (and set of laws) for a community, rather than solely on the existence of an elite that embodied perfect political knowledge.

Aristotle

It was one of Plato's students, Aristotle, who surpassed him and finally succeeded him in intellectual influence. After exploring with the utmost vigor the anatomy of his political ideal, Plato was reluctantly forced to return to the contemplation of actual political situations. Aristotle was concerned with political actualities from the beginning. Lacking Plato's attraction to the idea of developing a caste of rulers with full knowledge of the good, Aristotle stressed the importance of sound laws. He was concerned not so much with the philosopher-king as with the prudent and practical statesman. Most important, he recognized that there were a variety of different ways in which the affairs of the state could be organized to provide decent government. That is, he realized that differing political forms offered different strengths and advantages.

The members of Aristotle's own school engaged in a study of the variety of constitutions of the Greek city-states, and Aristotle borrowed from Plato and elaborated a sixfold classification of forms of government. Beginning with monarchy, aristocracy, and democracy, Aristotle then analyzed the perversion of each of these forms: dictatorship, oligarchy and mob rule, or ochlocracy. In a very modern-sounding way, Aristotl defined the constitution as the basic law and arrangement of magistrate establishing the structure of government. But he took great care t observe that the actual process of government may diverge from the forr of the constitution. Thus a constitution that is supposed to functio democratically may in fact have been captured by an oligarchy or led b a demagogue into dictatorship—even though officially nothing ha changed.

Rather than pursuing the construction of an ideal state, Aristotl concentrated on the exercise of describing the best practicable state. Fo Plato, the supreme virtue of citizenship had been to fit into the idea order. For Aristotle, virtue was commitment on the part of the individua to the joint enterprise of managing the community. In one of his mos famous observations, Aristotle characterized humans as political animals In other words, it is our natural, desirable lot to participate in the affair of the state, and our lives are to take meaning from that participation Without participation in a civic order, it is impossible to be fully human Thus the end of the good state is the moral perfection of the individual and the individual's moral salvation is impossible without membership i the state. The person outside the city-state, or polis, was bereft, maimed and permanently incomplete. In the best practical state, the constitutio would be of mixed form, containing elements of both oligarchy an democracy. Most important, it would have as its social foundation a larg middle class composed of virtuous citizens, neither very rich nor ver poor. Such a large middle class would give the state a wide base o support, and the citizens would be interested enough to hold the magis trates accountable for their actions.

Here, fully developed, were two political truths that have remaine valid to this day: the importance of the middle class, and the notion o mixed governmental forms.

The Romans

It is ironic that Aristotle died in 322 B.C. Building on the work of Plato he had provided a brilliant analysis of the possibilities of politics in th self-governing Greek city-state. But at the very time Aristotle was devel oping his analysis, the system of small self-governing units to which i was directed was declining. One of Aristotle's former pupils, Alexande of Macedonia, whom history knows as Alexander the Great, was reshap ing the world. It is a timeless comment on the complexity of the educa tional enterprise that Aristotle's views on politics seem to have had n particular impact on Alexander. Nor did Aristotle comprehend the wa in which Alexander's later conquests—drawing geographically dispersed heterogeneous populations into huge, loose political associations an breaking the old bonds of local community—had forever altered the political landscape.

Thus, at the very time that Aristotle was refining his ideas concerning the relationship of law and democracy to political stability, the world to which his ideas were addressed was disintegrating. No longer could persons find identity and complete self-fulfillment in their membership in the polis. The intimate political communities were gone, and empires were rising in their place. Peoples would be ruled from afar and would work out their individual salvations, rather than participating in a community life that gave existence full meaning. The paramount question of politics for the Greeks had been how to perfect the city-state, but that question was no longer relevant.

The process of bringing the whole of the Mediterranean Basin into a single governmental system, begun by Alexander of Macedonia, was perfected by Rome. The Romans erected the grandest system of law and public adminstration the world had ever known. Indeed, the world was to see no parallel for another 1,000 years.

The most famous expositor of Roman political ideas was the politician-philosopher Marcus Tullius Cicero (106–43 B.C.). Typically Roman, Cicero was a man of political action rather than a detached observer, such as Aristotle had been. Cicero was both a party leader in the Roman Senate and the governor of a Roman province. He strongly resisted the establishment of dictatorial rule by Julius Caesar, and although he took no direct part in Caesar's assassination in 44 B.C., he certainly favored it. He was a bitter enemy of Marc Antony; and when Antony was restored to influence under a new Caesar (Augustus), he succeeded in having Cicero put to death.

Cicero wrote political treaties called the *Republic* and the *Laws* (thus putting himself in the Platonic tradition in style, but not in substance). The modern historian of political thought George Sabine has written of Cicero's significance:

[His] true importance in the history of political thought lies in the fact that he gave to the Stoic doctrine of natural law a statement in which it was universally known throughout western Europe from his own day down to the nineteenth century. From him it passed to the Roman lawyers and not the less to the Fathers of the Church.[7]

For the Greeks, the primary question had been how to achieve stable self-government in the city-state. For the Romans, as reflected in Cicero, the question was how to discover the principles on which world rule could be based and justified. The answer was that there exists a universal law of nature "unchangeably binding upon all men and all nations. No legislation that contravenes it is entitled to the nature of law, for no ruler and no people can make right wrong."[8] And how is this universal law to be discovered? Cicero's answer was reason—or, as he phrased it, "right reason." The trained human mind could read the dictates of nature, and it was the duty of all to conform to these commands. Thus was developed what became the core idea of political philosophy not only for Rome, but also for 1,500 years to come: the idea of a higher law that commanded and justified participation in the civic life of a political unit. Individuals subordinated themselves to the lawful state because it was naturally right that they do so. The law of nature was seen by Cicero as the common property of all the people, but they ceded to their rulers the role of articulating particular *rules* (expressions of natural law divined through their right reason) for the polity. Because law was universal and comprehensive, there was powerful attraction in the idea of universal government as well. In this way, Rome's effort at world rule was legitimized.

Cicero's own preference was for a state—republican in form—in which governing power was vested in an assembly of representatives (such as the Senate of the Roman Republic before the Caesars). But whereas the authority to govern would flow from citizens to their representatives, it could be exercised (and ultimately justified) only in accordance with the law of nature.

THE MIDDLE AGES

The reasons for the decline of Rome in the sixth and seventh centuries after Christ are endlessly debated by scholars. What is not in doubt is the consequence of Rome's decline. There was no successor to Rome as the dominant world power. Instead, politics once again fragmented—not back to the city-states of classical antiquity, but into the welter of baronies, duchies, and principalities characteristic of the Middle Ages.

But although actual government was fragmented into 1,000 pieces in Europe, the ideal of the world state remained vigorous. By this time, the dominant intellectual force was organized Christianity—specifically, the Church of Rome. And the church had developed its own version of a universal state. In place of Cicero's nature, the fathers of the medieval church substituted God.

Inasmuch as salvation was the paramount end of all human endeavor, it was the responsibility of the state to further salvation. Humans were bound to obey the commandments of the state because the state was divinely ordained. Kings and princes held their civil authority by God's pleasure and thus were defied only at peril. It was the church, however, that ultimately held (in the hands of the bishop of Rome, the pope) the keys to the kingdom of heaven. Thus, in theory, the authority of kings and princes depended on their fidelity to their holy mission and, by implication, on their deference to the Holy Father.[9]

Augustine

Perhaps the premier expression of the medieval conception of the Christian commonwealth was contained in the *City of God,* a long essay written by Aurelius Augustinus (354–430), bishop of Hippo, who is known to history as Saint Augustine. Appearing in 412, the *City of God* saw all Christians as constituting a single society. Under God the society had two heads; the pope and an emperor. Although the religious and the governmental hierarchies performed different functions—spiritual and temporal—there was no theoretical division between the two. That is, they were united in furtherance of a single divine purpose, and it was their duty to subordinate themselves to that purpose in both dimensions of social life.

This division, which constituted the "official" world view of intellectuals at least until the eleventh century, was sadly at variance with the reality of medieval political life. There was no City of God on earth. By contrast, the most important political relationship of the Middle Ages was that between lord and vassal. This relationship was both political and economic, with the lords owing protection and certain economic advantages (the use of tillable land and access to mills for grinding grain) to the vassals. This relationship, referred to generally as *feudalism,* dominated the Middle Ages as completely as the city-state had dominated Greek antiquity. Thus did the ideal of the Christian commonwealth coexist uncomfortably with the reality of small political-economic units bound together on the basis of mutual need and worldly obligation.

In theory, the king might claim to represent the authority of God and to partake in the character of the emperor in the Christian commonwealth. In fact, the power of the king depended on his relationships with the great lords (who were technically his vassals); and their power, in turn, depended on their fiefs and on their vassals, whose primary loyalty was to them and not to the king. Central government administration was weak. Each local lord ran his own show, often administering justice, sitting as "court" himself, and interposing himself firmly between the authority of the central monarch and the inhabitants of his own province.[10]

Attempts to recreate a world of governmental order as a successor to Rome failed after periods of brief success and promise. In the ninth century, Charlemagne, a great warrior-king of the Franks (a tribe in western Germany), enjoyed some success in his attempt to unite Western Christendom.[11] The enterprise foundered after his death, however. And in any case, Charlemagne had never succeeded in uniting more than a portion of Western Europe under his leadership.

Machiavelli

By the fifteenth century, however, major changes—or at least the beginning of major changes—could be seen. These changes were both intellectual and governmental. Perhaps the most dramatic indication of an altered intellectual climate was the work of the Italian author and statesman Niccolò Machiavelli (1469–1527). Ignoring the universalistic theory of a divinely ordained natural law, Machiavelli concentrated on the everyday realities of practical politics. Unlike his medieval predecessors, his abiding preoccupation was not with how one divined the will of God, but rather with what a person could do to accomplish immediate objectives in the real world. This turning away from abstractions and concentrating instead on the realities of contemporary political life is what gives Machiavelli a distinctly modern look. His most famous work, *The Prince,* published in 1532 after his death, has often been criticized as cynical and immoral. In it Machiavelli seeks to counsel a secular ruler as to what he must do, tactically, if he is to succeed in maintaining his rule. However, the approach of *The Prince* is not to counsel the ruler to be evil, but rather to state the facts of life objectively. In another political work, *The Discourses* (finally published in 1531), it is clear that Machiavelli himself was committed to a republican view of government, which he derived from his studies of the ancient Roman writers—particularly Cicero. That Machiavelli's name has come to describe craftiness and dishonesty in politics is a terrible irony.[12]

Governmentally, what was beginning to happen at this time was the development of the nation-state—a new form of government organization that was finally replacing, especially in large sectors of Western Europe, the patchwork of medieval feudalism.

THE RISE OF LIBERALISM

By the fifteenth century, a new political world was emerging. Out of the sprawling maze of feudal provinces and nonexistent empires, there emerged a small number of governmentally integrated policies. In England, France, Spain, and Russia (with Germany's unification under Prussian leadership following later), there developed powerful central rulers who were able to subordinate the provincial nobility and to provide a degree of political integration, which distinguishes these polities from anything that had existed since the time of Rome.

The king and czar were now not simply the foremost nobles among many, but were also both central authority and visible manifestation of nationhood. Here and there, powerful provincial leaders might hold out for a while; but the tide was running toward the new centralized form of national government, which was able to provide uniform law and the rudiments of integrated governmental bureaucracy to large populations.[13] The creation of centralized nations allowed for economic intercourse of a sort that had been frustrated by the wildly divided and fractionalized politics of the Middle Ages.

But while these nation-states were evolving, there was (at least at first) no new political theory to match! The notion of temporal rulership as a grant from God continued as the theoretical basis of political authority. And whatever quarrels a Louis XIV of France or a Philip II of Spain or a Charles I of England might have with the pope, the ultimate justification for their kingships, and for the authority of the Russian czar, was that they ruled by divine right.[14]

The theory of divine right of kings did not necessarily imply absolutism. As a practical matter, kings granted concessions to important subjects and recognized certain traditional rights inherent in different classes, or estates, within the nation. This is particularly marked in England, where the right of commoners to petition the king for redress of grievances before voting taxes to support the royal exchequer was well recognized by 1500. Nonetheless, the basic theory of the matter was that the king was first on the ground and that his prerogative was not something conferred on him by the nobles, by the gentry, or by the people, but rather something he held from an authority beyond this world.

The carry-over of this essentially medieval theory into the age of the nation-state created problems. Under the medieval theory, not only was the ruler's authority derived from God, but also the ruler was obligated to conduct the affairs of the state in such a way as to facilitate the salvation of the citizens. However lightly some of the new national rulers may have treated this obligation, it was nonetheless fixed in the theory of their kingship: they were to direct the feet of their subjects on the path of salvation.

Hobbes

What made for problems, of course, was the Protestant Reformation. As long as the religion of the king and subjects could be taken for granted (it being that of the Church of Rome), there was little difficulty. A particular temporal prince might quarrel with a particular pope over money or marriage or the odd fiefdom, but the matter of religion did not generate internal division within the kingdom. By the seventeenth century—with European Christianity slivering into a number of differing pieces, each with its own religious style (and announcing that style as exclusively valid)—things changed. Russia and Spain remained largely immune from the contagion of sectarian warfare, but Central Europe and England were ravaged.

It was out of this experience of creedal strife, with contending sects vying for control of the mechanism of the state, that a wholly new approach to government was developed. The crucial contribution was made by Thomas Hobbes (1588–1679).[15] For Hobbes, the old central question of political thought had simply lost its relevance. Hobbes's question was radically different. To establish the authority of the state by reference to God had given rise to civil strife. For Hobbes, the main issue was how to protect people from the aggression of their peers and thus achieve a modicum of peace and stability in civil life.

The most important element of Hobbes's thought for the development of a new political theory was separation of church and state. Religion was to be a private matter, not the province of the monarch. Nor was the monarch any longer to be considered divinely ordained. The power of the state derived from the people, not from God; it was not rooted in the law of nature, but was wielded in the interest of the people. Here we have a revolutionary shift in perspective. No more was a person seen as naturally a citizen of the state, and no more was the state seen as having natural or heavenly presumptive rights to govern. The sole justification for the existence of the state was that it provided a service, and this was to be the hallmark of a new age in political theory. This insight marks the beginning of the modern period in political thought.

The view of the state as natural, or "organic," with preexisting constant claims on individuals was replaced in the seventeenth and eighteenth centuries by a view of the state as based on an agreement, or "contract," between the citizens who would be subject to the state. This

---

Box 2-1. The Protestant Reformation and the Rise of Liberalism

Both Luther and Calvin said, with some qualifications, that one must disobey but not resist such a ruler, for all rulers derive their power from God. Later, however, some of Calvin's followers concluded not only that resistance is sometimes justified, but that the people have a right to overthrow rulers who deny them freedom of religion. By this they meant everyone's freedom to practice Calvinism, to be sure. Yet their arguments for freedom of conscience, resting in part on the claim that government receives its authority indirectly from God through the consent of the people, planted the seeds of the argument in favor of religious toleration.

Without intending to do so, then, the Protestant reformers prepared the way for liberalism. By teaching that salvation comes through faith alone, Luther and the other reformers encouraged people to value the individual conscience more than the preservation of unity and orthodoxy. From individual conscience to individual liberty was still a radical step for the time, but it was a step that liberals took in the 17th and 18th centuries. For in those centuries liberalism emerged as an attempt to free individuals from the constraints of religious conformity and ascribed status in society—an attempt, that is, to work a fundamental transformation of society.

Source: *Terence Ball and Richard Dagger, "The 'L-Word': A Short History of Liberalism,"* Political Science Teacher *(Winter 1990): 2–3.*

notion of the limited "servant state" is the core of what came to be called *liberalism*.

In the beginning, liberalism did not look very liberal. Hobbes's own view of humans was pessimistic, and his fear of people's unbridled appetites was great. (Note, for instance, his famous comment that the life of a human being in the "state of nature" was solitary, poor, nasty, brutish, and short.) Hobbes saw an authoritarian state as necessary to protect people from one another. Individuals, of their own volition and for their own physical preservation, must submit themselves almost entirely to the rule of the state.

Locke

Later thinkers in the liberal tradition conceived of the role of the state very differently. Like Hobbes, they saw the state as essentially secular and as ordained by the governed people for their own convenience and protection. But in the thought of such writers as John Locke (1632–1704), the state was accorded far less control than in Hobbes's version.

Locke's *Two Treatises on Civil Government,* which appeared in 1690, are the classic expression of liberalism as a political theory.[16] The state is to protect individuals and their property against aggression from their neighbors; as with Hobbes, the state is to have no religious mission and is not to interfere in the spiritual life of the citizens. Unlike that of Hobbes, however, Locke's state would confine itself strictly to its policing and peacekeeping duties and would respect a substantial realm of privacy and individual autonomy. The citizens are to govern not only their own spiritual lives, but most other important aspects of their lives as well. They would do this on the basis of their own desires and initiatives as long as they respected the laws of the state. Individuals would find their important meaning and satisfactions in their private lives. Thus, although the theoretical foundations of liberalism were laid by Hobbes, its conception of the state was principally the work of Locke.

This liberal conception of the state was further refined by thinkers such as the Scottish philosopher and historian David Hume (1711–76) and the Scottish economist Adam Smith (1723–90). On the Continent, there were important additions to the liberal theory. In France, Baron de Montesquieu (1689–1755) argued the importance of building internal restraints into the liberal form of government such that the powers of a government would be separated and balanced. His essay *The Spirit of the Laws,* published in 1750, had considerable influence on the framers of the American Constitution of 1787. And Montesquieu's erratic but brilliant countryman Jean-Jacques Rousseau (1712–78) gave liberalism perhaps its most radical expression. Rousseau, far more than Locke, insisted that the mechanism of the state be democratic and based on the political equality of all citizens.[17]

Throughout the nineteenth century and into the twentieth, liberalism as a political world view commanded the center of the intellectual stage. In the same way, the theory of natural law had been central for the Romans, and the theory of the Christian commonwealth for medieval intellectuals.

THE MARXIST CHALLENGE TO LIBERALISM

However, liberalism has not escaped stern challenge. Although the theory and practice of liberal statecraft unleashed human energies that resulted in tremendous strides in science, technology, and the creation of material wealth, the human costs of this industrialization were considerable. The operation of the private sector, with individual initiative and the monetary incentive given free play, resulted in huge inequalities among the rich, the middle class, and the poor. By the latter decades of the nineteenth century, some thinkers were dissenting from the liberal orthodoxy and were casting about for a new theory of politics that would better respond to what was becoming their primary question: how can we retain the advances of the Industrial Revolution while providing more equal distribution of its benefits?

The basic answer to this question, to which innumerable variations and refinements have been added, came from a German scholar named Karl Marx (1818–83). Marx rejected the liberal theory of the relationship of the state to the individual. For Marx the great moral evil—to be opposed above all else—was not the tyrannical state, but the tyranny of the rich over the poor in the private sector. Whereas liberals celebrated the wealth created within the private sector, Marx argued that the operations of private business had resulted in absolute power being vested in a small class: the bourgeoisie, the capitalists. Through their control of natural resources and manufacturing plants (that is, the means of production), the capitalists had virtually enslaved the much larger class: the workers, the proletariat. The proletariat was, for Marx, the true producing class. The muscle and sweat of the workers were what gave value to raw materials, turning them into finished goods. Capitalists grew fat on the labor of the proletariat, and their appetite for ever-increasing profits forced further and further exploitation of the proletariat.

Marx was not the first thinker to wonder whether equality might not be the most important end of politics. Early socialist experimenters, such as Robert Owen (1771–1858) in England and Charles Fourier (1772–1837) in France, tried to engineer equality in small communities organized on "ideal" patterns. Results were mixed and were not, apparently, transferable to larger societies. A more thoroughgoing egalitarian thinker, Karl Marx, dismissed the early experiments of Owen and Fourier as "utopian."[18]

Box 2-2. Karl Marx (1818–1883)

Karl Marx, a middle-class German scholar who had studied philosophy at the universities of Bonn and Berlin, is the father of world communism. His philosophy of dialectical materialism provided the ideological weapons in the Russian Bolshevik Revolution, which brought Lenin—and later Stalin— to power. Marxism *was also an important force in the revolution Mao Tse-tung led in China. Marx saw the working class (the proletariat) in capitalist societies as developing a class consciousness that led inevitably to a struggle with the exploiting class. This, in turn, would lead to revolution and the dictatorship of the proletariat.*

Marx denied that he was the first to see the class struggle. Middle-class historians had done this before him, as Lenin later pointed out. But let Marx speak for himself:

> *What I did that was new was to prove: (1) that the existence of classes is only bound up with particular, historic phases in the development of production; (2) that the class struggle necessarily leads to the dictatorship of the proletariat; (3) that this dictatorship itself only constitutes the transition to the abolition of all classes and to the classless society.*[1]

Marx and Friedrich Engels, his close friend and collaborator, issued the Communist Manifesto *(1848), declaring that the class struggle holds the key to understanding all hitherto existing societies. Shortly thereafter, Marx found it wise to move to England with his family. Although he earned some money as an occasional journalist, and even prepared some articles for the* New York Tribune *during the American Civil War, he was frequently dependent on Engels, the son of a wealthy businessman, for money in order to support his family. Working in the British Museum and using official British documents depicting the harsh conditions in British factories, Marx wrote his major work* Das Kapital *in three volumes, two of which were edited by Engels and published after Marx's death in 1883. In essence, Marxism is a theory derived from experience in early British industrial capitalism.*

The leaders of great revolutions typically are well-educated members of the middle class. Marx is a prime example, as are Engels and Lenin.

Note:
1. Karl Marx, Selected Correspondence, *July 27, 1854, p. 71. An excellent summary of Marx's ideas, ideal for the beginning student, is found in George A. Sabine,* A History of Political Theory *(New York: Henry Holt, 1937), chap. 32.*

Marx saw all of human history and all of human affairs as determined by the prevailing economic arrangements within society. Looking back, Marx argued that in the Middle Ages the basis of wealth had been land. Land had been controlled by the feudal barons, and it was this control that gave them power and dominion over their vassals. The rise of the nation-state and of liberalism, Marx argued, had changed the primary means by which wealth was created. The primary means of creating wealth became manufacturing, and the bourgeoisie who owned the factories challenged and displaced the feudal rulers. By the nineteenth century, Marx concluded, the capitalists had consolidated their dominion over the mass of their fellow citizens.

What was needed—indeed, what was inevitable—was another alteration in the control of the means of production. Just as surely as the bourgeoisie had displaced the feudal overlords, so the proletariat would displace the bourgeoisie. This was for Marx the meaning of revolution: the proletariat would seize control of the means of production and run the economy not for the profit of the few, but for the equal division of rewards among the many.

Marx's theory of history—often described as *dialectical materialism*—received its premier expression in volume 1 of *Das Kapital,* which appeared in 1867. The essentials of Marx's view, however, were contained in his famous *Communist Manifesto,* published in 1848.

In *communist* thought—exemplified in the works of the Russian revolutionary Vladimir Ilyich Ulyanov (1870–1924), who is known by his revolutionary code name Lenin—emphasis is placed on the revolutionary aspect of Marxist thought. There is need for violence in the making of the revolution, and the revolution does not—indeed will not—wait for the mechanisms of electoral law or parliamentary politics. In a famous pamphlet entitled *What Is to Be Done?* (published in 1902), Lenin argued that only a disciplined party of dedicated professional revolutionaries could succeed in smashing the capitalistic order. Thus the Communist party was to be the vanguard of the proletariat.[19]

The other principal stream of contemporary thought that flows from Marx's work is *democratic socialism.* Rather than emphasizing the radical revolutionary aspect of Marx, democratic socialists—such as Eduard Bernstein (1850–1932) in Germany—envisioned the possibility of bringing about the demise of the bourgeoisie and creating common ownership of property through nonviolent means. While accepting Marx's analysis of history and his critique of liberalism, democratic socialists seek to achieve the fully socialized society through representative political processes.

Both streams of Marxist thought—communist and social democratic—have spawned a welter of variants. Marxist analysis, however, remains the most powerful critique of the political theory of liberalism. While liberals continue to emphasize the importance of individual initiative and a large private sector protected from government, persons more concerned with the inequalities of wealth and reward tend to gravitate toward Marxism. After all, greater equality can be achieved only through the vigorous intervention of the state. Whereas the liberal retains an abiding suspicion of the state and is willing to rely on it only intermittently to ameliorate particularly painful social conditions, the Marxist is ready to use it in a sustained and purposeful fashion to redistribute income and to mold society into a proper and more disciplined order.

Recently, a number of commentators have announced the "death of communism,"[20] and this is often coupled with suggestions to the effect that socialism is a proven failure as a mode of economic organization.[21] But while there is ample and accumulating evidence of the terminal decline of communism as an ideological force, it is far from clear that socialism, per se, is losing its appeal. Democratic socialism still had its powerful advocates in the 1990s, such as former West German Chancellor Willy Brandt, honorary leader of the German Social Democratic party and—before his death in 1992—a leading figure within the Socialist International. Furthermore, within the newly noncommunist states of Eastern Europe there is strong residual sentiment for retaining many of the economic programs and practices of socialism, which are thought to foster a more humane social order than that of liberal capitalist countries.[22]

SUMMARY

In this chapter we have touched on the major periods and figures in the development of systematic political analysis. It is important to remember that each period and school of thought focused on a particular core concern, or central question. These concerns and questions were dictated by the conditions of the times in which various thinkers lived and by the political realities they faced.

For the Greeks, the problem was discovering the proper governmental form for the city-state. For the Romans and the medieval church fathers, the problem was articulating a basis for a universal law that would undergird and justify a universal political order. For the "moderns" of the liberal tradition, the problem was devising ideas for limiting and containing the power of the governments of the new nation-states. And for the Marxists and other socialists, it was providing for greater economic equality of persons.

But although thinkers of the various schools were responding to different questions and concerns, this does not mean that their work was unrelated. The great periods or schools of political thought have successively enriched one another. Greek reflections on the difficulties of democracy enriched the thought of the American founders, even though this group was primarily within the liberal tradition. In the same way, socialist thought concerning equality has certainly entered into and enriched the American liberal tradition.

NOTES

1. On the American states themselves as political subsystems, see Alan Rosenthal and Maureen Moakley, eds., *The Political Life of the American States* (New York: Praeger, 1984).

2. For a biographical portrait of Trotsky, including the evolution of his thought, see Bertram D. Wolfe, *Three Who Made a Revolution* (Boston: Beacon, 1955), pp. 169–214.

3. From "Politics as a Vocation," in H. H. Gerth and C. Wright Mills, eds., *From Max Weber: Essays in Sociology* (New York: Oxford University Press, 1946), p. 78.

4. Ibid., p. 79.

5. David Easton, *The Political System* (New York: Knopf, 1953). This conception of the political system was refined in David Easton, *A Systems Analysis of Political Life* (New York: Wiley, 1965).

6. The comparison was suggested by the description of the polis in Alfred Zimmern, *The Greek Commonwealth*, 5th ed. (New York: Oxford University Press, 1961), pp. 139–79.

7. George H. Sabine, *A History of Political Theory*, 3rd ed. (New York: Holt, 1961), p. 163.

8. Ibid., p. 165.

9. See Michael Oakeshott's chapter, "The Nature and End of the Christian State," in his *The Social and Political Doctrines of Contemporary Europe* (London: Cambridge University Press, 1939).

10. Excellent background here is Helen Cam's chapter, "The Quality of English Feudalism," in her *Law Finders and Law Givers in Medieval England* (New York: Barnes and Noble, 1963).

11. See Norman F. Cantor, *Medieval History* (New York: Macmillan, 1963), pp. 226–38.

12. An excellent corrective in this respect is Giuseppe Prezzolini, *Machiavelli* (New York: Farrar, Straus, and Giroux, 1967). On the seminal influence of Machiavelli, a valuable book by a brilliant young British scholar (tragically killed in a mountain-climbing accident shortly before its publication) is Felix Raab, *The English Face of Machiavelli* (London: Routledge and Kegan Paul, 1964).

13. On the theme of nationalism and the development of the nation-state, see Carlton J. H. Hayes, *Essays on Nationalism* (New York: Macmillan, 1928).

14. On the sort of conflict generated, see Patrick McGrath, *Papists and Puritans under Elizabeth I* (New York: Walker, 1967). One of the best brief treatments of the period is Charles H. McIlwain, *The Growth of Political Thought in the West* (New York: Macmillan, 1932), pp. 201–363.

15. For an exploration of the essential modernity of Hobbes's thought, see

Maurice Goldsmith, *Hobbes's Science of Politics* (New York: Columbia University Press (1966).

16. For a relatively recent study, see Peter Laslett, *John Locke: Two Treatises of Government* (London: Cambridge University Press, 1967).

17. An excellent essay exploring the problematic and ambiguous aspects of Rousseau's thought is Andrew Hacker, *Political Theory: Philosophy, Ideology, Science* (New York: Macmillan, 1961), pp. 289–339.

18. For a fascinating treatment of the evolution of egalitarian–socialist–communist thought and action, see Edmund Wilson, *To the Finland Station* (Garden City, N.Y.: Anchor Books, 1961).

19. A useful introduction to communist thought is Alfred G. Meyer, *Communism* (New York: Random House, 1960).

20. Zbigniew K. Brzezinski, *The Grand Failure: The Birth and Death of Communism in the Twentieth Century* (New York: Scribner, 1989).

21. Michael Novak and Peter L. Berger, *Speaking to the Third World: Essays on Democracy and Development* (Washington, D.C.: American Enterprise Institute, 1985).

22. See, for instance, Henry Milner, *Sweden: Social Democracy in Practice* (New York: Oxford University Press, 1989).

SUGGESTED READINGS

Axelrod, R. *The Evolution of Cooperation.* New York: Basic Books, 1984. By comparing the success of game strategies, Axelrod illuminates a basic aspect of human political behavior: the circumstances under which persons are more, and less, likely to cooperate.

Charlesworth, J., ed. *Contemporary Political Analysis.* New York: Free Press, 1967. A collection that introduces the student to a variety of approaches to the study of politics.

Czudnowski, M., ed. *Political Elites and Social Change.* DeKalb: Northern Illinois University Press, 1983. A distinguished collection of political scientists' essays on the comparative roles of elites in various political systems.

Dahl, R. *Modern Political Analysis.* Englewood Cliffs, N.J.: Prentice-Hall, 1962. An excellent short introduction to the problems of political analysis as perceived by a leading American political scientist.

Downs, A. *An Economic Theory of Democracy.* New York: Harper and Row, 1957. A fascinating attempt at a restatement of democratic theory, using an exchange model of individual motivation—a model borrowed from economics.

Gutmann, A. *Liberal Equality.* New York: Cambridge University Press, 1980. Reconciling the imperatives of liberty and equality has been a central project of modern political theory; Dr. Gutmann's book represents a very sophisticated effort in that direction.

Janowitz, M. *The Reconstruction of Patriotism: Education for Civic Consciousness*. Chicago: University of Chicago Press, 1983. A distinguished political scientist argues that the American liberal consensus has become flabby, and suggests certain innovations—including a volunteer national service—that are sure to be controversial.

McIlwain, C. H. *The Growth of Political Thought in the West*. New York: Macmillan, 1932. An old book, but one of the most lucid expositions of the essentials of classical and medieval political thought.

Mackenzie, W. J. M. *Politics and Social Change*. Baltimore: Penguin, 1967. Particularly useful for its chapter on "social biology," this is one of the most controversial approaches to politics.

Macridis, R. *Contemporary Political Ideologies*, 3rd Edition. Boston: Little, Brown, 1986. A useful survey of the range of modern political belief systems.

Meehan, E. J. *The Homewood Foundations of Political Analysis: Empirical and Normative*. Homewood, Ill.: Dorsey, 1971. A challenging but highly rewarding exploration of traditional and nontraditional approaches to politics.

Neumann, F. *The Democratic and the Authoritarian State*. Glencoe, Ill.: Free Press, 1957. A collection of essays on the tensions between liberty and state power, by one of the most distinguished members of the "Frankfurt School" of political thinkers.

O'Sullivan, N. *Revolutionary Theory and Political Reality*. New York: St. Martin's, 1983. An interesting analysis and comparison of the ideas of various revolutionary leaderships.

Rosenblum, N. L. *Another Liberalism: Romanticism and the Reconstruction of Liberal Thought*. Cambridge, Mass.: Harvard University Press, 1989. A fascinating exploration of a body of liberal thought that has been underemphasized in standard accounts of the tradition.

Runciman, W. *Social Science and Political Theory*. London: Cambridge University Press, 1965. Brilliant essay by an English scholar on Max Weber, Karl Marx, and other theorists of the relationship between politics and society.

Schama, S. *Citizens: A Chronicle of the French Revolution*. New York: Knopf, 1989. The French Revolution was not only one of the great realigning events of world history, but a great intellectual event that is beautifully detailed in this book.

Spiro, H. H. *Politics as the Master Science: From Plato to Mao*. New York: Harper and Row, 1970. A very interesting short analysis of major schools of political thought.

3

Classifying
Political Systems

The most dangerous time for a bad government is when it starts to
reform itself.

—ALEXIS DE TOCQUEVILLE

A universal theory of the state is a chimaera, for historical
development and national character are the most important of all
considerations in investigating the laws of political development.

—JOHN NIVILLE FIGGIS

A WORLD OF DIFFERENCES

One necessary step toward achieving sophistication in political analysis
is to recognize how careless we all are in our ordinary conversation about
politics and how this carelessness is often reinforced by the way politics
and political systems are treated in newspapers and on television. It
seems, for instance, that in the conventional wisdom of journalism the
world is divided into good political systems (democratic, open, free) and
bad political systems (dictatorial, closed, authoritarian). Such a tendency
to dichotomize does violence to the rich variety of political systems that
exist in the world today, and it ignores the even greater variety of systems
that have existed at various times in human experience.[1]

Every day we speak of democratic systems in a casual, offhand way
but are uncomfortably aware, even as we do it, that the difference among
systems loosely characterized as democratic (such as the United States,
Great Britain, and Mexico) may be even greater than the differences that
separate one "democracy" (say, Mexico) from a system usually described as "authoritarian" (say, Chile under the rule of General Augusto
Pinochet). As we shall see again and again in our examination of politics,
the popular vocabulary is inadequate and sometimes misleading. More
variegated and subtle criteria of classification are required to meaningfully
characterize political systems.

PRIMITIVE POLITICAL SYSTEMS

In his classic essay *The Web of Government,* Robert MacIver, one of
the great modern political sociologists, wrote of the role of the family as

43

the building block of society and of the political system that operates in society. "Political government" MacIver pointed out, "is one form of social regulation, but by no means the only form."[2] Regulation of the behavior of individuals is a universal function performed in every society. Society, in MacIver's terms, is merely "a system of ordered relations." This ordering may be achieved via highly informal folkways, without specific institutions of a centralized sort making decisions for the society as a whole. Loose alliances of families (tribes and clans) may come together and form quite effective hunting/gathering or simple agricultural societies without ever evolving fixed mechanisms of government.

In its simplest form, the relationship among family, society, and state may be seen as pyramidal. The family provides regulation of individual behavior within its own boundaries of kinship. Kinship groups may be linked together in the tribe or the clan and their relationships one with another regulated by informal understandings or by intermittent authority, such as meetings of chiefs or elders or periodic councils of headmen. The step to the creation of the state establishes specialized institutions of government that, as we noted in Chapter 2, can make authoritative decisions for the society as a whole and back them up, if necessary, with legitimate uses of force. An *institution* is nothing more than a regular, recurring pattern of human interaction that is identifiable and that perpetuates itself in time. The regularly elected selectmen of a small New England town constitute a political institution, as does the Congress of the United States.

This evolution from family to interconnected network of families to clan and tribe and finally to formal institutions of government was first brought into focus by the British writer Sir Henry Maine in his book *Ancient Law,* published in 1861. It has been suggested that Maine's book did for the study of human institutions what Charles Darwin's *On the Origin of Species* did for the study of biological nature. Just as Darwin's great work emphasized the evolution of life from simpler to higher forms, so Maine's *Ancient Law* emphasized the evolution of societies from the more primitive to the more developed or modern. *Law*—the formal rules by which government is organized and by which it regulates the lives of individuals who live in the society—was not something that sprang up one day full-blown. Rather, it developed over centuries, at very different rates in different places.[3]

Thus, when we say that a political system is "primitive" or "traditional," we mean that the evolution from loosely ordered and rather informal social relationships to specialized regulation of certain aspects of life in the society by permanent institutions of government has not progressed to the point it has reached in a modern state. History is replete with examples of successful and unsuccessful transitions from pregovernmental (primitive) to modern governmental organization.

In the seventeenth and eighteenth centuries, five warlike tribes (Mohawks, Senecas, Cayugas, Onandagas, and Oneidas) of Native Americans in what is now Upstate New York made an attempt at governmental organization. Their creation—the Iroquois League—achieved considerable success and stability, succeeded for generations in eliminating war among the member tribes, and provided a way for the tribes to relate in a somewhat coordinated fashion to the growing European presence in North America. However, the coming of the Revolutionary War and the tensions generated by the split between those loyal to Britain and those siding with the American rebels proved too much for the league, and its fragile structure collapsed. It is interesting that, although the formal mechanisms of the league were well worked out and understood, its existence was only intermittent. The occasional meetings of tribal representatives in the central council were not supplemented by institutions operating through the year.[4]

Quite similar patterns of nation building are evident in Europe. In the thirteenth and fourteenth centuries, for instance, the wild clans of the Highlands of Scotland were drawn together under a central monarchy. Although it lasted longer than the Iroquois League would four centuries later, the Scottish monarchy remained a fragile government, able only with great difficulty to exercise authority over the fractious chiefs and regional barons. In the course of political evolution, the Scottish state was subsumed into the larger and more effective English governmental system.

CLASSIFYING MODERN POLITICAL SYSTEMS

"Discrimination" is a word that needs rehabilitation. In America it has become tainted by its association with racial discrimination, and persons of good will now tend to shy away from it in other contexts. This is too bad, because all serious intellectual work (of which political analysis is a branch) involves making intelligent distinctions (discriminations) between things that are grossly alike but subtly different. To do this necessary discriminating, we need criteria of classification that are both reasonably clear and reasonably well agreed on by other participants in the analytical enterprise.

Classification by Governmental Form

Perhaps the most familiar (and certainly the oldest) way to compare political systems is in terms of the *form* of government. Thus in Chapter 2 we found both Plato and Aristotle distinguishing among *democratic* forms of government (in which ultimate decisional power is vested in a group of voting citizens), *oligarchy* (in which the direction of affairs is in the hands of a ruling elite), and *monarchy* (in which the power to govern is vested in a single individual). Each of these three forms was seen to have its particular strengths and weaknesses, but all three were clearly preferable to *ochlocracy*—the breakdown of governmental forms into rule by the mob.

In fact, the Greek historian Polybius (203–120 B.C.) took these ideas a step further, developing a cyclical theory of governmental degeneration and succession. Each pure governmental form was flawed; it would inevitably decay, become corrupt, and give way to a successor form. Thus, the virtuous and effective king would die, and his son—a mediocre ruler—would only just get by. This son's offspring—an incompetent knave—would reduce the kindgom to near ruin. This degeneration would result in an oligarchy; leading persons within the society would seize control to put things right.

In the same way, however, the virtue and skill of these high-minded oligarchs was nonrenewable; as death forced the problem of succession, factional splits would deepen. Again discontent would grow. The oligarchs would be driven from power by a popular movement, and democracy established. Democracy, in turn, was subject to the fatal danger of demagoguery. Although the initial response of the participating citizens to the crisis brought on by the decaying oligarchy would be effective, sooner or later the losers in the conflicts of democratic politics would be tempted to make irrational appeals to the citizens. Such demagogic initiatives would be met by demagogic responses, and the polity would decay into ochlocracy (mob rule) with its anarchic chaos and paralysis of governmental structures. This situation would eventually be salvaged by the coming of a superbly talented leader who would be capable of gathering enough support to reestablish the state in his person; in other words, there would be a new king and a new beginning of the cycle.[5]

Of course, Polybius borrowed heavily from Aristotle. But he did sharpen one important idea in his classification of polities by governmental form. He refined Aristotle's suggestion that, given the inevitable decay one into another in the cycle of failure and replacement, long-term stability of government might be sought by mixing regimes. That is, a form of government with monarchical, oligarchical, *and* democratic aspects might have some chance of long-term survival. The strength of one element of the mixed constitutions would operate at times to offset the weaknesses of another. Democracy, for instance, could not degenerate into persecution of minorities, because either the king or the council of oligarchs would have enough power to restrain the majority and contain the disastrous effects of demagoguery. By the same token, prolonged inattention by the monarch or the oligarchs to pressing societal needs would result in democratic pressure on oligarchs or the monarch to respond to popular impulses.

Classification by Type of Regime

Recently, political analysts have grown dissatisfied with the classification of political systems according to the form of government. For one thing, by the middle of the twentieth century, few polities were formally describing themselves as monarchies. Most countries were—in name at least—"democracies," making some pretense of having representative institutions. Thus, the former Soviet Union had a very fine legislature (the Supreme Soviet), which did not in fact play any significant role in setting governmental policy; and the periodic elections held throughout the country were a sham.

Obviously, some sharper analytical tools than those provided by Aristotle and Polybius are needed to distinguish among polities. What has evolved is a classification system that looks not to the form of government, but rather to the relationship that actually exists between those who really control the mechanisms of the state and the rest of society. How, in short, do the rulers actually relate to the ruled?

Although each modern writer varies the terminology and definitions, three major *types* of political systems are characteristically identified: *pluralist* systems, *authoritarian* systems, and *totalitarian* systems.

Pluralist Systems

In governmental form, a pluralist system might be a republic or a constitutional monarchy or, not inconceivably, an oligarchy. What is important to the existence of pluralism is the capacity of a variety of groups within the population to have a sustained impact on the behavior of governmental decision makers. In its ideal version (which, of course, does not exist in reality), a wide variety of overlapping religious, economic, ethnic, and geographical groupings—operating through organizational elites—would compete and form alliances to achieve particular policy outcomes. In addition, the governmental decision makers would be required, as a prudential matter, to take into account the anticipated reactions of major groups within the population in making their decisions.

Certainly, the style of interest group activity differs from pluralism to pluralism; but the reality of group activity—of pressure and of governmental deference to the twistings and turnings of group wants and perceptions—persists. In the Netherlands, for example, interest group activity is highly regularized.[6] That is, the interest groups are formally represented within the structure of the governmental bureaucracy on various boards and commissions. Thus, an American political scientist writing on the systems of the Benelux countries (Belgium, the Netherlands, and Luxembourg) was told in all seriousness by Dutch officials whom he was interviewing that interest groups do not exist in the

Netherlands. All these officials really meant here was that interest groups do not operate with the same organizational style with which they operate in, say, the United States. In the United States, interest groups are formally quite separate from government, and their approaches to government are freewheeling, intermittent, and spontaneous.

Authoritarian Systems

Authoritarian systems, or "traditional dictatorships" as they are sometimes called, may be monarchical or oligarchical or democratic in governmental form. But in all of these systems, the activity of interest groups in attempting to exert pressure on and influence the governing elite is sharply restricted. The governing elite—be it a single "maximum leader" or junta—demands and achieves autonomy in matters of public choice. The leader or the oligarch may (and almost certainly will, in order to remain in power for any substantial period of time) take into account the anticipated reactions of major groupings within the population. But the free play of political forces with access to governmental decision makers is sharply limited.

Examples of traditional dictatorships include Spain under the late Generalissimo Francisco Franco,[7] Greece under the regime of the "colonels" who seized power in 1967 and ruled in authoritarian fashion until they were driven from power and elective politics was resumed in 1973, and the regimes governing Syria and Iraq today.

In authoritarian systems, political liberty is restricted, sometimes to the extent of violent repression of insurgent political groups. However, in nonpolitical areas of life (religion, commercial activity, scholarship, and the arts), considerable latitude for individual initiative and fulfillment may exist. As long as one conforms politically, one is allowed to lead one's private life relatively unsupervised and undirected by the state.

Furthermore, authoritarian regimes do not characteristically try to exercise the extensive controls over the lives of their societies that one sees in totalitarian cases. As Carl Friedrich and Zbigniew Brzezinski have pointed out, authoritarian regimes tend to be based on certain key powerful social institutions (the church, the army, the large landholders, the banks, the old established families, and so on).[8] The regime cannot undermine these crucial parts of the foundation that supports it. The object of the authoritarian ruler is maintenance of the status quo, not the remaking or mobilization of society.

Totalitarian Systems

The distinctive aspect of the contemporary totalitarian system of political organization was first placed in sharp focus by the late Hannah Arendt. Trained in philosophy, Arendt was a refugee from Hitler's

Germany and became one of the most sensitive observers of the twentieth-century political scene. Her 1951 book *The Origins of Totalitarianism* is a benchmark of political analysis. No longer was it possible to think of all dictatorial regimes as essentially similar.[9]

Today many commentators agree that totalitarian political organization is a recent, or "modern," phenomenon. That is, the kind of relationship between the rulers and ruled that characterizes the totalitarian system could be achieved in the twentieth century only after the advent of advanced technology, with its swift means of travel and rapid communications. By contrast, in traditional dictatorships there is no requirement that the population be drawn into vast, intricately monitored activity based on an ideology to which allegiance is required. Moreover, authoritarian regimes often allow the development of a diverse private sector including, but not limited to, economic enterprise. What is forbidden is political organizing in opposition to the regime, and criticism of the regime is sharply limited.

Such limitation of demands on the population is not characteristic of the totalitarian system. On the contrary, the population does not enjoy privacy and is not allowed to go about its own pursuits, satisfying its own social and economic impulses as long as it stays within the limits set by the regime. The characteristic feature of the totalitarian system is mobilization—a demanding outreach for not merely the acquiescence, but indeed the positive participation, of the population. The regime is interested not only in perpetuating itself and closing off alternatives and opposition, but also in managing society—in reconstructing the whole people on a model dictated by the ideology. Every institution of society must be drawn into the effort and must take, as its core mission, advancement of the program of the regime. Hence the omnipresent political officer and cadre. The authoritarian system may discourage the formation of labor unions because they may later emerge as rallying points for political opposition. The totalitarian system forms its own unions to serve as adjuncts of the regime and as tools for mobilizing, motivating, and disciplining the workers. As Brian Crozier has written,

Authoritarian governments seek to abolish politics; totalist [totalitarian] governments seek to involve the entire population in politics. In Franco's Spain . . . it was possible to live a full life so long as one did not indulge in politics outside the recommended forms. Citizens could travel freely, and . . . the economy was overwhelmingly in private hands. In China—the ultimate totalist regime—it was impossible to opt out of politics, since the entire people was kept permanently involved under the vigilant eyes of the Communist Party cadres. It is fair to add, however, that if ordinary people were far freer in authoritarian Spain than in totalist Russia, the lot of politically active dissidents was only marginally better for Spaniards than for Russians.[10]

To put it bluntly, authoritarian regimes look good only by comparison to totalitarianism. While limited pluralism may be allowed in an authoritarian setting, constitutionalism is always a casualty.

For anyone interested in understanding the ways in which social control and mobilization are attempted (and often accomplished) in a totalitarian system, there was no better example than the Communist Party of the Soviet Union (the CPSU) in the middle decades of this century. And the crucial links in the system of party control were the first secretaries of the regional *(oblast)* and territorial *(krai)* party committees. These officials made up almost two-thirds of the membership of the Central Committee of the CPSU before Mikhail Gorbachev's reforms began to take hold at the end of the 1980s. In their home territories they presided, with the broadest and most effective kind of political mandate, over all public activities and many that in the West would be considered private. The distinguished Sovietologist T. H. Rigby reminds us of what party control was like in the pre-Gorbachev Soviet Union: "there is scarcely an area of organized activity in this region on which the [party] secretary may not be called upon to make a decision, or a social institution or organization for whose performance he cannot be called to account."[11]

Some scholars have referred to this kind of party control as "penetration" of society, and it is a factor that powerfully distinguishes totalitarian from authoritarian systems. While party control disintegrated in the former Soviet Union, the example of the successful suppression of the prodemocracy movement by the hardline communist leadership of China is a sobering reminder of the persistence of totalitarianism.

We must remember, though, that abstractions such as "totalitarian" and "authoritarian" are ideal types and that real political systems will only resemble one type more than another. And there are close cases; you can get a lively debate among scholars, for instance, on whether fascist Italy (1928–43) under Benito Mussolini was more an authoritarian or more a totalitarian regime. How one ultimately answers this question is not nearly so significant as what one learns about fascist Italy in the process of analyzing it and comparing it to, say, Nazi Germany. The real utility of categories of classification is not that they clearly separate the close cases, but that they do so for the gross cases. We can argue about fascist Italy or contemporary Serbia, but we need to be able to distinguish quickly between Franco's Spain and Stalin's Russia.

CONSTITUTIONALISM

We have examined the classification of political systems by form of government and, in a more modern idiom, in terms of the relationship of the ruling regime to the mass of the population. There remains, however, one type of government that overlaps the others: *constitutional* government.

Just what is constitutionalism? And what does it mean to say that a particular political system is a constitutional system? Much ink has been wasted in describing the differences between written and unwritten con-

---

Box 3-1. Aspects of Law

A political system does not have to be constitutional to sustain a functioning and useful legal subsystem, although constitutional polities tend to have more extensive and better developed legal institutions than, say, primitive or totalitarian systems. In Chapter 10 we shall examine the functions performed by courts in the United States and in other systems. But here, while we are still developing our vocabulary, it is useful to familiarize ourselves with some basic legal terminology, which has a way of cropping up frequently in discussions of politics.

Law *itself, at its simplest level, is a binding rule that a state is prepared to use its coercive powers to enforce. Such rules may be promulgated by assemblies, such as legislatures or tribal councils; they may take the form of decrees by a dictator or an elected leader authorized to rule by decree in emergencies. Such rules may be customary or traditional—reflecting the way it has been and is—or they may be made by judges in the course of deciding on conflicting claims brought before them.*

Common law *is a body of rules evolved through the process of judges deciding particular cases, stating the reasons for their decisions, and thereby creating precedents. Following the principle of* stare decisis *("to stand by things settled"), other judges rely on the prior decision as authoritative, and a rule—a law—is born.*

Natural law *is a concept we have already encountered in Chapter 2. It is the conviction that some principles are basic and fundamental to human nature or God's plan for the universe. These "laws" are therefore morally binding whether or not governments have chosen (or been wise enough) to recognize them in the* positive law *(the enforced and consistently administered law) of the jurisdiction. For the medieval scholastics such as Thomas Aquinas, the task of "right reason" was to discover natural law and then see that it be implemented. The difficulty of doing this in larger pluralistic societies is that, whereas most of us probably sense that there are natural or divinely ordained rules that all should follow, these rules stubbornly refuse to reveal themselves to all of us in the same ways. It is impossible to base positive law on natural law without preferring somebody's vision over somebody else's. In a democracy the only way to do this is by counting noses. For this reason, democratic legal systems are best understood in terms of legal positivism, rather than natural law.*

stitutions. In fact, what is important is not whether a constitution is written down or whether it is written down in a single document, but whether the rules of constitutional law—be they customary or written, whether they evolved slowly over time or were adopted all at once— actually constrain governmental leaders in their uses of state power. This point may be obvious, but it is by no means trivial. It is the core of the matter.[12]

Constitutions characteristically purport to do two things: (1) describe the structure of government and the allocation of formal legal capacity among the elements of the government; and (2) place certain limitations on the way government can behave toward individuals. In performing this latter function, constitutions create individual civil rights. These formal allocations of governing authority and these limitations on government, which we call "individual rights," can be either taken seriously or ignored. The constitution may actually describe in rough terms the way the country is governed, or it may be quite irrelevant to an understanding of a particular political system. In the case of the old Soviet Union, for instance, the constitution of 1936 (substantially amended in 1977) did describe the structure of the Soviet state, but, until recently, the rules of the Communist party told us more about the structure of the actual governing capacity in the Soviet Union than the constitution did.[13]

This is not to say that, for a regime to be meaningfully constitutional, every jot and tittle of its formal constitutional language must be followed in every case. It is to say that first, there must be a substantial correspondence between the actual arrangement of governing power and that described in the constitution *and,* second, the individual's rights created by the constitution must be taken seriously by those who exercise governmental power.[14] Some constitutions have provisions for temporary suspension of certain individual rights in national emergencies. This does not necessarily invalidate the constitution or make it a mockery. However, if emergencies tend to be frequent or to become permanent, the exception has eaten up the rules, and the system can no longer be considered constitutional.[15]

DEMOCRACY

We have previously defined democracy as the ancients—Aristotle and Polybius—defined it: ultimate decisional power vested in a group of voting citizens. It is now time to do greater justice to the term. The term *democracy* carries with it a rich and varying baggage of meanings in contemporary political discourse; but until we had developed such terms as "pluralism," "authoritarianism," and "constitutionalism," it was not possible to discuss democracy as a criterion of classification in all of its richness. There are, in fact, several distinct schools of democratic thought today.

Representatives of what might be called the *traditionalist* approach to democratic theory stress the centrality of representative institutions, and the preservation of individual liberties through constitutionalism, as the defining qualities of democracy. Representatives of what might be called the *neorealist* approach to democratic theory stress the performance of the government in providing for the objective material needs of the citizens, and the extent to which the system fosters social and economic equality.

All students of democratic society agree, however, on a few fundamentals:

1. That there be periodic elections to fill the positions in which real governing power is vested
2. That there exist an independent political opposition to those in power and that the power holders be effectively restrained from suppressing this opposition
3. That opportunity be maintained for free political speech
4. That opportunity be maintained for some significant social and economic mobility, both upward and downward.[16]

With the much heralded "triumph of democratic values" in the late twentieth century, it is perhaps inevitable that there exists less and less agreement about what constitutes "real democracy." The more we have of it, the more we realize that democracy comes in many shapes and sizes; in the coming years, the debate will only intensify.[17] At its core, however, "democracy" will always refer to something like the four fundamental elements above.

FURTHER REFINEMENTS

Constitutionalism and democracy are familiar criteria of classification. They distinguish some political systems from others in a meaningful way. In recent decades, however, political scientists have developed other criteria that, though perhaps not so powerful for classification purposes as, say, constitutionalism, enable us to recognize subtle differences between political systems, which in turn enable us to recognize subtle distinctions between types of constitutional and democratic polities. Mexico and Italy are both democratic and constitutional systems; but one is characterized by a feisty competition of multiple political parties, and one by the relatively disciplined and orderly operations of a single party. Similarly, Sweden and the United States are both democratic and constitutional systems, even though the levels of political participation in

Sweden are far higher than those in the United States and the extent of government management control and intervention in society is far greater in Sweden than in the United States.

Polyarchy

In 1971 Professor Robert A. Dahl published a short book entitled *Polyarchy: Participation and Opposition.*[18] Dahl began by arguing that "a key characteristic of democracy is the continuing responsiveness of the government to the preferences of its citizens, considered as political equals." And he further stressed that the term *democracy* should be reserved "for a political system one of the characteristics of which is the quality of being completely or almost completely responsive to all its citizens." There were thus a number of political systems—both in the West and in the Third World—that, although not fully democratic (and perhaps not even constitutional in a strict sense), are nonetheless open and competitive. They are open and competitive in ways that totalitarian and authoritarian regimes, which concentrate political power in a single elite, are not. Dahl called all systems characterized by rule from the top "hegemonic." In a polyarchical system, by contrast, there is the continuing possibility of struggle over policy among contending elites—or, as Dahl puts it, the possibility of "contestation."

In further contrast to hegemonic systems, polyarchies are characterized by some considerable inclusiveness of citizens within the political process—that is, by meaningful levels and opportunities for participation in politics. In the polyarchical system, as opposed to the hegemonic, persons outside the governing elite can have impact on policymaking. (See Figure 3-1).

At first reading, Dahl's conception of polyarchy might seem a trifle artificial or strained. It might even seem that polyarchy is democracy traveling in semantic disguise. A moment's reflection, however, reveals that the term *polyarchy* enables one to distinguish between full-fledged democracies and other systems that, although not dictatorial in the pattern of rule, are not, for example, characterized by regular elections. If there are opportunities for contestation by alternative elites, and if there is an opportunity through interest groups or through a free press to urge alternative courses of action on the rulers, the system can meaningfully be described as polyarchical while being very imperfectly democratic.

Mass Societies

Polyarchy is a useful concept because it allows us to discriminate between regimes that are not dictatorial yet are not quite democratic or even constitutional. Another highly useful concept is that of the mass

Figure 3-1. Dahl's Typology

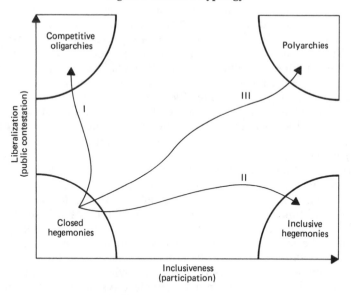

Source: Robert A. Dahl, *Polyarchy: Participation and Opposition* (New Haven: Yale University Press, 1971), p. 7. Reprinted by permission.

society, best developed by William Kornhauser in a book entitled *The Politics of Mass Society,* published in 1959.[19] This is a concept that enables us to distinguish between polities on the basis of the nature and dynamics of their social structures.

Kornhauser was fascinated by the problem of the modern large industrialized nation-state in which the traditional identifications of tribe, village, guild, and caste have broken down. If these basic social entities in which people lived and worked were not replaced by other kinds of mediating institutions, there was danger that the ruling elites of society could gain direct communications access to the undifferentiated and unorganized non-elites (the masses) and thereby manipulate them. Thus, mass society was a society vulnerable to totalitarian manipulation. The exploitation of modern electronic communication—facilitating direct links between a ruling elite and an atomized mass of individuals, without the necessity of operating through a network of traditional intervening institutions—was, Kornhauser thought, distinctly threatening. If, on the other hand, a rich infrastructure of intervening institutions existed, and a variety of interest groups and decentralized communities operated within the social system, the ability of a ruling elite to communicate directly with and manipulate the masses was reduced. Furthermore, in such a situation, the capacity of non-elites to have access to elites was enhanced.

In premodern societies (Kornhauser calls them "communal"), the traditional elites at the top were immune to the influence of non-elites; but the non-elites, in their turn, were insulated by the organization of feudal society—with its net of tight mediating structures—against unlimited manipulation by elites. In the totalitarian society, by contrast, the elites are immune to influence by the masses *and* the masses are not insulated by mediating structures and are susceptible to direct and sustained manipulation by the elite. (See Figure 3-2.) In pluralist societies, elites are highly accessible to non-elites, but a network of interest groups, local communities, and other associational structures provides insulation for the masses. The true mass society is characterized by highly available (unorganized and uninsulated) non-elites.

It is clear, then, that mass society is an inherently unstable social configuration. Indeed—like certain of the rare, more unstable elements—it infrequently exists in nature. In real-life transitions to modernity, the pressing and immediate question is whether the elites will solidify their position, isolate themselves from non-elites, and achieve manipulative control of the masses. Or will a process of organizational differentiation take place within the mass of the citizenry, resulting in the development of a network of mediating structures that will render the masses less available to elite manipulation and provide ways of taking advantage of access to elites in order that countervailing influence be exercised over policy? Consider, in this regard, the news in the summer of 1984 that the ruling party of Prime Minister Robert Mugabe in Zimbabwe had adopted a new party constitution calling for the eventual creation of an explicitly Marxist, one-party state.[20] This act does not necessarily mean movement in the direction of totalitarianism, but it did not augur well for the development of pluralism in that young nation.

The concept of mass society does more than provide a fancier, glorified way of distinguishing between totalitarian and pluralist political systems. It helps us understand why, in traditional societies, the kind of political

Figure 3-2. Kornhauser's Typology

AVAILABILITY OF NON-ELITES

		Low	High
ACCESSIBILITY OF ELITES	Low	communal society	totalitarian society
	High	pluralist society	mass society

Source: William Kornhauser, *The Politics of Mass Society* (Glencoe, Ill.: Free Press, 1959), p. 40. Reprinted with permission of The Free Press, a Division of Macmillan, Inc. Copyright © 1959 by The Free Press.

power typically exercised by monopoly elites in hegemonic modern societies is restrained. More important, it directs our attention to social features that may be harbingers of political change. Is a traditional infrastructure of mediating institutions breaking down? If so, it may bode ill for the political future of the society. Is the elite structure of society gradually becoming more available to mass access and influence? If so, this may indicate a traditional dictatorship evolving toward pluralism, or what Dahl would call "polyarchy."

This analytical tool is not so powerful as some others, but it gives us a subtle and very helpful way to approach societies and political systems in transition.

THOSE BLOCKBUSTER WORDS

We are now well on our way to developing a vocabulary of political analysis. We have waited until this point in our development of terms and concepts to reflect on a few very frequently used words requiring special consideration. They carry with them such resonances of "goodness" that they are overused and loosely used with wild abandon. In some cases, they are deliberately misused so that their aura of goodness can be borrowed and used to camouflage ideas that are very different from those to which the words are properly attached.

Liberty

The English political scientist Harold Laski (1883–1950) once remarked that *liberty* is the capacity of an individual to do what he or she "damned well pleases." Though it lacks elegance, this definition goes to the core of the matter. More specifically, liberty is the absence of restraint by the state on individual belief and action.

But although liberty has been a core value in the Western political tradition since at least the seventeenth century, it is a value that has its awkward aspects. Individual assertions of liberty may often run counter to the common good of the community. The capacity of the individual to say "No, thank you" to the state may result in the state's not being able to make some decision, enact some law, or implement some program that would be of general benefit to many people within the polity. More seriously, liberty will in many instances be contradictory to democracy. To mark off certain spheres in which the individual may decline governmental direction is to curb the capacity of the majority to use the instrumentality of the state as it wishes to advance the common good. But the most important value conflict produced by the assertion of liberty involves the conflict between liberty and equality.

Equality

Liberty was the ascendant political value in the West during the eighteenth and nineteenth centuries, but its dominance did not go unchallenged. Tom Paine (1737–1809) defended the American colonial revolt against British rule in his *Common Sense* (1776) and defended the French Revolution in his two tracts, *The Rights of Man,* published in 1790 and 1792. A self-taught political journalist, Paine was a proponent of the theory of natural rights. In this view, the state is obliged to respect a number of rights with which humans are endowed at birth. Among these is the right of *political equality* of all persons—a notion that by the early nineteenth century was being more and more commonly affirmed in the United States and Great Britain, and to a lesser extent in Europe. By the end of the nineteenth century, this understanding of equality as involving equal political status was established as an ascendant principle.

During the nineteenth century, political equality became coupled increasingly with another conception of equality: *equality of opportunity.* This concept suggests that a good society and its government provide conditions in which individuals are enabled to better their material lots in accordance with their ambitions and abilities, but within a system of laws requiring them to respect the lives and property of others. These two conceptions of equality—political equality and equality of opportunity— wound around and through each other through the political history of the emerging American nation and the British constitutional monarchy, and together they constitute today what may be called the "traditional understanding" of equality.

It is important to note that this traditional understanding is altogether compatible with extensive individual liberty; in fact, Tom Paine listed respect for private property along with political equality as among the natural human rights. But we have already seen another concept of equality that was developed in the nineteenth century (principally by adherents of Marx) and is still capable of attracting adherents in Western societies today. In this view, government has a positive responsibility not only to encourage conditions of equal opportunity, but also to engage in efforts to equalize social outcomes. That is, not only will individuals be guaranteed equal political rights, but they will also be assured by government that, within certain limits, the outcomes of social interaction will not vary dramatically. This is an equality not of opportunity but of results, or, as it is sometimes called, *egalitarianism.*

In contemporary America, egalitarians such as sociologist Christopher Jencks advance eloquent arguments for government activism to create more equal social outcomes, leading to what is often called "equality of condition." But there is no denying—nor do Jencks and those who agree with him attempt it—that government action aimed at eqalitarian outcomes will involve some infringement on individual liberty.[21]

Freedom

Certainly the biggest of all blockbuster words of politics is *freedom*. It s, at one and the same time, the most emotionally potent and the least pecific word in the lexicon of political analysis. The word is often used oosely in a fashion that makes it synonymous with liberty—the absence f restraint on an individual's behavior. This may be too old a sense of he word to exorcise, and yet it distorts the essential meaning of freedom.

Liberty is a perfectly useful concept to describe the absence of restraint nd the capacity to say "No" to government. Freedom is a wider, more pacious, and ultimately more important concept. It includes not simply he capacity to do what one pleases, but also the idea of a certain degree f success or individual fulfillment among the citizens of a particular tate.

To say that one is free is to say something more than that one is at berty to go about one's business, to develop a "lifestyle," to amass roperty, to rear one's children, and to speak one's mind independent of nterference by the state. Freedom also implies something more than here legal or economic equality. A person who is free possesses capaci-ies and achieves something—some state of being or consciousness that rings satisfaction and carries with it the confidence that he or she has enefited from the social order and from the operation of the system.[22]

Is freedom the capacity to satisfy material wants? Is freedom the erfection of one's spiritual life toward the end of salvation? Is freedom, s communist orthodoxy once decreed it, participation in the dictatorship f the proletariat that is proceeding through the phase of the construction f socialism toward the ultimate realization of pure communism? Is ndividual liberty or is the egalitarian engineering of outcomes more mportant to the nurturing of freedom?

There are no easy answers to these questions. We will return to them requently throughout this book in the course of considering the various olitical systems and the various conflicts that rage within them.

Justice

Finally, and almost as elusive as the concept of freedom, there is *ustice*. All sectors of all populations call for it, college students demand t of teachers and administrators, children call for it from their parents, nd all governments around the world pay it homage.

But that is the problem. Everyone extols it; everyone wants it. Yet we now that individuals, groups, and nations usually want many mutually xclusive things. The full-blooded cynic will argue that justice represents othing more than a particular individual's perception (or the perception f a group of like-minded individuals) about what outcome would be atisfactory in a particular situation. There is more force to this than

most of us like to admit, but it cannot be accepted as altogether true. I
is possible—we have the historical examples—for reasonable people to
agree to treat equal things equally and unequal things unequally, and then
to agree on rough rules for determining how one decides which things are
equal to which other things. But realizing that every concept of justice
has a substantial subjective component is the beginning of sophistication
in one's relationship with this powerful and evocative term. "Justice"
cannot, ultimately, be divorced from one's sense of what are appropriate
outcomes in particular situations. Although it is possible to work out
rough but serviceable agreements (laws and conventions) to guide the
resolution of particular types of social and even international conflict,
justice in the pure sense is an illusive and variable concept. One individual's sense of what is appropriate will often be different from another's.
And to sense that a particular outcome is appropriate may be altogether
different from recommending it as wise public policy to the community.[2]

Contemporary Liberalism and Contemporary Conservatism

It is easy to see the relationship between the basic idea of liberty and
the classical writers of the liberal tradition (such as John Locke and
Adam Smith), who conceived of the state as limited in its functions and
who saw most human achievements and satisfactions (freedom) proceeding from the free interaction of individuals in the private sector of society.
A hallmark of classical liberalism (see Chapter 2) was suspicion of and
restrained hostility to the coercive force of the state. Yet we sense that
the description ill fits those we call *liberals* in America today; that those
who hold such views are most often described as *conservative*. This
confusion is, however, easily dispelled.[24]

With the rapid industrialization that took place in America during the
latter decades of the nineteenth and early decades of the twentieth
centuries, more and more sensitive observers of our politics became
convinced that unregulated economic development was denying the essential conditions of freedom to too many citizens. The developing
extremes of wealth and poverty made equal opportunity a mockery.
Intervention by government was more and more often necessary to
regulate private economic power and to provide for basic fairness in
economic relationships. In short, many felt that the goal of freedom
required some sacrifice of liberty in order to equalize opportunity and to
provide minimally decent conditions of life to all persons. The shift from
classical liberalism to social-welfare liberalism was accelerated by the
Great Depression of the 1930s; more and more, social-welfare liberals
emphasized equality of result rather than equality of opportunity. By the
1970s a transformation had been effected by which American liberals,
while remaining committed to vigorous protection of individual civil
rights and liberties vis-à-vis government, had absorbed an essentially

Marxist preoccupation with equality and an eagerness to use government extensively as an instrument of social reform and management quite alien to the spirit of classical liberalism.

However, as Terence Ball and Richard Dagger point out,

This is not to say that neoclassical liberalism ever entirely disappeared. . . . In the 1970s and '80s, furthermore, neoclassical liberalism has enjoyed a revival. The emergence of the Libertarian Party is one sign of this revival, as is the admiration for "free market" policies so evident in the Thatcher and Reagan governments.[25]

SUMMARY

In this chapter our focus shifted from the history and vocabulary of political thought to contemporary political analysis.

We first surveyed the attempt to classify political systems by the prevailing form of government (monarchy, oligarchy, and democracy). The difficulty with this classification scheme is that the reality so often does not reflect the theory. Furthermore, there are few formal monarchies left in the world, and oligarchies habitually decline to identify themselves as such.

To overcome these difficulties, political scientists have developed a means of classifying political systems in terms of the type of regime actually operating (pluralist, authoritarian, or totalitarian). Here the critical issue is the extent to which the rulers must take into account the demands of the ruled and the extent to which society as a whole must respond to the demands for conformity and active support (mobilization) made by the state.

Next we considered the meaning of the term *constitutionalism*, stressing again the importance of looking beyond the form of a museum-cased document and observing the extent to which government is actually restrained by constitutional principles in dealing with citizens. Thus prepared, we moved on to explore some of the nuances—the shades of meaning—that are associated with the word *democracy*. Following this, we defined and considered the utility of the concepts of polyarchy (Dahl) and mass society (Kornhauser).

Finally, we commented on a small set of very highly charged but very broad terms—terms that occur so frequently that we tend to take them for granted. We should not; we should form the habit of insisting that people explain that they mean by words such as "justice" and "liberal"—lest the chance for a clear exchange of ideas be lost at the outset.

Perhaps nothing is more important to your own growing skill in political analysis than using words (the tools of analysis) in ways that are precise. To do this successfully, you must avoid the twin traps of emotionalism and sentimentality; they are to clear communication about politics what water is to gasoline.

NOTES

1. Consider, for instance, the Moslem variants discussed in Elie Kedourie, *Islam in the Modern World* (New York: Holt, 1980).

2. R. M. MacIver, *The Web of Government* (New York: Macmillan, 1947), p. 22.

3. Henry Maine, *Ancient Law* (London: J. M. Dent, Everyman's Library edition, 1960).

4. See James Thomas Flexner, *Lord of the Mohawks* (Boston: Little, Brown, 1979), pp. 28–42.

5. See the discussion of Polybius in George H. Sabine, *A History of Political Theory*, 3rd ed. (New York: Holt, 1961), pp. 154–56.

6. See Gordon L. Weil, *The Benelux Nations* (New York: Holt, 1970), esp. pp. 114–27.

7. See Arthur P. Whitaker, *Spain and the Defense of the West* (New York: Praeger, 1962).

8. Carl Friedrich and Zbigniew Brzezinski, *Totalitarian Dictatorship and Autocracy* (Cambridge, Mass.: Harvard University Press, 1956).

9. Hannah Arendt, *The Origins of Totalitarianism* (New York: Harcourt, 1951).

10. Brian Crozier, *A Theory of Conflict* (London: Hamish Hamilton, 1974), pp. 85–86.

11. See T. H. Rigby, "The Soviet Regional Leadership: The Brezhnev Generation," *Slavic Review*, 37, no. 1 (1978): 1–24.

12. See M. J. C. Vile, *Constitutionalism and the Separation of Powers* (New York: Oxford University Press, 1967), pp. 8–9.

13. Ivo Lapenna, "Marxism and the Soviet Constitutions," *Conflict Studies*, no. 106 (April 1979).

14. Still an excellent introduction to the intricacies of constitutional theory is Charles Howard McIlwain, *Constitutionalism: Ancient and Modern*, rev. ed. (Ithaca, N.Y.: Cornell University Press, 1947).

15. Paul Johnson, *Enemies of Society* (New York: Atheneum, 1977) p. 259.

16. An excellent recent collection of essays exploring the concept is J. Roland Pennock and John W. Chapman, eds., *Liberal Democracy: Nomos XXV* (New York: New York University Press, 1983).

17. See Benjamin Barber, *The Conquest of Politics: Liberal Philosophy in Democratic Times* (Princeton, N.J.: Princeton University Press, 1988).

18. Robert A. Dahl, *Polyarchy: Participation and Opposition* (New Haven, Conn.: Yale University Press, 1971).

19. William Kornhauser, *The Politics of Mass Society* (Glencoe, Ill.: Free Press, 1959).

20. *New York Times,* August 12 and 13, 1984.

21. See Christopher Jencks, et al., *Who Gets Ahead in America? The Determinants of Economic Success in America* (New York: Basic Books, 1979).

22. For an especially insightful exploration of the various nuances of the meaning of the term *freedom,* see Franz Neumann, "The Concept of Political Freedom," in Herbert Morcase, ed., *The Democratic and the Authoritarian State* (New York: Free Press, 1957), pp. 160–200.

23. Perhaps the single most important recent work dealing with these themes is John Rawls, *A Theory of Justice* (Cambridge, Mass.: Harvard University Press, 1971).

24. The classic on American liberalism is Louis Hartz, *The Liberal Tradition in America* (New York: Harcourt, Brace, 1955). In recent years Professor Hartz's approach has been criticized. See Thomas L. Pangle, *The Spirit of Modern Republicanism: The Moral Vision of the American Founders and the Philosophy of Locke* (Chicago: University of Chicago Press, 1988).

25. Terence Ball and Richard Dagger, "The 'L-Word': A Short History of Liberalism," *Political Science Teacher* (Winter 1990): 5.

SUGGESTED READINGS

Almond, G., and G. Bingham Powell, Jr. *Comparative Politics: A Developmental Approach.* Boston: Little, Brown, 1966. A classic statement of a framework for understanding political systems in terms of their degrees of functional specialization.

Brezezinski, Z. K. *The Grand Failure: The Birth and Death of Communism in the Twentieth Century.* New York: Scribner, 1989. An exploration of what is surely the greatest political change of our time, by one of the foremost American students of communism and former national security advisor to President Jimmy Carter.

Dahl, R. A. *Democracy and Its Critics.* New Haven, Conn.: Yale University Press, 1989. Exploration of the subtleties of democratic theory, by one of the most eminent political scientists of our time.

Finer, S. E. *Five Constitutions: Contrasts and Comparisons.* London: Penguin, 1980. Very useful treatment of the constitutions of the United States, West Germany, France (both Fourth and Fifth Republics), and the Soviet Union. Contains all the relevant texts.

Huntington, S. P. *Political Order in Changing Societies.* New Haven, Conn.: Yale University Press, 1976. Very important essay on the problems of developing a modern state mechanism.

Jagger, A. *Feminist Politics and Human Nature.* Totowa, N.J.: Rowman and Allanheld, 1983. A distinctively feminist dissent from the prevailing mode of classifying political systems.

Konrad, G., and I. Szelinyi. *The Intellectuals on the Road to Class Power.* New York: Harcourt, 1979. A chilling essay by two young Hungarians on the role of intellectuals, as a class, in the establishment of totalitarianism.

Lichtheim, G. *The Concept of Ideology.* New York: Random House, 1967. The significance of ideology in Marxist and other revolutionary movements.

Nolte, E. *Three Faces of Facism.* New York: Holt, 1966. Classic study of fascist movements in Germany, Italy, and France.

Olsen, M. *The Rise and Decline of Nations.* New Haven, Conn.: Yale University Press, 1982. An interesting attempt to relate social and political structure to the economic performance of systems.

Page, B. *Who Gets What from Government.* Berkeley, Calif.: University of California Press, 1983. A critique of American democracy from an egalitarian perspective.

Rae, D. *Equalities.* Cambridge, Mass.: Harvard University Press, 1981. A theory of democracy in egalitarian terms.

Rigby, T. H., A. Brown, and T. Reddaway, eds. *Authority, Power, and Policy in the USSR.* London: Macmillan, 1983. A collection of essays, dedicated to the distinguished sovietologist Leonard Shapiro, which brings together some of the most interesting recent thought on the structure of Soviet politics.

Wooton, G. *Interest Groups.* Englewood Cliffs, N.J.: Prentice-Hall, 1970. An excellent study of the importance and operation of interest groups in the British pluralist system.

Part II

Politics and Society

Public Opinion, Polling, and Political Culture

The public! The public!
How many fools does it take to make up a public?

—CHAMFORT

Since [President] Clinton's gotten in, and I will him all the best, I
have at this point contacted my Congressman, Senator and Mr.
Clinton about 10 times—by voice, speech, telegram and letter. I think
the only way these guys are going to wake up and smell the coffee is
because people like me are going to sit there and hound them.

—AMERICAN VOTER, 1993

The public buys its opinions as it buys its meat, or takes in its milk,
on the principle that it is cheaper to do this than to keep a cow. So it
is, but the milk is more likely to be watered.

—SAMUEL BUTLER

Public opinion in this country is everything.

—ABRAHAM LINCOLN

You may talk of the tyranny of Nero and Tiberius; but the real
tyranny is the tyranny of your next-door neighbor. . . . Public opinion
is a permeating influence, and it exacts obedience to itself; it requires
us to think other men's thoughts, to speak other men's words, to
follow other men's habits.

—WALTER BAGEHOT

WHO IS THE PUBLIC?

What a challenging and exciting world we face at the end of the twentieth
century! As we approach the end of the century, we stand confronted with
environmental and global economic changes of the first magnitude. The

67

breakup of the Warsaw Pact in Europe, together with the increasing economic and political integration of Western Europe, makes for challenges across a wide span of interests. The Middle East remains in turmoil.

Domestically, too, it is a time of promise and of challenge. The drug epidemic, the continuing challenge of AIDS, and other health-care issues all capture the public's concern. There is also the continued festering of the huge savings and loan bailout, as the budget deficit continues to trouble many Americans; and the abortion controversy seems no nearer solution than it did a decade, or even two decades, ago.

What do people want, and how can their government give them what they want? How can public opinion be harnessed to help sell a governmental program? How many "publics" are there, and how can the government listen to them all?

The introductory chapters in this book have indicated the extent to which all political systems—irrespective of size and ideology—do many of the same things for their citizens. They take all of the demands put forward by the citizens and turn at least some of them into action and results. They also seek to maintain the support of at least major portions of their citizenry by accomplishing tasks and giving rewards.

In the process, we are concerned with several important political concepts. How, for example, does a political system like that of the United States maintain itself? How does it educate its citizens to their responsibilities, and how does it mold their behavior to suit the demands of the state? How do citizens make their viewpoints known? How do they influence the government to follow their goals and achieve their ends? How does a government deal with the "real" world of international relations while at the same time taking public perceptions and misperceptions into account?

In this chapter we attempt to look at public opinion and at the various capabilities of political systems to see how they are intertwined. We shall examine the process of public opinion making, first to discern the basic aspects of political opinion and political change and then to look at a specific situation—one with a variety of dimensions that not only have a life of their own, but that also reverberate back onto the very public they are designed to serve.

REJUVENATIONAL CAPABILITY

In Chapter 13, we shall examine the political fact of life that all political systems face problems of change. The world is always changing, and a state must relate to those changes. Just as a society changes internally as certain economic and social (as well as political) forces shape its future, so too the international context will alter the way a state behaves and will issue a set of never-ending challenges to its leadership. The international environment produces change, and these changes impinge on each political system to varying degrees. In the case of the superpower United States, many of these changes in remote parts of the world have ramifications for its position in the world and the ability of its citizens to conduct their global business. The leaders of any political system must somehow come to grips with these changes, accepting them or opposing them or somehow modifying and changing them.

We term the ability of a political system to reinforce itself—to maintain and alter its institutions, structure, and process and to replenish its personnel—its *rejuvenational capability,* that is, its capacity to respond to change. This capacity to adjust to change has a variety of dimensions, but basically it refers to any political system's collective ability to deal with change from both within and without.

Although we term a political system's ability to adjust to change its rejuvenational capacity—implying that this capacity is an integrated whole—it actually consists of a variety of elements. For our purposes, we can break this down into its various components so as to examine each more closely: political socialization, political recruitment, the absorption of information, and the system's ability to *alter* its processes and structures to deal better with the forces of change.

Political Socialization

You are not born an "American." You are taught to be one. What we generally call *nationality* is often little more than a set of learned responses to certain symbols.[1] These responses may be taught in both formal and informal ways. Chances are, members of your family helped to teach you at an early age that you are an American. Later, in school, you were exposed to nationalistic elements. As a child, you were taught the pledge of allegiance. You were taught your country's history. You were, in short, taught *to be* an American. You were taught what a good citizen should say or do. In addition to your formal education, moreover, your life experience has influenced the way in which you look at your own political system.[2] The entire process by which members of a political system are civically educated and inculcated with the values of the system is termed *political socialization.*

Naturally, the leaders of any political system would like to have their citizens loyal and highly supportive of their government. For this reason, most formal political socialization is "positive." Of equal, if not greater, importance is the fact that the life experience of an individual citizen may or may not reinforce the formal teachings of the political system. In the United States, for example, racial minorities and the poor often face a set of learning experiences that run counter to the professed values of the system.

And many Americans have an aversion to many of the assumptions that the existence of a huge bureaucracy devoted to intelligence gathering and covert activities implies. Their "experience" has not been as positive as that of others who feel we have been well served by our intelligence agencies. In any case, both groups were "taught" their positions.

Political Recruitment

Another dimension to the rejuvenational capability is *political recruitment*. Political recruitment refers to the process by which a political system replaces its personnel or expands its membership in the bureaucracies, armed forces, law enforcement agencies, and other agencies of government. All political authorities—whether kings, presidents, generals, or prime ministers—must find ways of recruiting personnel. The ways in which they do so are important in determining the strength of the political system.

For example, are the personnel chosen on the basis of merit or on the basis of ethnic or linguistic background? Are they chosen because of their expertise or their loyalty? Do they come from primarily one socioeconomic group or from several? Are they given positions because of *who* they know or *what* they know? The staffing of the nation's bureaucracies is of critical importance because in many instances these bureaucracies keep the country running during times of stress or political upheaval.

If the people recruited are talented, energetic, and committed to the political system and if they are recruited on a more or less equitable basis, then the members of the bureaucracy may enable the political system to survive major problems, including the alteration or succession of governments. If political recruitment is done in a slipshod fashion, with tribal or political affiliation more important than an individual's performance or accomplishment, then—far from helping the political system—it may hurt. Those left out may well feel that they have no stake in the continuation of the system. Able people who are "turned off" can become dangerous rebels.

Information Utilization

The operation of a political system needs to be viewed also in terms of its ability to absorb and to utilize new information, information that is continually arising out of the domestic and international environments. The government's ability and/or willingness to utilize this flow of information is of such importance that some political scientists—most notably Karl Deutsch—have connected the self-destruction of a political system with "the process of self closure," or the shutting off of outside information.[3]

In order to survive, any political system must be able to accept a stream of information, process it, and utilize it. If a government fails to collect this new information, processes it improperly so that the decision makers do not have the correct picture, or fails to act on information it considers "bad news," it may encounter serious difficulties. For example, during the height of American involvement in the Vietnam War, then Secretary of Defense Robert McNamara instituted a computerized system that would indicate how many hamlets in South Vietnam were under government control and how many of the enemy had been slain (in other words, body counts). As weeks and months went by, the defense secretary was able to say with confidence that the United States was winning the war. In this case, however, the collection process proved faulty. The judgment about whether a particular village was "safe" or not came from the local Vietnamese political authorities and was not linked to any real test of safe versus unsafe (such as whether or not the authority spent the night in that particular village). High body counts were often the basis for promotion and were—it soon became clear—what McNamara wanted to hear. Dead civilians were counted along with dead soldiers. Thus, key decision makers in the United States made major decisions on the basis of faulty information.

Equally troublesome is the problem of bad news. No government likes to hear that its programs are failing or that its policies are incorrect. But pretending that a policy is working when it is not can seriously weaken a political system over time. For example, poverty and oppression in Latin America were widely reported and commented upon by the intelligence community long before a variety of countries in the region flared into open civil war and insurgency during the 1980s. The bad news that these disturbances were coming was simply turned aside by decision makers.

Of course, not all bad news comes true, either. During the Vietnam War, for example, it was widely alleged that, if South Vietnam fell to the North Vietnamese, the independent countries of Laos and Cambodia (or Kampuchea) would soon follow. It was also asserted that the fall of these three areas would be debilitating to the worldwide interests of the United States. By 1986, the first part of the bad news certainly had come true, with North Vietnam occupying and running all three countries; but the second had not, for the United States now seems far stronger and in a better global position than it was when it in fact was struggling to prevent North Vietnam from taking over South Vietnam.

One of the most important sources of "bad news" in any society comes from political opposition to those in power. Those outside the government often have a different perspective and tend to listen to different segments of the society. They may not always be right, and they are likely to take political advantage of a situation in which the government in power has made a mistake. But on balance, it is usually beneficial to the system *as a whole* to have opposition points of view taken into account. For, bad news is still news—providing new (albeit unfavorable) information that the government *must* take into account if it is to function effectively.

Change Capability

Another dimension to the rejuvenational capability that needs to be examined is the ability of the political system to change its institutions and processes. Given the dynamic nature of the internal and external environments it faces, a political system must be able to change if it is to survive.

Some political systems—for example, Sweden and Switzerland—have developed successful techniques for changing slowly but continuously, thus meeting the challenges of different ages. Other systems—such as czarist Russia or Iran under the shah—have exhibited a marked inability to adjust to new internal forces.

How do successful systems cope with change? We have suggested how important it is to keep lines of communication open with various groups in society, including those that might oppose specific policies, in order to ensure that they remain "loyal" opposition. Another indication of a system's adaptability is the existence of legal procedures by which portions of the political system can be altered without entailing its complete destruction. For example, in the two centuries since the founding of the United States, the Constitution and the amendment procedure associated with it have enabled the system to change—to "learn" to "grow" without jeopardizing the entire system.

NATIONAL CHARACTER

It has been argued that some people may be easier to rule than others. Some social and political observers would agree with Hans Morgenthau that *national character*—or persistent patterns of cultural, intellectual, and emotional characteristics—can be assigned to one people or another.[4] Morgenthau points to the differing behavioral patterns of the Americans, the Russians, the British, and the Germans to illustrate the importance of national character. This tricky concept bears closer examination.

It is important to focus on this concept, for if there were such a thing as national character, it would be of vital importance in both the process of political socialization and the formation of public opinion. It would form an important conceptual bridge in linking these two concepts. It might provide a key to rational assessment of the role of the government in determining the former and in reacting to the latter.

We must ask ourselves this question: is there a fixed national character that endures through the ages? Morgenthau uses a number of examples that, we would argue, speak against the very concept, or at least suggest that what he terms "national character" is really not immutable at all, but is continually changing under a variety of diverse influences.

What are we to make of the facet of German "national character" that he terms "militarism" and that presumably played an important role in both World Wars I and II? The Germans make good soldiers because it is part of their national character, so the argument runs. But surely it makes a difference *when* one looks at this so-called national character. During the Napoleonic era, the Germans were widely regarded as militarily hopeless. Their failure to stand up to the "bellicose" French during this period was seen as a given.

Morgenthau points to another aspect of the Germans' national character: their "lack of moderation."[5] The proof of this, he argues, is seen in the German attack on the city of Stalingrad during 1942—an attack that continued until the Russians finally surrounded and destroyed the German Sixth Army.[6] For Morgenthau, "this lack of moderation has proved to be the one fatal weakness of the German national character."[7]

Yet the Battle of Stalingrad emerged as a critical turning point *despite* its omission from the German high command's list of critical targets. It was Adolf Hitler who kept the German troops assaulting the city long after it had lost its strategic value; Hitler, however, was not a German, but an Austrian. Besides, many German military decision makers, including those directly concerned with the Sixth Army, opposed making it such a do-or-die effort. The Battle of Stalingrad might as easily be used to illustrate Russian national character, since it was the Russians who persisted in making the battle a do-or-die effort by steadfastly refusing to give up the city. One could argue that it was *their* "lack of moderation"— not the Germans'—that made the battle what it was. (It could also be argued that Stalin was a Georgian, not a Great Russian.) Today, with the two Germanys united, the world again grapples with these stereotypes.

We would argue that what looks like immutable national character is more likely to be a set of learning experiences determined through the process of political socialization. The Japanese people—so "bellicose" before and during World War II—became remarkably "pacific" and "passive" after their defeat, when a new government was installed by an American general. The Chinese—so "disorganized" and "corrupt" during the 1930s—became highly "organized" and "incorruptible" following the founding of the People's Republic, with its concomitant dedication to these characteristics as primary national goals.

What appears to be national character, we believe, is really simply patterns of behavior conditioned by time, circumstance, and the political and economic system that happens to be operative at the time. This behavior, we would argue, is actually more a reflection of *national will,*[8] or *national morale,* or the willingness of a people to follow certain national goals, or simply their national mood at a given time.[9] The national mood may or may not reflect government policy or its recent history of accomplishment or lack thereof; it may reflect deep-seated yearnings on the part of the population, or merely a passing or transitory feeling.

In any case, the feelings and desires of a population are important to the government, in terms of both the goals it is seeking and the limits that hostile opinion may place on its pursuit of certain goals. The national mood is important. If you as a leader of Chile are anxious to engage Argentina in a struggle over islands in the South Atlantic, for example you had better have a sense of what your own people want and will allow. At the same time, what people want can change or can be made to change. We shall return, in the next section, to this elusive notion of "public opinion."

One fascinating example of a potential change in the orientation of the national character is post-communist, independent Russia. Under centuries of domination by oppressive czarist and then communist regimes, Russian society never developed a political culture (the collection of attitudes and orientations toward the political system) that was conducive to stable democratic participation in the affairs of state. As voluntary democratic linkages between an independent society and a responsive state failed to develop during the turbulent years of Russian history, scholars were faced with a conundrum. Was there something inherent in the Russian character that led Russian society to seek authoritarian rule, whether in czarist or communist form, that would drown out the cacophony of public opinion and act without reference to the voice of the people? Or did a succession of Russian leaders from Ivan the Terrible to Stalin suppress Russian society, one willing and able to articulate its demands, for the sake of consolidating absolute power?

Whatever the source of the historical passivity of Russian society in using the collective voice to positively influence political outcomes, it has led some scholars to refer to the Russian case as a *subject political culture*—one in which the people's orientation to the political system is presided over, shaped, and controlled by a strong leadership. For example, in Soviet Russia society on the whole seemed to accept the stultifying domination over every aspect of citizens' lives by the pervasive Communist party and state bureaucracies. During the Soviet period, almost every citizen voted in every election—not because of loyalty to the Communist party or the belief that their vote could affect political outcomes, but because voting was made mandatory by a Communist party that used controlled participation to legitimate its rule. Any independent political activity, even the expression of unsanctioned opinions, was considered *dissent* and not the normal stuff of everyday political life. Many in the West mistook society's complacency as support for the Communist regime, which had successfully put a lid on the sometimes disrupting effect of the expression of conflicting ideas which inevitably emerges in any independent society.

When Mikhail Gorbachev came to power in the Soviet Union in 1985, he intended to gradually increase the opportunities for people to express their opinions about social problems and politics. His intent was to allow citizens to vent their frustrations and propose creative solutions to problems. Not only would this be essential for the well-being of a vibrant polity but it would also help the Communist party in its effort to rule over an increasingly complex society. No one was prepared for the response. When given the opportunity to express independent opinions and take independent action, Russian citizens (along with all the other nationalities in the former Soviet empire) did so with a vengeance. They took to the streets by the tens of thousands, demanding political change and the accountability of their once all-powerful political leaders. In February 1990 more than 100,000 citizens held a six-hour rally on the eve of a Communist party Central Committee meeting to demand that the party relinquish its monopoly of political power. (Two days later, it did.) They carried out letter-writing campaigns to Russian newspapers to complain about social life and the country's bloated bureaucracy. They held public meetings and demonstrations to pressure politicians to respond to their demands.

Inch by inch and issue by issue, Russian citizens broadened the boundaries of accepted participation under Soviet rule. They discovered a new source of power in their ability to influence political leaders newly concerned with public opinion. Like the mother who cried, "I won't give up my son!" when the Soviet army called up young Russian reservists to police violent demonstrations in the (then) Soviet republic of Azerbaijan—Russian citizens realized the impact of the public's voice on powerful state institutions. This massive outpouring of public opinion and independent activism not only shocked the Communist leadership, it was instrumental in the demise of communist rule (see Chapter 12).

These are all signs that the Russian national character is developing into a *participant political culture*—one in which citizens perceive that they have the potential to influence politics and are provided the means to participate in public and political life. Russian society in the post-Communist period may be moving toward this political culture of pluralism, which accepts that a conflict of opinions and of opposing interest groups can positively affect the political system as long as everyone agrees on the basic rules of the political game. This last point, however, leaves a big question mark hanging over the issue of the Russian national character and its impact on the political system. It is by no means certain that Russians can agree on the political rules of the game in the post-Communist period. If this is the case, an uncontrolled outpouring of conflicting opinions and opposing interests could lead to chaos or to the welcoming of yet another period of strong-arm rule. Russian society has indicated its capacity to use public opinion and social activism to overthrow a despised regime. But can it use these same things to create a new political system based on a state that is responsive to the articulated needs of free citizens and an independent society?

PUBLIC OPINION

What is *public opinion?* The respected political scientist V. O. Key perhaps put it best when he noted that public opinion consists of "those opinions held by private persons which governments find it prudent to heed."[10] In other words, relevant public opinion is that which has some influence on policymakers within the government. The opinion of a person in Tennessee that the weather is too hot in August is of little consequence for the conduct of government. However, this same citizen's opinions about government regulation of the tobacco industry may have more relevance, depending on a number of other factors.

How much relevance is accorded to any opinion depends on the *intensity* of force with which the opinion is held and the number of people holding that opinion, as well as where they are located within the social structure. Many Americans may feel we need a CIA, but relatively few Americans feel very strongly about it. For Key, there is a difference between the mythical public opinion often referred to by politicians and leaders and the media (say, "The people want price controls") and the actual sets of different public opinions. In truth, except for the consensus seen in the tiniest small-scale communities, an organic agreement—a single public opinion—is impossible.

And it makes sense that there is no single public opinion. There are only the opinions of a variety of special "publics."[11] For example, there is not one American, but many. There are millions of Americans who live in rural areas; millions more who live in cities. There are Americans who work for a living; there are those who do not. Some Americans are black; others, white or brown. There are Americans who are economically poor, and those who are economically well off. Some are religious; some are not. There are 230 million Americans spread throughout the United States, coming from a vast variety of backgrounds and wanting different and often conflicting things. Because of our different wants, we perceive events differently.

In addition to the interactions among the various factors making for diversity and those making for commonality, between differing heritages and common experiences, between the present realities and the future (or past) dreams, there are many forces at work on individual Americans and their political system. In a real sense, the political system must come to grips with this diversity and the process of change.

In some respects, the way in which our political process works depends on such gross features as the diversity and the range of backgrounds, hopes, and achievements of so many different Americans. Reading political science or political philosophy textbooks about alternative political forms, one might easily get the impression that any political system can be superimposed on any society, that one is always free to pick a particular political system.

This impression is probably not correct. People—at least in the abstract—may be able to choose what sort of economic arrangements they want or what kind of ideology they wish to pursue. But once having chosen these goals, they cannot have any sort of *politics* they want.

Box 4-1. *Soviet Opinion*

HOLD THE PHONE

New apartments are being built in Alushta, and telephones are being installed in apartments for people who are coming to live in the city. Our district was built in the 1950's, but underground telephone cables were not planned for, so we were left with no telephones. I have lived in the city for 32 years, worked hard all my life and grown old here. You can imagine, then, how angry I became when I asked a telephone worker when our street was finally going to get telephones, and he said, "Buy a telephone pole, put it up, buy a telephone cable, string it up, buy a telephone set— and then we'll hook you up."

Excuse me, but where can I get a telephone pole?

T. Zakharova
Alushta

SINGLE MOTHER'S PLEA

A. Solovyev [a previous letter writer] proposes prosecuting single mothers who leave their children in orphanages for the state to raise. But here is another question: How is a young, single woman supposed to raise and educate a child with a monthly state allowance of 20 rubles? . . .

The bureaucrats who allocate the funds to care for abandoned children moan that this costs the state . . . 300 rubles per month! But a single mother for some reason gets 20 rubles a month, and they think that's enough.

Do people like Solovyev know how hard it is for a young, single woman to decide to have a baby? And once she has decided, she and her child are left in unbearable financial conditions; 20 rubles is no solution to the problem. At the same time, the state spends 300 rubles a month on an orphanage child.

What kind of logic is that? If you want fewer children to be abandoned, then give 100 rubles a month to the single mother and let her raise her son or daughter to her heart's content. And the state will get a normal, healthy citizen and save 200 rubles.

V. D. Zhulyev
Yurevo, Sumskaya Oblast

A DEAD END

I don't support the idea of reburying the remains of people who are guilty of crimes against the Soviet people. I say the dead should be left where they are—including those who are buried at the Kremlin wall—but their tombstones should be marked with the words "Guilty of bloody crimes against the nation and humanity."

Also, streets in Moscow need to be renamed. After all, there are plenty of dead-end streets there. They should be named "Stalin Dead End" or "Brezhnev Dead End." Such names would serve as a memorial and at the same time be symbolic.

By throwing part of our nation's history out of our memory forever, we may pave the way for even bigger mistakes.

A. S. Karpov
Scientific research worker
Place of residence unknown

Source: *"Dear Comrade Editor" (Letters to a Soviet Magazine)*, New York Times Magazine, September 9, 1990, pp. 69–70.

Politics can affect society, economics, and even, perhaps, basic beliefs. "The future of political attitudes will depend far more on future social and political events than on the dynamics of demographic change."[12] But politics is itself to some extent a contingent activity. Here we are concerned with looking at the ways groups of people, through interest group activity (see Chapter 5) and the rejuvenational expression of public opinion as outlined above, influence the course of their lives.

If you were an elected official in the United States—say, a member of Congress—how would you find out what was on the minds of the people about a subject such as U.S. covert aid to rebels in the Sudan or Iraq? Would you listen only to the people who call you on the telephone? If you do, you would not be listening to those who do not call you—either because they do not know your telephone number or because they don't want to spend the money or because they don't want to take up your time, assuming (quite rightly, perhaps) that you have better things to do.

Would you listen only to the people you meet when you return home to your district? If so, you are not listening to the vast majority of your constituents whom you do not encounter in a weekend of public events—those who stay at home, live at the other end of your district, or who see you but wouldn't want to give you their opinion in public.

Would you pay attention only to your mail? If so, how? Would you count the letters for and against a particular bill? Would you discount the intensity of feeling for or against an issue in order to count simply the volume of letters? If so, you might be ignoring the vast majority of your constituents who never write you letters or feel so excited they cannot calm themselves enough to commit their emotions to paper.

What about polling? Since the methods above are likely to be unscientific and are not likely to let you determine with assurance exactly what the majority of your constituents actually believe on a given issue, why not just conduct a series of polls to determine how you will vote? Over the years, polling has become more refined and sophisticated; now, with the addition of computers, it has come to have, if properly done, considerable predictive value. Still, many people ask, how can the pollster, by questioning 600 voters in a state, predict how 2 million voters will react? How can a sample of 1,500 people interviewed throughout the United States actually reflect the sentiments of 230 million Americans?

The answer is that the best polling firms, using carefully worded questionnaires and proper techniques, may predict with reasonable accuracy the opinions of that universe. "Reasonable accuracy," however, depends on what you want to know. A first major "if" associated with polling is the size of the sample. In a universe of 1 million people, a proper sample of 600 will yield a sampling error of plus or minus 5 percent. That is, if you asked the people of southern Iowa whether they preferred a strong military to the United States's losing influence abroad and the answer came back 40 percent yes, 35 percent no, and 25 percent undecided, you could not be sure that the side favoring a strong military was ahead 40 percent to 35 percent. This would be an opinion "too close to call." With a sample of 300 you raise the error possibility to 6 percent; with a sample of 200, it increases to 7 percent.

Therefore if you were looking for the answer to a question of whether the people in your district favored aid to Romania and the result came back 75 percent yes, 20 percent no, and 5 percent undecided, you could be quite sure that a majority of people in your district favored such a course of action. You might or might not have reached the same conclusion from your mail and district visits.

A second major "if" associated with polling is the timing of the poll-taking operation. Polls do not tell you what is going to happen. In fact, they do not tell you what is happening at the moment you are reading them. They can tell you only what was happening at the time the poll was taken. Therefore, polling data can "age" if public opinion is changing. Many of the celebrated polling failures can be traced to changes in public opinion that took place after the actual interviews. Given the fact that a major poll involving 600 interviews may take a week or more to conduct and the computer analysis an equal amount, the situation may already have changed by the time you get the results to read. Compare, for example, the two polls reported in Boxes 4-3 and 4-4, taken in Moscow in May 1988 and December 1989. Far fewer people in 1989 believed that Gorbachev's policies would succeed than were indicated in 1988, and a greater number of respondents perceived that their economic situation had deteriorated in 1989 than had perceived this in 1988. Note also the *generational differences* in both polls. Soviet citizens of the older generation tended to distrust independent social activity (such as street demonstrations in 1988 and private enterprises in 1989) much more than the younger generation. The "over 60s" also put more trust in the leadership and its policies than the generation more exposed to alternatives. Nevertheless, public opinion on most issues does not change as rapidly as in these two Moscow polls; and a series of polls taken at, say, monthly intervals should give you a good sense of which way public opinion is moving—if in fact it is moving at all.

A third major "if" associated with polling—and perhaps the most important one in terms of accuracy—is the makeup of the voter sample. More critical than the number of people interviewed is the nature of those interviewed. If your pollster called 600 people and 375 of them were senior citizens, the opinions you received concerning free prescription drugs for those over 65 or free college tuition for anyone wishing to go to college would be heavily weighted, or slanted, in terms of the interests of this particular population group.

Therefore it is vital that any polling sample accurately represent the demographic makeup of the population in your district. If 17 percent of the people in your district are over 65, then 17 percent of the sample

Box 4-2. The Poll Gorbachev Hated,
from Argumenty i Fakty

Last summer, the weekly Soviet newspaper Argumenty i Fakty *asked its readers to express their opinions on the "outstanding" members of the Congress of People's Deputies, which had just completed its first session. Fifteen thousand postcards and letters came in response.*[1] *To gauge public sentiment, the editors counted and recorded the strongest opinions about the deputies; mild views were dropped from the tally. Tactfully,* Argumenty i Fakty *excluded two notables when publishing its results: President Mikhail Gorbachev and Vice President Anatoliy Lukyanov.*

Deputies with the highest number of positive votes tended to belong to the Interregional Deputies Group, a radical faction that advocates free-market restructuring of the Soviet economy, and criticizes Gorbachev for the sluggishness of perestroika.

Perhaps for that reason, Gorbachev soon attacked the poll in a private meeting with leading members of the press. Argumenty i Fakty *editor Vladislav Starkov was then called into Communist party headquarters and asked to accept other work. Support by the newspaper's staff helped him defy the offer and keep his position; he was still editor of the newspaper in mid-December. But the newspaper did publish two later polls that repudiated somewhat the "unscientific" method of the first.*

Orbis *has ordered the scores of the poll data to clarify the relative support for, or opposition against, a deputy. If the deputy has greater support than opposition, then the score is* + *(pro/con). If the opposition is greater, then the score is* − *(con/pro). Thus positive sentiment for Moscow Prosecutor Ivanov (*+ 14*) is about as strong as the negative sentiment against Vice President Lukyanov (*− 15*).*

In addition, the table also indicates whether a deputy has membership in the Communist Party of the Soviet Union; the Interregional Deputies Group; and the Supreme Soviet (the main legislative body in the Soviet Union). The social organization or geographical district that elected the deputy is also noted.

—The Editors

Notes:

1. Argumenty i Fakty, *October 7–13, 1989; in Foreign Broadcast Information Service,* Daily Report: Soviet Union, *October 19, 1989.*

Source: Orbis *(Winter 1990); 107–8.*

	Responses[1]			Membership[2]			
Deputy	Pro	Con	Score	CP	Sov	IR	Organization or Area
Popov	432	2	216	X	X	X	Engineering Society
Bykov	70	1	70				Lenin Children's Fund
Yemelyanov	202	3	67				Moscow District
Likhachev	83	1	83				Soviet Cultural Fund
Shmelev	285	4	71				Academy of Sciences
Zaslavkiy	50	1	50			X	Moscow District
Gayer	144	3	48	X	X	X	Vladivostok Region
Kazannik	287	6	48		X		Omsk Region
Afanansyev	390	16	24			X	Moscow Region
Bunich	63	2	31	X			Academy of Sciences
Obolenskiy	290	12	24			X	Leningrad District
Sobchak	258	8	32	X	X	X	Leningrad Region
Vlasov	361	15	24	X		X	Lublin Region
Chernichenko	196	9	22	X		X	Journalists' Union
Stankevich	67	4	17	X		X	Moscow District
Yeltsin	394	24	16			X	Moscow District
Ivanov	156	11	14			X	Leningrad Region
Yevtushenko	287	21	14				Karkov Region
Gdlyan	187	15	12			X	Moscow Region
Oleynik	47	5	9	X	X		Communist Party
Adamovich	130	16	8				USSR Film Union
Sakharov	609	79	8			X	Academy of Sciences
Zaslavskaya	49	9	5	X		X	Academy of Sciences
Karyakin	73	15	5	X		X	Academy of Sciences
Rasputin	74	69	1				Irkutsk Region
Medvedev	32	33	−1	X	X		Moscow Region
Belov	21	51	−2	X	X		Communist Party
Kasyan	18	53	−2	X	X		Krasnodarsk Region
Aytmatov	30	100	−3	X	X		Communist Party
Gorbachev*	50	189	−4	X	X		President
Chervonopiskiy	24	219	−9	X	X		Communist Youth
Nishanov	10	108	−11	X	X		Uzbekistan District
Rodionov	10	136	−14				Tbilisi District
Lukyanov*	12	177	−15	X			Vice President
Meshalkin	4	155	−39	X			Soviet UN Association
Samsonov	7	304	−43	X			Novospasskii District
Sukharev	2	154	−77	X			Moscow District
Shevchenko	1	91	−91		X		Ukraine District
Kazakova	0	68	—				Tashkent Region

Argumenty i Fakty *Poll*

Notes:

1. *Pro = Positive Comments; Con = Negative Comments.*

2. *CP = Communist Party; Sov = Supreme Soviet; IR = Interregional Deputies Group.*

Gorbachev and Lukyanov were not included in the initial publication of the poll.

Box 4-3. Voices From Moscow: What They Say about Their System

	Age				
	18–29	30–44	45–64	65 +	Total
One-party system in U.S.S.R. promotes development of democracy					
Agree	46%	50%	53%	60%	51%
Disagree	34	32	25	13	28
Elections to regional Soviet should be conducted under a multi-candidate system					
Yes	80	83	76	65	77
No	2	3	5	4	4
Interests of minority groups in U.S.S.R. are infringed on					
Not at all	61	65	65	84	66
Partially	27	22	20	6	20
Severely	4	2	1	1	2
It is acceptable for people with grievances to hold street demonstrations					
Yes	44	40	34	13	35
No	49	48	56	75	54
Support Gorbachev's domestic policies					
Completely	65	74	85	94	78
Less than completely	32	23	14	4	19
Support perestroika					
Strongly	65	66	83	83	73
With reservations	31	33	13	11	23
Material wealth of family over past three years has:					
Improved	31	40	30	27	33
Not changed	53	47	57	56	53
Worsened	15	11	12	13	12
Standard of living in next five years due to perestroika will:					
Get better	43	40	36	48	40
Won't change	18	18	18	17	18
Get worse	19	21	17	12	18
U.S. policies:					
Threaten U.S.S.R.	50	57	52	46	52
Do not threaten U.S.S.R.	32	27	29	29	29
When countries ask for military help, the Soviet Union:					
Should send troops	57	62	60	61	60
Should not send troops	21	20	24	12	20
Soviet troops in Afghanistan have fulfilled their goals					
Completely or basically	47	42	47	64	48
Partly fulfilled	23	28	21	17	23
Not fulfilled	11	14	10	2	10

Note: *Based on a poll of Moscow residents conducted by The Institute of Sociological Research of the Soviet Academy of Sciences for the* New York Times *and CBS News. A total of 939 Moscow residents were interviewed by telephone on May 7, 8, 14, and 15.*

Source: New York Times, *May 27, 1988, p. 7.*

Box 4-4. Perestroika in the USSR

At the end of last year Moscow's Centre of Political and Sociological Studies, led by Igor Mintusov, conducted a survey among 922 Moscow residents regarding perestroika in the USSR . . . The persons polled come from all strata of the population. . . . (The responses shown are percentages.)

1. Do you think that in the last 3–4 years the Soviet Union's economic position has become:

a. Better	4	c. Unchanged	11
b. Worse	82	d. Undecided	3

(Editor's Note: *The only significant variation by sex or age-group is among 20- to 29-year-olds, with slightly lower percentage "worse" and slightly higher "unchanged."*)

2. Has your own position in recent 3–4 years:

a. Improved	24	c. Remained unchanged	41
b. Worsened	33	d. Undecided	2

(Editor's Note: *Among the 20–29 age-group somewhat greater optimism: slightly higher "improved," slightly lower "worsened." N.B. also that 74 percent of the total sample say "unchanged" or "worsened."*)

3. Which of the following statements on perestroika would you subscribe to?

a. *The policy is right; it should be pursued at the present stage* 17
b. *The policy is wrong; we must go back to our previous politics* 5
c. *The policy is right, but changes should be made faster* 71
d. *Undecided* 7

(Editor's Note: *Very wide disparity among the over-60 age-group: significantly higher "present stage" and significantly lower "faster."*) . . .

13. Do you agree it should be possible for individuals to set up and own enterprises in the Soviet Union?

a. Yes	57	c. Undecided	12
b. No	31		

(Editor's Note: *Same pattern as in two previous questions. Among over-60s, however, 50 percent say "no."*)

14. Do you agree it should be possible to organize independent trade unions in the USSR?

a. Yes	69	c. Undecided	14
b. No	17		

(Editor's Note: *The pattern holds. In this case, over-60s say "yes," 48 to 32 percent.*)

15. Do you think Gorbachev's policy will succeed during the next five years?

a. Yes	26	d. No	14
b. More yes than no	31	e. Other, undecided	10
c. More no than yes	19		

(Editor's Note: *On this final question, about 50 or so, in most age groups, cluster around "yes" and "more yes than no," with over-60s most positive. Among 20–29 age-group, least optimism: 42 percent "no" and "more no than yes."*)

Source: World Affairs, *152, no. 2 (Fall 1989): 98–99.*

should include respondents from this group. Likewise, you would want to have other age, sex, and ethnic groupings well represented in terms of their actual portion of the population. If you represented a district with a large number of union members, you would want them accurately represented; the same would hold true for other income categories.

It is not necessary that the actual sample correspond exactly to the demographic pattern as long as the end product is made statistically accurate. In other words, if your sample consists of only 15 percent senior citizen responses and the actual population is 17 percent, you can weight the 15 percent by adding an additional 2 percent to the final outcome. This matching of responses with the actual population "grid," or mix, is very important in making sure that your polling results accurately represent the population whose opinions you are sampling. For example, the Arab–Israeli conflict is of critical concern to many Americans, but of greater concern to American Jews than to American Indians. Depending on the relative number of each in your district, you will want to make sure that the proper number of each is asked the questions.

A fourth major "if" associated with polling is the wording of the questions themselves. Some questions are easy to understand and to ask. For example, you might have been interested in knowing whether or not your constituents thought that President Bill Clinton is doing a good job. You could state the question as follows: "Do you approve or disapprove of the job President Clinton is doing?" This question would likely give you a more accurate set of answers than one worded like this: "Considering all of the wonderful things he promised, don't you think that President Clinton is not doing as good a job as he should?"

Or, if you were interested in finding out how a majority of your constituents felt about a proposed dam, you would want to say "Do you favor the building of the Cherokee Dam?" rather than "Do you favor the building of the Cherokee Dam, which will flood 54,000 acres of our precious state and cost a billion dollars?" In other words, polls are not conducted to educate the public or to give people your views on issues; they are carried out to find out the public's views on the issues. Consequently, you do not want to "skew," or slant, the answers in one direction or another (although you may want to skew your own answer the next time you answer positively on the question of the Cherokee Dam after finding that 65 percent of your constituents oppose it and only 15 percent favor it).

But if the issue is very complex—such as the question of CIA support for governments *or* insurgents in Latin American countries—it is imperative that a series of carefully worded questions be asked. Many Americans might approve of such action if they thought it would be successful. Many Americans might approve of the action in principle, but not if the death toll from resulting operations mounted. Many Americans might disapprove of such action even if they thought it would be successful. Many

Americans might disapprove of CIA intervention in other countries' affairs, even if no one died as a result. How much, then, do Americans have a right to know, in forming their opinions?[13]

Let us look at the phenomenon of public opinion and a particularly vexing issue: abortion. People who want to ban all abortions try to make their view prevail. People who want to limit abortions to specific situations (such as rape and incest) try to influence public opinion. People who want all women to have the right to an abortion (even if it is at government expense) want their view to be the one the government supports.

What does polling tell us about this important issue?

First, it is clear that polling reflects the questions asked as much as the answers received. Therefore, if you ask "Do you approve of the murder of unborn children?" you are likely to get a different response than if you ask "Do you favor the right of women who need them to get safe and medically approved abortions?"

Box 4-5. RU-486: The Answer?

Part of the difficulty with the abortion issue is its very public nature, particularly as it relates to policy formation and the federal and state funding of it. RU-486 is a pill developed in France that provides a woman with an option to pursue abortion in her own home and in private. RU-486 is a synthetic steroid that interferes with the action of progesterone, which helps prepare the lining of the uterus to retain the fertilized egg. When RU-486 is used in conjunction with prostaglandin, the fertilized egg is expelled 95 percent of the time.

RU-486 would remove at least part of the debate from the public arena. It would be available through physicians and could be used by women as a "morning after" pill to provide a nonsurgical abortion in her own home without public interaction with the clinic site—the setting of clinic rules and client–patient relations. Used in the early stages of pregnancy, it may arouse less public opposition than surgical abortion.

Currently the drug is not available in the United States, and no manufacturer or distributor of pharmaceutical products has been willing to assume liability for the marketing of RU-486 in the United States. Still, with the examples of cocaine and steroids clearly in mind, it seems unlikely that RU-486 can be kept out of the country indefinitely—especially since the American Medical Association endorsed it in 1990.

But the same forces that battle for and against surgical abortion may also work in this arena, making the drug itself as controversial as surgical abortion. In any case, the viewpoints of many publics will have to be taken into account as the controversy unfolds.

Second, in addition to the variety of loaded questions, it may well be that the public wants at least two somewhat contradictory results and that this expectation skews the data depending on the sequence of questions. For example, many Americans believe that a woman should have access to an abortion *if she needs one,* but different Americans define the need differently. For some, need involves only saving the life of the mother. For others, it means only when rape or incest is involved. For still others, it is for the mother-to-be's mental health. For still others, it is whenever a woman wants to rid herself of a fetus.

Third, many Americans oppose abortion in principle—"I wouldn't have one"—but approve it for others: "It's all right if it's necessary." But many believe that abortion should be "safe and legal" even if they aren't too clear in their own mind what is a justifiable reason.

Fourth, through the late 1980s and early 1990s, the national polls have tended to show that approximately 45 percent believe abortion should be "legal as it is now," while another 40 percent believe abortion should be legal "only in cases such as rape, incest, or to save the life of the mother." Approximately 10 percent would ban all abortions.

Fifth, these basic numbers change if questions are asked differently and different organizations have a stake in both changing the numbers toward their groups' philosophy, and in making sure that lawmakers *interpret* these findings to the groups' advantage. For example, the National Right to Life Committee (NRLC) is an interest group anxious to limit abortions to as small a number of specific cases (such as to save the life of the mother) as possible. The National Abortion Rights Action League (NARAL) seeks to make abortion a viable option for all women who want or need it.

Consider the various philosophical aspects of the debate before making up your own mind (or feeling confident you have the answer already).

1. Is abortion "murder"? Obviously, if you define abortion as murder (and can get society to agree with you), it would be difficult for anyone to make a case that this type of murder is more acceptable than other types.
2. But the definition of "murder" requires an acceptance that the fetus is a person. We accept the notion that, when the fetus leaves the womb after nine months, it is a child and thus a life, and killing that child would be murder.
3. Where, then, does life begin? At conception? At viability? At the end of pregnancy? Does the fertilized egg have a "soul"? Does the baby have a "soul," for that matter?
4. Should a woman have control over her own body? Most Americans agree that abortion is permissible to save the life of the mother. That

seems to suggest a hierarchy of values. So too does the notion that a women should have control over the destiny of her body and *anything within it.* As of 1993, we as a society have generally accepted the primacy of a woman's rights in this instance, over the rights of the fetus and the father of the unborn child. Should we continue to do so?

5. Since the Supreme Court decision in *Roe v. Wade* in 1973, which created the right of a woman to have an abortion, there have been more than 1.5 million abortions a year—4,000 a day for most of this period. Abortion is an intrinsic part of our current social fabric. Should it be one in the future?

6. Now, for many Americans the issue of abortion is an unpleasant one. We generally don't like the idea of abortion, but many of us don't like the alternatives to it (that is, no legal abortions). Most of us Americans accept the right of women to have abortions, but we differ a great deal (by region, religion, socioeconomic status, and psychographics) as to what are proper situations for which to espouse abortion.

7. Most Americans accept the notion that abortion should be available to women, even if we don't particularly like the act (and might prefer more widespread use of birth control). Yet, is this the answer? Many of the groups who argue most vociferously against abortion are also adamantly against birth control, as well. Is this a case of wanting to have it both ways? Is it realistic to think that not having sex is a viable option for those wanting to avoid unwanted pregnancies?

8. Most Americans accept the premise that women should have the choice of having an abortion or not. But most also favor restrictions on abortions. Those interest groups that favor women's having abortions at any time for any reason at government expense, and those that favor society's prohibiting any abortions for any reason, do not now speak for the majority of Americans. Yet, Americans feel more strongly and act more concertedly as interest groups than an equal number of unaffiliated Americans do, so the groups *seem* to be speaking for a greater number.

9. You can see from what we have outlined here that there is both overlap and underlap in these concepts. Not all Americans agree on every aspect of abortion, yet we as a society have to make laws to reflect that pluralism. This is especially true since the 1989 *Webster* case in which the Supreme Court left the matter of abortion up to the states. This means there are now 50 battlegrounds in the abortion conflict, in addition to the national battleground.

10. As we enter the twenty-first century, the issue of abortion prevades our society and our political culture, and the political landscape is strewn with the bodies of those politicians who paid attention to the wrong interest groups (or paid attention to the right interest group at the wrong time). There is no easy answer to the abortion controversy that will satisfy all or even most Americans, let alone all or most interest groups.

Abortion remains a powerful example of an insoluble problem in a pluralistic society.

SUMMARY

In this chapter, we have looked at a variety of dimensions of public opinion and the rejuvenational capability of political systems. How political systems seek to reinforce themselves and socialize their members into supporting the system were covered. In the process, we looked at such aspects as political recruitment, change capability, national character, and the ways states take into account the diversity of their population.

We also explored the concept of public opinion—noting that there is not one public opinion but many and that there are a variety of ways of sampling public opinion or opinions, and concluding that polling is a difficult but rewarding way to deal with them, at least in a democracy where free expression is not punished.

We did demonstrate, however, that some issues—like abortion—are very difficult to "solve" in a pluralistic society.

NOTES

1. Boyd Shafer, *Nationalism: Myth and Reality* (New York: Harcourt, Brace, and World, 1955); and R. Dawson and K. Prewitt, *Political Socialization* (Boston: Little, Brown, 1969).

2. For an overview of many of these points on political socialization, as well as a critique of V. O. Key, see Forrest P. Chisman, *Attitude Psychology and the Study of Public Opinion* (University Park: Pennsylvania State University Press, 1976).

3. Karl W. Deutsch, "Communications Models and Decision Systems," in James C. Charlesworth, ed., *Contemporary Political Analysis* (New York: Free Press, 1967); and Karl W. Deutsch, *Nerves of Government* (New York: Free Press, 1963).

4. Hans Morgenthau, *Politics among Nations* (New York: Knopf, 1966), pp. 126–33.

5. Ibid., p. 132.

6. For an in-depth examination of the "might have beens" concerning the Battle of Stalingrad military campaign, see C. P. Potholm, *Strategy and Conflict: The Search for Historical Malleability* (Washington, D.C.: University Press of America, 1979).

7. Morgenthau, *Politics*, pp. 132–33.

8. This element of national will is central to Ray Cline's *World Power Assessment* (Washington, D.C.: Center for Strategic and International Studies, 1975).

9. In fairness to Morgenthau, he devotes considerable attention to this na-

tional morale ingredient, calling it "more elusive and less stable, but no less important than all the other factors in its bearing upon national power." See Morgenthau, *Politics,* pp. 133–35.

10. V. O. Key, Jr., *Public Opinion and American Democracy* (New York: Knopf, 1961), p. 14. For an engaging look at the process and institutions of free speech, see Frederick Schauer, *Free Speech: A Philosophy Enquiry* (New York: Cambridge University Press, 1982).

11. See the various essays in Norman Luttberg, ed., *Public Opinion and Public Policy: Models of Political Linkage* (Homewood, Ill.: Dorsey Press, 1968). For an analysis of the "public opinions" by reference to the organizing concepts of coalitions, elites, and masses, see Harry Holloway and John George, *Public Opinion: Coalitions, Elites, and Masses* (New York: St. Martins Press, 1982).

12. Paul R. Abramson, *Political Attitudes in America* (San Francisco: W. H. Freeman, 1983), p. 316.

13. For an interesting analysis of the public's right to know and the controversy about that right, see David M. O'Brien, *The Public's Right to Know: The Supreme Court and the First Amendment* (New York: Praeger, 1981).

SUGGESTED READINGS

Abramson, R. *Political Attitudes in America.* San Francisco: W. H. Freeman, 1983. A wide-ranging and engaging study of political attitudes, emphasizing continuity and change in such important areas as party loyalties, political efficacy, and political trust.

Bennett, W. *Public Opinion in American Politics.* New York: Harcourt, Brace, Jovanovich, 1980. A standard text that covers the recent academic literature well; a useful book for beginning undergraduate readers.

Brown, Archie, and Jack Gray, eds. *Political Culture and Political Change in Communist States,* 2nd Edition. New York: Holmes and Meier Publishers, 1979.

Dalton, Russell. *Citizen Politics in Western Democracies.* Chatham, N.J.: Chatham House, 1988. An informative source that focuses on answering this question: why does the public form the opinions it does about politics in different political situations?

Davis, Nanette. *From Crime to Choice.* Westport, Conn.: Greenwood Press, 1985. Describes the abortion market and the business of performing abortions. An interesting detailed look at many sides of the abortion issue.

Entman, Robert M. *Democracy without Citizens.* New York: Oxford University Press, 1989. An insightful look at the media and how it influences and manipulates the public's opinions.

Ginsburg, Faye D. *Contested Lives.* Berkeley: University of California Press, 1989. An examination of the early legal battle over abortion, from the trial of *Roe v. Wade* to an interesting look at both pro-choice and pro-life stories—all accounts of real people who have closely dealt with abortion in one form or another.

Holloway, H., and J. George. *Public Opinion: Coalitions, Elites, and Masses.* New York: St. Martin's Press, 1982. A fine study of the process of mass participation in politics and the roles of family, education, religion, ethnic differences, and social class as dimensions of public opinion.

Kleppher, P. *Who Voted? The Dynamics of Electoral Turnout 1870–1980.* New York: Praeger Publishers, 1982. The definitive account of those who vote, and why, as looked at through the prism of American presidential politics. Gives the reader a firm understanding of the trends in voter turnout and the reasons for those changes.

Lovenduski, Joni, and Joyce Outshoorn, eds. *The New Politics of Abortion.* Beverly Hills, Calif.: Sage, 1986. Not only does this book look at the politics of abortion in America, but it also takes an interesting look at the abortion conflict in France, Great Britain, Ireland, Italy, and other countries, showing that this is an international issue and not one that is solely a problem in the United States.

Mickelson, Sig. *From Whistle Stop to Sound Bite.* New York: Praeger Publishers, 1989. A look at television from the very beginning and how over the years it and various other forms of media have influenced and shaped political campaigns.

Neuman, W. Russell. *The Paradox of Mass Politics.* Cambridge, Mass.: Harvard University Press, 1986. An analysis of the masses and their involvement in politics. An examination of their opinions and also a look at their participation in elections.

Piven, Frances, and Richard Cloward. *Why Americans Don't Vote.* New York: Pantheon Books, 1988. A detailed study of what makes Americans not want to vote. How many registered voters there are, how many of them vote, and the factors in history that have caused nonvoting are all examined to determine why the American public is not showing a high voter turnout.

Rodman, Hyman. *The Abortion Question.* New York: Columbia University Press, 1987. Looks at the controversy that surrounds abortion from moral, medical, and psychological sides. A good source for learning about the abortion controversy and what its future issues and choices will be.

Rubin, Eva R. *Abortion, Politics, and the Courts.* Westport, Conn.: Greenwood Press, 1987. Analyzes the legal side of the abortion issue by using different case studies, and gives an excellent chronology of the different problems and issues that faced the legal side of abortion from 1980 to 1986.

Tucker, Robert C. *Political Culture and Leadership in Soviet Russia: From Lenin to Gorbachev.* New York: Norton Publishing, 1987.

Wennberg, Robert. *Life in the Balance.* Grand Rapids, Mich.: William B. Ferdmans Publishing, 1985. A close study of the moral implications surrounding abortion. The right of the fetus is discussed, as well as the role of religion and the law and how we might be able to make a decision about the abortion controversy.

5

Interest Groups and Political Parties

The "lobby" and the "pressure group" are familiar to many, but they are accepted in the way that typhoid bacillus is, as an organism that is a feature of civilized existence but must be eradicated if society is to develop and prosper. The interest group as defined in these pages is far less familiar.

—DAVID B. TRUMAN

In our age there is no such thing as "keeping out of politics." All issues are political issues, and politics itself is a mass of lies, evasions, folly, hatred, and schizophrenia.

—GEORGE ORWELL

How can one conceive of a one-party system in a country that has over 200 varieties of cheeses.

—CHARLES DE GAULLE

Damn your principles! Stick to your party.

—BENJAMIN DISRAELI

The miners asked me to tell you that this is not a revolt, it is not a spontaneous outburst of discontent. Everything is much more serious. We have often heard from the mouths of executives what a good working class we have. But now this class has gone out into the streets and squares and the executives didn't recognize what was happening. . . . [A] strike is a gesture of demonstration, when other methods fail to get through to leaders.

—SOVIET DEPUTY TO PRESIDENT MIKHAIL GORBACHEV OF THE FORMER USSR

POLITICS AS PROCESS

"Politics" usually means talking about an election campaign, an election, or, more frequently, current issues of high visibility featured on the evening news: mounting budget deficits, a crisis in the Persian Gulf, or a high rate of unemployment. Suppose, however, that you feel so strongly about an issue—whether it be taxes, the environment, or foreign policy— that this time you are not content merely to talk about it with your family and friends. Rather, you are so angry or frightened or just plain concerned that you want to make your opinion known where it will count and to those who appear to be in positions to *do something*. But, you are likely to wonder, will my individual views or opinions carry any weight? Who cares about how I feel about the price of gasoline or hospital care or reinstating the draft? What possible impact can I have on our nation's stance in the Middle East or in the Caribbean?

One of the ways in which citizens have traditionally tried to give their individual opinions greater clout with the policymakers has been to band together with others of similar persuasion. They form *interest groups*— people who share the same opinion about a particular issue, program, or policy. Those who oppose abortion join with thousands of others who also oppose it. Their combined weight *as a group* surely exerts more influence than the voice of a lone dissenter. Those who favor arms- control negotiations join with like-minded people. They are opposed in turn by a coalition of groups whose members believe the United States needs to maintain its defenses in a still dangerous and uncertain world.

The sheer complexity and diversity of the modern economy give rise to an array of *economic* interest groups. Because government, through its laws, regulations, and bureaucratic activity, is intimately involved in the everyday workings of the economy, these interest groups have come to play a major role in making public policy.

James Madison—sometimes referred to as the father of the U.S. Constitution—foresaw this development with remarkable insight. Writing in the *Federalist* No. 10, in 1787, Madison observed that "a landed interest, a manufacturing interest, a mercantile interest, with many lesser interests, grow up of necessity in civilized nations, and divide them into different classes, actuated by different sentiments and views."[1]

Madison was writing as an American, and there is no doubt that he accurately portrayed the kind of intense interest-group activity we have in this country—especially that of our great economic groups, such as business, labor, and agriculture. Madison also foresaw that the conflicts among these interests would necessitate the involvement of government in controlling them. Madison was suggesting that similar patterns of economic interests *necessarily* develop in all civilized nations. This is not something peculiarly or uniquely American.

Of course, there are "interests" other than those pursued by economic groups. David B. Truman, author of a classic work on the activity of groups in American government, defined an interest group as a collection of people who share some particular attitude and who, as a group, make "certain claims upon other groups in the society for the establishment, maintenance or enhancement of forms of behavior that are implied by the shared attitudes."[2] By broadening the concept of interest group to include commonly shared *attitudes,* Truman has moved beyond the economic factor—important though it is. He has also moved closer to the real world, in which people differ and engage in conflict over many things other than economic interests. Abortion is such an issue. So, in part, is affirmative action. So was our involvement in Vietnam—an issue that tore this country apart in the 1960s. In this decade of the 1990s, the question of nuclear weapons and their control touches a raw nerve here and abroad. To be sure, powerful economic interests are well organized to pursue their goals and protect themselves. So are environmental, ethnic, veterans', professional women's, religious, and ideological groups. Indeed, the past two or three decades have seen an expansion of the U.S. policy agenda accompanied by the proliferation of organized groups.

LINKAGE MECHANISMS: INTEREST GROUPS AND POLITICAL PARTIES

Political scientists are fond of referring to interest groups in terms of their *linkage* function. What does this mean, and is it of any interest to students of politics? As emphasized in Chapter 1, politics is concerned with those who exercise power. People who exercise power are in a position to affect the lives of others in vital ways: their livelihood, their schooling, their leisure, and even their very existence. Serious students of politics are therefore very much interested in understanding any institutions, mechanisms, or procedures used to "link" the interests and opinions of ordinary people with those who exercise power over their lives. In a so-called open society, one expects to find that those in power are subject to some real constraints imposed by "We, the People," to quote the Preamble to our own Constitution. In "closed" or authoritarian systems (see Chapter 3), on the other hand, those in positions of power are relatively free to make their own decisions and to frame their own policies without regard to the wishes or opinions of ordinary citizens. In an open society, those devices that serve to link the bulk of the population with elite levels of power and leadership are thought to have special importance in preserving this quality of openness. In turn, the openness of the system is thought to make democracy more stable! Actually, as we shall see, even in relatively closed societies there are linkage devices present; they are used in subtle ways to help maintain the patterns of control between those in power and the general citizenry.[3]

The *political party* is another important institution enabling citizens to participate in the process of governing. Viewed historically, the party is a relatively recent phenomenon. Party systems as we know them in the contemporary era are the result of nineteenth-century developments.

Americans were among the first to invent a party system as a means of linking government with the ordinary citizen. As a consequence, we have come to place special significance on the health of our own party system. If the parties are in trouble—as is often charged these days—Americans are likely to conclude that their democracy is threatened. Unless we have a strongly competitive two-party system, how can the views of the great mass of people have any impact on those who hold political power?

This kind of argument has traditionally been instilled in Americans from early childhood. Belief in the value of parties, election campaigns, and election contests as a means of keeping a check on those who govern us is basic to the process of political socialization in this country. American political scientists repeat similar themes as gospel. One of the most respected authorities on American parties summed up the matter in these words: "The political parties created democracy and . . . modern democracy is unthinkable save in terms of parties."[4]

Experts on "political democracy"—as the term is used here and in other "free" and "open" political systems—have looked to political parties to perform a number of vital functions: linking government with public opinion, selecting political leaders, organizing the "public will," and instilling a general sense of civic awareness. Although Americans were among the first to develop this system and its rationale, we have no monopoly on it. Much the same kind of thinking permeates the British political system, as it does several Western European countries, Canada, Australia, New Zealand, and Israel. In all, some 30 nations practice some form of democracy—from tiny Costa Rica to India with its 700 million people, many of them poor and illiterate. Furthermore, as events in Eastern Europe, Latin America, and even Russia suggest, the democratic universe (and hence the importance of party systems) is expanding.

On the other hand, in this century authoritarian and even totalitarian political systems have found it useful to employ mechanisms called "parties." To be sure, a totalitarian party system is strikingly different from our so-called two-party system. Nevertheless, totalitarian regimes find that the political party serves an important purpose in linking the mass of the citizenry with the centers of governmental power and authority.

For this reason, some political scientists often find it useful to study parties in terms of different types. A simple classification scheme consists of the two-party system, the multiparty system, and the one-party system.

Two-party System. Two parties share the bulk of the votes and public offices between them, with each of the two dominant parties winning majorities in a substantial number of elections. There may be other minor parties, but they are not able to gain control of the directing personnel of government. Both the United States and the United Kingdom are frequently cited as having two-party systems, although the United Kingdom has several parties, most with a few seats in the House of Commons. Third parties are also fairly common in American national politics, though only the Republicans and Democrats ever gain control of the federal government.

Multiparty System. Three or more parties share the bulk of the votes and public office, and no single party is consistently able to win a majority of votes or offices. France provides the classic example of several parties holding seats in the national legislature; consequently, French governments usually have been coalitions of parties. We shall see some of the practical consequences of this arrangement later in the chapter, when we examine Charles de Gaulle's leadership in the Fifth Republic and the Socialist government of President François Mitterrand in the current era.

One-party System. One-party systems come in all shapes and sizes. In the former Soviet Union, for example, the Communist party (CPSU) was the sole legal party from 1918 until 1990, and its apparatus controlled all other institutions of society—government, labor unions, the armed forces, and universities. Another form of one-party system developed in Mexico where the ruling Institutional Revolutionary Party (PRI) dominated politics from 1929 to 1988. Controlling the selection of candidates to political positions in Mexico's 32 states, the PRI used this extensive patronage system to establish its one-party dominance. In 1988 the dominance of the PRI was broken, however, when newly elected President Carlos Salinas de Gortari proclaimed, "The era of the virtual one-party system has ended." Still another example of one-partyism is Kenya, in which, over the past few years, there has been a wrenching struggle on the part of opponents of the ruling Kenya African National Union (which is the only legal party) and its leader, President Daniel Arap Moi. Political scientists have long debated the extent to which one-partyism is compatible with democracy.[5] A guarded answer might be that in some cases—where the one-party system is fairly flexible and permeable, and its rule not enforced by legal mechanisms or a political police—limited democratic politics can take place. But in the former Soviet model, and probably the present Kenyan model, the answer is clearly no.

Interest groups and political parties are invariably ranked among the most important of the linkage mechanisms. What specific functions are they likely to perform? Can we expect to discover significant differences among political systems by examining the uses they make of basic linkage devices such as interest groups and political parties?

We turn our attention first to the United Kingdom, a country that has had long experience with both interest groups and parties. It also features a political system that is generally considered one of the most "open" in the world. Next we examine another democratic political system where interests are represented much differently and in the context of many political parties. Does the multiparty system of France make that country more or less democratic or representative? Finally, we turn our attention to a "closed" regime—the former USSR—and ask how interests were (or were not) represented in the absence of democracy and under the watchful eye of a single political party.

POLITICAL LINKAGES—THE UNITED KINGDOM

Actually, the British party system is a two-party system by one measure alone: since 1945, only the Conservative party or the Labour party has been able to form a government in the House of Commons. By electoral measures, Britain has a lively multiparty system. The Liberal party—a major party until about 1920—still runs third and wins several million votes in general elections. In 1981 the Liberals joined with a new Social Democratic party, led by several former prominent Labour MPs (members of Parliament) who were thoroughly disenchanted with the divisive factions within Labour, to form the "Alliance." There is also a tiny Communist party and two nationalist parties: the Scottish Nationalists and Plaid Cymru (Welsh). With the exception of the Communists, all of these lesser parties are represented in the House of Commons. Indeed, the Labour government of 1974–79 did not have a majority of House seats and so depended on the support of Liberal and Nationalist MPs. When the Liberals withdrew that support on a vote of confidence in 1979 (following a winter of labor unrest), the government of Prime Minister James Callaghan collapsed. Shortly thereafter, the Conservatives led by Margaret Thatcher launched their "counterrevolution."

Richard Rose describes the situation faced by British voters.

> As it stands, the electoral system faces voters with much the same choice as a vote of confidence in the House of Commons: a choice between two parties, the Ins and Outs. A voter can vote for or against the governing party and the opposition. Most voters are prepared to accept this choice, some with a marked preference for one party, and others reduced to choosing between the lesser of two perceived evils.[6]

When voters do find themselves choosing between the lesser of two evils, they are likely to incline toward apathy and independent voting. About a quarter of the British electorate now abstains from voting in general elections, and each general election finds more citizens moving away from traditional voting habits than would have been the case 10 or 15 years earlier. (Remarkably similar conditions have characterized the typical voting behavior of Americans in the current era—a subject we return to at the end of Chapter 6.)

Labor Unions

The United Kingdom—or England, as it is usually called by most Americans—is a highly industrialized country. In fact, the Industrial Revolution began in the United Kingdom. Because it came so early in the nineteenth century, the original English factory system created a raw and ugly scene: bleak factory towns and cities, wretched housing for workers and their families, pitifully low wages, child labor, poor schools, and inadequate medical care. So far as the new industrial workers in the coaling villages of Wales and the factory towns in the northern and middle counties of England were concerned, industrial capitalism in its original version decreed lives of poverty and ignorance for hordes of ordinary people. To make matters worse, this development occurred in a society with rigid lines of demarcation between social classes. If one were born into a working-class family, one had very little prospect of ever rising above this level. Even language separated the classes; members of the working class spoke crude dialects of their own.[7]

People who find themselves leading lives of desperation and degradation while their neighbors are living well are not likely to accept the difference *permanently*. This is especially true if they are citizens in a society that presents an opportunity—through its relative openness—for them to join forces in ways that challenge the status quo.

This was the situation in Britain at the turn of the twentieth century. Middle-class democracy had been achieved by this time. Furthermore, thanks to a Conservative ("Tory") prime minister—Benjamin Disraeli—some industrial workers had been given the vote. There are still important traditional centers of conservative strength in several working-class communities. Furthermore, conservatives drew working-class votes, especially in the southern and western areas of England, under Margaret Thatcher's leadership.

The industrial workers in England, Wales, and Scotland had seen great concentrations of capital amassed to mine the coal, build the railroads, and create the factories. Up to this point, the workers had faced this concentration of economic power as *individuals*. But having learned the painful lesson that the individual worker was virtually powerless to affect wages or working conditions and that a worker who protested too loudly was likely to be put out of work, they turned to building their own *trade unions*.

These industrial workers, following much the same kind of approach used in Western Europe and the United States, decided to join together in unions of their own in order to increase their *bargaining power* with the capitalist owners; they would bargain "collectively" rather than individually. If the owners resisted this collective approach, the workers would all go on strike, closing down the plant. It would no longer be a matter of summarily firing an individual worker who protested. *All* of the workers would be without work and income so long as the strike lasted; but now the owners would be without a functioning plant, without goods to sell, and without profits. In a test of wills, the strike became a worker's weapon in the fight for better wages and improved working conditions.

Needless to say, the capitalist owners were less than delighted with these early small unions. The initial attempts to organize British workers in the coal mines and in the textile factories encountered fierce and often brutal employer resistance. One result of this reaction was to "radicalize" the workers. Another was to stiffen their solidarity. Even today it is virtually impossible to work in a coal mine in Wales without holding a union card.

Democratic Socialism

By the end of World War I, the trade unions were well established in the United Kingdom. In the meantime, some labor leaders and a small group of Fabian Society intellectuals (among them George Bernard Shaw, the dramatist) had been attracted to *democratic socialism*. They agreed with Karl Marx that industrial capitalism—based on private ownership of the means of production—featured a sharp division between the classes, with the capitalist owners on one side and the workers on the other. They did not agree with Marx, however (or with the Russian Bolsheviks, for that matter), on the historical necessity of having a "dictatorship of the proletariat" (a dictatorship of the working class).[8] Generally speaking, most of the English socialists shied away from violent revolution. They believed society would permit an evolutionary move toward socialism that would preserve the traditional liberties of the English under the parliamentary system of government. In short, they felt that the system was sufficiently open to permit their ultimate triumph.

This arm of the workers' movement was not content to rely on collective bargaining and the strike weapon. Rather, it saw the need for a political party that would compete in general elections and develop enough strength at the polls to form a government. In the meantime, the workers had gained the right to vote.

The terrible economic depression of the late 1920s and the 1930s soon put this approach to democratic socialism to a severe test. The older industrial economy of Britain was hit hard during the worldwide depression. Millions of workers whose standard of living was low even when they were working were now without any work, and many were desperate. Collective bargaining and the strike weapon were almost useless in these circumstances.

As fate would have it, the first Labour government—headed by Prime Minister Ramsay MacDonald—was in power in 1931 when the full force of the economic collapse hit Britain. MacDonald's government proved weak and was replaced not by a swing to political extremism, but by a coalition government of Labour, Conservative, and Liberal leaders.

Although some British intellectuals and a few labor leaders were at this time attracted to communism, most were not. Then suddenly, in 1939 after Hitler attacked Poland, the British found themselves engaged in an all-out struggle for national survival. In Britain's "finest hour"—to borrow the language of the wartime prime minister, Winston Churchill—the people were distracted from the struggle between capitalism and socialism. Besides, many of the workers were now employed in the military forces. (Mobilization for war is a sure cure for massive unemployment, as both British and American experiences clearly demonstrate.)

By the time the war was over and Hitler's regime had been crushed, the British nation had developed a powerful labor movement, including a Labour party to which the unions and their members gave much of their voting strength. In 1945 the British public elected a Labour government dedicated to putting its own version of democratic socialism to work by nationalizing a number of basic industries. It also brought to fruition a modern welfare state, including a national health program for all ("socialized medicine," as it was labeled by its critics).

What had started nearly a century earlier as modest and humble efforts by ill-educated small groups of coal miners and factory workers had become a mighty social force. Labor in the United Kingdom today is both an interest group and a political party. This *organized* force has utterly transformed the social, economic, and political landscape of the United Kingdom. The trade unions and the Labour party have come to play an enormously important role in "linking" the interests of the working-class population with those who exercise power.

At the same time, however, the worker's movement is far from monolithic. If all the workers in Britain were to support the Labour party at the polls, Labour would enjoy a permanent political majority in the House of Commons. Instead, Labour has a hard time winning in most general elections. One special problem is the historic presence of some 1.5 million workers who traditionally vote for Conservative candidates. In a real sense, these voters are the descendants of those working-class families who supported Disraeli a century ago. Thus we see that the pursuit of pure economic or class interest is modified in Britain by other factors, which are bound to confuse the outside observer. In addition, many rank-and-file workers appear disenchanted with the Labour party, and their support helped Thatcher's Conservative party come to power in 1979 and remain in power through election victories in 1983 and 1987.

The Iron Lady

Prime Minister of Great Britain Margaret Thatcher—a grocer's daughter who studied chemistry at Oxford and later became a lawyer and a politican—was the first woman to head the British government as well as the first to lead a major Western nation. Prime Minister Thatcher came to power in May 1979 when her Conservative party gained a solid 43-seat majority in the House of Commons, thus unseating a Labour government headed by James Callaghan. As a result, Britain had a majority government for the first time in five years. The Callaghan government had been forced to rely on a shaky alliance between Labour and tiny Scottish and Welsh nationalist delegations; when this alliance came apart, the Callaghan government was finished.

The conservative victory in 1979 ushered in more than a decade of what some would call the "Thatcher revolution." Driven by a strong political will and indefatigable energy, Margaret Thatcher set out to do nothing less than "dismantle the welfare state," which she claimed had made Britain the "sick man of Europe" in the 1970s. Holding strong free-market convictions, the new prime minister vociferously argued in Parliament that the democratic socialist consensus between the Conservative and Labour parties was responsible for Britain's dismal economic performance. The state had nationalized too many industries, making the economy inefficient and discouraging productive business competition. The welfare system was also inefficient and overly protective, stifling private initiative in the marketplace. Most importantly, according to Thatcher, the labor unions had too much power to sabotage the capitalist economy by calling for widespread strikes and demanding higher wages than the national budget would allow.

Thatcher set out to change drastically the terms of Britain's state–society relationship. She denationalized many industries, hoping to encourage more private ownership. She tried to reduce the scope of state-subsidized services offered to British citizens. Finally, she tried to break the power of the large labor unions, using political control to prevent strikes and to limit the bargaining power of unions vis-à-vis British management and the government.

Thatcher's economic policies were designed to stimulate the British economy and make it competitive on the world market. The Thatcher government reduced the income taxes paid by the middle and upper classes, but increased the "value-added tax" (the VAT—a kind of national sales tax on almost all products) to 15 percent. In attempting to streamline an inefficient economy, Thatcher's economic policies led to a sharp increase in unemployment, which shot up from its already high level of 900,000 in May 1979 to 1.5 million during her first year in power. Incredibly, this was to double to more than 3 million during Thatcher's first term—a level not seen in the United Kingdom since the Great Depression of the 1930s.

These policies—tax breaks to the well-off and increased unemployment—would seem to undermine the interests of the British working class. Wouldn't we expect that British workers would have flocked to their political party—the Labour party—as a vehicle to oppose Thatcherism in the halls of Parliament and at the highest state level? It wasn't that simple. Thatcher avoided alienating the workers by co-opting them into her new program of "popular capitalism." Conservative party billboards in London proclaiming "Go Tell Sid" were aimed at getting workers to buy shares in newly privatized companies, like British Gas. Thatcher encouraged workers to buy their own homes and get out of their "council houses"—those subsidized by the state. The positive workers' response to Thatcher's initiatives led many to call her plan one of "embourgeoisement"—co-opting workers into the capitalist middle class by raising their standard of living and giving them a stake in the ownership of private companies.

Meanwhile, the Labour party was shooting itself in the foot. As a response to Thatcherism, Labour turned left at the beginning of the 1980s, becoming more radical and voicing anticapitalist policies. The new radicalism, which the conservative press called "the loony left," alienated many of Labour's more moderate followers. It was at this point that four leading Labour leaders broke from the party to form the Social Democrats, which aligned with the small Liberal party to form the Alliance, as mentioned earlier. But neither the Labour party, under the leadership of Neil Kinnock, nor any of the smaller parties could break the momentum of Thatcherism throughout the 1980s. More workers started voting Conservative; and the power of the labor unions, at least for the moment, had been deflated by Thatcherism's appeal to a working class that saw its needs fulfilled by a more productive economy.

By the 1990s, however, the momentum had waned. The pace of economic growth started to slow down, and Thatcher's determined political style—once the source of revitalization to a depressed British electorate—began to appear uncaring and unresponsive to Britain's poor and to changing social interests. Finally in 1990, after bitter infighting in the top ranks of the Conservative party, Margaret Thatcher resigned her post as prime minister given that she had lost the confidence of her party and the electorate. John Major—proponent of a kinder, gentler Thatcherism—was chosen by Conservative leaders to replace Thatcher as prime minister. He retained this post through a popular election in the spring of 1992 after the Conservative party won parliamentary elections. Demoralized and distraught after four consecutive Labour losses, Labour leader Neil Kinnock resigned, conceding that the Labour party had no clear mandate from Britain's working class.

Does the decline of the Labour party indicate the end of *class politics?* Has the Labour party lost its *social base,* as workers switch their political allegiance to the Conservative party? Has Thatcherism ended the political influence of a working-class movement in Britain? Only by constantly analyzing the changing nature of working-class (and other social) *interests* and their representation in *political parties* will we be able to answer these questions as Britain heads into the twenty-first century.

POLITICAL LINKAGES—FRANCE

The paradoxes of French political culture and politics extend to the activity of interest groups and political parties. We might expect that the country in which the modern nation erupted on the scene with the historic force of the 1789 *Révolution* would provide an example of strong representative institutions between the state and society. The values of that revolution—liberty, equality, fraternity—might lead us to expect a dogged determination on the part of the French public to defend its rights and organize its interests against a traditionally strong state. With French society sharply divided—historically—on issues of class (workers versus business), religion (clericalism versus secularism), ideology (socialism and communism versus classical liberalism and conservatism), and region (the urban middle class and rural agrarians), it would seem logical that linkage mechanisms play a strong role in representing various social interests. Logic, however, is not one of the prevailing characteristics of the French political system.

Even after the 1789 revolution, French politics tended toward authoritarianism and centralization under Napoleon Bonaparte. These tendencies had some positive outcomes, such as the establishment of universal and standardized education, the emergence of an efficient administrative bureaucracy, the codification of laws, and the transformation of an ethnically diverse, multilingual society into a modern nation-state. On the negative side, the tradition of the strong state meant that, when governments changed hands, it was difficult to wrest power from the center; political changes were thus not orderly alternations of parties within a commonly agreed upon system, but rather drastic changes in the political system itself. Thus when France changed its governments throughout the eighteenth and nineteenth centuries, it alternated from *République* to dictatorship to monarchy and back.

These two characteristics—strong state, and drastic swings in types of political system—have had two effects on interest group politics and political parties in France. The first is that gravitation toward strong central rule discouraged the development of effective and independent societal interest groups. Partly because state administrative organs took the lead in dealing with social problems and partly because of the distaste inherent in French political culture for organizing and mobilizing social interests, group activity has not played the role that it has in the United States or, to a lesser extent, in Great Britain.

The second effect is the weakness of representative institutions. While France is a multiparty system, the main representative forum of party politics—the National Assembly (parliament)—has traditionally been either ineffective, weak, or impotent in comparison with the French executive. Citizens tend to distrust political parties and the way they jockey for power; they therefore have not imputed significant power to a national parliament, where party politics could cause drastic swings in state power. Unlike in Great Britain, where the Labour and Conservative parties came to agree on the basic rules of the political game after World War II either by consensus or political expediency, in France it was feared that a change in party rule would lead to drastic changes in the political system. We'll see how that fear was unfounded; but the fear itself has been a determining factor in the divisive and relatively weak operation of party politics in France.

Interest Group Activity

To continue with our example of the working-class movement, we'll see that the trade union movement was never as unified or organizationally coherent in France as it was in Great Britain (through voluntary association) or the USSR (by Communist party *diktat*). Working-class consciousness didn't develop as early in France as it did in Great Britain since, in the former nation, industrialization came about at a much later date and French peasants and farmers have proved a much more formidable political force than their British counterparts. A working-class outlook did not emerge as ferociously as the party-inspired brand in the USSR because of what political scientists call the existence of "cross-cutting cleavages" in French society. That is, not all workers identified with other workers based only on their role in the economic system. Some workers identified more with religiously like-minded people; some allied with the communists, and others with the more reformist socialists. So the working-class movement in France has been traditionally weak based on *social factors:* later industrialization and a variety of interwoven interests that united workers with other members of the polity.

The working-class movement remained weak because of *institutional factors.* For example, when the workers did attempt to organize interests, they did not band together behind one political party, as was the tendency in Great Britain (though we've seen that the Tories have been quite successful in co-opting many of the British workers). Whereas the left in Great Britain generally agreed that democratic socialist measures were to be instituted though a reform of the accepted parliamentary sytem, the left in France diverged after the Russian Revolution of 1917—with the more militant members splitting off to form the Communist party, and the reform-minded members fashioning a new Socialist party. Some white-collar workers tended to associate with moderate or conservative elements. The affiliation of the divided interest-group movement with various political parties is as follows:

Labor Union	Description	Party Affiliation
Confédération Générale du Travail	blue-collar workers	PCF
Confédération Français Démocratique du Travail	blue-collar workers	PS
Force Ouvrière	white collar	independent
Conseil National du Patronat Français	French employers, management	tends toward right
Fédération Nationale des Syndicats des Exploitants Agricoles	French farmers	tends toward left[9]

This division has meant that the French working class has traditionally not had as much leverage against its employers (whether the employer is an independent business concern or the state) as in Great Britain or the USSR (where, even though the Soviet worker didn't have much power over the state, it was difficult or impossible for an enterprise manager to fire any worker). This is due largely to the traditions of *étatisme* (the strong presence of the state in societal affairs) and *dirigisme* (state participation in voluntary economic planning). In other words, the state—administrative bureaucracies of the governmental ministries, legal system, and the economic and social planning councils—had played a large role in mediating conflicts in society and in directing economic development. John Ardagh provides an example of how this worked until the government of Jacques Chirac tried to "roll back the State" in 1986.

> If an electrical firm, say, wanted to increase the price of some model, it had to get together with its competitors and prepare a joint dossier showing how production costs and other factors affected business. It took this to the Ministry of Finance which then weighed the economic and social implications. After much haggling, the decision on a new price—to be applied by all firms—was taken by the bureaucrats.[10]

This type of state mediation is sometimes referred to as *neocorporatism*—the involvement of state institutions with social groups to solve a social conflict or problem. The neocorporatist state tries to use its powers to mediate among conflicting groups to solve a policy problem without dominating the policy process. The goal is to prevent social devisiveness and move more effectively toward a common solution by using the resources of the state administration. It is different from pluralism in that the state assumes a larger role in the policy-mediating process. Whereas in a pluralist system the state might be just one actor among equal actors, in a neocorporatist system the state is definitely first among equals.[11]

This might make the policymaking process more efficient, but some argue that it results in not only a weakening of democracy, but a general weakening of representative processes. This has dire effects on French political participation, for it means that at intervals the French citizens—frustrated by their lack of opportunity to make significant contributions to the policymaking process through strong representative institutions—engage in more anarchic and socially disruptive forms of participation than might otherwise be the case. The students and workers' strike of May 1968 and the public services strike of the 1980s are often given as examples of this phenomenon.

The French Multiparty Political System

If interest group activity in France has traditionally been relatively weak, how have the broader and more comprehensive parties fared as a linkage mechanism between the diverse French society and the strong French state? As alluded to in the de Gaulle quote at the beginning of this chapter, the diversity of French society has indeed resulted in a plethora of ideologically varied and fractious political parties. Unlike the one- and two-party systems, a multiparty system such as that in France will witness a more transient rise and fall of smaller parties, a jockeying among political parties to accrue the most political advantages in elections, and the formation of governing coalitions when a single party does not enjoy a majority of the public's vote. The apparent instability fostered by the interplay among small and ideologically varied parties is counteracted by the continuity of the French state and administration. In fact, some argue that it is because the political parties were unable to agree on government policies when they had the chance (that is, during the Third and Fourth Republics, when the National Assembly had the potential to be relatively influential) that the French administrative bureaucracy has grown so strong.

In the Third Republic (1875–1940), French political parties in the National Assembly voted down 100 governing coalitions, making politics dependent on personalities, ideology, and political favors. In the Fourth Republic (1946–58), politics suffered the same instability, with six political parties preventing an efficient input into the crucial policymaking necessary to rebuild the country after World War II. It was as a result of the ineffectiveness of multiparty politics that Charles de Gaulle, who wanted to operate in the name of France above the fray of party politics, was led to create a relatively weak National Assembly in conjunction with a relatively strong dual executive (the president and the premier) as the linchpin of the constitution of the Fifth Republic (1958–present). Thus, while a vote (with conditions attached) in the National Assembly can bring down the government (the premier plus cabinet) of the day, the president can dismiss the National Assembly and call for new elections.

De Gaulle made liberal use of referenda—thus bypassing the national legislature—as a way to assess national approval of his policies, and he violated the constitution on a number of occasions to push his policies through a recalcitrant National Assembly.

Since de Gaulle resigned in 1969, party politics have come to play a more central role in national policymaking, and the party system has tended to coalesce around a loose left–right spectrum.[12] The major parties in France today are the RPR (the rightest Assembly for the Republic), the UDF (the center-right Union of Democracy, and the PS (Socialist Party). The PCF (Communist party) was one of the strongest Eurocommunist parties in the 1950s, 1960s, and 1970s, and four of its members held major cabinet positions in the Socialist government elected in 1981; but it has since lost much of its standing in French politics, given its relatively inflexible party program and recent changes in the French electorate. The FN (National Front) is a party that appeared on the scene only in the early 1980s, basing its platform on chauvinistic anti-immigration policies that appealed to those French workers displaced by cheap foreign labor and to other groups in French society who felt alienated from the political process and who wanted to register a protest vote. The RPR and UDF have formed coalitions in recent years to strengthen their rightist and centrist positions; the PS has held the major position on the left, adopting and abandoning the PCF as political expediency required.

The fortunes of political parties depend not only on their social bases of support, but also on *political organization*—most notably, the type of electoral system a country employs. A "winner-take-all," "first-past-the-post" electoral system means that whoever gets the most votes wins—even if it's not a majority—and there is only one winner per district, regardless of the relative distribution of votes. This tends to perpetuate the two-party dominant system in Great Britain and the United States because a small party doesn't have much of a chance to get its candidate elected, since people don't want to waste their vote. In a proportional representation (PR) system, electoral districts are composed of two or more seats that are filled by representatives according to the proportion of votes received. The PR electoral system tends to perpetuate a multi-party system because small parties can win seats even if they don't receive a majority of the vote in a district. France has employed PR throughout much of its political history, which helps to explain its unruly multiparty system.

To promote political stability, the single-member-district, two-ballot electoral system prevailed in the Fifth Republic, except for 1986 when the Socialist government reverted to a PR system to prevent a landslide rightist victory in the legislative elections of that year. The two-ballot system allows voters a choice among many political parties in the first ballot, but also eliminates the potential instability of such a wide variety by placing on the second ballot only those legislative candidates who received 12 percent of the vote. In presidential elections, the top two candidates—receiving the most number of votes in the first ballot—then run off in the second. This causes parties to form electoral coalitions for the second ballot, which tends to offset the ideological fractionalism of a multiparty system.

Parties and Power

Throughout the first two decades of the Fifth Republic, the right and center-right parties dominated French politics under the leadership of de Gaulle, Georges Pompidou, and Giscard d'Estaing. After the economic hardships and failure of the rightist governments to solve problems of unemployment and inflation in the late 1970s, the left came to power in 1981, under the leadership of François Mitterrand and his reconstituted Socialist party. *L'alternance*—a change from tried and true conservative rule to a Socialist-dominated legislature and executive—was the first test of the durability of the institutions of France's Fifth Republic.

Many French citizens feared that the Socialists would radically change French social and economic structures; the French economic elite was especially concerned that state nationalization of industry and central control of banks would threaten France's economic competitiveness. The Socialists did, in fact, attempt to institutionalize economic changes that would create more public property and systematically provide enhanced worker benefits and increased control of the workplace. They were hampered in their efforts, however, by the needs of a modern economy and by other more conservative French institutions, such as the Economic and Social Council, the Senate, and the Constitutional Council.

In 1984, Mitterrand removed the four Communist party cabinet ministers he had appointed in order to get PCF support in his election campaign, and instituted a set of economic austerity measures to get the economy moving again. Since economic growth and worker benefits are not always compatible, it appeared as if Mitterrand was abandoning some of the socialist goals of the PS in order to ensure economic pragmatism.

The result was that leftist voters became disenchanted with the Socialists because they appeared to have reneged on their party platform. Rightist voters, while convinced that the PS-controlled executive and legislature would not undermine French traditions, nonetheless saw the PS as pursuing the same policies as the right and center-right, only less effectively. This dissatisfaction with the Socialist regime led to the PS's defeat by the parties of the right and center-right in the 1986 elections to the National Assembly. The election of a conservative parliament (RPR and UDF) during the term of a socialist (PS) president resulted in the second test of the Fifth Republic institutions: *cohabitation*.

"Cohabitation" here refers to a division of France's dual executive—the president and the premier—between two different political parties.

This situation can occur because the president is popularly elected every seven years and the premier, who represents the dominant political forces in the National Assembly, is chosen after legislative elections held every five years. Up until Mitterrand's election in 1981, the center-right presidents appointed ideologically sympathetic premiers, which made sense for the coherence of policymaking, and which was possible because of the mandate provided by a majority of right and center-right deputies in the National Assembly. When Mitterrand was elected president, he dissolved the National Assembly to call for new elections (this being his prerogative as president), in order to try to get a majority of leftist deputies in the national legislature. It would have been difficult to get PS policies passed through the conservative-dominated legislature that had been elected under d'Estaing in 1978. The new president was successful, and 55 percent of the deputies in the 1981 legislative elections were sympathetic to Mitterrand and his policies.

However, in 1986 a legislative election was due—two years before Mitterrand's term as president was over. Because of the dissatisfaction of French voters with PS policies, they voted into power a right and center-right dominated National Assembly. Even though Mitterrand could appoint his own premier, it was understood that the president chooses a representative of the dominant political forces in the legislature. And so, Jacques Chirac—the mayor of Paris and a member of the RPR—became the premier under Mitterrand's presidency. This cohabitation meant that there was a great potential for policy conflicts and battle over the turf of the national executive, based on ideological and party platform issues. It was also a test of the division of powers within the dual executive.

Whereas the president is supposed to represent French national interests and protect the constitution, the premier is responsible for the mechanics of policymaking and setting the political course of the government of the day. De Gaulle usurped all of the premier's powers, claiming that this was all for the greater good of France. In 1986—with two different conceptions of what the greater good of France was—there was potential for a paralysis of the executive and a threat to the very institutions of the Fifth Republic.

The political system passed the test, however, and Mitterrand and Chirac developed a working relationship based on a separation of executive power, even though there were some points of disagreement (such as who should represent the French nation at international gatherings). From 1986 to 1988, cohabitation signified that the days of ideological party politics were at an end. Even though the socialists and conservatives shared the executive, there were no decisive ideological battles that threatened the stability of the French political system. Clearly, the Fifth Republic *political institutions* have proven strong enough to withstand even the most unusual quirks of the French *political process*.

Box 5-1. 1988 French Presidential Elections

First round of elections—Realignment of support for two final candidates. As stated, in the first round of the election on April 25 M. Mitterrand and M. Chirac were placed first and second respectively. The National Front candidate, M. Le Pen, won a considerably higher percentage than the opinion polls had predicted and ended up in fourth place, in front of the official Communist Party candidate, M. Lajoinie. The final voting figures published by the Constitutional Council were as follows:

	Votes	Percentage of valid votes	Percentage of total electorate
M. Mitterrand	10,367,220	34.09	27.19
M. Chirac	6,063,514	19.94	15.90
M. Barre	5,031,849	16.54	13.19
M. Le Pen	4,375,894	14.39	11.47
M. Lajoinie	2,055,995	6.76	5.39
M. Waechter	1,149,642	3.78	3.01
M. Juquin	639,084	2.10	1.67
Mlle Laguiller	606,017	1.99	1.58
M. Boussel-Imbert	116,823	0.38	0.30

Second round. *The results of the second round as proclaimed by the Constitutional Court of May 11 were as follows:*

	Votes	Percentage of valid votes	Percentage of total electorate
M. Mitterrand	16,704,279	54.02	43.76
M. Chirac	14,218,970	45.98	37.25

In this round, out of a registered electorate of 38,168,869, a total of 32,085,071 went to the polls, the abstention rate being 15.8 per cent. Of the votes cast 3.7 per cent were blank or void.

Source: *Roger East, ed.*, Keesings Contemporary Record of World Events, *Longman Group, 34, no. 6 (June 1988): 35979, 35980–81.* Reprinted by permission.

At the next presidential elections in 1988, Chirac decided to quit the premiership and run against Mitterrand in his bid for the reelection to the presidency. Mitterrand won a decisive victory in the second-round vote of the elections, but the PS could not gather a majority in the legislative elections called after Mitterrand's victory. The Socialists won a plurality—allowing Mitterrand to choose a PS premier, Michel Rocard—but

Box 5-2. 1988 French Legislative Elections

The second round of voting on the distribution of seats in the National Assembly on June 12, which was a run-off in each constituency between candidates who had failed to win outright with the required overall majority in the first round but who had won 12.5 per cent or more of the vote, produced a relatively close result. The Socialist Party failed to win an absolute majority even though it increased its representation and remained the largest single political party in parliament.

The results of both ballots, as published on June 6 and 13 by the Ministry of the Interior were as follows:

	First ballot		Second ballot	
	Votes	Percentage	Votes	Percentage
Registered vote	37,945,582		30,045,772	
Votes cast	24,944,792	65.73	20,998,081	69.88
Valid votes cast	24,432,095	64.38	20,303,575	67.57
Abstentions	13,000,790	34.26	9,047,691	30.11
Extreme left	89,065	0.36	0	0
PC	2,765,761	11.32	695,659	3.42
PS	8,493,702	34.76	9,198,778	45.30
MRG	279,316	1.14	260,014	1.28
Presidential				
Majority[1]	403,690	1.65	421,587	2.07
Ecologists	86,312	0.35	0	0
Regional lists	18,498	0.07	0	0
RPR	4,687,047	19.18	4,688,493	23.09
UDF	4,519,459	18.49	4,299,370	21.17
Various right[2]	697,272	2.85	522,970	2.57
FN	2,359,528	9.65	216,704	1.06
Extreme right	32,445	0.13	0	0

Notes:

1. Comprised "various left" candidates.
2. Joined RPR and UDF to campaign as URC in second round.

In the second round, when the abstention rate was 30.1 per cent, a total of 48.7 per cent of the vote was cast for those parties constituting the presidential majority, 46.8 per cent for the URC (which in the second round comprised not only the RPR and the UDF but also "various right" candidates), 3.4 per cent for the Communist Party and 1.1 per cent for the National Front.

The national council of the Greens (Les Verts) had decided at a meeting on May 13–15 not to present any candidates in the general election on the grounds that the way in which the campaign was conducted favoured parties already represented in the National Assembly and that the battle between the two major blocs impoverished the political debate. The movement also expressed itself in favour of a return to the proportional system as the only means of combating the National Front. At its meeting the council agreed to set up a permanent five-member leadership structure led by M. Jean-Louis Vidal, who for the time being would be the Greens' national spokesperson.

Source: *Roger East, ed.,* Keesings Contemporary Record of World Events, *34, no. 10 (October 1988): 36228.*

lid not get a strong enough mandate from the voting public to guarantee
hat their policies would be passed in the National Assembly. What can
xplain the support for Mitterrand, given voters' uncertainty about his
arty, the PS? It seems that Mitterrand, after his first term in office, came
o think of himself (and to be thought of by the population) as more a
epresentative of France (as the French head of state) than the leader of
. political party with a specific policy agenda. Ironically, Mitterrand has
ollowed in the footsteps of his one-time ideological adversary, Charles
le Gaulle, in claiming to represent the interests of France—interests that
ie above the fray of party politics.

POLITICAL LINKAGES—THE USSR

For over 70 years, the Communist Party of the Soviet Union (CPSU)
vas the only existing and legitimate political party in this country of more
han 280 million people, including more than 100 ethnic groups. Whereas
n two-party or multiparty systems, the linkage mechanism works in an
pward direction (with the interests and demands of the population being
ommunicated to the political parties, which compete for office), in the
joviet case it worked in a downward direction (with the single party
ommunicating its goals and policies to the population). In contrast to the
3ritish case where workers expressed their interests through a party that
iad to compete with other parties representing different interests in order
o gain office, in the USSR the workers' interests were considered the
nly true interests. Since the CPSU—by virtue of its role in spearheading
he 1917 revolution—was the only representative of the working class, it
laimed a legitimate monopoly on power.

While national and local elections were held periodically with an almost
00-percent turnout (since voting was mandatory), the function of elec-
ions was not to select among parties' candidates, but to legitimate single-
arty rule. By voting for party-sponsored candidates (with only one name
n the ballot), society registered its "support" for CPSU policies and
ersonnel. The events of the late twentieth century, however, have shown
hat this support was illusory and based largely on the population's fear
f punishment or its resignation to communist control and the lack of any
eal choice. Before examining how free choice has affected the mush-
ooming of interests and political parties in ex-communist countries, we
urn now to the development and role of the CPSU and of the trade
nions, as an interest group, in the former Soviet Union.

The USSR: A Workers' Society?

According to Marx and Lenin, the working class represented the
lriving force of history. It was by virtue of the labor of workers that

societies developed and bore fruit. Historically, the workers had been exploited by economic and political elites; to systematically fight that exploitation, they needed to develop a *working-class consciousness*. Lenin argued that the democratic socialist route taken by European countries such as Britain was merely a sham to trick workers into believing that their needs would be met within the boundaries of a parliamentary, Western-style democracy. Reform within the system was not enough for Lenin: he believed that only a complete change of the system through revolution would elevate the worker and workers' interests to their rightful place in history.

However, in the historical conditions in Russia, the workers were not yet ready to rule themselves. After years of czarist oppression, they had no self-rule experience. The group that would represent the interests of the workers and that would be the *vanguard of the working class* and would "spark" a continuing revolution in Russia and around the world was the Communist party. This party was not to be one among many, because it did not represent only one interest or social group among many. It represented the only legitimate interest: that of the workers.

Thus, every other party was illegitimate, in the logic of Marxism-Leninism. Rather than viewing a two-party or multiparty system as a vehicle for democracy or pluralism, the Russian revolutionaries viewed it as merely a showpiece for the exploitation of the workers by the economic and political elite. Worker parties in the West were granted concessions but never allowed to gain significant power. The reasoning by the revolutionaries was that, if one party could fulfill the needs of society and represent the only true social interest, then other parties and interest groups would only undermine its efforts and promote social devisiveness. Thus the one-party system was born in the USSR—a system that lasted, in one form or another, from 1917 to 1990.

The Trade Unions: Then and Now

Trade unions, as they developed in the industrial nations of the West, existed only in minor form in the Russia of 1917. Though trade unions became well developed under Communist rule in the USSR, they were— unlike the unions in Britain and to a lesser extent in France—not a major force in the making of public policy. Their linkage function, therefore, was quite different from that performed by trade unions in the West.

In Britain, powerful trade unions could put pressure on the Labour party (which also represented other interests) to implement policies favorable to the workers, threatening to withdraw their support for the party if their demands were not met. In the USSR, the CPSU did not rely on the support of the trade unions to stay in power; rather, the party used the trade unions to act as "transmission belts" (as Stalin called them) to the workers. Trade unions became the mechanism by which the CPSU leadership channeled its policies to the Soviet people at their places of work. Since the party-state owned all of the factories and businesses, controlled all of the wages, prices, and production targets, and established all economic policies, the trade unions had no leverage against the party in making its demands. In other words, the trade unions were not autonomous organizations. They depended on the party for their very livelihood.

While the Soviet trade unions were not used as vehicles to relay workers' interests to the party, they were used to protect workers' rights, as defined by the CPSU. For example, the All Union Council of Trade Unions (the Communist-sponsored national union organization) protected workers' jobs (making it very difficult for enterprise managers to fire their employees), granted liberal leaves of absence for female workers (who constituted over 50 percent of the Soviet workforce) for child care, and guaranteed workers inexpensive housing, utilities, and heavily subsidized vacations at communal workers' health resorts (called "sanatoriums").

Nevertheless, workers continued to encounter many frustrations that the CPSU-dominated trade unions could not or would not resolve. Poor working conditions (such as outdated or dangerous equipment), lack of consumer goods on which to spend disposable income, and limited housing availability (leading to cramped and shoddy living conditions) were just some of the workers' complaints. Yet there was no formal organized method of voicing these complaints other than through party-sponsored organizations. The strike—a tool used by workers in other countries to force management and/or the state to listen to their demands—was not illegal in the USSR, but was discouraged by threat of arrest and other sanctions.[13]

As we shall see in Chapter 14, when Soviet citizens were denied an effective official forum for voicing their real opinions, they tended to withdraw from formal politics and turn to apathy or indifference. In this case, being denied the tool of the strike, many Soviet workers became disinterested in their jobs (since it was difficult to advance or earn wage increases) and turned to alcohol, absenteeism, and a thriving black market (the "unofficial economy") to offer their services for higher wages and to purchase scarce goods. Needless to say, this had devastating effects on the Soviet economy, with one Soviet source estimating that worker alcoholism cost the USSR $100 billion annually in revenues and losses.[14]

When Mikhail Gorbachev came to power in 1985 and encouraged Soviet workers to offer constructive criticism concerning their working conditions, the issue of the strike as a legal action subject to formal arbitration emerged in official policymaking circles. This issue became especially acute in the summer of 1989 when coal miners in Kemerovo—a coal-rich region in the Kuznetsk Basin—refused to work in the mines as a way to protest working and living conditions, low wages, and lack of basic consumer goods.

What began as a walkout of 77 miners turned into a massive strike involving more than 100,000 workers throughout nine cities. The miners' demands at first centered around economic concerns at the workplace: poor equipment, irrational production quotas, low quality of workplace food, lack of material goods, and inadequate vacation time. Soon these specific economic demands escalated into a broad package of social and political demands: economic independence from the state for the coal mines and all enterprises, new elections to the local city councils ("soviets"), and the end of one-party rule.

The significance of the strike is that, when workers turned to their local CPSU committees and official trade union councils, they found resistance and opposition to workers' demands. As one Soviet legal scholar noted during the crisis, "Stalinism turned [trade unions] from agencies for the protection of working people's rights and legitimate interests into hostages of the apparatus. In their current form . . . they are hardly capable of performing their intended functions."[15] Because the official unions were so unhelpful, the workers formed their own strike committees—similar to those formed by the Polish trade union Solidarity under the communist regime in 1980—which were independent of the CPSU apparatus and state. These strike committees formulated worker demands, kept order and sobriety at all times among the striking workers, and acted as the link between the workers and the state in negotiating an end to the strike.[16]

The strike committees are a clear example of how interest groups emerged in reforming communist states: party-state official organizations proved incapable of responding to the needs of certain social groups. As citizens took advantage of the opportunities for political action (provided by the leadership's need for active citizen involvement in reform), they formed independent organizations as a vehicle to express their needs and demands to the ruling group.

This nascent form of interest group organization was not always appealing to many Soviet citizens accustomed to social *order* and the pervasive power of the CPSU party-state in preventing any social disruption. During the strike, many Soviet citizens voiced their horror at the ability of a minority of workers to disrupt the general social order by making specific and narrow demands. They called upon Gorbachev and top party leaders to use whatever means available to end the strike and restore normal working and living conditions.

Gorbachev and sympathetic reformers knew that it was not so easy: order had to be restored by the *consent* of the new strike committees, which represented the legitimate demands of the workers, and not by *coercion* justified solely by the CPSU's interpretation of what was in the workers' interest. So, reformist political leaders negotiated with the strike committees and acceded to some of their demands, while warning that the leadership and society in general would not tolerate the economic and social disruption of repeated strikes.

The Soviet example illustrates a fundamental tension inherent in interest group activity in all political systems: how can leaders and citizens reconcile the legitimate interests of *part* of society with the *common good* of the whole country? What we must ask ourselves in order to answer that question is this: who gets to define the "common good"? In the Soviet Union, it used to be the Communist party. With the advent of *glasnost* and *perestroika,* it became far less clear.

Dismantling Central Control in the USSR

It is understandable that the CPSU leadership was wary of allowing Soviet coal miners to form an independent trade union; after all, for more than 70 years the party dominated all decision-making processes and steered the course of all social processes in the Soviet Union. To be sure, social groups—such as the Central Trade Union Council, the Writer's Union, the Soviet Peace Committee, the Union of Journalists, and other organizations—existed under the single-party regime, but they were all under the wing of the party apparatus. Every group, in order to be assured a meeting place, funding, and freedom from police harassment, had to be registered with the state and conform to party-defined social goals. Nevertheless, the party actively encouraged citizen participation, which was guaranteed by the 1977 constitution.

What can explain this paradox of single-party domination of interest groups and its promotion of citizen participation? Why did the party want citizens to participate if it controlled all of the public organizations? The answer is that interest group activity in the single-party system performed a different function than it does in a two-party or multiparty system. In the single-party system, interest group activity was not designed to actually affect policymaking or to convince the ruling party or coalition to change or modify its political programs. Citizen participation was designed to legitimate the party's policies, to channel party goals to society, and to give active citizens an outlet for expressing particular needs.

One should not infer from this that the CPSU acted in one voice before Mikhail Gorbachev introduced his momentous reforms. While before 1987 the top leadership kept intraparty conflicts behind closed doors, there were different points of view within the party and state bureaucracies, especially concerning the allocation of resources. Western Sovietologists—using a practice called "Kremlinology"—sought out policy disagreements by looking for acerbic remarks, personnel changes, and predominance in public functions or public photographs to see who was in and who was out in the Soviet leadership. They discerned, in part, that various institutions—especially the military and the economic ministries—developed interests peculiar to their work and fought for these interests with the CPSU bureaucracy to get more funding, a greater share of scarce resources, and more personnel. The pattern of bureaucratic and institutional interest articulation was consistent enough for some scholars to argue that a form of "institutional pluralism" characterized policymaking throughout the communist period.[17]

But this limited pluralism never escaped the boundaries of single-party rule. While bureaucratic infighting influenced the formation of policies and while CPSU-sponsored public participation affected the *implementation* of policies, there never developed autonomous social groups that could question not just the methods of CPSU rule, but its very goals. Not until, that is, Mikhail Gorbachev appeared on the scene in 1985 and decided to democratize the Communist party.

In the first five years of his rule, Gorbachev never intended for the CPSU to relinquish its monopoly of political power. He called any move toward a multiparty system "rubbish" since he, along with many other Soviet citizens, believed that only the single-party system could simultaneously provide the democracy and social order necessary to reform the Soviet system. Gorbachev's original aim was simply to make the CPSU more *effective* in its policymaking and implementation, by bringing it closer to the actual needs and interests of the Soviet population.

As democratization was introduced into the ranks of the CPSU hierarchy, splits within the leadership increasingly emerged. Since Gorbachev liberalized media exposure to the inner workings of CPSU decision making, these emerging factions in the CPSU became more and more public. Soviet and Western observers alike were amazed to see a public airing of sharp differences between party leaders, since the CPSU was careful to present a united front to the public before 1985. While most of the CPSU leaders agreed that there had to be serious reforms in Soviet society, they disagreed vehemently as to the nature and pace of those reforms.

Initially, the disagreements coalesced around two extremes: one represented by Yegor Ligachev, who felt that perestroika and glasnost' were going too fast and threatening Marxist-Leninist values; and Boris Yeltsin, who argued that the reforms were too slow and were not fundamental enough to instigate meaningful change in Soviet society. Gorbachev tried to strike a balance between the "hardliners" and the "radicals." Finally, after much emotional debate, the Central Committee of the CPSU (the party's main policymaking forum)—with the prodding of Gorbachev—agreed to renounce its claim on single-party monopoly and voted to allow the creation of a multiparty political system in the USSR.

As more frequent splits within the ranks of the CPSU became increasingly public, individuals and groups became bolder and more organized in articulating their interests and alternative visions of the future path of

Soviet development. By 1990, more than 60,000 "informal groups" (groups not registered with the state or sanctioned by the CPSU) had sprung up across the USSR. These groups represented a broad spectrum of interests that developed throughout the vast reaches of Soviet society but that never surfaced under the watchful eye of the CPSU, as it strove to maintain social order at all costs.

Many of the new groups represented the interests of the various nationalities in the USSR. "Sajudis" in Lithuania, "Rukh" in the Ukraine, and the Latvian Popular Front all struggled with the central party-state leadership to make their native tongues the official languages of their republics, to devise their own sets of laws, and to gain autonomy or independence. Environmental groups—such as "Green World" and the "Socio-Ecological Union"—attempted to repair the damage done to lakes, rivers, and cultural monuments by the Stalinist industrialization drive; many of the groups later formed political parties. Russian nationalist groups—such as "Pamyat" (Memory)—struggled against those reforms that they believed to be dangerous to the interests of the Russian nation: Westernization, pluralism, and the alienation fostered by a market economy. Entrepreneurial, military, parliamentary, religious, and workers' groups all sought to organize, present a program or set of demands, and mobilize their members to attain their goals either through their own efforts or by lobbying local or national party and state leaders.[18]

As we shall see in Chapter 14, the Communist party and Soviet state could not survive the explosion of independent interests that emerged during the Gorbachev era. Communist linkage mechanisms—the single party and the official trade unions, for example—proved incapable of channeling freely expressed independent opinions and interests to state bodies of power. In the end, the Soviet state was destroyed—an extreme example of how social interests can affect politics when there are no satisfactory political links between an independent citizenry and the state.

The rise of political leader Boris Yeltsin—the ex-communist official who rose to power by fighting the entrenched Communist party and defying the Communist coup plotters in August 1991—was due largely to his ties with the Russian population. As president of Russia (the successor state to the old Soviet Union), Yeltsin, along with other political leaders and activists, is attempting to formalize links between Russian citizens and the new Russian state by creating institutions in which popular participation can influence the policymaking process.

The Soviet single-party political system has been replaced by a Russian multiparty system. This new party system is still in its infancy: the configuration of Russian social interests has not yet made itself clear after years of Soviet domination; the political parties are weak and do not clearly represent specific social groups or interests; and political parties still play an insignificant role in the political process even a year after Russia became an independent state. While there are more than 20

Russian political parties ranging from monarchists to anarchists to neo-Stalinists, they have not yet proven effective in channeling independent social interests to a newly forming political system.

The case of Russian workers illustrates an alternative to political parties as a linkage mechanism. In Russia (unlike in Great Britain or France), workers and trade unions have tended not to align themselves with any political party. After decades of domination by one oppressive Communist party, they don't trust that parties will truly represent their interests. Yeltsin—hoping to prevent disruptive strikes and to co-opt workers into his economic reform program—has encouraged a process of *social partnership* among the Russian government, independent trade unions, and business organizations. To use a term introduced above in our discussion of France, this "neocorporatist" form of linkage is designed to encourage the cooperation of the worker and business groups in working out policies based on each of their interests, bypassing the sometimes devisive and disruptive political party system. Neocorporatism, as embodied in Yeltsin's social partnership, is designed to link social groups to the Russian state while at the same time maintaining order through consensus and compromise.

The Russian case provides a fascinating study of the construction of linkage mechanisms between a newly independent society and a democratic state still in the process of formation. Will workers become an influential force in Russian politics, or will they be eclipsed by a new class of entrepreneurs? Will the workers and the entrepreneurs continue to cooperate with government representatives in forming public policies through a social partnership program? Or will these groups turn to opposition political parties to counter government policies once the political party system becomes more entrenched? While only time will answer these questions, one thing is certain. For the first time in the state-dominated history of their country, Russian citizens have the chance to articulate freely their own interests and to participate in the arduous process of building a democratic political system in which those interests can be freely expressed.

SUMMARY

This chapter has emphasized the importance of linkage mechanisms in the political system as a way to connect "the people" to the policymaking process dominated by government elites. Recalling the importance of public opinion (dealt with in Chapter 4), we focused here on interest groups (especially workers and trade unions) and political parties. Different types of political party systems—single, two, and multi—have different strengths and weaknesses and significantly affect the way interests are (or are not) channeled from society to the state. Three case studies—

Great Britain, France, and the Soviet Union—illustrate the variety of linkage mechanisms in modern political systems. Linkage mechanisms are affected by changes in both government policy and society; whether or not a dynamic equilibrium between state and society can be maintained depends on how effective the linkage mechanisms are in channeling social interests to bodies of state power.

NOTES

1. In Roy Fairfield, ed., *The Federalist* (New York: Doubleday/Anchor, 1961).
2. David B. Truman, *The Governmental Process,* 2nd ed. (New York: Knopf, 1967), p. 33.
3. This is not to be confused with "linkage theory" in international relations.
4. E. E. Schattschneider, *Party Government* (New York: Farrar and Rinehart, 1942), p. 88.
5. *New York Times,* Aug. 5, 1990.
6. Richard Rose, *Politics in England* (Boston: Little, Brown, 1980), p. 259.
7. For an interesting study of this crucial aspect of English society, see Richard Hoggart, *The Uses of Literacy* (London: Pelican Books, 1958). Professor Hoggart, who was born into a working-class family, argues that British society remains class structured.
8. An excellent summary of Marx's ideas—ideal for the beginning student—is found in George A. Sabine, *A History of Political Theory* (New York: Henry Holt, 1937), ch. 32.
9. From John Ardagh, *France Today* (New York: Penguin Books, 1988), p. 101; Mark Kesselman et al., *European Politics in Transition* (Lexington, Mass.: D. C. Heath, 1987), pp. 206–8; and Colin Campbell et al., *Politics and Government in Europe Today* (New York: Harcourt, Brace, Jovanovich, 1990), pp. 198–201.
10. Ardagh, *France,* p. 57.
11. Some scholars prefer not to use the somewhat tainted "corporatist" label (the term originated with fascist policies in the early twentieth century) and characterize state–society relations in France as *state-dominated pluralism.* See, for example, David Wilsford, "Tactical Advantages versus Administrative Heterogeneity: The Strengths and Limits of the French State," *Comparative Political Studies,* 21, no. 1 (April 1988): 126–68, at pp. 159–60.
12. Traditionally, the left end of the spectrum has meant either communist or socialist parties—those that based their policies and membership on the working class and that desired, in greater or lesser degrees, to change the existing social structure to give more benefits to the relatively poorer members of society. The traditional right has meant, in the case of France, those parties concerned with preserving the status quo, maintaining private property and landed interests, and preserving religious values in society. We might see necessary changes in the depiction of this continuum, given the need for communist and socialist parties to

reevaluate their policies and the emergence of "green" parties and "postmaterialist values" that don't fit precisely into a left/right categorization.

13. Gordon B. Smith, *Soviet Politics: Continuity and Contradiction* (New York: St. Martin's Press, 1988), p. 207; see pp. 189–221 for a thorough discussion of the Soviet economy, its workforce, and the structure and function of the trade unions.

14. Ibid., p. 207.

15. S. Shishkin, "Is the Strike Legal?" *Izvestia*, July 14, 1989, p. 3, in *Current Digest of the Soviet Press*, 51, no. 28 (August 9, 1989): 5.

16. The striking miners attempted to break all ties with the official CPSU-sponsored All Union Council of Trade Unions to form an independent trade union. See Bill Keller, "Soviet Miners Seek Control of Union," *New York Times*, September 17, 1989.

17. See Jerry Hough, *The Soviet Union and Social Science Theory* (Cambridge, Mass.: Harvard University Press, 1977), for an argument based on this approach. For a different point of view, see Alexander Groth, "U.S.S.R.: Pluralist Monolith," *British Journal of Political Science*, 9, pt. 4 (October 1979): 445–64.

18. See Vera Tolz, "The Emergence of a Multiparty System in the USSR," *Report on the USSR*, 2, no. 17 (April 27, 1990): 5–11.

SUGGESTED READINGS

Group Theories

Dahl, R. *The Dilemmas of Pluralist Democracy: Autonomy vs. Control*. New Haven, Conn.: Yale University Press, 1984. An analysis by America's leading theorist of pluralism, in which he examines the importance of corporate power.

Greenstone, J. D. "Group Theories." In Fred I. Greenstein and Nelson W. Polsby, eds., *Handbook of Political Science*, Vol. 2. Reading, Mass.: Addison-Wesley, 1975. A summary review of pluralist theories.

Truman, D. B. *The Governmental Process*. New York: Knopf, 1971. The standard study of groups in our governmental process.

Interest Groups

Salisbury, R. H. "Interest Groups." In Fred I. Greenstein and Nelson W. Polsby, eds., *Handbook of Political Science*, Vol. 4. Reading, Mass.: Addison-Wesley, 1975. A summary essay on interest group activity.

Political Parties

Epstein, L. D. "Political Parties." In Fred I. Greenstein and Nelson W. Polsby, eds., *Handbook of Political Science*, Vol. 4. Reading, Mass.: Addison-Wesley, 1975. A summary essay surveying the scholarly literature.

Politics in France

Ardagh, John. *France Today*. New York: Penguin Publishers, 1987. An information-packed, colorful, and fast-paced account of politics, society, and culture in contemporary France.

Ross, George, Stanley Hoffmann, and Sylvia Malzacher, eds. *The Mitterrand Experiment: Continuity and Change in Modern France*. Oxford, U.K.: Oxford University Press, 1987. An insightful collection of essays on various successes and failures of "the left in power" from 1981 to 1986.

Wilson, Frank L. *Interest Groups Politics in France*. Cambridge, U.K.: Cambridge University Press, 1988. Using interviews with interest group leaders, the author explains the weak position of interest groups in France in light of domineering executive and administrative branches.

Politics in the United Kingdom

Hattersley, Roy. *Choose Freedom: The Future of Democratic Socialism*. London: Michael Joseph Publishers, 1987. An insider's view from a deputy leader of the British Labour party on the party's goal of democratic socialism.

Kavanaugh, Dennis. *Thatcherism and British Politics: The End of Consensus?* Oxford, U.K.: Oxford University Press, 1988. A rich assessment of the philosophical and policy-oriented goals of Thatcherism and their implications for British politics and society.

Tivey, Leonard, and Anthony Wright, eds. *Party Ideology in Britain*. New York: Routledge, Chapman, and Hall, 1989. An interesting examination of the principles on which British political parties construct their platforms and orient their policies.

Politics in the USSR

Brzezinski, Z., and S. P. Huntington. *Political Power: USA/USSR*. New York: Viking/Compass, 1965. An important comparative study of the two superpowers.

Byrnes, R. F., ed. *After Brezhnev: Sources of Soviet Conduct in the 1980s*. Bloomington: Indiana University Press, 1983. A comprehensive, multidisciplinary series of essays by several authorities, emphasizing how internal and external factors influence one another in shaping Soviet behavior.

Hahn, Jeffrey W. *Soviet Grassroots: Citizen Participation in Local Soviet Government*. Princeton, N.J.: Princeton University Press, 1988. A thorough and interesting account of political participation in communist countries, with a focus on citizen input into Soviet local politics.

Smith, Gordon B. *Soviet Politics: Continuity and Contradiction*. New York: St. Martin's Press, 1988. An excellent text on the tensions that emerged in Gorbachev's USSR in the fields of socialization, the party and state apparatus, regional politics, law, and the economy.

6

Elections, Campaigns, and Voting

> Talents for low intrigue, and the little arts of popularity, may alone
> suffice to elevate a man to the first honors in a single state; but it will
> require other talents and a different kind of merit, to establish him in
> the esteem and confidence of the whole Union, or of so considerable
> a portion of it as would be necessary to make him a successful
> candidate for . . . President of our United States.

> —ALEXANDER HAMILTON IN *Federalist No. 68*
> (EXPLAINING THE ADVANTAGES OF THE ELECTORAL
> COLLEGE OVER DIRECT ELECTION OF THE
> PRESIDENT)

> There aren't any poor PACs or Food Stamp PACs or Nutrition PACs
> or Medicare PACs.

> —SENATOR ROBERT DOLE

> To oversimplify and exaggerate slightly, if one generation of
> Republican politics began with the election of Ronald Reagan as
> California governor in 1966, another generation may well have started
> with Pete Wilson's takeover of that office in 1990.

> —DAVID S. BRODER

THE UNIVERSALITY OF ELECTIONS?

There was a time—and not so very long ago at that—when in an
introduction to political science, such as this book, it would have been
pointed out that elections are the means used for choosing and changing
rulers in only relatively few countries of the world. It would have also
been pointed out that, even in some countries where the forms of electoral
selection existed, the reality was selection through the internal co-
optation processes of a single ruling party. In other settings, so the lesson
would have gone, leadership passed from junta to strongman to junta in
successive military coups. There were even a few examples remaining
where leadership succession was hereditary. (The king of Nepal agreed
only in early 1990 to permit the beginnings of electoral politics.)

There are still examples of most of these things: authoritarian regimes
such as those of Syria and Iraq, totalitarian regimes (albeit wobbly) such

as those in Cuba and China, and a variety of military regimes such as those of Haiti and Nigeria. But as Francis Fukuyama observed in the article ("The End of History") we discussed in Chapter 1, we are living in an era of the steady expansion of the practice of liberal democracy. Events in Eastern Europe and Russia, along with the passing of authoritarian regimes in countries such as Chile and Argentina in the late 1980s, constitute powerful evidence for Fukuyama's thesis. While we argue that history is not about to end (because there are many other sources of conflict between people and between nations than the clash between authoritarianism and democracy), there is no question that elections are becoming more and more important—for the simple reason that, in more and more settings, actual transfers of power are being effected through electoral means. In the second edition of this book, discussion of elections was tucked away in chapters on classifying regimes and on political parties, public opinion, and interest groups. It is a measure of the new importance of elections—perhaps their coming ubiquity—that we here devote a chapter to the subject of elections, campaigns, and voting. For instance, in Myanmar (the nation formerly known as Burma), we are witnessing a protracted struggle to establish a system based on free elections. This involves wresting political power from a military elite that has governed for decades. A national election in May 1990 was held with apparent success, but the entrenched military regime promptly began delaying tactics to postpone its loss of power. By early 1993 the military was still in control but, under increasing international pressure, was being forced to make concessions. Most observers expect the transition to democracy to be successful sooner rather than later.

ELECTIONS

Elections come in a whole variety of shapes and sizes. There can be direct and indirect elections: under the original U.S. Constitution, for instance, the Senate was indirectly elected, with its members chosen by the state legislators; this was changed by the Seventeenth Amendment in 1913 to the present system of direct election. There can be election of candidates for office, and there can be elections (usually called "referenda" or "plebiscites") on questions of public policy. And elections can be organized in a variety of different ways, with very different consequences for the operation of the respective political systems.

The Legal Context

In 1967 Douglas W. Rae, of the political science department at Yale, published a book titled *The Political Consequences of Electoral Laws;* a second edition was published in 1971.[1] The book has won praises and respect over the years and—while not beyond criticism—serves as the standard work in the field.[2] We will not be able to present the richness of Rae's argument here, but we shall borrow from his terminology.

A first and obvious question pertaining to any electoral system comes down to this: how is representation *apportioned?* Is the polity treated as one electoral jurisdiction with representatives elected *at large*—where voters vote for all the places to be filled by selecting a slate or choosing the requisite number of names from the list? Or is the electoral jurisdiction broken down into *districts?* And if so, are the districts *multimember* or *single member?*

One of the great debates among political scientists in the twentieth century has been over the relative merits of *proportional representation* (PR) as against *single-member districts.* In a PR system, which works best in at-large elections or where there are multimember districts, the voter votes essentially for a party label, and a slate of candidates and representation is awarded proportionally on the basis of a party's success. In the single-member district, it is a case of winner-take-all. This is one of the important ways in which electoral law affects the party system of a polity. Proportional representation is thought to encourage the development of multiple parties, whereas single-member districts militate toward two-party systems—since there is a premium on the formation of majority coalitions to win the single seat.

Even here, however, there can be interesting variations. A single-member district may operate on a plurality formula or a majority formula. The requirement of a majority clearly is the strongest electoral reinforcement of two-partyism, while allowing a winner of an electoral plurality to take the seat opens the way to third parties.

This is far from being an uncontroversial, strictly technical matter. As with all the choices that must be made by a polity, when decisions are taken as to how its elections are to be legally structured, some group's electoral interests will be advanced and some other group's electoral interests will be set back. The choice between a plurality and a majority is being hotly debated in the American South with regard to the aspirations of black voters and candidates. Many states in the region require majority victories in both *primary elections* (which decide who shall be the official nominees of the parties) and also in the *general elections.* If there is no majority winner in a particular race (say, a race for governor in which there are four candidates—Democrat, Republican, and two independents), a runoff election is held among the top finishers—and, if necessary, another runoff, until a majority victor emerges. The problem for blacks is that, while they tend to vote as a block, there is no state in which blacks constitute a majority. Under a plurality system, black candidates who finish first in the field with, say, a third of the vote would win office. Under a majority requirement, the white vote—split between the candidates the first time around—can (and often does) come together in the runoff behind the surviving white candidate, giving him or her a majority and leaving the black candidate—still with one-third—a loser. Blacks complain that they can finish first but never win. Some whites respond that the community will be better governed and the people as a whole better represented by public officials who have garnered majority support. Blacks reply that majority requirements discriminate against them and possibly violate the Voting Rights Act of 1965, which prohibits electoral arrangements and devices that are racially discriminatory. We shall find out, because in the summer of 1990 the U.S. Justice Department announced it was filing suit under the act against the State of Georgia's requirement of a majority in primary elections.[3]

Another familiar way in which electoral laws affect the outcome of elections is through the process of *districting* (deciding on the geographic boundaries of electoral jurisdictions) and *apportionment* (deciding how many voters will choose how many representatives in what size districts). In the United States, the Supreme Court has decided that the equal protection clause of the Fourteenth Amendment to the Constitution requires the number of people in electoral districts to be roughly equal so as to satisfy the principle of "one-person-one-vote."[4] In other political systems, however, the equality-of-population approach is not so strictly followed.[5] A familiar problem with respect to districting is the potential for *gerrymandering* (the drawing of the district lines in ways that further the electoral prospects of the party or group in power, and diminish those of its opponents).

Even the form of the ballot (*ballot structure*) may be significant and may favor some kinds of outcomes over others. For instance, Douglas Rae distinguishes between "ordinal ballots," which allow voters to distribute their vote among candidates of different political parties, and "categorical ballots," which require the voter to register all choices along party lines—voting only for candidates of one party identification. It is suspected that ballot structure affects the contours of the political party, but the relationship has proved hard to pin down.

The Party Context

In the preceding chapter (Chapter 5), we discussed the types of party systems. And we have already touched here on the much argued relationship between PR and multipartyism. The seminal work on the relationship between matters of electoral law and types of parties was done in the early 1950s by the French political scientist Maurice Duverger.[6] What became known as "Duverger's law" posited that "the plurality system (in single-member districts) tends to lead to two-party competition."[7] PR, Duverger said, tends to lead to multipartyism. Later students and commentators have divided between those who think that "electoral systems

Box 6-1. *Affirmative Action and Abigail Thernstrom*

The passage in 1965 of the federal Voting Rights Act represented a crucial step forward in guaranteeing the promise of the Fifteenth Amendment to the Constitution of the United States that all citizens would have the right to vote without regard to "race, color, or previous condition of servitude." Throughout the South prior to the passage of the act, millions of black Americans were effectively excluded from the electoral processes by a variety of devices such as poll taxes and literacy tests. Furthermore, district lines were often drawn (gerrymandered) in ways that made the election of black public officials difficult or impossible. Under the Voting Rights Act, the Justice Department was able to seek the elimination or change of large bodies of state election law.

With the demise of the cruder exclusionary laws, there was a massive increase in black political participation. But by the late 1980s some blacks were asking whether certain electoral arrangements, which were on their face not racially discriminatory at all, were in fact still holding back black political progress, in violation of the act. Principally at issue were so called at-large elections. In such an arrangement, all the voters within a jurisdiction—say, a city—vote for all the places that will be filled on the city council. Thus, if there are 30 people on the city council, a voter would vote for 30 names from a list of candidates. In jurisdictions where whites and blacks tend to vote as blocks and where the black vote is less than a majority, blacks may find they can never elect black candidates under at-large arrangements. This has led to lawsuits under the Voting Rights Act that are aimed at persuading judges to order the replacement of at-large systems with systems of single-member districts, with the district lines so drawn as to guarantee that a number of black candidates would be elected roughly proportional to the size of the black vote within the jurisdiction. Opponents charge that for the court to adopt such an interpretation of the Voting Rights Act would, in effect, be to require legally a kind of proportional representation by race that is alien to the spirit of the law and of the Fifteenth Amendment.

In 1987, political scientist Abigail M. Thernstrom published a study of the problem titled Whose Votes Count? Affirmative Action and Minority Voting Rights. *The following is from the conclusion of her book.*

At various points in this book I have touched upon the potential costs attached to maximizing minority office holding. Perhaps the most important danger is that categorizing individuals for political purposes along lines of race and sanctioning group membership as a qualification for office may inhibit political integration. As James Blumstein argued at the 1982 Senate hearings [on amendments to the Voting Rights Act], such categorization amounts to a racial "piece of the action approach," perhaps freezing rather than thawing the previous system of racial politics. The heightened sense of group membership works against that of common citizenship. As Donald Horowitz pointed out at those same hearings, ethnic boundaries, by diminishing the sense of common citizenship, may "ultimately smother democratic choice and threaten democratic institutions."[1]

Note:

1. *Abigail M. Thernstrom,* Whose Votes Count? Affirmative Action and Minority Voting Rights *(Cambridge, Mass.: Harvard University Press, 1987) pp. 242–43.*

affect politics [party patterns]," and those who think that party systems affect electoral systems.[8]

In political science—as in social science generally—we must wrestle with this problem of the "direction of causality." We observe that two or more things affect one another, but (in the technical language of science) we do not know which is the "independent" and which is the "dependent" variable. And this difficulty is nicely illustrated by the relationship between electoral laws and political party forms. As Douglas Rae puts it,

> party systems are influenced by many variables—social, economic, legal, and political. [The] electoral law . . . is to be counted only one of the many determining forces. And it is . . . impossible to sort out all the contributing factors, or to assign even approximate weights to them. Worse yet, electoral laws are themselves shaped by party systems.[9]

In other words, causality runs *both ways* in this case.

CAMPAIGNS

How do people become candidates for public office, and how do they go about attempting to prevail in electoral competition with other candidates? While the ways are many and various across the different kinds of political systems that incorporate free competitive elections, there are some aspects or dimensions of the processes that provide points of comparison.

Recruitment is the term employed by political scientists to focus attention on the kinds of people who are drawn into electoral politics in different systems and in different periods in the evolution of a particular system. What classes, ethnic and age groups, occupational groups, tribes, or regions tend to produce candidates? At one time in Great Britain the candidates of the Conservative party tended to come from solidly upper-class backgrounds, and those of the Labour party from working-class backgrounds, especially from the trade union movement. This sharp difference in recruitment patterns had a polarizing effect on the entire political system. Today, British recruitment patterns are more fluid. Margaret Thatcher, as often remarked, is the daughter of a grocer; her Conservative successor, John Major, is of equally humble origin. Tony (Anthony Wedgewood) Benn, one of the most radical Labour members of Parliament, refused an inherited peerage to continue to serve in the House of Commons. In America, one of the most important recent changes in recruiting patterns involves the increasing number of women successfully entering electoral politics, with an especially large number of U.S. Senate candidates in 1992—leading journalists to refer to it as "The Year of the Woman."

How *nominations* to electoral candidacy are bestowed is another useful point of comparison between systems. Turning to Britain again, nominations for seats in Parliament are controlled by the central offices of the political parties with the approval (usually) of a committee of the party faithful from the constituency (district) for which the candidate is being chosen. In the United States, we have in recent decades placed increasing reliance on primary elections to choose the nominees of the major political parties, Democratic and Republican. In the late nineteenth century and the earlier decades of this century, the political party organizations themselves (at the ward, municipal, county, and state levels) chose the candidates who would run under the party banner. While this selection was often formally accomplished by caucuses or conventions, the leaders of the party organizations—especially the city, county, and state organizations—exercised important, often decisive influence. These political "bosses" tended to reserve nominations for persons who had loyally served and worked their way up within the party organization—or, as it was called by its critics, the "machine." The primary election was the favored device of "progressive" reformers who sought to break the control of the bosses and the machines over nominations. They certainly succeeded, but the result has been the breakdown of party organizations generally. Among the first to note this with alarm was V. O. Key, Jr.,[10] who was concerned about the turbulence and lack of structure in American electoral politics as party organizations declined and nominees became independent political freebooters. Whether, in retrospect, there was more to be said for bosses and machines than early twentieth-century reformers thought is a question now being seriously considered by some political scientists.[11]

It is also important to consider the *ground rules* under which electoral campaigns are conducted. Both legal ground rules (involving matters such as the duration of the campaign) and ground rules derived from the political culture (such as the permissible styles of political rhetoric) are important.

In America—unlike, for instance, the democracies of Western Europe—there are no formal limits on the duration of electoral campaigns. The traditional date for the beginning of presidential election campaigns is Labor Day, with election day the first Tuesday in November. But—first in presidential campaigns, and then in Senate, House, and gubernatorial races—summer campaigning has become common. Increasingly, general election campaigns begin right after nomination, and primary election campaigns (seeking the nomination) many months in advance. It has been observed with only modest exaggeration that in America we are in a permanent political season—a state of perpetual campaigning.

Furthermore, many observers see the traditional limits on *political rhetoric* as slipping away, and campaigning becoming more negative and bitterly personal rather than being addressed to the great policy issues of the day. In fact, negative attacks on opponents have long been a part of the American campaign style; but with the rise of electronic media as the principal means of communication with the voters—and especially the rise of the brief television "spot"—the phenomenon of "negative ads" is obtrusive, and it worries us. It worries us, but the political consultants who orchestrate campaigns find such attacks effective. And there is no indication, especially after the bitter Bush–Clinton race of 1992, that negative campaigning is abating.[12]

Finally, this leads us to the matter of money—of *campaign finance*. Not only do we campaign a lot and often bitterly, we campaign very expensively in America. As Larry J. Sabato, a political scientist at the University of Virginia, puts it,

> Just about everyone agrees that there is a problem with the system of American campaign finance, but there is far from a consensus about what the problem actually is, much less what should be done about it. Some reformers say that the central difficulty is special interest financing of electoral campaigns, a development represented by the rapid and massive growth of political action committees (PACs) over the past two decades. . . .
>
> Some observers claim that the most vital issue of campaign finance goes beyond PACs to the skyrocketing costs of modern electioneering in general, a condition that forces candidates and office holders to spend too much time on fund-raising and deters many good people from running for public office.[13]

The costs of television time, and of the myriad pollsters and consultants who are adept in its effective use, have to be (along with longer campaigns) major factors in the cost spiral. Not only must the expensively purchased air time be used to maximum effect, but great amounts of time and talent are expended pursuing the attention of the "free media," as political consultants often refer to the news shows. (Some newspersons have responded primly by referring to themselves as the "earned media.") "Media events" are staged to have the cameras, speeches, press conferences, and announcements timed with reference to the evening news shows, and on-camera statements by the candidate most always lead off with some brief but forceful few phrases that can be turned into a 10- or 15-second "sound bite."

A frequently discussed response to the cost problem is providing more completely free television time. Again, many Western European systems do so routinely. But then the solution creates its own problem. In Europe, all or some of the television outlets are government owned, and it is far easier to lay down the law to them about what to show, and how much, and when. In America, taxpayer dollars would have to pay for the time, or an intricate requirement for free political time would have to be made a legal condition of a station's relicensing. Nor is it easy to design free media systems that are neutral between incumbents and challengers or between established major-party candidates, on the one hand, and independents and insurgent candidates, on the other. And finally, there is the question of limiting media access. It would make little sense to establish a generous system of publicly financed free media time for campaigning, and then have those candidates who are able and motivated buy still more. The whole point is to remove the pressure to raise big bucks for TV time. But in America there are First Amendment (freedom of speech) concerns triggered as soon as we even start to discuss limiting anyone's capacity to engage in political speech. We take a broader view of free speech than any other democracy. Such factors as these—deriving from political culture and constitution—are important to the style and ground rules for electoral campaigning.

BALLOT MEASURES

One type of election that is growing in popularity across the United States is the *referendum* or "ballot measure." In this type of election, everyone—regardless of party affiliation—can vote yes or no on a variety of issues such as shutting down nuclear plants, saving threatened and endangered species, cutting automobile insurance rates, calling for deposits on returnable containers, and so forth.

In many states—California and Oregon, among them—it is not unusual for there to be 20 different questions on the ballot in a given election cycle. In other states as well, the device is becoming more and more popular.

Why? One reason is that citizens seem to feel remote from Congress and their state legislatures. By collecting the signatures necessary to put a referendum on the ballot—most states require a percentage of the votes cast in the previous election—citizens can feel empowered and feel they have a bigger stake in the government.

Once on the ballot, these questions become subject to voter approval. Again, individual citizens or groups can go forward without the approval of either major political party. Most referenda are nonpartisan; and while the competing groups might like the endorsement of the Republicans or the Democrats, such is rarely needed.

What are the essential ingredients of a ballot measure campaign? Box 6-2 indicates what one consulting firm believes are the essential requirements for a successful effort in this arena. But as far as the process is concerned, here are some aspects to consider:

1. Ballot measures typically depend on citizen initiative to get on the ballot and to get the process moving; but often, interest groups jump in to try to influence the course of events. In a recent California situation, the insurance industry spent $75 million to defeat a referendum calling

---

Box 6-2. Ballot Measures

Consider the following standard advice given by one political consulting firm to prospective clients interested in supporting or defeating a ballot measure.

Requirements for Successful Ballot Measure Campaigns. *Ballot measure campaigns are unique. Parallels drawn from normal candidate electoral experiences are inappropriate and the requirements for successful ballot measure campaigns must be present for consistent success in this area.*
These include:

1. *Control over the wording of the ballot measure*
2. *Extensive research opportunities at the front end of the election cycle*
3. *Control over the spokespeople, especially the "leaders," for the referendum—those engaged in the free media and debate situations*
4. *Sufficient control and direction over the formation of the umbrella committee*
5. *Complete control over all aspects of the paid media, including the choice of authority figures and themes*
6. *Sufficient financial resources to give a responsible hope for success, irrespective of the opposition's activities*
7. *Sufficient time to develop the proper themes and to control all aspects listed above*
8. *Sufficient time and penetration opportunities to enable the position we take to establish itself first, in order to frame the debate*
9. *Assurances that the client be represented by experienced, aggressive, tenacious legal council*
10. *Control over the timing and content of all free media efforts.*

Source: *Command Research.*

---

for a 20-percent cut in auto insurance rates. (Incidentally, that effort lost.)

2. "Framing the question" becomes of vital importance. With candidates, voters make up their minds on a variety of issues and aspects. But in a ballot measure, it is critical that the debate be framed so that the voter goes into the booth already committed to one image or another. For example, in referenda dealing with nuclear power, those persons who favor nuclear power try to frame the debate in terms of "the costly alternatives" or "dependence on foreign oil," while those persons who oppose nuclear power try to focus on "health and safety concerns."

3. "Driving the ballot" is what a referendum is all about; both sides try to place the voter in a psychological situation where he or she will

gladly vote for one position because the other is made to appear far more unpalatable.

4. Referendum campaigns, then, are not League of Women Voters–type debates with an accent on fairness, rationality, or even common courtesy. Many referenda are decided on the principle of "fear drives out favor," in which both sides try to paint their opponent and the referendum outcome in the darkest possible terms.

5. While not all ballot-measure campaigns require television, television is the preferred media for those who can afford it, precisely because the 30-second (or even 10-second) spot message can impart such a powerful sense of need and obligation ("the future is now; we must act").

One thing is certain: in the 1990s, the American political system—and probably other political systems around the world—will see more ballot measures, not fewer. And strange as it may seem, some observers are beginning to question whether so much direct democracy is healthy for the American system, or even constitutional![14]

VOTING

What do we know about voters and the dynamics of voting? British political scientists refer to the subfield of "cephalogy" or the study of electoral results and behavior; but it is the American voter who has been most exhaustively studied, and our discussion will be restricted to this breed. Is the American voter the rational and attentive citizen we were all taught in school to regard as the ideal? Or is the voter a slothful creature activated only for single-issue crusades or taxpayer revolts?

Much of the discussion of the voter in our popular culture is a result of the idealistic picture mugged by mundane reality; this leads to a wild overreaction in which ordinary Americans are belabored as lazy boobs. Realism in considering voters is essential, but that is not the same thing as cynicism.

The locus classicus of the realistic depiction of the American voter is Walter Lippmann's *Public Opinion,* first published in 1922.

> The amount of attention available is far too small for any scheme in which it was assumed that all of the citizens of the nation would, after devoting themselves to the publications of the intelligence bureaus, become alert, informed, and eager on the multitude of real questions that never do fit very well into any broad principal.[15]

But this *does not* imply that Lippmann despaired of the *good sense* of the electorate—far from it. He noted that, while the average person had little attention span left for politics after the immediate business of holding job and family together, there was (as we discussed in Chapter 5) a rich structure of groups and individuals who are both attentive (those whom Gabriel Almond later came to call "attentive publics")[16] and relatively expert. The less attentive majority of us tend to identify with trusted elites. Far from seeing the general public as being an undifferentiated "mass public," Lippmann saw it as sorting itself out in a complicated but meaningful "structure of opinion" that registered itself in a general—but coherent and significant—way at election time.

Low "issue orientation" was also one of the major findings of the first really rigorous study of American electoral behavior: *The American Voter* by Angus Campbell, Philip Converse, Warren Miller, and Donald Stokes, published in 1960. This work was based on elaborate interview data (survey research).[17] Here the voting choice was envisioned as resulting from a "funnel of causality" in which various factors operated on the prospective voter, with the most important ones becoming dominant as election day approached. Among the factors usually predominating were found to be party identification (often inherited) and candidate orientation. Issue orientation paled by comparison. It is worth noting, however, that the research design of *The American Voter* set very high standards for responses to be classed as issue oriented or "ideological." And even so, the voters did not emerge as "Boobus Americanus." Party identification for Campbell and his coauthors—the most important structuring variable in American electoral behavior—was correlated with issue orientation, with the stronger party identifiers possessing higher levels of intellectual organization in their perception of issues. As with Lippmann, the picture emerged of a low-attention, noncerebral public that was yet able to register its preferences in broad and general terms at the polls.[18]

Nonetheless, V. O. Key, Jr., became concerned by the early 1960s that his colleagues were selling their fellow citizens short. Key set out in a short but trenchant book, The *Responsible Electorate,* to argue the thesis that "the voters are not fools."[19] Key administered a very important corrective to the conventional professional wisdom concerning issue orientation, while not doubting the essential outlines of the picture of the voting public as it emerged in the work of Campbell and his coauthors. Key, looking back over aggregate voting data for elections between 1940 and 1960, concentrated on the difference between those who switched from one party label to another and those who did not. Key found that certain general issue perceptions were associated with switching, and that this pattern of switching could be decisive of outcomes.

The reworking of the somewhat dismal picture painted by *The American Voter*—begun by Key, continued in the work of later scholars such as Norman Nie, Sidney Verba, and John Petrocik in 1976,[20] and especially Morris P. Fiorina in 1981.[21] Two points emerged: not only had party identification been somewhat overemphasized by the Campbell group; but as the 1960s gave way to the 1970s, the identification with party was, in real terms, declining in importance relative to other factors influencing voter choice.

By the time Professor Fiorina's *Retrospective Voting in American National Elections* appeared in 1981, he was inclined to conclude that the correction itself may have gone too far.

> Though the revisionist studies are in part convincing, the picture of the electorate that emerges from them is not so impressive that one can revive civics-book democratic theory. Just as an older generation of scholars apparently understated the attention and responsiveness of the electorate, the revisionists are prone to overstate it.[22]

Seeking a balanced realism, Fiorina argued that voters tend to know one very important thing every time an election rolls around: they know "what life has been like during the incumbent's administration."

> They need *not* know the precise economic or foreign policies of the incumbent administration in order to ascertain whether the incumbents have performed poorly or well. . . . Rather than a prospective decision [based on what candidates are saying they *will* do], the voting decision can be more a retrospective decision.[23]

Professor Fiorina sustains his analysis through data from the elections of 1960 through 1972 and concludes that the voter can be seen as a "reasonably rational fellow" so long as "rationality" is not defined as "the purest form of issue voting."

But what about nonvoting and "low turnout"? What sorts of people are nonvoters, and what should one make of the relatively low turnout that characterizes the American political system?

An excellent study of the nonvoter is Arthur T. Hadley's *The Empty Polling Booth*,[24] published in 1978. Hadley's conclusions have been generally borne out by later work, as well. His principal conclusion is that nonvoters are socially, economically, and demographically more *like* voters than *unlike* them.

Hadley finds that two of the most widely propagated notions about nonvoters are myths: first, that nonvoters are a poor, uneducated, dispossessed, and generally alienated lot; and second, that archaic and complicated registration and other legalistic requirements keep large numbers of people away from the polls.

> Far from being ignorant and belabored, the majority of those who today find themselves physically disenfranchised are kept away from voting because their success leads to mobility and thus causes them problems in meeting residency requirements. The stereotype is not merely wrong; it's backwards.
> Yet, the myth of the ignorant, poverty-stricken, physically disenfranchised

non-voter continues to be strongly held for powerful political and psychological reasons.[25]

Hadley calls nonvoters "refrainers" (an odd choice of term since, as his own data suggest, one common thread running through the very different kinds of people who do not vote is a degree of self-absorption that works against their going to the polls) and divides them in the following fashion.

The "positive apathetics" could not be more different from the "Boobus Americanus" of the stereotype; they are "by and large a group of young, educated, happy refrainers" who find their lives "too full of other satisfactions for voting to matter." These make up 35 percent of those not voting, and this conclusion fits nicely with the importance accorded to apathy by modern voting studies beginning with that of Bernard Berelson and his colleagues in 1954.[26]

The "bypassed" constitute 13 percent of the nonvoters. These most closely resemble the stereotype in the sense that they are somewhat more southern, somewhat less educated, and somewhat poorer than nonvoters generally. Interestingly, Hadley found that they were only slightly (4 percent) more black than nonvoters generally. These folks do feel impotent and unable to plan and control their lives for anything more than the very short term. They are, in every sense of the term, marginal people.

The "politically impotent" are in some ways similar to the bypassed, but they differ in a crucial respect: the impotents are solidly middle class. They are not conspicuously young or conspicuously black or conspicuously southern or conspicuously poor. What they are, according to Hadley, are conspicuously fatalistic. As he puts it, they share most of the characteristics of voters but also possess an extreme belief in the importance of luck. The politically impotent "have the knowledge, skills, and competence to handle their lives," and in "many ways they are doing it quite well." They "have the capacity to vote," but do not. Unlike the positive apathetic, they appear to take politics seriously, feel guilt about not voting, and therefore have a high emotional investment in invoking fatalism as the excuse for their nonperformance.

The "physically disenfranchised," who make up 18 percent of nonvoters, are again a group resembling the stereotype, but a small one. Here legal reasons, high mobility, and poor health keep away people who otherwise, apparently, do want to vote. In its other attributes, this group is most like voters, and it is likely that a change in polling arrangements could draw in a portion of this population; but Hadley stresses that registration difficulties are the least of the problems involved. The harder problems involve the actual physical difficulty experienced by the ill and handicapped in getting to the polls, getting an absentee ballot, or otherwise engaging in the electoral system.

The "nay sayers" make up a small group of nonvoters—only 6 per-

ent—but it is highly informed, highly attentive to politics, and intellec-
ually aggressive. Like famous British cynic Lady Astor, these folks
"never vote because it only encourages" the politicians. These are, on
he whole, economically successful people. Hadley's data show no single
eason for principled abstention; there are nay sayers both on the left and
n the right. What defines them is that their convictions about nonvoting
re intense.

Then there are the "cross-pressured" nonvoters—another small group.
These are only 5 percent of Hadley's refrainers; and once again, the
xistence of this segment in the electorate bears out a strand of research
hat goes back to Berelson and his colleagues. Here we have mixed
marriages and families with one member holding a political patronage
ob. Then, for some, it is really an intellectual matter. Things about both
andidates, or both parties, or both sides of the referendum question
xcite them and turn them off. Since cross-pressuring involves increasing
ain as the moment of decision approaches, the easiest way to reduce the
ain is to remove the necessity for decision.

Beyond these six categories there are, in Hadley's data, a fascinating
1 percent of the people who *do* vote who strongly manifest the charac-
eristics of nonvoters. Hadley calls this group of voters the "vergers,"
nd pointedly asks what we can expect to happen to the turnout figures if
his marginal cohort of voters slips to nonvoting. They are, Hadley notes,
"as unlikely to discuss politics as refrainers," and they are just as self-
entered and a little poorer, economically, than refrainers generally.
Thus, not only do nonvoters tend to resemble voters, but a significant
hunk of voters display the characteristics of nonvoters. Looked at in
his way, the recent decline in electoral participation in America—absent
ome dramatic crisis—seems likely to continue.

The bottom line is, we know quite a lot about the nonvoter—and the
icture that emerges is not very attractive. While there are among the
bypassed" (and perhaps the "politically impotent") certainly some
esemblances to the stereotype of the alienated/excluded individual, the
enerality of nonvoters does not bear out the stereotype.

Who benefits from the perpetuation in the popular culture of the myth
f the excluded and the alienated? The desire to believe in a "silent
majority" that is out there just waiting for a candidate with a program
lear enough to rally them is persistent on both the left and the right of
merican politics. And perhaps this in itself is a partial explanation. Or
erhaps what is at work is a simple phenomenon of mirror imaging—in
which persons who feel a duty to vote, and want to vote, and do vote,
ssume that all other reasonably intelligent people must feel the same
ay. Therefore, if these others do not vote, malevolent forces must be at
ork. The 1993 election saw a modest upturn in voting (at least at the
residential level), but it remains to be seen whether this is the beginning
f a trend.

SUMMARY

Noting that elections and voting are becoming more important in mor places around the world we turned first to a consideration of the ways i which elections are organized, and to the complicated relationship between the structure of elections and political party systems. Next w examined the ways in which people come to be elected to office, wit attention focused on recruitment, nominations, campaign practices, an campaign finance. We then paused to consider the phenomenon of ballc measures and referenda—a sector of American electoral politics that i growing in importance. Finally we briefly touched on the highlights of th large literature on voting behavior in America, and concluded with consideration of the nonvoter and the significance of low turnout.

NOTES

1. Douglas W. Rae, *The Political Consequences of Electoral Laws,* 2nd ee (New Haven, Conn.: Yale University Press, 1971).

2. See Arend Lijphart, "The Political Consequences of Electoral Laws, 1945 85," *American Political Science Review* (June 1990): 491–92.

3. *New York Times,* August 9, 1990.

4. *Reynolds v. Sims,* 377 U.S. 533 (1964).

5. See Rein Taagepera and Matthew Soberg Shugart, *Seats and Votes: Th Effects and Determinants of Electoral Systems* (New Haven, Conn.: Yale Unive: sity Press, 1989), pp. 14–18.

6. Maurice Duverger, *Political Parties: Their Organization and Activity in th Modern State* (New York: Wiley, 1954).

7. Taagepera and Shugart, *Seats and Votes,* p. 50.

8. Ibid., p. 53.

9. Rae, *Political Consequences,* p. 141.

10. V. O. Key, Jr., *American State Politics* (New York: Knopf, 1956).

11. See John M. Allswang, *Bosses, Machines, and Urban Voters,* rev. ee (Baltimore: Johns Hopkins University Press, 1986).

12. *New York Times,* September 9, 1992.

13. Larry J. Sabato, *Paying for Elections: The Campaign Finance Thick* (New York: Priority Press, 1989), p. 1.

14. Julian N. Eule, "Judicial Review of Direct Democracy," *Yale Law Journ* (May 1990): 1503–90.

15. Walter Lippmann, *Public Opinion* (New York: Free Press edition, 1965).

16. Gabriel Almond, *The American People and Foreign Policy* (New Yor Harcourt, Brace, 1950).

17. Angus Campbell, Philip E. Converse, Warren E. Miller, and Donald I Stokes, *The American Voter* (New York: Wiley, 1960).

18. Ibid., pp. 188–215.

19. V. O. Key, Jr., *The Responsible Electorate* (Cambridge, Mass.: Harvard University Press, 1966).

20. Norman H. Nie, Sidney Verba, John R. Petrocik, *The Changing American Voter* (Cambridge, Mass.: Harvard University Press, 1976). See also Michael Margolis, "From Confusion to Confusion: Issues and the American Voter (1956–1972)," *American Political Science Review* 31 (1977); and Gerald Pomper, *Voters' Choice* (New York: Dodd, Mead, 1975).

21. Morris P. Fiorina, *Retrospective Voting in American National Elections* (New Haven, Conn.: Yale University Press, 1981).

22. Ibid., p. 5.

23. Ibid., p. 6.

24. Arthur T. Hadley, *The Empty Polling Booth* (Englewood Cliffs, N.J.: Prentice-Hall, 1978).

25. Ibid., p. 28.

26. Bernard R. Berelson, Paul F. Lazarsfeld, and William N. McPhee, *Voting* (Chicago: University of Chicago Press, 1954).

SUGGESTED READINGS

Crew, I., and D. Denver, eds. *Electoral Change in Western Democracies: Patterns and Sources of Electoral Volatility*. New York: St. Martin's Press, 1985. Chapters on the recent electoral histories of 13 modern democracies make this an exceedingly useful book for comparative purposes.

Ginsberg, B., and A. Stone, eds. *Do Elections Matter?* Armonk, N.Y.: M. E. Sharpe, 1986. An interesting collection of essays, dealing mostly with America, that reflect on the various and sometimes surprising ways elections impact on other aspects of the political system.

Grofman, B., and A. Lijphart, eds. *Electoral Laws and Their Political Consequences*. New York: Agathon Press, 1986. A valuable collection, updating and correcting Rae's work.

Rokkan, Stein, with Angus Campbell, Pes Torsvik, and Henry Valen. *Citizens, Elections, Parties: Approaches to the Comparative Study of the Processes of Political Development*. New York: David McKay, 1970. Fourteen studies of the dynamics of the extension of citizenship and the electoral franchise to previously nonparticipating "masses."

Sabato, L. J. *The Rise of Political Consultants*. New York: Basic Books, 1981. The first major analytical work calling attention to the existence of this new force in American electoral politics—a force that is fast being internationalized.

Sorauf, F. J. *Money in American Elections*. Boston: Scott Foresman/Little Brown, 1988. A very useful survey. A good starting point for a term paper.

Part III
Structures of Government

7

The Age of the Executive?

No man is fit to govern great societies who hesitates about disobliging
the few who have access to him for the sake of the many he will never
see.

—THOMAS BABBINGTON MACAULAY

Put not your trust in princes.

—LORD STAFFORD, FAITHFUL MINISTER OF CHARLES
I (ON HEARING THAT THE KING HAD JUST ACCEDED
TO HIS DEATH SENTENCE)

Energy in the Executive is a leading character in the definition of
good government.

—ALEXANDER HAMILTON IN *Federalist* No. 70

LEADERSHIP IN A WORLD OF CHANGE AND CONFLICT

In a world seething with change and violent conflict, and at a time
when one century draws to an end while a new era dawns, where are the
heroic leaders? Who are the political leaders of the great nations? What
characterizes their leadership? What are the principal sources of executive leadership in contemporary society? Do you see a leader whom you
are prepared to follow with enthusiasm, a leader who offers a striking
vision of the future? Is the world perhaps changing in fundamental ways—
and so quickly that neither leaders nor ordinary citizens are able to keep
pace in trying to shape a common destiny?

An essential question has intrigued political thinkers and ordinary folk
since the beginning of recorded history. The same question persists
today. To what extent do great leaders shape the future? Are they capable
of directing the course of change? Or are they (and we) helpless objects
tossed about on the tide of events? Will conflicts grow so intense that
leadership is overwhelmed by them?

These timeless questions take on a special meaning in "the age of the
executive," a phrase that has frequently been used to describe the
twentieth century. The tumultuous events of this century have been
accompanied by the emergence of powerful political leaders—*executives*.

143

In the United States, Franklin D. Roosevelt provided a highly personalized brand of leadership as our nation struggled through the Great Depression of the 1930s and then played a decisive role in World War II. Winston Churchill almost single-handedly inspired the British people in their stubborn resistance to the Nazi war machine. Adolf Hitler, an evil mad genius, rearmed the mighty German nation and then led it to the brink of ruin, while also directing the systematic slaughter of 6 million European Jews and countless other victims. V. I. Lenin brought about a Marxist revolution in backward, nonindustrialized, and peasant Russia. Joseph Stalin grimly and ruthlessly led the Russian masses to industrialization within a totalitarian garrison state.

Asia too has produced its share of impressive executive leaders in this century: Mahatma Gandhi in India and Sun Yat-sen and Mao Tse-tung in China are leading examples.

This brief listing suggests that strong twentieth-century executive leaders in the past have not always been attractive or "good." Nor have the results of their leadership always been benign. No necessary relationship exists between the powerful executive and a commitment to "democracy" or to the general welfare of the people. The powerful executive may become the feared tyrant, as Stalin and Hitler did. As the twenty-first century dawns, exploding technology, huge permanent bureaucracies, rapid growth in the world's population, and vast disparities in living conditions for the world's masses make the challenge of leadership extraordinarily complex.

Each of the twentieth-century political leaders we have mentioned could claim not merely to have reacted to events but also, by dint of intelligence and will—political skill—to have redirected the course of history. Earlier in this century the American philosopher Sidney Hook, discussing the role of the heroic leader in history, drew the following distinction between the "eventful" leader and the "event-making" leader:

> The eventful man in history is any man whose actions influenced subsequent developments along a quite different course than would have been followed if these actions had not been taken.
>
> The event-making man is an eventful man whose actions are the consequences of outstanding capacities of intelligence, will, and character rather than accidents of position.[1]

The twentieth century created conditions that brought forth a number of political executive leaders who were "event makers" and who redirected the course of history.

TRANSACTIONAL AND TRANSFORMATIONAL LEADERSHIPS

In his 1978 study called *Leadership,* James MacGregor Burns—biographer of Franklin D. Roosevelt and John F. Kennedy and author of several important studies of American politics—draws a sharp distinction between "transactional" and "transformational" leadership.[2] *Transactional leadership* refers to the kind of leadership that is often associated with the real world of messy politics in which chief executives bargain with other powerful powerbrokers, constantly engaging in a process of give-and-take, bullying, persuading, and horse trading in an effort to gain support for programs they favor. *Transformational leadership,* as Burns defines it, seems closer to the event-making brand of leadership Hook described many years ago. Burns however, views the transformational leader as the heroic executive who uses great ideas to move people and, in doing so, brings about profound transformations in the society and possibly in the world as well. Moreover, the transformational leader succeeds in lifting people out of their everyday lives so that they are morally enlarged. It is doubtful that Lenin, Stalin, and Hitler uplifted many souls, but they were event makers who nonetheless changed their nations and the world, for better or for worse.

The 1970s seemed a poor decade for executive leadership around the world, and some observers wondered whether transformational (or even strong transactional) leadership was possible under modern conditions. The decade of the 1980s—with the impact of Ronald Reagan on the American political agenda, the desocializing of Great Britain under Margaret Thatcher, and the struggle for change that took place in the Soviet Union under Mikhail Gorbachev, now taking place in Russia under Boris Yeltsin—has revived optimism in the matter of leadership.

But to understand why strong leaders emerge, it is useful to go back a bit.

CONDITIONS CONDUCIVE TO EXECUTIVE LEADERSHIP

The rise of strong, powerful executives earlier in this century did not occur in a social vacuum. Underlying changes in the economy and technological changes help explain the development of conditions that encouraged the growth of executive leadership as well as the relative decline in the power of legislative bodies.

The United States is a case in point. American national politics during the last quarter of the nineteenth century featured congressional politics. Presidents were seldom large or dramatic figures. In 1885 Woodrow Wilson, then a young scholar, wrote a book called *Congressional Government.* The world of Washington policymaking, as Wilson saw it, was a world dominated by Congress and especially by key figures inside Congress. He observed, "I know not how better to describe our form of government in a single phrase than by calling it a government by the chairmen of the standing committees of Congress."[3]

But with the turn of the century, the scene shifted almost overnight. The assassination of President William McKinley in 1901 brought young Theodore Roosevelt to the White House. Roosevelt was not only the youngest president in our history, but he may also have been the most energetic. As Henry Adams, who knew him well, observed,

> Power when wielded by abnormal energy is the most serious of facts, and all Roosevelt's friends know that his restless and combative energy was more than normal. Roosevelt, more than any other man living within the range of notoriety, showed the singular primitive quality that belongs to ultimate matter—the quality that medieval theology assigned to God—he was pure act.[4]

Furthermore, Theodore Roosevelt's "restless and combative energy" was soon addressed to the expansion of American power in world politics. He was an ardent and avowed expansionist, a leading architect of U.S. sea power who used the "bully pulpit" (as he called it) of the presidency to preach his doctrines to an adoring public.

Our first strong executive leader of the twentieth century spoke for a new political generation. This generation looked uncritically to the White House for leadership and direction. Alfred Kazin, noting the importance of this connection between leader and public, assessed Theodore Roosevelt's leadership as follows:

> He was blindly ambitious, he did not always have a proper respect for the truth, and he worshipped pure energy. Yet because he believed with fierce and emotional patriotism . . . that the history of America was the central event in the history of the world, he made a whole generation believe it.[5]

Roosevelt's experience in the White House also led Woodrow Wilson to revise his earlier views of American government. Watching Roosevelt in action, Wilson was one of the first Americans to appreciate the growing importance of presidential leadership. Shortly thereafter, Wilson left the presidency of Princeton University and was elected governor of New Jersey. Elected president of the United States in 1912, Wilson—like Theodore Roosevelt—proved to be a strong executive. He was also the first president to understand how greatly industrialization was changing American society.

The Industrial Revolution and the Centralization of Power

The expansion of executive leadership is directly related to the growth of industry and the increasing need for government to regulate the centralization of economic power. Once again, the American experience illustrates the trend. Power in world politics in this century is the direct consequence of a nation's gaining industrial and economic strength. During the age of congressional government, the United States was still considered a second-rate power. The great powers of Europe seldom assigned one of their top diplomats to Washington, D.C., in the 1880s. This situation was to change, however, with astonishing abruptness. The underlying reason was the incredibly rapid expansion of American industrial power. Between 1880 and 1910, the United States underwent "the most rapid economic expansion of any industrialized country for a comparable period of time."[6] Just at the turn of the twentieth century, the United States managed to outpace the rest of the world, including the great powers of Europe, in the production of iron and steel. The United States was soon recognized as a great power because of its industrial might.[7]

In turn, industrial power was soon translated into military power. The policy of expansion so favored by Theodore Roosevelt gave this country a Pacific empire following the annexation of Hawaii and the conquest of the Philippines after the Spanish–American War. The United States already had Alaska, thanks to a purchase from czarist Russia arranged by Secretary William H. Seward in 1867 for a bargain price: $7.2 million. Indeed, an American commodore had opened medieval Japan to the Western world and had initiated the process of modernization during the administration of Franklin Pierce, *before* the Civil War.

The United States needed a powerful navy if it was to claim the Pacific Ocean as a kind of American lake, and the buildup of the navy was begun during the 1880s. We also needed a professional army if we were to control native resistance in the Philippines following the Spanish–American War. Elihu Root, a close advisor to Presidents McKinley and Theodore Roosevelt during this period, was principally responsible for creating an army staff and the Army War College. Not to be outdone, the navy was already on its way to becoming the first important U.S. military bureaucracy.

When the general war broke out in Europe in 1914, it seemed only a matter of time until the new American industrial giant would be drawn into this terrible conflict. And so it was, under the leadership of President Wilson, a man who had previously declared himself and the nation "too proud to fight." The essential fact was that U.S. military and industrial power proved to be the decisive factor in determining the outcome of World War I. The United States was a world power with heavy responsibilities (although the nation often did not accept these responsibilities during the 1920s and the 1930s).[8] The United States had become a major force in determining the future course of international conflict.

Once again in World War II—a truly global conflict—it was American industrial–military power that finally tipped the scales against Nazi Germany and Japan.

Modern War

Thus we note still another vital connection between the age of the executive and important changes taking place inside the society (or system). Executive leadership in this century has often been spurred by the conditions of modern warfare. Twice in this century, great industrialized nations have fully mobilized their human and national resources in wars aimed at destroying the enemy's total economy (and this *before* the development of nuclear weapons and intercontinental missiles). Such mobilization requires the merging of great public and private bureaucratic organizations.

Since the development of nuclear weapons and modern missiles, the specter of global and total wars has involved the possible annihilation of human civilization as an additional risk. This risk has served to further the centralization of authority; few could wish to entrust this issue to a large number of diverse decision makers. At the same time, the technological complexity of the new weapons systems makes it even more crucial for decision makers to have access to expert technical advice.

Bureaucratization of the Executive

Executive leadership in a highly industrialized society is also increasingly bureaucratized. A permanent large navy soon spawns a permanent large naval bureaucracy. A large standing army and a sophisticated modern air force also contain permanent bureaucratic structures. Each of these military bureaucracies, like all bureaucracies, is intent on promoting and protecting its own organizational purpose and integrity.[9] The navy is intent on controlling the seas. The army wants to be prepared to fight effective land battles around the globe. The air force views the skies much as the navy views the ocean. Both the air force and the navy have developed elaborate and expensive nuclear missile systems.

The Welfare State

The chief executive of a great industrialized nation in this century thus faces a series of competing and contesting executive bureaucracies. Of course, they are not all military bureaucracies. Today, thanks to the steady growth of the human-welfare state, vast bureaucracies on the domestic side of government may very well be larger, more numerous, and more expensive in their program activity than those involved in national security. This is the case in the United States and the United Kingdom.

These matters are addressed in Chapter 9. Here we wish to emphasize that the age of the executive has been transformed into the age of the bureaucratized executive. The more unwieldy the mechanisms of government grow, the less likely our leaders are to emerge as "heroic."

The Mass Media

When our founding fathers were busy drawing up the Constitution of the United States in 1787, they were embarking on a bold experiment, something the world had never seen before: a "large" republic. The population of the 13 colonies at that time was about 4 million, of whom some 700,000 were slaves. By the time Franklin D. Roosevelt entered the White House, there were 120 million Americans; there were more than 250 million in 1990. Thus, some 130 million Americans have been added to the nation's total population within the lifetime of citizens still alive.

The implications of this population growth for political leadership are enormous. Twentieth-century political executives must find ways of communicating with, and possibly inspiring, millions of people. It is not surprising that political leaders have increasingly come to rely on the mass media—especially radio and television—as means of reaching masses of people instantaneously. Unfortunately, mass-media communications are a one-way street. Millions listen when the leader speaks, but they have no direct means of talking back. In this sense, there is no real communication between the contemporary political executive and the ordinary citizen unless other means are devised. In the meantime, more and more citizens in the United States depend on TV news as the major source of their information on politics and government.

In a society that professes to being "democratic," the emergence of the mass society—industrialized, centralized, and bureaucratized—poses serious problems in remaining "democratic." A. D. Lindsay, a respected English student of democracy, put it this way: "The real issue between the democrats and the anti-democrats is that democrats think of a society where men can do and act as responsible persons. The anti-democrats talk of the mob, or the herd, or the crowd."[10]

The problem, as Lindsay well understood, is that twentieth-century mass society—with its slick instruments of mass persuasion—makes it all too easy to treat millions of people as though they were a crowd, rather than a community of human beings. At the same time, the growth of huge centralized bureaucracies poses a threat to effective political leadership. Little wonder, then, that leaders appear essentially unresponsive to the needs and feelings of the ordinary individual. As Lindsay notes, "The isolated individual is always powerless against great organizations."[11] Bear in mind that the mass media are also large organizations of power and influence. We shall return to examine the role of the mass media in national politics more closely later in this chapter. The authentic democratic leader must somehow find ways of encouraging mutual understanding of commonly shared objectives so that ordinary citizens do not feel left out. And this is no easy feat in a mass society. How often do *you* feel that our leaders are being responsive to your interests and needs?

CONSTRAINTS ON EXECUTIVE LEADERSHIP

History is full of ironies. One of them is that this century of the executive has placed heavy constraints on political leadership, especially in the industrialized Western world. Whether similar constraints will be felt as the newer nations of the Third World advance technologically remains to be seen. Be this as it may, four major constraints deserve our attention.

Bodies of Opinion

First of all, there are the *constraints or limitations imposed by bodies of opinion*. A contemporary political leader is seldom free to act without the support of influential groups within the society. And the opinions of these influential groups may very well conflict. A British prime minister today normally expects sharp differences of viewpoint between the trade unions and British industry. Whatever economic course this British leader and his or her advisors chart, they are limited by opposition to that course from powerful groups that it affects adversely.

There is no reason to assume that political leadership in a garrison state such as the former USSR was entirely free to act as it chose. There were important differences of opinion between the Soviet military establishment and the scientific community, for example. Limited resources channeled into the development of military strength were not available for the millions of eager Soviet consumers, who were increasingly aware of the higher standard of living enjoyed by many of their contemporaries in other countries.[12]

In the democratic nations of the West, where a free press and the freedoms of assembly and speech are guaranteed, the opinions of ordinary citizens are sufficiently important that political leadership invests a great deal of energy in trying to shape favorable bodies of opinion at the level of mass society.

As one moves up the social and economic ladder to upper-middle-class and elite levels, the presence of an educated and attentive public serves as an influential constraint on executive leadership.

Parties and Elections: Popular Controls

Since the early nineteenth century, Western constitutional regimes have placed a special emphasis on *competition between political parties* in free elections as a means of bringing forth alternative leaders and controlling their behavior in office. In this kind of political system, even the most dynamic executive leader must face the ultimate control of the electorate. Franklin D. Roosevelt, who shattered all American precedents by triumphing in four consecutive presidential elections, nonetheless faced able opponents each time he ran. He won solidly three times and swept to a landslide victory once (in 1936); but even at the peak of his power, he realized that millions of Americans were opposed to his administration. They happily voted against him and his policies! This psychological constraint on leadership can be very real.

Of course, most presidents do not win in landslide elections (though Lyndon Johnson did in 1964 and Richard Nixon did in 1972). Some manage to eke out rather narrow margins of victory, as John Kennedy did in 1960 and Jimmy Carter did in 1976. Others win comfortably but by less than landslide proportions as with Ronald Reagan in 1980 and 1984, and George Bush in 1988. Kennedy, who was keenly aware of the slimness of his margin, liked to quote Thomas Jefferson: "Great innovations should not be forced on slender majorities."[13] Executive leaders who face the voters periodically at the polls may understandably be reluctant to force "great innovations." This is especially true when millions of citizens appear indifferent or antagonistic toward politicians and "politics as usual." Elections—as a means of sampling the opinions of millions of citizens—often provide a basis for executive leadership, but they also serve to constrain that same leadership.

Independent National Legislatures

There is not a more effective constraint on executive activity than an *independent national legislature that is doing its job.* Many observers believe that the complexity of the issues, together with the centralizing tendencies of industrial society, has simply overwhelmed legislative bodies, which have fallen easy prey to extraordinary assertions of executive power. There is some truth to this. However, we believe that it is also true that great national legislative bodies have sometimes been all too prone to succumb to executive authority. They have sometimes seemed incapable of asserting an institutional will to resist executive encroachment.[14]

In the case of Congress, it is difficult to argue that our national legislative body—in existence since the founding of the Republic—need be an embarrassed phantom in policymaking. The Constitution arms Congress with ample powers over war making, taxation, regulation of commerce, and public spending, to name only the most obvious "positive powers." Congress also has the power to override a presidential veto, to investigate virtually any aspect of executive performance, and to impeach. These are hardly sources of inherent weakness.

Box 7-1. Taming the Prince

One of the most interesting recent books on executive power comes from a political scientist who is not, primarily, a student of presidents and prime ministers, but of political philosophy. In late 1989 Harvey C. Mansfield, Jr., of the Harvard University department of government, published Taming the Prince: The Ambivalence of Modern Executive Power, *arguing that the American president is a constitutionally and democratically domesticated version of Niccolò Machiavelli's prince (see Chapter 2)—the first and classic rendition (the prototype, in fact) of the modern, secular, political executive. In this analysis, the legislative and judicial branches of government appropriately act and speak in general terms—by stating rules and appealing to principle. The executive is the seat of discretion in government; it can act with particularity, with "secrecy and dispatch," and without necessity for specific legal rationalizing of every step and initiative. For this reason, laws and constitutions can never wholly or perhaps even adequately confine and control executive behavior. There is no legalistic substitute for virtuous executives. Executives naturally come to predominate over legislatures, but it is also this centrality of the executive in modern governments that makes responsibility and accountability possible.*

That the separation of functions [between legislation and execution] has not worked does not mean that the separation of powers should be abandoned or that the American way of confusing the functions should be exchanged for the British one. But Locke's intended division of responsibility between generalizing by law and using discretion has been overcome and—not surprising to anyone schooled by Machiavelli—to the advantage of the power closer to the deed. As a sign of this universal tendency, one may remark that it is quite possible to use the term "leadership" without seeming to favor monarchy. In executive leadership, bygone partisans of monarchy do not quite have all they ever wanted, but they have enough to satisfy them that modern republicans have unwittingly admitted much truth in the monarchist cause.[1]

Note:
    1. Harvey C. Mansfield, Jr., Taming the Prince: The Ambivalence of Modern Executive Power *(New York: Free Press, 1989) pp. 293–94.*

How an "imperial presidency" managed to develop in the face of these great powers would require a more complete analysis than this brief chapter affords. But the point is not difficult to see: powerful executives arose in this country typically with the support of the public and Congress! Theodore Roosevelt captivated a political generation of enthusiastic followers. Woodrow Wilson—elected originally as a minority president in 1912 due to a deep division within the Republican majority—managed to establish his own strong popular base by showing himself to be the master of Congress in the domestic arena. FDR's first 100 days have seldom, if ever, been equaled in the degree of congressional and popular support afforded executive leadership in meeting a domestic crisis of major proportions.

Nevertheless, even the strongest twentieth-century presidents have eventually felt the restraining hand of Congress—a fact often slighted or ignored in recent writings about presidential leadership. Theodore Roosevelt engaged in a running battle with the leaders of his own party in Congress. Woodrow Wilson's dream of leading the United States into the League of Nations was shattered in the Senate. Congress humbled FDR when he attempted to "pack" the Supreme Court, and Congress stopped his New Deal reform program in its tracks after 1938. His foreign policy initiatives were severly limited by a series of neutrality laws that Congress passed between 1935 and 1939. And look what happened to Presidents Johnson and Nixon when they overreached: Johnson chose not to run for another term, and Nixon resigned in disgrace rather than face an impeachment trial in the Senate. And Ronald Reagan, despite his popularity and early successes with Congress, ended his second term with greatly diminished power and "standing" as a result of the Iran–Contra Affair.

Independent Judiciaries

Another kind of limitation on executive power involves the courts. In the United States, the *capacity of courts to check the executive* is particularly dramatic and extensive. At the national level, the judiciary is a separate and coequal branch of government (along with the executive and legislative branches), and the Supreme Court exercises judicial reviews: it can nullify actions of the other branches that it finds contrary to its interpretation of the Constitution. The 50 state supreme courts exercise similar power over governors and legislatures with respect to their state constitutions.

In no other political system in the world do courts have quite so much formal power to check executive initiatives, but this does not mean that courts elsewhere are insignificant as countervailing institutions. The courts of India, for example, administered a severe (but not then fatal) check to the late Premier Indira Gandhi by finding her guilty of election fraud in 1974. This did not involve a judicial or a constitutional veto; it was an ordinary administration of the criminal law.

Courts need not possess the power of American-style judicial review to be governmentally significant. What they must possess is enough independence from the executive to administer existing law fairly, without politically motivated interventions forcing them to go easy on certain defendants and to bear down on others. If politically important people can be brought to trial for corruption, and if judges can resist pressure to punish dissidents in the absence of any evidence of crime, then courts can check executives.

If the American experience is any indication, the age of the executive also yields examples of presidential leadership that manages from time to time to rise above the ordinary limits on executive power—at least long enough to alter the direction of public policy. We turn now to a case study of the presidency of Ronald Reagan as a means of examining more closely the complex and frustrating role of executive leadership in an age of political stalemate.

RONALD REAGAN—CASE STUDY IN EXECUTIVE LEADERSHIP

President Ronald Reagan celebrated his seventy-fourth birthday a few weeks after his second inaugural. The oldest president in American history, whose life spanned most of the twentieth century, also proved to be one of the most difficult to pigeonhole. An ideological conservative and an ardent anticommunist, President Reagan presided over a government that enormously expanded federal budget deficits, offered nuclear technology to the world's largest communist regime, the People's Republic of China, and facilitated the end of the Cold War.

A radio/television performer and movie actor who spent 30 years working in Hollywood dream factories and living surrounded by super-affluence, Reagan, then in his mid-fifties, turned to electoral politics shortly after Senator Barry Goldwater, an authentic conservative, suffered overwhelming defeat at the hands of Lyndon B. Johnson in November 1964. Two years later, Reagan trounced Pat Brown, the incumbent Democratic governor of California, who had served eight years. Governor Reagan was easily elected to a second term as governor of the nation's largest state in 1970. By this time, he had emerged as the special favorite of conservative Republicans whose cause he had made his own. It was Reagan's good fortune to finally gain his party's nomination in 1980 just as the Carter presidency was unraveling at the seams. Ronald Reagan offered an alternative, a change of course.

President Reagan in the White House exhibited many of the same traits he had earlier revealed while serving as governor. An amiable and genial personality who knew how to use radio and television to advance his cause, Reagan also demonstrated a remarkable capacity for evading public rebuke for official mistakes and failures, including the loss of some 300 American marines in Lebanon in 1983–84. He combined these gifts with a firm determination to stick by his own simple views and traditional values (nation, family, self-reliance, and supply-side economics) in the face of ambiguous and complex realities. As president, Reagan also displayed a capacity for making pragmatic adjustments on matters of substance while continuing to profess articles of conservative dogma.

Reagan's administrative style (as became clear in the wake of the Iran–Contra Affair) was similar to that of a chairman of the board. That is, he delegated very large operating responsibilities to a few trusted staff members, thus freeing himself to concentrate on "the big picture." This style contrasted sharply with the Carter presidency, in which the man in the Oval Office took unto himself virtually every difficult problem he could lay his hands on. Carter often seemed determined to master personally the technical details of each and every complicated issue. Reagan, on the other hand, was notorious for being casual about matters of complicated substance. As in his college days, he relied on a "quick study" the night before the big exam.

Once in office, President Reagan moved swiftly and surely, displaying a fine instinct for transactional leadership as he pushed his own primary program objectives to center stage. The permanent Washington power brokers on Capitol Hill—in the executive bureaucracies and the permanent special-interest lobbies—were visibly impressed. Reagan most assuredly was not another Jimmy Carter. Early in his first term, Reagan managed to gain acceptance of the essentials he sought: a massive tax reduction, a sharp increase in defense spending, and a slowing of the growth in spending on domestic programs. In essence, this was more a political than an economic strategy; the basic aim was to reorder the nation's basic public-policy priorities—a supremely difficult task in an era of political stalemate.

By the end of his first term, after weathering a severe recession, Reagan saw the American economy pass into its longest period of sustained postwar growth. Whether this growth was altogether healthy and balanced is a matter of sharp debate, and whether Reagan left the economic landscape well prepared or ill prepared for his successor, George Bush, is also debatable.[15] What is not debatable is that the Reagan presidency made a difference. Whether one wishes to speak of a "Reagan revolution" or not, the face of American politics was changed dramatically, purposefully, and by the chief executive.

How much of this was due to the fact that Reagan was "The Great Communicator"? Was his use of the media, in fact, all that good? And most importantly, what have the past couple of decades of American politics taught us about the importance of the media?

REEXAMINING PRESIDENTIAL LEADERSHIP: THE PRIME-TIME PRESIDENCY

The changing nature of the political and social influence wielded by the mass media requires that we carefully reexamine the politics of presidential leadership. A free press has been seen as being of fundamental importance in the American version of "democracy" since the days of

Thomas Jefferson. We have long recognized the vital role the press plays in informing citizens and in providing a forum for leadership to present its views and for political opponents to offer alternatives. Television has the unique capacity of putting the picture and the sound of live events (and pseudo-events) into the American living room. In doing so, television has subtly transformed the nature of political news and altered the relationship between leadership and the public. By the middle of the 1960s, this new instrument had transformed the techniques of political campaigns and elections, bringing into being a new form of presidential politics. Since then, television has emerged as the primary source of news—including political news—for the majority of the public, including that portion of the public (audience) which is largely "inadvertent," that is, those millions among us who watch the evening newscast absentmindedly while waiting for a "sitcom" or a game show. Television—in bringing politics, Washington, and a view of the world into our living rooms so vividly—may also assault the ordinary passivity of a mass (inadvertent) audience, thus increasing the "volatility" of the public response.

Given this aspect of changing reality, the practical capacity of a president—any president—to lead the nation depends on his or her and his or her media managers' ability to *exploit* the all-seeing eye of the TV cameras. This becomes an exceedingly tricky business—and not simply for technical reasons. The rise of television news has altered the relationship among president, the permanent community of Washington power brokers (including, ironically, the press corps), and the public.

The importance of this change for presidential leadership may be illustrated best by turning to Professor Richard Neustadt's influential theory.[16] Reduced to essentials, Neustadt's original (1960) interpretation of the politics of presidential leadership emphasized the president's *bargaining* relationship with other key actors: wily congressional oligarchs, entrenched bureaucratic chieftains, influence-peddling lawyer-lobbyists, the skeptical press and inflated media pundits—all members of the permanent community of Washington, all "good ole boys" and power brokers. The presidency, as Neustadt saw it in 1960, was an office made to order for the transactional leader, assuming he was clever enough to handle the job. Neustadt presumably wrote (as did Machiavelli) from his own recent experience as a young staff member in Harry S. Truman's budget office and as a sometime member of the White House staff, and he also reflected on Dwight D. Eisenhower's experience in the Oval Office. Neustadt's theory held that the other key actors in Washington policymaking were engaged in the continuous business of "president watching," assessing the chief executive's every move, looking for signs of strength or weakness. At the same time, the president as political-policy leader was (or should have been) busily engaged in trying to persuade, bully, or cajole these power barons into moving in the direction *he* wished to go. The role model for this kind of presidential leadership was clearly FDR—Neustadt's favorite "heroic" president.

A president so engaged is well advised to be careful in guarding his own potential for influence; if this potential is seriously weakened for whatever reason, he is in mortal peril as policy leader. Furthermore, the president alone is fully aware of what *his* power stakes are. He alone is principally interested in protecting them, so Neustadt's original argument runs.

A president who is to be at all effective as a transactional leader within the permanent Washington community depends mightily on his "professional reputation" within the same community. Furthermore, this reputation and the way he is "read" by Washington's power brokers depends on their assessment of his standing with "the public." When this standing weakens or is perceived as weakening, the president's bargaining position also begins to weaken. At the same time, the president's professional reputation is damaged, and his power to persuade wanes.

What videopolitics has done to Neustadt's interpretation is to stand it on its head. Once TV news becomes the primary source of political information (or misinformation), the president's standing with the public (which is by no means as simple a relationship as Neustadt's theory implies) depends largely on how his or her presidential performance is presented in bits and pieces, day after day, night after night, by CBS, NBC, ABC, MacNeil–Lehrer, and cable TV news. Among those who are chiefly engaged in "translating" the president's effectiveness are important members of the Washington community: reporters, pundits, editors. Consequently, the vital matter of the president's standing with the public (the television audience) is, in considerable measure, the by-product of *their* activity. The media technicians—in their presentation of presidential activity (much of it managed by the president's advisors)—project an "image" of presidential leadership or lack thereof to the rest of us. The Reagan administration mastered this process.

Further complicating the vital interrelationships among the president, the Washington power brokers, and the public (audience) is the mounting suspicion that the power brokers—for all of their presumed sophistication and cynicism—themselves respond, as the public does, to the images they see and hear on the nightly news. This certainly seems to have been the case during the Reagan years.

IRON TRIANGLES AND ISSUE NETWORKS

Prior to Ronald Reagan's presidency, serious, sober, and intelligent people expressed concern that television appeared to be weakening the base of popular leadership in an age of continuing stalemate. Whether or not the mass media could succeed in shortening the time span of effective presidential leadership, a president intent on bargaining in Neustadtian fashion certainly faces a far more complex set of key bargainers than was the case in 1960. Indeed, the president's own inner circle of top advisors now contains its own array of conflicting "bureaucratic" interests. Furthermore, the persistent stalemate in the center of national politics has taken on an added dimension of some importance in terms of frustrating White House policy leadership: the rise of huge "complexes" or "iron triangles." First to gain notoriety was the military–industrial–congressional complex—a product of the Cold War that was originally called to the public's attention in President Eisenhower's farewell address. To this have been added other complexes: welfare, education, health, energy, and employment training, to name a few. These complexes are based on triangles of power in which bureaucracies and subbureaucracies, special-interest groups, and "issue networks" of experts, congressional committees, and subcommittees and their staffs interlock and, in so doing, create structures of power that are semiautonomous. Once established, most of them are here to stay; as these complexes incline toward permanence, presidents remain conspicuously impermanent. It is worth noting that the Reagan administration, which intended the expansion of the military–industrial complex and the substantial reduction of most domestic complexes, succeeded only in sharply reducing employment training and energy; it eliminated *none*.

Furthermore, the permanent Washington executive bureaucracies—linked as they are with the bureaucratic root structures at the state and local levels—remain effectively responsible for implementing policies and programs. Their permanence (which is based on genuine expertise), their importance to their national constituencies, and their relative freedom from effective presidential control endow these organizations with an inertial force of their own. A painful lesson each president has learned is that he must often face a protracted uphill battle in "faithfully executing" the laws (implementing national programs)—even those closest to his heart.

Of course, ours is not the only society in which profound structural and generational–demographic changes establish new value and interest conflicts, thus complicating the role of executive leadership. For another recent example of a modern democracy featuring a contemporary executive leader who assumed power determined to alter the course of national policy, we turn briefly to the United Kingdom.

THE IRON LADY AND HER CIVIL SERVANTS—CASE STUDY

We conclude this introduction to the age of the executive, and this discussion of some of the serious political questions it raises, by viewing very briefly the case of former Prime Minister Margaret Thatcher, the first woman to lead a British government.

Prime Minister Thatcher Faces Her Civil Servants

Consider Prime Minister Thatcher's experience soon after she took over the responsibilities of executive leadership in the British government in 1979. As noted in Chapter 5, Thatcher and her government—following a decisive victory at the polls in May 1979—came to office determined to alter the direction of public policy in important ways. The Thatcher government was convinced that public spending, especially for domestic programs, needed to be curbed. This would require a reduction not only in the level of public services, but also in the number of civil servants (bureaucrats) administering the programs. Thatcher was further determined to curb double-digit inflation, to discipline the trade unions, and to increase productivity.

Within six months, public resistance to Thatcher's program cuts had grown vocal. Specific groups affected by cuts in school lunches, hospital care, and educational programs made their unhappiness known through every public forum available to them. More troublesome for the government, however, was the resistance mounted by members of the permanent civil service. This quiet resistance was felt within weeks of Thatcher's assumption of executive responsibility.

For example, soon after taking office, Thatcher perceived that the Treasury Department—home of the most powerful senior civil servants—was dragging its feet in establishing the level of public expenditure cuts she was looking for in her first budget. It couldn't be done, said the Treasury "mandarins" (as they are familiarly known in the United Kingdom). Thatcher summoned the Treasury minister, his four subordinate ministers, and the five highest ranking Treasury senior civil servants to her office at 10 Downing Street. According to Adam Raphael, a respected journalist of the *London Observer,* "They came out shaking from what was an unprecedented dressing-down. A week later the Treasury came up with £1000 million in cuts."[17]

Prime Minister Thatcher had established her credentials as a chief executive determined to have her policy initiatives taken seriously. On the other hand, the senior career officials who run the Treasury (and who, many think, actually run the British government) have seen prime ministers come and go. Thatcher, by force of her personality, had won round one. But what about the rounds to come?

Despite the usual reluctance of British officials to discuss publicly these power relationships between political leaders and career civil servants, there is reason to believe that Thatcher soon encountered new forms of resistance to her government's basic policies—especially those calling for reduction in government personnel. For example, the *Economist*—a

Box 7-2. The Long Career of Margaret Thatcher

Feb. 11, 1975   *Margaret Thatcher, a Member of Parliament since 1958, defeats Edward Heath in a contest for leadership of the Conservative Party.*

May 4, 1979   *She becomes Prime Minister when the Conservatives win a parliamentary majority in general elections.*

April 2, 1982   *Argentine forces invade the Falkland Islands, a British colony claimed by Argentina. Mrs. Thatcher sends a naval task force, which retakes the South Atlantic islands June 14–15 after a war costing 255 British and 650 Argentine lives.*

July 9, 1982   *She begins a second term as Prime Minister after the Conservatives win general elections.*

March 12, 1984   *The National Union of Mineworkers, opposing plans to close 20 unprofitable mines, begins a strike to challenge Mrs. Thatcher's attacks on union power.*

March 3, 1985   *After a 51-week strike, the longest and most violent in British history, the miners vote to return to work without a settlement.*

Jan. 6, 1986   *Defense Secretary Michael Heseltine resigns in a dispute over the American-led takeover of Westland, a helicopter manufacturer.*

June 11, 1987   *Mrs. Thatcher becomes the only British Prime Minister of the 20th century to win three consecutive elections.*

July 24, 1989   *The Foreign Minister, Sir Geoffrey Howe, is removed and given the honorary but empty post of Deputy Prime Minister after disagreeing with Mrs. Thatcher over monetary strategy.*

Oct. 26, 1989   *Nigel Lawson, Chancellor of the Exchequer, resigns following conflicts with Mrs. Thatcher over monetary policy.*

Nov. 1, 1990   *Sir Geoffrey resigns the Deputy Prime Minister's post over Mrs. Thatcher's resistance to European union.*

Nov. 13, 1990   *Sir Geoffrey tells the House of Commons that Mrs. Thatcher is jeopardizing British interests and dividing the Government.*

Nov. 14, 1990   *Mr. Heseltine challenges her for the party's leadership and the prime minister's job. He is Mrs. Thatcher's first serious challenger after 15 years at the helm of the party and more than 11 in power.*

Nov. 20, 1990   *Mrs. Thatcher fails to defeat Mr. Heseltine in a party election, forcing a second round.*

Nov. 22, 1990   *After talks with supporters, Mrs. Thatcher announces her resignation.*

Source: New York Times, *November 23, 1990.*

magazine noted for its reliable information on politics inside the British government—reported in October 1979 that Lord Peter Carrington, who served as foreign secretary in the first Thatcher government, had allowed his senior civil servants to propose cutting the BBC's radio and television overseas services as substitutes for pruning the Foreign Office itself.

Prime Minister Thatcher had been in office only a short time when her government ran up against the stern reality that domestic and foreign policy concerns today are hopelessly intertwined. Just as she was establishing her government's intention to hold firm in requiring a sharp curb in public spending, Treasury officials reported that Britain's participation in the European Common Market was costing at least £1 billion annually above and beyond any possible economic benefit to the nation. The publication of this key fact, just as the Thatcher government's first-round cuts in schools, hospitals, and colleges and universities were being felt, caused acute embarrassment. Almost immediately thereafter, Thatcher embarked on the difficult and frustrating task of trying to convince her European allies that they should ease her country's economic burden— and her own political dilemma. And Thatcher had a point; her country and Italy—the two economically weakest foreign partners—were paying disproportionately into the European Economic Community while more affluent countries—most notably Germany and France—were getting the best of the bargain. Not too surprisingly, Thatcher discovered that political leaders in France and Germany were only moderately sympathetic to her arguments. They seemed very slow to accept the notion that Britain should pay less and they more!

The Iron Lady Twelve Years Later

Thatcher proved to be a remarkably determined, persistent, and durable chief executive. Her standing with the British public rose dramatically during the Falkland Islands conflict, costly though it was; and this, combined with a badly divided Labour party, brought her Conservative government a clear-cut reelection in 1983. In the meantime, Thatcher held to her domestic course despite extraordinarily high levels of unemployment. There were 3 million jobless in the United Kingdom month after month—about twice the already high level that existed when she came to power in 1979. Double-digit joblessness on a continuing basis was a social cost the prime minister seemed quite prepared to impose on her people so long as inflation was slowed and productivity showed some signs of increasing. Moreover, on the occasion of her fifth anniversary as prime minister, Thatcher said she intended to seek an unprecedented third term. Her objective, she made it clear, was to continue the task of replacing "socialism," which she found "debilitating," with her brand of "modernization" and "individualism."

And how was Thatcher viewed by the British people? A poll taken in

April 1984 for the *London Observer* showed that four out of five British citizens regarded the Iron Lady as being as "tough" as Winston Churchill, the heroic leader during World War II. The same poll, however, revealed that many ordinary people did not like either her "style" or her program. Presumably, part of the reason for Thatcher's success at the polls was the weakness of her opposition parties among the general public.[18]

As for those high-ranking civil servants who play such an influential role in the British government, there was reason to believe that the prime minister had greatly strengthened her control of central policymaking. As the usually well informed *Economist* reported in March 1984,

> Mrs. Thatcher wants a cadre of top officials (i.e., senior civil servants) who are, in the words of the German civil service statute, "in continuing agreement with the basic political views and aims of the government." The permanent secretaries at most major departments are now known as Mrs. Thatcher's personal appointments, often promoted over the heads of more senior candidates.[19]

Thatcher went on to win a resounding victory in the 1987 general election. However, early 1990 found her in political hot water over local-government tax reform. In November a revolt within her Conservative party in the House of Commons freed her to step aside in favor of her handpicked successor, Chancellor of the Exchequer John Major. While much of the welfare state of Great Britain remains, it is also the case that the face of society has been changed dramatically from what it was before Margaret Thatcher rose to power.[20]

SUMMARY

The twentieth century has been viewed as the age of the executive—an age in which a number of major figures have crossed the world stage: Franklin D. Roosevelt, Winston Churchill, Adolf Hitler, V. I. Lenin, Joseph Stalin, Mahatma Gandhi, and Mao Tse-tung, among others. In these cases, executive leadership played a key role in altering the society and, sometimes, in shaking the world.

In the 1970s, though, we had cause to wonder whether "the age of the executive" was an appropriate label for the era in which we were living. The examples of Ronald Reagan, Margaret Thatcher, and Mikhail Gorbachev seem to have resolved that doubt in favor of executive leadership.

Nevertheless, we can probably expect executive leadership in our time to be cast in a less heroic mold than in the past. The conditions that gave rise to heroic executive leadership included industrialization, rapid technological change, wartime conditions, and the rise of mass media in communications. But these same developments, which have contributed to a centralization of power in modern societies, have enormously complicated the matter of providing executive leadership. The very mass media that in their inception were an opportunity for the exercise of heroic leadership are today a check on it. And even the examples of Reagan, Thatcher, and Gorbachev can be interpreted as much as lessons in constraint on executive leadership as examples of heroism.

Traditionally, one thinks in terms of four major constraints on executive leadership: (1) the opinions of large bodies of people; (2) political parties and elections; (3) an independent national legislature; and (4) independent judiciaries. Bureaucracy should now be included as an additional constraint.

NOTES

1. Sidney Hook, *The Hero in History* (New York: John Day, 1943), p. 154.

2. James MacGregor Burns, *Leadership* (New York: Harper and Row, 1978).

3. Woodrow Wilson, *Congressional Government* (New York: Meridian, 1956), p. 82.

4. Henry Adams, *The Education of Henry Adams* (New York: Modern Library, 1931), p. 417.

5. Alfred Kazin, *On Native Grounds* (New York: Reynal Hitchcock, 1942), p. 104.

6. Reinhard Bendix, *Work and Authority in Industry* (Berkeley: University of California Press, 1974), p. 254.

7. See Ernest R. May, *Imperial Democracy: The Emergence of America as a Great Power* (New York: Harper and Row, 1973).

8. Selig Adler, *The Uncertain Giant 1921–1941: American Policy between the Wars* (New York: Macmillan, 1965); also Robert Devine, *The Illusion of Neutrality* (New York: Times Books, 1962).

9. See Anthony Downs, *Inside Bureaucracy* (Boston: Little, Brown, 1967) for a careful examination of the highly technical literature on organizational behavior.

10. A. D. Lindsay, *The Modern Democratic State* (New York: Oxford University Press, 1943), p. 280.

11. Ibid., p. 258. For a brilliant diagnosis of the forces behind totalitarianism, see Hannah Arendt, *The Origins of Totalitarianism* (New York: Harcourt, 1951), previously discussed in Chapter 3.

12. A recent careful examination of the role of the military in what was the USSR is found in Timothy J. Colton, *Soldiers and the Soviet State: Civil Military Relations from Brezhnev to Gorbachev* (Princeton, N.J.: Princeton University Press, 1990).

13. Arthur M. Schlesinger, Jr., *One Thousand Days* (Boston: Houghton Mifflin, 1965), p. 709.

14. Arthur M. Schlesinger, Jr., makes this argument in *The Imperial Presidency* (Boston: Houghton Mifflin, 1973).

15. See Martin Anderson, *Revolution* (New York: Harcourt, Brace, Jovanovich, 1988). But to the contrary see Kevin Phillips, *The Politics of Rich and Poor* (New York: Random House, 1990).

16. Richard Neustadt, *President Power: The Politics of Leadership* (New York: John Wiley, 1980).

17. Adam Raphael, "At the Court of Queen Maggie," *London Observer,* October 7, 1979.

18. *London Observer,* April 29, 1984. The poll was conducted by Lou Harris, a prominent American pollster.

19. *Economist,* "No Other Goals but Mrs. Thatcher's," March 10, 1984, p. 58.

20. One of the best recent assessments of change in British politics and government over the postwar years is Lord Quintin Hailsham, *A Sparrow's Flight* (London: Collins, 1990). And for an argument that the changes Thatcher has wrought have been insufficiently profound—have not reformed the *institutions* or *forms* of policymaking in Great Britain—see Walter Williams, *Washington, Westminster, and Whitehall* (Cambridge, U.K.: Cambridge University Press, 1988).

SUGGESTED READINGS

Arendt, H. *The Origins of Totalitarianism.* New York: Harcourt, 1951. A brilliant study of totalitarian society and leadership.

Boulding, K. *Three Faces of Power.* London: Sage Publications, 1989. A suggestive, wide-ranging essay by one of the most distinguished social scientists of our time.

Burns, J. MacG. *Leadership.* New York: Harper and Row, 1978. A distinguished political scientist's major cross-cultural and cross-disciplinary study of leadership.

Grover, W. F. *The President as Prisoner: A Structural Critique of the Carter and Reagan Years.* Albany: State University of New York Press, 1989. An interesting recent study that addresses the "political structure" of the American presidency, arguing that the " 'impasse' between public expectations of economic prosperity and military supremacy, and the waning ability of the state to furnish them, has produced declining confidence in government generally, and in the president as head of government."

Hook, S. *The Hero in History.* New York: John Day, 1943. An American philosopher contrasts two basic kinds of leadership.

Lindsay, A. D. *The Modern Democratic State.* New York: Oxford University Press, 1943. A British scholar examines the nature of democratic leadership.

Lowi, T. *The Personal President: Power Invested and Promise Unfulfilled*. Ithaca, N.Y.: Cornell University Press, 1985. An expression of nagging doubt on the possibility of strong presidential leadership, given the patterns of political recruitment in America and the favored styles of leadership.

Schlesinger, A., Jr. *The Imperial Presidency*. Boston: Houghton Mifflin, 1973. The American historian and biographer of FDR and JFK offers a critical view of the contemporary presidency.

8

Legislative Assemblies

In those days, there was no king in Israel: every man did that which
was right in his own eyes.

—JUDGES 21:25

In practice, responsibility in politics today is to be found in executive
leadership. . . . Everywhere but in America the legislative function
has fallen into the hands of the executive, and in America, Congress
has sustained its not-quite-equal position only by invading the sphere
of the executive by means of its committees and their staffs.

—HARVEY C. MANSFIELD, JR.

WHY STUDY LEGISLATURES?

Why should you study or think about national legislatures? Why should
you care one way or the other what goes on within the Congress of the
United States, much less the British House of Commons? What does a
legislative assembly have to do with you or me? War? Peace? The cost of
living? The control of nuclear weapons? Who cares about or pays any
attention to the activities of Congress or the British Parliament?

The shortest answer to these questions is that, for free peoples,
legislatures have often proved rather handy institutions in the struggle to
become free and especially to remain free. Legislatures are marvelous
institutions for practicing representative self-government, and they have
also been useful in asserting popular claims against excessive displays of
executive authority. We Americans are a special case in point—or so, at
least, it seems to us.

While they were still subject to both royal and parliamentary authority,
colonial Americans developed a special fondness for their own legislative
assemblies and learned self-government in them. In the process, American colonists were developing an almost instinctive distrust of executive
authority long before 1776.[1] When the time came to make the break for
independence, eighteenth-century Americans turned almost as a matter
of course to a legislative body—the Continental Congress—to serve as
the chief governmental institution throughout the tortuous course of the
revolutionary struggle. The first American national government, established under the Articles of Confederation (1781–89), also featured a
Congress, virtually no executive, and no central judiciary.

The Constitution of 1787 was designed to correct some of the more glaring weaknesses of this first government under the Articles. While it provides for a president and a system of federal courts, the Constitution also places Congress first in the document, and more than half of it is devoted to a detailed listing of the powers of Congress. These are very great powers, as we shall note later.

But these are references to the seventeenth and eighteenth centuries, when people in the Western world were engaged in an initial struggle to establish representative government in an age of absolutism. What does this have to do with us today?

Today, at the close of the twentieth century, the world is different from what it was when our founding fathers created institutions of representative government. Our incredible technological capabilities have enabled us to send objects that penetrate deep into outer space. The speed of change in contemporary society is dazzling. Ours is a society in which there are no easy answers to complex public problems, such as unemployment and inflation. Whether one speaks of the latest weapons system, the development of a national health insurance plan, or the control of hazardous wastes, one immediately encounters enormously complicated technical details, which only experts have the competence to sort out.

Serious questions must be faced. Are legislatures effective in making policies for today's complicated and interdependent world? Can committees of nonexperts be expected to make "rational" judgments about weapons systems and health plans? Is it possible for a legislative assembly to compete with the expertise of modern bureaucracies? Why are modern legislatures generally held in low esteem by many citizens? In short, are legislative assemblies in danger of becoming obsolete?

To answer these and similar questions, we shall take a closer look at contemporary legislative bodies, asking ourselves what basic functions they serve and how significant these functions are. We shall also examine briefly the careers and activities of a few leading legislators in the United States and in Britain. In so doing, we hope to shed some light on the present condition of one of the Western world's most interesting political inventions: the representative, legislative assembly.

BASIC FUNCTIONS OF LEGISLATURES

Historically, legislative bodies have performed several basic governmental functions. Although they have often been thought of as essentially lawmaking agencies, legislatures have also served as vital instruments in placing restraints on the exercise of executive authority. In some countries—Britain being a leading example—the national legislature has also had the capacity to make and unmake governments. In the United

Kingdom the chief executive, called the prime minister, and his or her cabinet are elected by a majority in the House of Commons. A third major function is representation. National legislatures developed as a means of providing representation in the affairs of state to groups whose interests had not been adequately represented by royal authority. For example, throughout most of the seventeenth century, Britain was engaged in a long and often bloody struggle between the monarchy and Parliament, with the landed interests generally looking to Parliament as their institution. The so-called Glorious Revolution of 1688 marked the end of royal absolutism in Britain, as Parliament and the forces it represented gained ascendancy. *Civil Government,* John Locke's famous treatise, offers a brilliant rationalization of this constitutional settlement. This book took on additional significance later; the opening paragraph in the Declaration of Independence, drafted by Thomas Jefferson, paraphrases the essentials of Locke's thinking.

Thus legislative assemblies have at least three major functions:

1. Lawmaking
2. Oversight of executive activity
3. Representation

If any of these functions were seriously eroded, the legislature would face an altered—and probably weakened—role.

The twentieth century has often been referred to as the age of the executive, and the decline of the legislature is thought to be a common phenomenon throughout the Western world. We know, for example, that the U.S. Congress enjoys no great prestige. Its inner workings are too complex for ready display, even on C-SPAN. Indeed, the public's respect for Congress as an institution has deteriorated steadily in recent years. For this reason alone, we need to examine carefully how national legislatures are discharging their traditional responsibilities in the current era. The decline in public prestige does not necessarily reveal the real importance of legislative bodies, however. In fact, it may mislead us, causing us to overlook one of the real centers of action.

For example, the combination of functions—and especially the representative and lawmaking ones—places the contemporary national legislature squarely in the midst of many divisive issues and sharp conflict. Many difficult issues face national legislators these days: inflation, unemployment, the quality of the environment, human welfare, health, education, and national security, among others. Consequently, legislative politicians live with the uneasy assignment of finding either some means of resolving complex and contentious issues or, failing in this, some way of blunting the issues so as not to intensify domestic conflict any further.

THE BRITISH PARLIAMENT

Let us first turn to England and the mother of Parliaments. Here we find a *bicameral* (two-house) national legislature: the House of Commons and the House of Lords. Although the House of Lords retains a few residual functions, which are mostly ceremonial, it has no real authority in making legislation. For this reason, we will focus our attention on the House of Commons, the site of political power in the United Kingdom.

The House of Commons: A Sense of Crowd and Urgency

An American entering the House of Commons for the first time is struck by the smallness and compactness of the chamber. After the old House of Commons was damaged in an air raid, the decision was made to rebuild a small chamber. Winston Churchill, speaking as prime minister in 1943, explained why.

> If the House is big enough to contain all its members nine-tenths of its debates will be conducted in the depressing atmosphere of an almost empty or half-empty chamber. The essence of good House of Commons speaking is the conversational style, the facility for quick informal interruptions and interchanges . . . but the conversational style requires a fairly small space and there should be on great occasions a sense of crowd and urgency. There should be a sense of the importance of much that is said, and a sense that great matters are being decided, then and there, by the House.[2]

The atmosphere in the House of Commons is rather similar to that of a private club; the style of debate, conversational. As Walter Bagehot, a learned student of the English government, observed more than a century ago, "You have not a perception of the first elements in this matter till you know that government by a club is a standing wonder."[3]

Standing wonder or not, the new member of the House enters an ancient institution with an atmosphere all its own and a set of rules and norms governing official behavior. Very little of this is written down. New members are soon socialized into the club—even those who represent fairly extreme positions in British politics.

Many years ago, Harold Laski explained the importance of being a House member. His insight remains valid today.

> The easy thing, of course, to say . . . is that the House of Commons is an attractive club, with all the habits that pertain to this special institution . . . but, in fact, these habits serve another purpose of immense importance. The impact of a member upon the House is a very good way (though it is not the

only way) of testing his ability for ministerial position. A man who is to rule a department well must have the qualities which enable him to be acceptable to the House of Commons.[4]

Anthony Sampson, a keen observer of contemporary Britain, has noted that "the building itself has an overpowering atmosphere for any new member, and even when, as in 1945 or 1964, there is a great inrush of tough new members, they are easily intimidated by the traditions and rules."[5] Aneurin Bevan, the Socialist minister who brought the national health program to Britain after World War II, reflected that, when he first entered the House from a background in a poor Welsh mining village, he felt that he was entering a place of worship—or, as he put it, "ancestor worship."

Parliament is distinctly British, just as Congress is unmistakably American. Some of the differences between the two national legislative bodies are explained, no doubt, by the way politics is organized in the two countries and by important differences in political "culture" (norms, values, ideas, and patterns of behavior). Traditionally the individual member of the House of Commons has found it easy to accept the clublike atmosphere, in part because he or she is a member of a cohesive national political party that exerts considerable influence over members' voting. As recently as the early 1970s, two knowledgeable students of political change in Britain offered this assessment:

> Politics in Britain, to a remarkable degree, are based on the competition between cohesive parties which act together in the national legislature and offer unified appeals for the support of the mass electorate. A member almost never goes against the party whips in the division lobbies, and very few candidates diverge from the party line in their election appeals. The familiar American phenomenon of the candidate who plays down his party affiliation and emphasizes local, rather than national issues is much less common in Britain.[6]

As we have noted throughout this book, the processes of change work inexorably on the institutions and practices of government. Great Britain is no exception to this rule. Hence, by the mid-1980s, informed students of British politics found that the declining cohesiveness of political parties was having certain consequences for the behavior of members of the House of Commons. It was no longer the case that "a member almost never goes against the party whips." Both the Conservative and the Labour parties contained members who refused to toe the party line, and cross-voting occurred with increasing frequency. And, as we noted in Chapter 5, the House of Commons now includes representatives of several parties, including Conservatives, Labourites, Liberals, and Social Democrats, as well as Scottish and Welsh nationalists. To some extent, the clublike atmosphere of the House is bound to change under these conditions.[7]

So substantial was this change in the voting behavior of members of Parliament that Samuel Beer, a longtime American authority on British politics, labeled it "the cross-voting explosion," and added, "This break with previous behavior came fairly suddenly and dated from the turn of the decade into the 1970s. In the next ten years more MP's rebelled than at any time since the latter part of the 19th century. They rebelled more frequently, in larger numbers, and over more important issues."[8] Indeed Margaret Thatcher was elected party leader in 1975 as the result of back-bench rebellion in the Conservative party. During the 1980s, dissent within the Labour party also reached new heights.[9]

In the U.S. Congress, the influence exerted by party leaders on the voting decisions of individual members of the House and Senate seldom matches the British model. Most votes cast on major controversial issues reveal a bipartisan majority against a bipartisan minority; a few moderate Republicans are likely to join a "liberal" Democratic majority in the House, whereas a bloc of "conservative" Democrats, mostly from the South (the so-called boll weevils) often join the majority of the Republican representatives, especially on domestic issues. A somewhat similar pattern is found in the Senate, where the Democrats assumed majority control following the 1986 election.[10]

Probably the most important single difference between the U.S. Congress and the British Parliament is that our national legislature is separated from the executive (thanks to the separation of powers specified by the Constitution), whereas their House of Commons is linked directly to the executive via the cabinet and its principal figure the prime minister, leader of the majority party. Rather than being separated, the legislative and executive branches in Britain are *fused*. This has important consequences for the way the British national legislature works and for the ways in which members' careers develop within the House of Commons.

In order to have any real hope of being a prominent political leader within a British political party and of eventually becoming a leader within a government, the ambitious politician must first gain a seat in the House of Commons and must then proceed to earn a reputation as an able House member. He or she must "join the club" and demonstrate a capacity for leadership inside the parliamentary party. This is far more important than serving one's constituents or gaining personal popularity with the folks back home. Although it would not be accurate to suggest that the legislator's "home style" is of no importance in British politics, it definitely has far less operational significance than in the United States. Yet here again, changes taking place in both societies appear to be making service to constituents a key to legislative behavior now that the bureaucratized welfare state is here to stay.

The House of Lords

Unlike the House of Commons, the House of Lords has a very limited legislative role. It can debate and make minor technical amendments in legislation, it can exercise a "suspensive veto" forcing Commons to revoke something of which it disapproves, but it cannot turn down legislation that has received majority support in the House of Commons, an elected body.

Most members of the House of Lords are hereditary peers, their seats having been handed down from father to eldest son; most of these peers are seldom present in the House of Lords. There are also some life peers, created by each government in power as a means of honoring individuals. For example, both Harold Wilson, the former Labour prime minister, and George Brown, his longtime colleague and rival in the House of Commons, were elevated to the House of Lords when their usefulness to the Labour party in the House of Commons had ended. Finally, there are the so-called law lords—eminent jurists who perform an important judicial function, serving as the ultimate court of appeal in civil and criminal cases.

Professor Richard Rose labels the House of Lords "an historical anachronism." Although in form it is the second chamber of Parliament, in practice "it is an institution that facilitates the making of policy," and it survives because "it has not interfered sufficiently strenuously in the past forty years to make its opponents wish to take the trouble to abolish it."[11]

THE CONGRESS OF THE UNITED STATES

Our national legislature—the Congress of the United States—enjoys an institutional existence independent of the executive branch. Rather than fuse these two political branches of government as in the British cabinet–parliamentary system, our founding fathers deliberately chose to separate the presidency and the Congress, causing them to engage in a continuous struggle over the making of public policy. Rooted in Article I of the Constitution, Congress is armed with great powers, including the power of the purse, taxation, promoting the general welfare, and regulating commerce.

There are important differences between the two houses of Congress. For one thing, a U.S. senator serves a six-year term, whereas members of the House of Representatives, who serve two-year terms, always seem to be running for reelection. Richard Fenno finds that the Senate, with only 100 members compared to 435 House members, has a "small town sense of community"; but paradoxically, the small size also tends to create prima donnas. "It's like a colony of movie stars," Fenno observed.[12]

Norman Ornstein, another political scientist who concentrates on ob
serving Congress, describes the Senate as "a funny place, a strang
place. Senators know their colleagues in ways that House members don't
But there are very few durable friendships in the Senate. Senators know
their colleagues on a superficial basis, while House members develop
durable friendships."[13]

In nine cases out of ten, service in either the House of Representative
or the Senate is likely to lead only to a long career in Congress. Althougl
five recent presidents served first in the Congress—Kennedy, Johnson
Nixon, Ford, and Bush—most of our national legislators do not seek t
build political careers that will culminate in positions of leadership in th
executive branch.

Congressional representatives are generally career politicians. Becaus
the two major parties are less cohesive and less disciplined than Britisl
parties are, individual congressional hopefuls must build their own coali
tions of support among their local constituents. Richard Fenno's carefu
probing has revealed just how important the matter of "home style" ha
become in perpetuating a career in Congress. The telling fact is that, onc
one is elected to the House or Senate, one's chances of being reelecte
are excellent, especially in the House.[14]

Although most members of Congress do not realistically expect t
become president, speaker, or majority leader, many of them like workin
in Washington and being part of the action. Indeed, they lead incredibl
hectic lives, leaving all too little time for thought or reflection on th
larger issues of the day.

The legislative pace in the House of Commons is less hectic, but i
general the pace of life in Great Britain tends to be less frantic than th
hustle and bustle of American life. The heavy reliance placed on legisla
tive committees in Congress, in contrast to their relative unimportance i
shaping legislation in Britain, may account for some of the difference
Pressures from constituents on members of Parliament to intercede o
their behalf with unresponsive government bureaucracies are growing i
Britain, but they do not approach the volume or intensity that they hav
reached in this country.

Perhaps more important, the proliferation of the staff system is not ye
a major phenomenon in Parliament, as it is in the United States. Perhap
the British realize that staff members are at best a mixed blessing for a
busy legislator. On the one hand, they are there to help him or he
respond to the many demands of the legislator's job. On the other hand
staff members have to be dealt with, they tend to generate more work
and they can be persistent in promoting their own policy agendas and pe
projects.

Why, then, would anyone aspire to be a legislator-representative? Fo
one thing, the pay is good, and the chances for a lengthy career ar
excellent. In England, a member of Parliament has the additional advan

tage of joining an exclusive club. No doubt the social life in Washington, D.C., is stimulating, and London is clearly more cosmopolitan than Cardiff or Leeds. A national legislative career has many advantages to offer, but undoubtedly one of the greatest attractions is having power and exercising power. Washington and London are where the political action is. And political action necessarily means struggling with the great issues of the day.

Congressional Leaders: Personality before Ideology

Those who rise to the top of the congressional system do so partly on the basis of seniority, partly on party ideology, and to a great extent on personality. Indeed, recent scholarship suggests that Senate and House members in the 1980s are seeking leaders with whom they feel personally compatible.

"It is hard to know what these guys want, or who they feel comfortable with," said Richard Fenno, who conducted an in-depth study of eight senators. "What they want to know is, What will my life be like with him as a leader? Is he the kind of guy I can work with? Is he the kind of guy I can approach?"[15]

George Mitchell, the Democratic majority leader in the Senate, is a case in point. He was chosen in 1989 to replace the colorless Robert Byrd because it was thought that the intellectually nimble Mitchell would function as a more effective opposition spokesman and critic of the Republican administration. But he was also chosen because he was well liked and trusted within the party. Senator Robert Dole, the Republican minority leader, offers something of a contrast. As Professor Robert Peabody once observed when Dole was Republican chairman of the Senate Finance Committee, senators "really don't want somebody too far out in front, too dazzling." But then Peabody added, "On the other hand, Dole has more chits than anyone else."[16] In other words, despite his occasionally sharp tongue, the senator from Kansas is a consonant cooperator with his fellows on particular legislative projects.

The Staff Army of Our Billion-dollar Congress

One of the reasons why many of our national legislators are reelected with relative ease is that Congress is now staffed in a fashion that virtually guarantees it. Indeed, David Mayhew has gone so far as to argue that the principal objective of Congress today is to bring about the reelection of incumbents.[17] Whether or not Mayhew has overstated this aspect of congressional experience, each member of Congress—Senate or House, newcomer or veteran—is paid, staffed, and otherwise provided for beyond the wildest dreams of a British member of Parliament. (Even a key member of the British House of Commons has a "room," or office, so small that it would be looked on with contempt by a legislative assistant on Capitol Hill, and most members of Parliament have no offices and no staff.) The annual salaries paid to members of Congress have no counterpart in any other great national legislature. It now costs almost $2 billion a year simply to keep Congress in business.

Our national legislators are not only well paid (despite the furor in 1989 over their latest raise) and provided with excellent fringe benefits (including free medical care, generous pensions, and travel allowances), but they also provide themselves generously with staff assistance. The number of congressional staff people virtually tripled between 1967 and 1983, and the trend is steadily upward.

With even the most junior member of the House allowed 18 staff members, and with a junior senator from a tiny state such as Rhode Island or Vermont allocated half a million dollars annually for staff, one can easily see that our representatives in Washington have taken a long step toward maximizing their chances at reelection.

In addition to their personal staffs, Washington legislators have access to more staff personnel on the various committee staffs. A senior senator who chairs a major committee and several subcommittees has available scores of staff experts and can avail himself or herself of their specialized knowledge on vital issues. Clearly, any anonymous challenger has a hard time launching a successful campaign against an incumbent possessed of this built-in advantage.

What do these staff assistants do? They answer the phones, type letters to constituents, prepare postage-free newsletters for mass mailings to constituents, and talk with bureaucrats, reporters, constituents, lobbyists, and other staffers. They also write speeches for their bosses, help them prepare for committee hearings, draft legislation, negotiate legislative compromises, advise their bosses on how they should vote, and try to mold public opinion. They also work hard in political campaigns; *their* jobs too are at stake! These are good jobs on Capitol Hill. The hours are long, but the salaries are excellent and so are the fringe benefits, because congressional representatives take very good care of their own. It is fair to say that congressional staff constitute the mostly invisible and steadily proliferating third house of our national legislature. One excellent recent study refers to the staff members as our "unelected representatives." Another labels congressional staffs "the invisible force in American lawmaking."[18]

A Collection of Committees

Once the representative or senator has arrived on Capitol Hill, a principal key to the nature of his or her legislative career in Washington is committee assignments. Unlike the British House of Commons, which until recently used committees only sparingly, Congress does most of its essential business in committees. It is only a slight exaggeration to suggest that Congress is really a collection of committees that come together from time to time in the House and Senate to ratify agreements previously made by a committee. Thus, committee assignments help shape the role the legislator chooses to play in Washington. The reforms of recent years that have opened the internal workings of congressional committees—thus altering the rules—have not seemed to diminish the exceptional power and influence of politically skillful chairpersons such as Senator Robert Dole or Representative Dan Rostenkowski.

Power: Coin of the Realm

Power—getting others to do as we wish (see Chapter 1)—is the common coin of the world of politics, though experts frequently disagree about the nature of power and how and why it is employed. Still, only the most naive person would not soon realize that those who participate seriously in legislative politics are also engaged in a continuing power struggle *to influence public policy*. Some legislators, as we have discovered, prove far more effective than others in shaping policy. Those who are influential are said to have "power," whether they deny it or not.

How does this work in the real world of policymaking?

Former Secretary of State Edmund S. Muskie—one-time chairman of the Senate Budget Committee, a candidate for the vice-presidency in 1968, a contender for the presidential nomination in 1972, and previously state legislator and governor in Maine—offered this view after spending his adult life in politics, two decades of that in the Senate.

"Power, power," says Muskie impatiently. "People have all sorts of conspiratorial theories on what constitutes power in the Senate. It has little to do with the size of the state you come from. Or the source of your money. Or committee chairmanships, although that certainly gives you a kind of power. But real power up there comes from doing your work and knowing what you are talking about. Power is the ability to change someone's mind. *That* is power around here. . . . The most important thing in the Senate is credibility, CREDIBILITY! *That* is power."[19]

Continuing on this theme, Muskie then noted how the way the Senate does business has changed in twenty years.

"One of the things that has changed is that the floor is not the place it used to be for changing minds. There was a time, not many years ago, when a good debate would attract a good many Senators, and some would make up their minds on the basis of what was said. Today hardly anyone has time to go to the floor except for votes because the work has proliferated so much.

So many more issues, so much more committee work to take care of, to become expert in."[20]

Muskie was asked whether the power to change minds is evident in the cloakroom, where senators and House members meet informally.

"The cloakroom!" Muskie scoffs. "In *committee,* not the cloakroom. *Nothing* happens in the cloakroom. *Nothing.* The cloakroom is where you go to rest your ass."[21]

WHAT NATIONAL LEGISLATURES REALLY DO

It is time to ask ourselves what it is that a great national legislature—such as the British Parliament or the U.S. Congress—actually does, in this day and age, that is worth our attention here. Have national legislatures declined in importance as well as in prestige?

Although we live in an age of strong executive rule, that age has also brought the ever growing activity of bureaucracies to the fore, and national legislatures continue to play a major role in shaping national policy. In both Britain and the United States, the rise of the modern welfare state was possible only after lengthy and intense political struggle within their respective national legislative arenas. This is not to downplay the importance of the executive leadership or the continuing activity of public bureaucracies in implementing their vast programs. But no one should minimize the extent to which these expensive and complicated programs depend on legislative authorization and funding for their continued existence.

The two national legislatures are also deeply involved in debate and discussion concerning vital defense and foreign-policy matters. Throughout the twentieth century, Congress has been a prime shaper of our national security policies. It was Congress that warmly supported Theodore Roosevelt's attempts to extend American power into the Pacific Ocean area at the beginning of the twentieth century. The decision *not* to participate in the League of Nations after World War I was forced by stubborn Senate resistance to the treaty. Congressional isolationists wrote a series of neutrality laws in the 1930s aimed at limiting President Franklin D. Roosevelt's discretion in world politics. Aid to Western Europe following World War II depended on congressional funding. The Cold War, down to and including Vietnam, required solid support in Congress. The president alone cannot bring a Panama Canal Treaty to fruition or ratify a SALT agreement or maintain a firm position in the Middle East without congressional backing. And it requires an act of Congress to draft young Americans into the armed forces.[22]

Not many Americans appreciate the extent to which foreign-policy and defense issues have colored contemporary political discussion in Britain, despite Britain's greatly reduced role in global politics. Some of the most heated and divisive debates in British domestic politics have stemmed from sharply differing views of Britain's role in its continuing partnership with the United States and of Britain's participation in the European Common Market. Hence it seems myopic to view these two national legislative assemblies as being in a state of serious decline when it comes to influencing domestic and foreign policies.[23]

Perhaps we need to look elsewhere for signs of decline in the importance of national legislatures. How about the historic importance of legislatures in overseeing and checking the activity of the executive? This seems to offer more promising substance largely because, as we have noted throughout this book, huge bureaucratic structures stand tall wherever we look across the landscape of big government. In Great Britain, with its mixture of private enterprise and modified socialism, public bureaucracies are a major institutional presence. Furthermore, for more than a century, the people of Britain have been accustomed to having their civil servants play a major role in running the country. (It is almost a cliché in British middle-class society to say that it doesn't really matter whether the Labourites or the Conservatives are the government of the day, because the civil servants remain in charge.)[24]

In the United States we have been slower, perhaps, to recognize just how large a role these huge public bureaucracies play not only in implementing policy but also in shaping it in the first place. (We discuss this more fully in Chapter 9.)

Making the Executive Behave

The vast expansion of public programs in recent years, their incredible technical complexity, and their enormous costs pose a real problem for national legislatures. How is a body of politicians—nonexperts—ever to devise effective mechanisms for "controlling" this massive governmental machinery, reaching, as it does, into every nook and cranny of everyday life? The British rely heavily on two simple techniques, neither of which appears to be entirely adequate in today's world.

Controlling the Executive in Britain

Although the British prime minister, who has the support of a disciplined majority in the legislative arena, enjoys an advantage over an American president, this does not mean that there are no constraints placed on the exercise of executive power in Britain. Two mechanisms stand out as most important in this respect: the loyal opposition and the question time.

Loyal Opposition. The British have institutionalized "opposition" in the House of Commons. The leader of the opposition, who is paid a salary, and fellow members of what is called the *shadow cabinet* are seated directly across from the front benches, where the prime minister and cabinet officers sit as leaders of the majority party. Day after day, the opposition is there, engaging in free debate with one principal objective in mind: as the London *Economist* put it, "to make life very difficult for the government."[25]

Whereas bipartisan coalitions often take shape inside Congress, the House of Commons features sharp party differences on virtually all important public issues. It is the principal task of the opposition to keep these differences alive and visible to the general public.

Question Time. This ancient custom affords any member of the House of Commons an opportunity to question government ministers. The British place an unusual reliance on "the ability of opposition MP's to make ministers look foolish, obstructive, secretive or just plain wrong in debate, or more often at question time, and the effect of the resulting publicity."[26] The procedure works this way: question time is scheduled in the House of Commons every day except Friday from 2:45 to 3:30 P.M., although the prime minister may be questioned only on Tuesdays and Thursdays. The other ministers take turns at intervals of about ten days.

Every member of the House has the right to question a minister and may be content to receive a written answer. A member who wants an oral answer to a written question must "star" the request, giving two days' notice.

The process has been described by a British political scientist as follows:

> At question time the member rises and, addressing the speaker, refers to his question. The minister rises and reads his reply. On answering, the ministers may expect a veritable drumfire of supplementary questions. Where the issue is controversial, the process turns into a cross-examination of the Minister by all the House. And sometimes the question or answer is dynamite.[27]

Critics of the Parliament charge that a loyal opposition—even buttressed with free debate and the question time—is not sufficient in an age of all-pervasive bureaucracy. Partly to meet this line of criticism, in 1967 the British created the parliamentary commissioner for administration. This official, who reports to a select committee of the House, serves as a kind of ombudsman, reviewing cases of maladministration referred by individual members of the House.

As is the case in the United States, there is long-standing unease in Britain about Parliament's ability to scrutinize the budget. There is a public accounts committee in the House of Commons that has been strengthened in recent decades. It now has an able staff, but doubts remain that this committee is able to get very deeply inside the complexities of a modern budget prepared by the executive branch.

Controlling the Executive in the United States

The United States has three major weapons with which to combat executive arrogance, bureaucratic indifference and inefficiency, and extreme cases of executive willful abuse of power. It is doubtful that any other national legislature possesses a comparable arsenal.

Power of the Purse. Historically, Congress has relied mostly on the appropriations committees in the House and Senate to oversee spending by the departments and agencies of the federal government. Especially during and after World War II, the ability of these committees to keep pace with the mushrooming activities of government was severely strained. As a practical matter, the appropriations committees delegated this responsibility to small subcommittees.

In addition to the increasing sums of money involved, and the increasing complexity of the programs these monies fund, there are three other factors that have operated to make the task of budget oversight more difficult. First, Congress has, over the past 20 years, been delving into proposed budgets in greater detail (especially the proposed accounts for the Department of Defense). Second, the looming specter of the budget deficit has increased pressure to effect savings. Third, and most important, a variety of factors—including changes in the patterns of recruitment and election of representatives and senators (see Chapter 6)—have resulted in increasing *decentralization* of power in Congress.[28]

In 1975, in an attempt to tighten up its system of budgeting, Congress created a set of new structures: budget committees for both houses, and a joint Congressional Budget Office (CBO), which, it was hoped, would generate economic estimates and forecasts that could be used to counter those of the President's Office of Management and Budget (OMB). One effect of this, however, was to multiply to *at least six* (and often more) the number of congressional panels that become involved with a budget request as it passes through the process. As Senator Sam Nunn, chairman of the Senate Armed Services Committee recently put it,

the extent to which we have wrapped ourselves around the budget axle is exacerbated by the growing tendency to examine budget proposals in even finer, almost microscopic, detail. The Armed Services Committee now authorizes almost every element of the defense budget each year, down to almost the last screw and bolt. . . . At its worst this tendency has spurred not unreasonable charges of congressional "micromanagement." . . . But even more troublesome, this trend to micromanagement has the staff and members focusing on the beach while we should be looking over the broad ocean and beyond the horizon.[29]

Investigations. From its earliest hours two centuries ago, Congress has looked on its power of investigation as a major instrument in the continuing struggle with the executive branch. Today the congressional prerogative to investigate virtually anything it wishes to investigate—most notably, the activity of an agency in the executive branch—is well established. For example, a Senate investigative committee performing before television cameras first exposed the Nixon administration to the harsh light of publicity in the so-called Watergate Affair.

Congress also has an important staff agency of its own: the General Accounting Office (GAO), which has developed a strong investigative arm during the past two decades. For example, the GAO played a key role in uncovering a large-scale pattern of fraud inside the General Services Administration in 1978–79. It also found serious misuse of procurement practices in the Pentagon during the Reagan administration.

Impeachment. The fact that Congress has the constitutional power to impeach executive and judicial officials is perhaps a more theoretical than a practical curb on the abuse of power *most of the time*. Still, we have the recent example of President Richard Nixon resigning the office in disgrace largely because the House was prepared to vote articles of impeachment charging an obstruction of justice inside the White House. Fortunately, President Nixon was not prepared to put himself and the nation through the ordeal of an impeachment trial in the U.S. Senate, as President Andrew Johnson did more than a century earlier. And in the Iran–Contra Affair of 1986, it is likely that one reason the Reagan administration was so readily forthcoming with documents and witnesses was a concern that, otherwise, a move for impeachment might begin to take shape.

Representation

Historically, legislative assemblies were created in order to represent important groups whose interests were being ignored or neglected by executive authorities. In both Britain and this country, national legislatures were developed to serve as instruments of popular rule and popular control. Furthermore, as we moved through the nineteenth century into the twentieth, national legislatures came to represent the ever growing diversity of industrial society.

How well is this representative function being performed today? Do we Americans feel that our congressional representatives and senators are accurately representing our interests? How do the ordinary folk of Britain feel about their representatives in the House of Commons?

These are difficult questions to answer because of a conspicuous paradox. In both countries there is a growing feeling that national legislatures are in a state of decline relative to the awesome power of the executive and the public bureaucracies. Legislative bodies often seem to be in danger of becoming mere rubber stamps, while the key decisions affecting people's welfare are made elsewhere. On the other hand, individual legislators in both countries have astonishingly little difficulty getting reelected time after time after time. The unpopularity of the legislature as an institution does not seem to carry with it unpopularity as an individual legislator.[30]

It is also apparent here and in Britain that most national legislators are career politicians who are intensely interested in staying in power. Hence they must *appear* to represent us well, whether they do in fact or not. And this is all the more difficult because, on both sides of the Atlantic, most national legislators are far from typical citizens. In general, they are more affluent, better educated, and better connected than are most of their constituents. National legislators are drawn from the ranks of "professionals": doctors, lawyers, businesspeople, professors, and so on. One does not often find dirt farmers or mechanics serving as legislators in Westminster or on Capitol Hill.

In practice, the representative function depends not so much on the social and economic background of legislators as on their *responsiveness* to the demands and needs put forth by organized groups. In a very real sense, these groups are the "representative" agencies in our society.

For example, there were at least 20 millionaires serving in the U.S. Senate during the 1980s. Obviously, millionaires do not comprise 20 percent of the U.S. citizenry. Yet these senatorial millionaires differ widely on issues of policy. For example, Senator Edward Kennedy, Democrat of Massachusetts, was an ardent spokesman for the poor, members of minority groups, the elderly, and disadvantaged.

One might assume that, in Britain, members of the House of Commons who "represent" the interests of working men and women in the Labour party would be products of working-class society. This is not exactly the case, however. There are Labour MPs from working-class backgrounds. However, the majority of Labour MPs—like their Conservative opponents—tend to be relatively affluent people with university degrees, whatever their social origins may have been. So whom they represent or how well they represent them is not a function of their present position in the economic and social structure of English society.

Perhaps the only conclusion we are justified in reaching is that, during this period in history, the representative function—like the legislative and oversight functions—appears to have meaning in established Western parliamentary regimes, though in an ever changing context. How much meaning this Western political invention may have for governing in the Third World remains to be seen.

SUMMARY

We are forced to the conclusion that modern national legislatures, such as the U.S. Congress and the British Parliament, are very much alive as the twentieth century draws to a close. They may be weakened, both in general public esteem and in their battles of strength with the huge executive bureaucracies, but they are far from irrelevant. Also, their functions appear to be changing as conditions change. Less important as initiators of legislative policy (because so much technical expertise resides in executive hands), legislative bodies may gain in importance when it comes to exercising legislative oversight, assuming that they develop new and better techniques for controlling the details of executive activity.

Parliament in the United Kingdom is bicameral. Effective legislative power is lodged in the House of Commons, which reflects popular majorities; the House of Lords survives as a historical anachronism that exercises very little legislative authority. Parliamentary politics in the United Kingdom is a product of competition between two cohesive and disciplined political parties. Margaret Thatcher's career in the House of Commons affords a unique study in the way legislative, executive, and political party leadership are combined in British experience.

The U.S. Congress is given comprehensive powers in Article I of the Constitution. Congressional representatives are products of a political system that places a premium on strong ties with local constituencies. Reelection becomes a prime objective for these career politicians, whose "business" has become a billion-dollar annual operation featuring a proliferation of staff. The role of Robert Dole as chairman of the Senate Finance Committee (before his election as Senate majority leader in early 1985) affords insight into the key role that senior committee chairpersons play within the congressional system. In effect, Congress functions as a collection of committees.

Although the pace of Washington legislative life leaves little opportunity for reflection on great issues, members of national legislatures are nonetheless deeply involved in shaping national-security and domestic policies. They also have a vital interest in making the executive "behave," that is, in controlling the power of the executive branch. The British employ two basic techniques: question time, and the loyal opposition. Congress, by contrast, relies principally on its power to control the purse strings, to conduct committee investigations, and to threaten or carry out impeachment.

How representative these legislative bodies are is a good question. Their membership is drawn disproportionately from professional, upper-middle-class people who are responsive to the interests of powerful groups whose support they rely on in gaining election.

NOTES

1. See B. Bailyn, *The Ideological Origins of the American Revolution* (Cambridge, Mass.: Harvard University Press, 1967).

2. Quoted in K. C. Wheare, *Legislatures* (New York: Oxford University Press, 1968), p. 5.

3. Quoted by Anthony Sampson in *The Anatomy of Britain Today* (New York: Harper Colophon Books, 1965), p. 38.

4. Harold Laski, *Parliamentary Government in England* (New York: Viking, 1947), pp. 129–30.

5. Sampson, *Anatomy of Britain,* p. 38.

6. David Butler and Donald Stokes, *Political Change in Britain* (New York: St. Martin's, 1971), p. 217.

7. See Max Beloff and Gillian Peele, *The Government of the United Kingdom: Political Authority in a Changing Society* (New York: Norton, 1980); they reported cross-voting in at least 20 percent of the divisions between 1970 and 1974, with the increase especially marked in the Conservative party (p. 188). Douglas E. Ashford, writing from a perspective that places British politics within the framework of a changing policymaking environment, notes similar changes at work. He, moreover, would suggest that the clublike atmosphere of the House of Commons is based on an elite consensus that has been under severe strain in recent decades. See Douglas E. Ashford, *Policy and Politics in Britain, the Limits of Consensus* (Oxford, U.K.: Basil Blackwell, 1981).

8. Samuel Beer, *Britain against Itself: The Political Contradictions of Collectivism* (New York: Norton, 1982), p. 180.

9. Ibid., pp. 180–83.

10. David J. Vogler, *The Politics of Congress,* 4th ed. (Boston: Allyn and Bacon, 1983); see especially pp. 107–16 for an intelligent presentation of the various "cues" a member of Congress turns to in deciding how to vote.

11. Richard Rose, *Politics in England* (Boston: Little, Brown, 1964), p. 216. See also Kenneth MacKenzie, *The English Parliament* (London: Pelican Books, 1951). MacKenzie's little book is a gem, offering an erudite survey of the historical development of Parliament and of how and why it works as it does.

12. Quoted in the *New York Times,* September 9, 1983.

13. Ibid.

14. See Richard Fenno, *Home Style* (Boston: Little, Brown, 1978).

15. Quoted in Martin Tolchin, "Personality Put First in Congress," *New York Times,* September 4, 1983.

16. Ibid.

17. David Mayhew, *The Electoral Connection* (New Haven, Conn.: Yale University Press, 1975).

18. Michael Malbin, *Unelected Representatives: Comgressional Staff and the Future of Representative Government* (New York: Basic Books, 1980). See also Harrison W. Fox and Susan Webb Hammond, *Congressional Staffs* (New York: Free Press, 1977).

19. Bernard Asbell, *The Senate Nobody Knows* (New York: Doubleday, 1978), p. 210. See also Elizabeth Drew, *Senator* (New York: Simon and Schuster, 1979).

20. Asbell, *Senate Nobody Knows,* pp. 210–11.

21. Ibid., p. 211.

22. Thoms M. Franck and Edward Weisband, *Foreign Policy by Congress* (New York: Oxford University Press, 1978).

23. Two recent studies by well-established senior political scientists argue that Congress has been in a state of resurgence since the 1970s and that its internal workings reveal not simply wheeling and dealing, but actions taken to serve the common good. See James Sundquist, *The Decline and Resurgence of Congress* (Washington, D.C.: Brookings Institution, 1981), and Arthur Maas, *Congress and the Common Good* (New York: Basic Books, 1983).

24. See Richard Rose, *Politics in England,* 3rd ed. (Boston: Little, Brown, 1980), for an intelligent and up-to-date discussion of the influential role that Whitehall (the civil service) plays in British policymaking.

25. *Political Britain* (London: *Economist* Newspapers, 1976), p. 7.

26. Ibid.

27. S. E. Finer and Michael Steed, "Politics of Great Britain," in Roy C. Macridis, ed., *Modern Political Systems: Europe,* 4th ed. (Englewood Cliffs, N.J.: Prentice-Hall, 1978), p. 81.

28. See William M. Lunch, *The Nationalization of American Politics* (Berkeley: University of California Press, 1987), pp. 95–130.

29. Quoted in Mackubin Owens, "Micromanaging the Defense Budget," *Public Interest* (Summer 1990): 134.

30. Recent studies suggest that the similarities between national legislators in the United States and Great Britain may be greater than once thought and that they include looking after the interests of the people back home. See especially "The House Is Not a Home: MP's and Their Constituencies," Bruce E. Cain, John A. Ferejohn, and Morris P. Fiorina, a paper prepared for the Midwest Political Science Association meeting in Chicago on April 19–21, 1979. Compare "The Roots of Legislator Popularity in Great Britain and the United States" by the same authors, published as Social Science Working Paper 288 by the California Institute of Technology in October 1979. This latter paper was presented in an earlier version at the 1979 annual meetings of the American Political Science Association. Both papers were supported by a National Science Foundation research grant.

SUGGESTED READINGS

Ashford, Douglas. *Policy and Politics in Britain: The Limits of Consensus.* Oxford, U.K.: Basil Blackwell, 1981. A well-informed American examines British government in terms of the politics of policymaking in a bureaucratized welfare state.

Beer, Samuel. *Britain against Itself: The Political Contradictions of Collectivism.* New York: Norton, 1982. A noted American authority on British politics describes a system undergoing profound change.

Cain, B., J. Ferejohn, and M. Fiorina. *The Personal Vote: Constituency Service and Electoral Independence*. Cambridge, Mass.: Harvard University Press, 1987. A beautifully disciplined study of the ways in which the imperatives of constituency service drive the congressional process in subtle ways. Published well before the savings and loan scandals broke.

Fenno, Richard, Jr. *Home Style*. Boston: Little, Brown, 1978. An informed view of the importance of the local constituency to the national legislator.

Fiorina, M. P. *Congress: Keystone of the Washington Establishment,* rev. ed. New Haven, Conn.: Yale University Press, 1989. A very perceptive work on Congress *within* the system; established now as a minor classic.

Longley, L. D., and Oleszek, W. J. *Bicameral Politics: Conference Committees in Congress*. New Haven, Conn.: Yale University, 1989. The first really thorough study of a crucial aspect of the congressional process: the dynamics of conflict in the conference committees that "hammer out" differences between House and Senate versions of legislation.

Malbin, Michael. *Unelected Representatives: Congressional Staff and the Future of Representative Government*. New York: Basic Books, 1980. Case studies illustrating how powerful and diverse staff influence is within the policymaking processes of Congress.

Mann, Thomas, and Norman J. Ornstein. *The New Congress*. Washington, D.C.: American Enterprise Institute, 1981. Two Washington-based political scientists describe the inner workings of the contemporary Congress.

Ornstein, N. J., ed. *The Role of the Legislature in Western Democracies*. Washington, D.C.: American Enterprise Institute, 1981. A useful collection of comparative essays.

Parker, G. R. *Characteristics of Congress: Patterns in Congressional Behavior*. Englewood Cliffs, N.J.: Prentice-Hall, 1989. One of the best recent studies in the behavioral tradition.

Ripley, R. B. *Congress: Process and Policy,* 4th ed. New York: W. W. Norton, 1988. Perhaps the best general survey work available.

Rose, Richard. *Politics in England: An Interpretation for the 1980's,* 3rd ed. Boston: Little, Brown, 1980. A solid text on British politics and policymaking revised for the present decade.

Sundquist, James. *The Decline and Resurgence of Congress*. Washington, D.C.: Brookings Institution, 1981. A detailed analysis of the role of Congress in national policymaking, looking toward a resurgence of congressional influence in the 1980s.

9

Bureaucracies and Politics

In a modern state the actual ruler is necessarily and unavoidably the bureaucracy.

—Max Weber

The budget, for all its intimidating detail, might be seen . . . as the Ultimate Cookie Monster. Its excessive tendencies toward consumption are not exactly ennobling. (It does not ordinarily present itself as seriously concerned with investment.) But at the same time, its underlying motivation is clearly not malevolent. What harm it may cause is largely unintended. Its massive presence might be understood as little more than a compilation of cookies received, cookies crumbled, and crumbs spewed forth.

—Richard G. Darman
President George Bush's budget director

Delegation . . . was Reagan's Achilles heel. Reagan's practice was to make decisions on the basis of the options his aides presented to him. He did not question those options, or seek to refine and shape them himself. Therefore when he had competent aides, as in his first term, things tended to go well. When his aides were deficient, as in the case of the triumvirate of Donald Regan, John Poindexter and Oliver North, the results could be catastrophic.

—Fred I. Greenstein

THE BUREAUCRACY PROBLEM

Like many Americans, you may not have a favorable view of bureaucracy. Perhaps you would prefer not being labeled a "bureaucrat." The chances are excellent, however, that sooner or later you will find yourself employed in a bureaucracy. At present, nearly one American worker in every six is employed by a government organization. Many others have jobs that depend directly or indirectly on public funds. Many more spend their entire working careers inside the huge organizations of the modern business corporation, including the multinationals. These, too, are bureaucracies. As you know, colleges and universities are bureaucratized. So are churches and trade unions. Many farms are owned and operated by gigantic agribusiness combines. Unless you expect to be a poet or a basketweaver, your chances of joining the ranks of bureaucratic society are excellent.

Organization in our age equals *bureaucracy*. Bureaucracy provides a way of getting things done in a complex technological and interdependent mass society. It provides a way of getting goods made. General Motors is a huge, bureaucratized, industrial corporation capable of mass-producing complex machines. Bureaucracies offer a way of getting huge quantities of items distributed. The U.S. Postal Service has more employees than General Motors—more than half a million—and distributes several billion pieces of mail a year. It is a public corporation.

Bureaucracy is also a way of governing. As we noted in Chapter 7, the presidency has been bureaucratized. Presidential leadership is filtered through a small set of specialized bureaucracies such as the White House staff and the Office of Management and Budget. Congress is becoming increasingly bureaucratized. The huge bureaucracies of the great federal departments—Defense, Health and Human Services (HHS), Transportation, Housing and Urban Development (HUD), and so on—now constitute a fourth major branch of government rivaling the presidency, Congress, and the courts in terms of influence exerted on public policy.

Many of the forces, such as industrialization, rapid technological change, and centralization, that have helped make this century the age of the executive (as discussed in Chapter 7) have in turn transformed contemporary society into the bureaucratized society. Wherever we turn today—whether it be toward Russia, France, Great Britain, China, India, or the United States—we find large bureaucratic organizations, both private and public, dominating the landscape.

But, you may ask, hasn't bureaucracy been around for a long time? After all, the ancient Roman Empire was administered by bureaucrats. Pontius Pilate was a Roman bureaucrat. The Roman Catholic Church has been administered by a clerical bureaucracy for centuries. Czarist Russia contained a huge and cumbersome bureaucracy long before the Communist oligarchs established the contemporary bureaucratic empire we know as the former USSR.

The important difference is that bureaucracy in the late twentieth century is tied directly to technology and to mass society in the postindustrial era. Contemporary bureaucracy has developed as an *organizational response*—as a means of dealing with bewildering complexity in a world of rapid and incessant technological change. Bureaucracy is no longer simply a set of arrangements, procedures, and people for implementing and administering public policy. At present, large public bureaucracies also play a major role in initiating new programs and policies. In short, bureaucracy has become an important policymaker, as well as a policy implementer. And like other policymakers, bureaucracy is engaged in the conflicts and struggles of contemporary politics. Bureaucratic organizations exert enormous power over the lives of ordinary people.

Hence we have the phenomenon best known as "bureaucratic politics." A major portion of this chapter will address this subject. But first we need to understand the elements of bureaucratic organization.

BUREAUCRACY AS ORGANIZATION

Bureaucratic organization is hierarchical. There is an ordered structure of ranks from the top of the organization down to the bottom level. Bureaucratic organizational charts are typically pictured as pyramids, with the command posts at the apex. The theory holds that commands move downward through this structure while responsibility moves upward.

The basic organizing principle of a bureaucracy is a high degree of *specialization of function* based on an elaborate division of labor. Thus the U.S. Bureau of Labor Statistics does nothing but compile and refine "labor statistics." However, this responsibility includes categories as diverse as monthly figures on unemployment rates and the cost-of-living index. Those statisticians who help calculate the monthly rates of unemployment live in a world of statistics vastly different from that of their colleagues whose specialty is manipulating data in such a way as to calculate rises in the cost of living. Bureaucracy is a way of responding to or dealing with *complexity and large numbers.* (Bear in mind that there are more than 240 million Americans, not to mention a billion Chinese and 750 million in India.)

In theory, bureaucratic organization provides a means of offering *uniformity of treatment* (millions of war veterans are eligible for the same benefits); *accountability* (program dollars are spent according to law and elaborate sets of regulations); *efficiency* (more than 36 million Americans routinely receive their Social Security checks each month in a highly computerized operation, just as many millions more routinely receive their income tax forms early in January each year, often before they have taken down the Christmas tree); and *responsiveness* to the needs of individuals in a mass society.

Why, then, do problems arise? Part of the difficulty is that the working elements of bureaucratic organization do not necessarily follow the lines of the organizational chart. The formal organization also contains an *informal organization,* a matter we discuss shortly. But the other difficulty is that the objectives of bureaucracy—uniformity of treatment, accountability, efficiency, and responsiveness—may conflict or may be inconsistent with one another. Or they may be honored in the breach, as, for example, when program dollars are spent irresponsibly or in a corrupt manner.[1] For example, corruption evidently permeated the bureaucracies of the former Soviet Union and was serious enough to impede program objectives.

Max Weber, a great German social theorist (1864–1920), was one of the first to perceive the major role that bureaucracy would play in this century, and he made it a central concept in his influential writings. In Weber's formulation, bureaucracy emerged as an organized attempt to maximize efficiency in nation-states during an age of industrialization. His "ideal" form would feature "subordination," "discipline," and "rationality"—all as part of the ordered hierarchy we have described. Weber was ahead of his time in seeing that the growth of bureaucracy would also pose a serious threat to individual freedom of action. He warned that "the dictatorship of the official" was gaining ground, rather than Karl Marx's "dictatorship of the proletariat."[2]

BUREAUCRATIC POLITICS

Weber anticipated *bureaucratic politics*—a subject that has become very popular with a number of academic political scientists in recent years. There are really two kinds of bureaucratic politics. The first has to do with the way the bureaucracies function *internally*—how the informal organization makes the organization work in ways never dreamed of by those who like to draw organizational charts. This aspect has drawn most of the attention of sociologists, students of public administration, and corporation executives. The second type of bureaucratic politics, which is currently fascinating students of politics, derives from the fact that bureaucratic organizations are also political actors in the larger realm of politics, government, and policymaking and that bureaucracies have *their own interests and objectives,* which they pursue with skill, vigor, and persistence in the larger political arena.[3] Later in this chapter we offer case studies illustrating important aspects of bureaucracies as political actors.

Informal Organization

The politics of the informal organization inside bureaucracy is often seen by students of administration and management in terms of patterns of *communication*. The theory holds that the chief executive at the top of the hierarchy issues the order (or policy), which is then transmitted downward through the superstructure by policy and administrative assistants to the middle and lower levels of the complex organization, where it is obeyed and carried out. As you can well imagine, this theory grossly oversimplifies reality.

A complex organization rapidly develops an informal organization, or *communications network,* alongside the purely formal structure. It may very well be that some of the top officials around the chief executive are not very able or effective; it may also be that, once one reaches the middle levels, one may find some staffers lacking in credibility. The middle level usually contains some "old pros" who have been around a long time. They have seen the bright young types around the chief come and go over the years. Besides, they have had enough experience to know their parts of the organization better than anyone else.

It may even be that the order or policy as they receive it from above has already been altered, consciously or otherwise, by the administrators above them. In any event, these middle-level old pros have a way of hearing what they want to hear and of discounting heavily what they don't want to hear from the officials just above them.

And so it goes, down through the various levels of the pyramid. It is a notorious fact within large organizations that the communication received at the operating levels is likely to be different from the one originally issued by the chief.

Put as simply as possible, the informal organization has developed its own communications network. Anyone who has served at the top of a large bureaucracy will testify to the reality of this network.[4]

The organization, with its own communications network, frequently displays a remarkable capacity for frustrating leadership at the top by altering and, indeed, ignoring orders from above. American presidents are among those who experience this phenomenon. For example, during the tense moments of the Cuban Missile Crisis in 1962, President John F. Kennedy discovered to his chagrin that his orders to the State Department to negotiate the dismantling of obsolete missiles in Turkey—orders that he had relayed 18 months earlier—had not been carried out.[5]

Bureaucratic Types

The internal politics of bureaucracy also features different types of bureaucratic behavior. There have been a number of attempts to classify bureaucrats into distinct categories. Anthony Downs offers one of the most elaborate classification schemes. He lists five types of bureaucrats. He sees "climbers" and "conservers" as purely self-interested officials who are motivated almost entirely by goals that benefit themselves rather than their bureaus or society as a whole.

Climbers consider power, income and prestige as nearly all-important in their value structures.
Conservers consider convenience and security as nearly all-important. In contrast to climbers, conservers seek merely to retain the amount of power, income and prestige they already have, rather than to maximize them.[6]

Box 9-1. FDR's View of Bureaucracies

The Treasury is so large and far-flung and ingrained in its practices that I find it almost impossible to get the action and results I want—even with Henry [Morgenthau] there. But the Treasury is not to be compared with the State Department. You should go through the experience of trying to get any changes in the thinking, policy, and action of the career diplomats and then you'd know what a real problem was. But the Treasury and the State Department put together are nothing compared with the Na-a-vy. The admirals are really something to cope with—and I should know. To change anything in the Na-a-vy is like punching a feather bed. You punch it with your right and you punch it with your left until you are finally exhausted, and then you find the damn bed just as it was before you started punching.[1]

Source: *Marriner S. Eccles,* Beckoning Frontiers *(New York: Knopf, 1951), p. 336, as quoted in Richard E. Neustadt,* Presidential Power: The Politics of Leadership from FDR to Carter *(New York: Wiley, 1980), p. 33. Reprinted by permission.*

No doubt there are people who function within organizations primarily with their own self-interest in view. In fact, Downs's study argues that every organization functions partly because the people in it see their own self-interest in the organization's functioning effectively. But these labels are merely attempts at classification. You may have known someone, for example, who started out as a climber and later decided to hang on as a conserver. These are not hard-and-fast categories in the real world of bureaucracy.

Downs offers three other types. These types are all "mixed-motive" officials whose goals combine self-interest and loyalty to larger values, but the mixture varies from one type to the next.

Zealots are loyal to relatively narrow polities or concepts. . . . They seek power both for its own sake and to effect policies to which they are loyal.

Advocates are loyal to a broader set of functions or to a broader organization than zealots. They also seek power because they want to have a significant influence upon policies and actions concerning those functions or organizations.

Statesmen are loyal to the society as a whole, and they desire to obtain the power necessary to have a significant influence upon national policies and actions. They are altruistic to an important degree because their loyalty is to the "general welfare" as they see it. Therefore, statesmen closely resemble the theoretical bureaucrats of public administration textbooks.[7]

Most officials probably seek power for its own sake *and* in order to effect policies, and they are engaging in a political process no matter whether they are motivated by selfish or altruistic purposes.

As with his first two categories, Downs is imposing abstractions on reality. Rarely does a particular flesh-and-blood bureaucrat fit one of these pure types. Nevertheless, the categories do help us explain the kinds of behavior that actually take place inside large organizations. Do you doubt that a zealot is likely to behave differently from a statesman? As we have suggested, a lot depends on *which* type is located *where* inside the bureaucracy. A zealot in a key middle-level slot may be in a position to weaken and frustrate the purposes of a statesman a level above. A climber in a middle-level slot may prove troublesome to a conserver who is his or her superior. Therefore the conserver may see to it that the climber's contributions are not widely recognized. Bureaucracy, seen from the inside, soon becomes a very human organization, and the organization shapes the behavior of the human beings who work in it.

The Pursuit of Organizational Interests

The same bureaucratic organization that has developed its own complex internal communications network and internal patterns of politics also exhibits political behavior *externally*. The bureaucracy has its own organizational interests to pursue in the larger world of politics and policymaking. The organizational interests that the Navy pursues are quite different from those of the Army or the Air Force. For that matter, the organizational interests of the nuclear Navy are different from those of the nonnuclear Navy. In a similar fashion, the organizational interests that the Department of Health and Human Services pursues are markedly different from those pursued by the Labor Department. They are also far more complex and diversified because HHS employs 100,000 bureaucrats and sponsors programs that cost in the hundreds of billions of dollars annually, whereas the Labor Department has only 18,500 emloyees and has under $10 billion of annual expenditures.

Whether the bureaucracy is as large as HHS or as relatively small as Labor, whether it deals with national security or domestic concerns, it is bound to protect its organizational turf. Each bureaucratic organization has its own set of goals and objectives, and it fights to fufill them. In order to survive, public bureaucracies need people and dollars, that is, bureaucrats and program funds—both of which are authorized by legislative bodies. It is both logical and obvious, then, that bureaucracies have a basic organizational self-interest in seeing to it that the legislature provides enough people and program dollars to keep the organization going. This basic fact of life puts bureaucracies into the legislative political arena, along with the chief executive, the political parties, and the private-interest groups. As a matter of fact, government bureaucracies often join with private groups in lobbying inside legislative bodies at both state and national levels of government. Government bureaucracies compete for resources (money, people, technology) just as private-interest groups do. The two frequently work hand in glove pursuing similar objectives.

The Army Corps of Engineers: An Example of Organizational Politics at Work

The Corps of Engineers is both a civil and military engineering and construction agency. As a military unit, the Corps is broadly responsible for military construction, military engineering supply, and military engineering training programs. As a civil construction agency, the Corps is responsible for the design, construction, operation, and maintenance of navigation and flood control improvements and related work.[8]

So wrote Professor Arthur Mass in *Muddy Waters,* a study that offers a critical analysis of the way in which the Army Corps of Engineers—beginning in the 1820s with internal improvements projects (navigation improvements of the Ohio and Mississippi rivers and the building of the Chesapeake and Ohio Canal)—gradually built a bureaucratic empire of its own, closely tied to private construction companies, labor unions, members of Congress, and congressional committees. Indeed, the civil activities of the Army Corps of Engineers now constitute the major portion of the federal government's pork barrel. Each year, the appropriations for "rivers and harbors" feature a multibillion-dollar struggle between regions, communities, and their congressional representatives for a share of the "pork." It is a weak and pitiful representative who cannot obtain a harbor dredging, a dune saving, a flood-control dike or dam, or a hydroelectric project for the folks back home. Needless to say, the corps now is virtually independent of effective control by the Army chief of staff (much less the president) in its civil activities. Putting aside for the moment its military responsibilities, it is accurate to say that the Army Corps of Engineers has become a semiautonomous operating agency of Congress. The corps is a powerful bureaucratic–political actor. Early in his term of office, President Jimmy Carter decided to oppose a number of these pork-barrel projects. This proved to be a serious error. Individual legislators and the corps fought back successfully; and in the process, the president lost some of his influence among the permanent Washington power brokers.

A classic pork-barrel project, the Tennessee–Tombigbee Waterway was completed in 1984, a decade and a half after the Army Corps of Engineers first broke ground. The waterway, intended to carry barge traffic from Appalachian coalfields to the Gulf Coast, cost some $2 billion; it runs the length of western Alabama and Mississippi—a total of 232 miles. The project survived attacks by environmentalists and by railroads competing for Tenn–Tom shipping. But it had powerful friends in Congress, especially on the House and Senate appropriations committees and subcommittees chaired by senior legislators from Alabama and Mississippi.

A bureaucracy fights hardest, naturally, when its own existence is threatened, but bureaucratic organizations rarely find their existence threatened. Most of the time, bureaucracies are involved in the politics of policymaking *so as to keep on doing what they have been doing.* This is the normal bureaucratic tendency. It is also natural for bureaucracies to want to grow and develop. Hence bureaucracy, in addition to administering and implementing policies, is also intimately involved in initiating and developing new programs and policies. In this fashion, it gains more personnel (bureaucrats) and additional program dollars. Admiral Hyman G. Rickover, a high-placed zealot type in the nuclear Navy, led the way in developing more nuclear submarines and aircraft carriers armed with ever more complicated weapons systems. On the other hand, a top officer in the nonnuclear Navy would see his or her bureaucratic interest best served by supporting the development of more guided-missile frigates or by rejuvenating World War II battleships during the Reagan era of generous military spending. In order to accomplish either objective, the admirals join forces with those private interests that build the ships and their related weapons systems. Then they work together to influence decision making within the Defense Department, the institutionalized presidency, and the Congress.

Bureaucratic Bargaining

Resources, both human and natural, are limited even in the richest and most advanced societies. Therefore, bureaucracies inevitably find themselves competing for shares of available resources. Once again, competition for limited resources leads us to politics.

In order to compete with other organizations, each bureaucracy engages in a bargaining process. Bureaucratic officials must negotiate and compromise, just as elected politicians do.

Morton Halperin, a political scientist who served at a high level in the Defense Department in the 1960s, has given an insider's account of the bureaucratic politics surrounding the development of the Sentinel antiballistics missile system in 1967.[9] This development was under way in the midst of military escalation in Vietnam. President Lyndon B. Johnson and Robert McNamara, his secretary of defense, were faced with heavy costs involved in the fighting in Vietnam. At the same time, the United States had reached the stage where technology permitted the development of an antiballistic missile (ABM) system that could be used to protect its land-based Minuteman missile sites against future attack from the Soviet Union. The military had an organizational interest in developing the new system, as did certain private corporations. But the Johnson administration was reluctant to support openly an overtly anti-Soviet ABM system, because doing so would jeopardize the president's chances of obtaining a nuclear nonproliferation treaty with the USSR. And McNamara feared that a full-scale development of the new system would escalate the nuclear arms race—a consequence we could ill afford.

On the other hand, if the administration did nothing or did too little, there would be severe criticism from the military-bureaucratic interests, as well as from those in Congress who were concerned about the growing size of the Soviet missile force.

The administration tried to have its cake and eat it too by developing a "thin" version of the ABM system, saying publicly that the system was to be designed to protect us from attack by the Chinese. The possibility of a serious missile attack launched from China bordered on the absurd, however, so this "compromise" position was received skeptically on Capitol Hill and, no doubt, inside the Kremlin as well.

Actually, the administration was finally forced to admit in congressional testimony that, in proceeding to build the thin anti-Chinese system, it left open the possibility of later expanding it into an anti-Soviet defense.

The Sentinel system, as the anti-Chinese system was called, affords a view of the competing interests involved in the decision—or nondecision—made in 1967 to build an expensive antiballistic missile system at a time when Vietnam was costing the United States $25 billion each year.

Muddling Through: Incremental Change

Once bureaucratic organizations are recognized as political actors engaged in a bargaining process with other powerful forces and interests, they are revealed as part of a complex process that is likely to be directed not by "rational planning," but through bargaining and compromise among competing interests, including bureaucratic interests. This view, at any rate, is held by those who are skeptical of rational planning.

Professor Charles Lindblom of Yale is probably the most noted exponent of this view. In place of rational planning, he offers us "the science of muddling through"—a "science" that features a process of "mutual adjustment."[10] Bureaucratic society as Lindblom sees it (and he draws heavily on American experience) is one that tends to make changes in increments, that is, in bits and pieces. Most of the time we make changes not by launching grand new programs wholesale, but by altering ongoing programs *at the margins*. And when we do launch new programs, we tend to do so tentatively and in relatively small proportions. This course of action fits in nicely with the bureaucratic way of doing things.

BUREAUCRACY IN THE UNITED KINGDOM

Do you find it hard to imagine that an analogous process may also be at work inside the massive bureaucracies of China? Or those of France and the United Kingdom—two nations in which career civil servants are known to be highly influential policymakers?

It would be a serious error to assume that a process featuring incrementalism, bargaining, and compromise is somehow unique to American bureaucratic-political experience. A study of the former Soviet system as it functioned during the Brezhnev era in the 1960s and 1970s refers specifically to "a policy process which relied decisively on bargaining, compromise, and incrementalism; by the promotion of change and adaption to new conditions by gradual and cumulative policy changes."[11]

Modern bureaucracy finds one of its best expressions in the British civil service. In England, public employees are usually referred to as "civil servants" not as "bureaucrats." The civil service in England offers a career ladder leading to positions of great prestige, as well as to power, influence, and authority. Those who make it to the higher levels are largely responsible for administering the activities of the British government, including a well-developed modern welfare state. Although the official lives of these "mandarins" (as they have often been labeled) are normally veiled in anonymity and secrecy, there is good reason to believe that the civil servants, whose authority carries to the highest levels of the government, are also influential in *making* public policy. They are more than administrators and implementers. They are a force to be reckoned with in British politics.

R. H. S. Crossman: A Cabinet Official Faces the Civil Service Bureaucrats

Unfortunately for students of politics, the British—and this includes most British political scientists—have shown remarkably little curiosity about the policymaking role of their civil servants. R. H. S. Crossman, a political scientist by training and a career politician who served more than 25 years in the House of Commons and held top cabinet posts, has helped lift the veils of secrecy and anonymity in three volumes of diaries covering the period of his service as cabinet minister (1964–70).

Crossman's experience reveals the close working relationship that exists between a cabinet minister and the high-ranking civil servants on whom the minister must rely for administration of the department. Every British ministry (department of government) has a permanent secretary. The permanent secretary is a member of the civil service, normally with 25–30 years of administrative experience. Except for two or three personal assistants (often younger civil servants), the cabinet minister—a politician and elected official—finds that the entire ministry is run by the career civil service headed by this experienced and sophisticated permanent secretary.

Crossman describes one of his first conversations as minister of housing with his permanent secretary, George Moseley, in October 1964.

[I] said, "Now you must teach me how to handle all this correspondence," and he sat opposite me with his owlish eyes and said to me, "Well, Minister, you see there are three ways of handling it. A letter can either be answered by you personally, in your own handwriting; or we can draft a personal reply for you to sign; or, if the letter is not worth your answering personally, we can draft an official answer." "What's an official answer?" I asked. "Well, it says the Minister has received your letter and then the Department replies. Anyway, we'll draft all three variants," said Mr. Moseley, "and if you just tell us which you want, ..." "How do I do that?" I asked. "Well, you put all your in-tray into your out-tray," he said, "and if you put it in without a mark on it we deal with it and you need never see it again."[12]

Minister Crossman soon realized that, if he were to have a positive role of his own to play, he would have to find ways of making the career civil servant responsive to his leadership. Otherwise, the ministry would keep on running without his leadership.

The Administrative Class

Mr. Moseley, the permanent secretary in the ministry of housing, was a senior member of the administrative class—the key to the functioning of the English bureaucracy. There are some 4,500 people in the administrative class, from junior officials to senior mandarins. A person is recruited into the administrative class right out of the university, usually with no more than a bachelor's degree. Historically, Oxford and Cambridge have produced most members of the administrative class. This base has been broadened in recent years, although Oxford and Cambridge graduates continue to dominate the system.

The administrative class does not knowingly recruit fools or indifferent students. It seeks talent—those with strong academic records. A premium is placed on ability to write and speak the English language with some distinction. Historically, the administrative class has sought generalists rather than specialists. A classics major is as likely to be chosen as anyone else. The concept behind the system is that a young well-educated amateur with skill in the language and analytical ability, fresh out of the university, can be trained within the administrative class for two or three decades to serve effectively as a mandarin when the time comes. As a mandarin, he or she will have developed the skills needed to run a ministry and advise the minister, his political chieftain.

Political Neutrality?

If this system is to work in a society that features competition between different political parties (in this case, parties that tend to disagree rather

---

Box 9-2. Whitehall: A Village

"Whitehall" is a word used to describe the center of bureaucratic-political power in the United Kingdom—the place where ministers, who are elected politicians, meet face-to-face with the senior civil servants who effectively run the government. Richard Rose, a British political scientist, describes Whitehall as being like *"a village where most people feel that they belong to a community. . . . Whitehall is in many respects a small community. . . . The people who work there spend most of their working hours together, developing an intimacy like that found within a small American liberal arts college. . . . Within this village, everyone knows or knows about everyone else's strengths, weaknesses, opportunities, and ambitions."* Rose also observes that, while ministers and governments come and go, the civil servants remain forever.[1]

The consequences for the workings of the British government are important.

"The ethos of Whitehall is set by civil servants rather than ministers, because they are more numerous as well as durable. At any time, about ninety ministers and twenty times as many senior civil servants are likely to be working in Whitehall. Of these, it can be reckoned that only a dozen or two ministers carry much political influence; they must work in tandem with several hundred very influential civil servants."

Note:
1. Excerpts are from *Richard Rose,* Politics in England *(Boston: Little, Brown, 1980), p. 99.*

---

sharply about the direction of public policy), it is imperative that the civil servants remain neutral in the usual political sense. They must be as prepared to serve a Labour (moderate socialist) government as they are to serve a Conservative government. Prior to 1945, there were those who doubted that the British civil service—many of whose senior members were products of middle-class and upper-middle-class society—would be able to serve a socialist government with neutrality and effectiveness. Those doubts have been stilled by more than 30 years of subsequent experience.

This does not mean, however, that civil servants do not have their own views of where their particular ministries should be heading. Once again, we must remind ourselves that a bureaucratic organization has its own bureaucratic "essense" to protect. English bureaucracies are no exception to this rule; indeed, they were early pioneers in this aspect of bureaucratic politics.

The Department of Health and Social Security (HSS) was created on November 1, 1968, and Richard Crossman became its first secretary of state (minister). In effect, the new department combined two existing bureaucracies, each with its own essence and each with different missions and ways of doing business. Getting these two bureaucracies to work under one minister would not be easy. Naturally, there would be a civil service mandarin to serve as permanent secretary. There would also be a civil servant as undersecretary for health, and another for social security. Minister Crossman, of course, was the political chieftain and a prominent member of the Labour government's cabinet. He was a close ally of Prime Minister Harold Wilson.

Sir Clifford Jarrett, who was the permanent secretary, and Minister Crossman did not work well together, possibly because Jarrett—nearing the end of a long career—did not apparently relish this assignment. By April 1970 (with Jarrett's retirement scheduled for July), Crossman was clearly anxious to find a replacement who would be more to his liking. Seeking new talent, Crossman turned to Sir William Armstrong, another mandarin who headed the civil service. By this time, Crossman's own preference was for Sir Denis Barnes, the permanent secretary in the Department of Employment and Productivity (DEP); and therein lies a tale.

An Atypical Mandarin

Sir Denis Barnes was in one sense a typical senior mandarin, having entered the administrative class in 1937 after a distinguished undergraduate career at Oxford. This part of his history was perfectly normal. On the other hand, he was quite atypical. Brilliant and independent-minded, Barnes was known to have his own ideas about how things should be done. For example, rather than belong to one of the clubs famous for including mandarins as members, Barnes preferred a "more interesting" club—one that featured journalists, artists, and intellectuals among its members. Moreover, Barnes's wife was a successful novelist, whereas the typical mandarin's wife generally lived in her husband's long shadow.

Although Crossman did not know Denis Barnes well, he had met him socially and had certainly encountered Barnes and his handiwork professionally. Crossman seemed to enjoy crossing swords with Barbara Castle, another Labour minister. His diary reveals a number of episodes in which Crossman went out of his way to frustrate Castle's bureaucratic and political plans. Sir Denis at this point was permanent secretary in Barbara Castle's ministry. In fact, Barnes had recently been a key actor in a struggle between Castle's ministry and Crossman's.

The Department of Employment and Productivity in 1970 was well advanced in an effort to modernize itself and to improve its bureaucratic image. Formerly the Ministry of Labour, which was a small and unglamorous department, DEP saw a chance to alter and enhance its role. Sir Denis Barnes, who had served inside this agency for 30 years, was a leading figure in the transformation.

Barnes in 1970 was at the peak of his power. Sir Clifford Jarrett, on the other hand, appears as a somewhat burnt-out case. In any event, he was in a position not particularly to his liking, and he was working for a minister who did not have a great deal of confidence in him.

Fateful Meetings of the Mandarins

About this time, fateful meetings were taking place between the two ministries. These meetings dealt with the future organizational (bureaucratic) location of the Public Employment Offices. These employment offices had been lodged in the Ministry of Labour and were now located in its successor, DEP. Unfortunately, the employment offices did not mesh well with DEP's new image. Products of the Great Depression of the 1930s, they were still viewed by rank-and-file people as "unemployment offices." They were offices to which one went when out of work, or "on the dole," as the English say.

Minister Castle and Sir Denis Barnes would have been happy to have the distribution of unemployment checks handled elsewhere. Accordingly, at meetings of the two ministries—with Barnes representing DEP and Jarrett representing the Department of Health and Social Security—an agreement was reached under which the issuing of unemployment checks was eventually to be transferred to Minister Crossman's department. Minister Crossman, who was not present at these meetings, was not a party to the bargain.

When he learned of the arrangement worked out by the two permanent secretaries, Crossman exploded. His reaction is recorded in his diary.

This afternoon I found Mildred Riddelsdell [a civil servant undersecretary] and Clifford Jarrett waiting to talk to me . . . on the subject of the extraordinary joint official paper on the future of D.E.P. and D.H.S.S. We had a tremendous row and it became very clear how badly the Department had behaved. This was not just a recommendation from an inter-departmental committee because the matter had also gone to a meeting at the very top between Denis Thingammyjig [Barnes] and Clifford Jarrett. This ridiculous proposal had been supported without their speaking to me.[13]

Crossman, as minister of health and social security, was understandably furious to discover that his own civil servants, headed by the permanent secretary, had been outmaneuvered by Sir Denis Barnes and colleagues into accepting a function—the passing out of unemployment checks—that hardly added to the prestige of HSS. Worse still, the organization plan had been worked out without prior consultation with the *minister!*

The outburst recorded above took place on February 24, 1970. Several weeks later—in April—the Crossman diary records conversations with

Sir William Armstrong in which Crossman tried to get Sir Denis Barnes as *his* permanent secretary, replacing Jarrett who was scheduled to retire soon. But DEP's minister, Barbara Castle—who was Crossman's cabinet colleague and sometime antagonist—apparently would not let Barnes go.

The episode suggests that British civil servants are not mere "implementers" of policy, that the relationships between the minister and the highest level civil servants in his or her department are critical to his or her overall "success," and that it behooves the elected cabinet minister to assert policy leadership as strongly as possible in a system with an entrenched and able civil service bureaucracy. Either that or get the best civil service mandarin available!

It would be a mistake to jump to the conclusion that the two mandarins in this episode were simply shuffling papers. To the contrary, the career people who head up permanent bureaucracies are frequently engaged in bloodless conflicts involving organizational images. Nowhere is this more important than in efforts aimed at reorganizing bureaucracies—an activity very common in the world of bureaucratic politics. And this truth is as fundamental in Washington, D.C., as it is in London.

POLITICAL STYLE AND BUREAUCRATIC ENVIRONMENT

The style of political leadership varies considerably with the bureaucratic environment in which it is located. In Britain, for example, the cabinet minister is expected to realize that his or her highest ranking civil servants will not merely offer advice, but will also try to nudge the minister in directions the department wishes to go.

Professor John Mackintosh—an authority on the British government, a former member of the House of Commons, and a friend of Richard Crossman—explains it this way:

> It is now fully accepted that civil servants should recommend what seems to them to be the correct course of action. The Civil Service Commission's note to entrants says that one of the tasks of the Administrative Class is to "advise ministers on the formation of policy." Sir Edward Bridges has described how "there has been built up in every department a store of knowledge and experience in the subjects handled, something which eventually takes shape as a practical philosophy, or may merit the title of a departmental point of view."[14]

One can assume that Sir Denis Barnes in the foregoing case study was following his *department's point of view* in trying to foist the unemployment checks onto another department. Richard Crossman, a sophisticated student of British politics as well as an elected politician, surely was not too surprised by this maneuver, however unhappy it may have made him. And shortly thereafter, he wanted Sir Denis Barnes to come and work for him!

Sir Denis Barnes: British Mandarin

Soon after he retired from the civil service, Sir Denis Barnes wrote a book describing in intricate detail the struggle between three successive British governments—those of Harold Wilson, Edward Heath, and James Callaghan—and the trade unions (1964–79). During most of this period, Barnes served as the top civil servant involved in shaping governmental policy in this vital area. Unfortunately, his book—unlike the Crossman diaries—betrays reluctance to discuss the role that Barnes played in all of this, though Barnes is quite explicit about the political nature of the process he describes. Reading between the lines, however, one suspects that Barnes personally encouraged ministers (his political bosses) to develop legislation aimed at disciplining the unions. This much is clear: trade union resistance to governmental policies was a decisive factor leading to the eventual defeat of all three governments—two Labour and one Conservative.[15]

There is every reason to believe that the relationships between political leadership and the bureaucracy are greatly influenced by the nature of the political society. In the United States where presidents and cabinet officers always bring their own staff assistants with them (assistants who are *not* members of the permanent bureaucracy), the struggles between policy leaders and the permanent civil service are continuing and intense. It often appears to presidents and their key aides that it is a matter of the bureaucracy *versus* the president. Jimmy Carter had been in office less than a year when he admitted that he had seriously underestimated the independent power of the bureaucracy. As he put it,

> Before I became President, I realized and was warned that dealing with the federal bureaucracy would be one of the worst problems I would have to face. It has been even worse than I had anticipated.[16]

Richard M. Nixon, who brought about more basic reorganization of the higher levels of the federal bureaucracy than any other president since FDR, felt the same sense of frustration at times. Here he is exploding at George Shultz, his secretary of commerce (and, later, Ronald Reagan's secretary of state):

> Yea. One of the reasons, George, that you got to act on that SBA (Small Business Administration) guy—I don't care if he's a guy with eighteen kids—is that we have no discipline in this bureaucracy. We never fire anybody. We never reprimand anybody. We never demote anybody. We always promote the sons-of-bitches that kick us in the ass. That's true in the State Dept. It's

true in HEW. It's true in OMB, and true for ourselves, and it's got to stop. This fellow deliberately did not—I read the memorandum—he did not carry out an order I personally gave. I wrote the order out. . . . And the son-of-a-bitch did not do it. Now, I don't care what he is. Get him out of there.[17]

The fascinating aspect of this is that the president of the United State was reacting to bureaucratic resistance on the part of a federal officia located *not* in Washington, D.C., but in a regional office in Californi: The man who had aroused President Nixon's ire was by no means a higl ranking key official close to the center of national decision making; h was a middle-level bureaucrat thousands of miles away from the Ov: Office. This illustrates at least two important points: first, that command from above in a complex bureaucratic organization are often altered, i not resisted, by the time they reach the middle level; and second, tha nine out of ten federal employees—many of them at the middle level an below—live and work outside Washington. They live and work among th IRS agents, air traffic controllers, crop and soil specialists, census taker: meteorologists, FBI agents—you name it.

Presidential frustration in the face of bureaucratic resistance, which i common in all administrations, was well expressed by Arthur M. Schle singer, Jr., historian and one-time presidential assistant, in his insider' account of President Kennedy's "thousand days."

> The Presidential government, coming to Washington aglow with new ideas and a euphoric sense that it could do no wrong, promptly collided with the feudal barons of the permanent government, entrenched in their domains and fortified by their sense of proprietorship; and the permanent government, confronted by this invasion, began to function . . . almost as a resistance government.[18]

Imperial Bureaucracy and Public Frustration

It isn't merely presidents who are frustrated by the permanent bureau cracies. Increasingly, ordinary Americans perceive bureaucracy as : threat to their individuality. In the era of FDR, government was ofte: viewed as a solution to deep-seated problems; but today, government—and especially government *bureaucracies*—are seen as part of the prob lem. This perception is shared by leaders and the public alike.

Alpheus Mason, professor emeritus of politics at Princeton and distin guished biographer of Justices Louis Brandeis and Harlan Stone, ha: expressed his concern that out of the "imperial bureaucracy" a crisis i emerging as momentous as the Civil War or Watergate. After tracing : series of earlier constitutional crises, Mason observes,

> The great risk has always been that a drive for excessive power—or the counterdrive it arouses—will not be stopped; that one branch of our system

will cripple or destroy the vibrations of the others. . . . [Bureaucracy may offer a special case.] The bureaucracy will be peculiarly difficult to stop because it is not one of the traditional parties to our system. It was not foreseen, and therefore not limited, by the Constitution. It does most of its work in secret; it mushrooms out of good intentions . . . and it pervades the government at all levels, fusing executive, legislative and judicial functions. Once an administrative agency is in orbit, there seems to be no effective control.[19]

Time will tell whether Professor Mason's premonitions about an imperial bureaucracy are justified, but there is already abundant evidence testifying to the frustrations and difficulties recent presidents have experienced leading the nation in an age of permanent huge executive bureaucracies. If they are to be successful, political leaders must find ways of working together with the heads of the permanent bureaucracies.

The complex interrelationships between political leaders and the higher levels of the permanent bureaucracies are especially difficult to fathom in the United States because the line has not been clearly drawn between the two. As a result, permanent members of the civil service may occupy policymaking positions that virtually make them members of the administration in power. Moreover, there are others who are explicitly political appointees of the White House; such individuals may be selected principally on the basis of their expertise, not their previous political activity. These political appointees may come to reflect more emphatically the program of the bureaucratic agencies to which they are attached than the changing political needs of the White House. Hugh Heclo's probing examination of the activity of political executives in Washington argues that the high-level career civil servants and the political appointees of any administration all share an ambivalent leadership position. Heclo describes the continuing struggle between these forces as they try to develop working relationships.[20]

The pattern of relationships between elected officials and the permanent civil service is somewhat different in the United Kingdom, as we have seen, because a very thin layer of ministers at the top confronts the permanent mandarins who have long been accustomed to asserting significant influence on policymaking. In France it is customary for the political leaders in a new government to reach into the permanent civil service for top policymakers, who then became active partisan participants in that government. Thus François Mitterrand's Socialist regime relied heavily on high-ranking and able civil servants to carry out its program of internal reform although few (if any) of them were avowed "socialists."

We may assume that a somewhat different pattern prevailed in the former Soviet Union, because party leaders were also members of a party bureaucracy that ran the government on a permanent and continuing basis. The professional politician in the Soviet Union functioned entirely in a bureaucratic environment. The Soviet politician's attitude toward bureaucracy was thus bound to be different from that of a political leader in Britain, France, or the United States.

Whatever these national differences, politicians in all major countries must be prepared to deal with bureaucracy as a significant institutional force—a force that often constrains (when, indeed, it does not frustrate) political leadership.

Richard E. Neustadt, a perceptive student of these matters, offered this generalization drawn from American experience: "Bureaucracy has brought a new contestant into play: the great prospective struggle is between entrenched officialism and politicians everywhere."[21]

Everywhere? This covers a lot of ground. But it certainly applies in the United States and Great Britain, and it probably applies in Russia and China as well, to say nothing of Germany, France, Sweden, Canada, and elsewhere.

What do you think? What are the implications? Especially, what are the implications for "democratic" control over those who exercise political, economic, and military power?

GROWTH OF BUREAUCRACIES

Although probably no one understands all the implications of bureaucracies' steady growth, we suggest three adaptational effects that seem especially important to students of politics. Bureaucracies affect human behavior while raising important questions about responsibility and the exercise of authority.

Ways of Adapting

We human beings are extremely adaptable. If we live in a society dominated by huge organizations—bureaucracies—then we find ways of adapting. Robert Presthus, a profound student of *the organizational society,* as he labels it, believes that such adaptation has already taken place. More and more of us spend our working lives inside these large organizations with their bureaucratic structures, procedures, and politics. But we don't all take to them in the same way. Presthus describes three basic types who display strikingly different patterns of adjustment to work and life inside this organizational society.[22]

The Indifferents

Many people are basically indifferent to working inside huge bureaucracies. Indifference or withdrawal is the typical pattern of accommodation for the majority of organization people, according to Presthus. The *ndifferents* are found chiefly among the great mass of waged and salaried employees. Many of these people are shut off from real participation in centralized decision making. They come to work, do their jobs, and go home. They are frequently discouraged by the work itself, which is characterized by machine processing and assembly-line methods. Their real interests have all been redirected toward off-the-job satisfactions.

Many of the indifferents have working-class and lower-middle-class backgrounds. They do not necessarily share middle-class and upper-middle-class values; they are often able to separate their work experience from their personal lives *outside* the organization. Presthus sums up their attitude this way:

Indifferents . . . tend to find their real satisfactions in extravocational activities. While the upward-mobile "carries his job home with him," indifferents separate their work from their "personal" experiences and work is often repressed as something unpleasant. The pay check is what counts.[23]

The Upward-Mobiles

The *upward-mobiles* thrive in the organizational society, and they are the ones who make it go. They contrast sharply with the indifferents in class background, attitudes toward work, and personal satisfactions.

The upward-mobiles, Presthus says, are chiefly products of the middle class and especially the upper middle class. Many of them are graduates of elite institutions of higher learning. They are certainly not indifferent toward large organizations. Indeed, they have adapted to them very nicely. They are the "winners." As Presthus notes, "Upward-mobiles are typically distinguished by high morale; their level of job satisfaction is high."[24]

Identifying their own personal goals with those of the organization, they derive strength from their involvement. In return, they reap a disproportionate share of the organization's rewards in power, income, and ego-reinforcement. They are loyal to the organization and are highly sensitive to status and power. Their personal lives are closely tied to work and career objectives. They want to succeed in the organization, and they often do. Summing them up, Presthus observes,

Despite any conflict between their personalities and their roles, upward-mobiles are characterized by an ability to overcome doubt and ambivalence. They do not perfect causes, and their devotion to prestige and power characteristically enables them to reach a satisfactory personal accommodation. This is putting the matter too negatively, however; it is clear that they find the bureaucratic situation congenial, and that they can often adapt with relatively little strain.[25]

There is little reason to doubt that the upward-mobiles will continue to flourish in a bureaucratic society. Organizational society breeds its own organizational men and women.

The Ambivalents

Although many workers remain indifferent toward large organizations in which they work, and though many executives, administrators, and technicians are happy upward-mobiles, there are a good many others who remain ambivalent. Their feelings about working and living in a bureaucratic setting are decidedly mixed, and so too is their essential pattern of accommodation.

Presthus finds this "disenchanted minority" to be both creative and anxious; these *ambivalents* hold personal values that frequently conflict with bureaucratic claims for authority and adaptability.

> While the upward-mobile finds the organizational congenial, and the indifferent refuses to become engaged, ambivalents are a small residual category who can neither reject its promise of success and power, nor play the roles required to compete for them.[26]

The ambivalent minority nevertheless plays an important role. Intellectual by nature, honoring knowledge, skill, and theory, these people are sensitive to the need for change in a rapidly changing world.

But they are not happy. They tend to distrust the upward-mobiles in authority above them. Their personal lives are often marked by anxiety and ill ease. As Presthus puts it, "they care too much, but can do too little" in a bureaucratic setting. "Alienated by bureaucratic conditions and by their own distortions of them, they can find little satisfaction in work."[27]

The implications for politics in a bureaucratic society are quite real. A large body of citizens is likely to feel cut off from participation in centralized decision making. A creative minority, sensitive to the need for change, feels frustrated and alienated from the larger organizational purposes. Meanwhile, those who have adapted readily to the bureaucratic setting find success and a sense of personal achievement in making the system work. How do you think you will adjust to a position in our organizational society? Will you be an upward-mobile, an indifferent, or an ambivalent? Or some combination?

Iron Triangles and Issue Networks

In the United States, the growth of bureaucracy has been accompanied by the rise and proliferation of subsystems. This fragmentation of policy making has rendered control by the citizenry even more difficult.

Dwight D. Eisenhower was the first president to call attention to an *iron triangle* ("the military–industrial complex," as he labeled it), and he waited until his farewell address to do so. He was referring to the linkage of the Pentagon with defense contractors (such as General Dynamics, Lockheed, and Electric Boat) and the supporting congressional committees and subcommittees. In the decades since Eisenhower issued his warning that this powerful subsystem might veer out of control, the steady expansion of the policy agenda has given rise to any number of these iron triangles: health, welfare, education, environment, and so on. More recently, Hugh Heclo has argued that the concept of the iron triangle "is not so much wrong as disastrously incomplete."[28] He finds relatively open networks of policy specialists (technocrats) who move with a certain nimbleness of tread back and forth among the bureaucratic agencies, the staffs of Congress, private think tanks and interest-groups, corporations, and major law firms. Most of the issue-network people are anonymous so far as the general public is concerned.
This is Heclo's view:

> The notion of iron triangles and subgovernments presumes small circles of participants who have succeeded in becoming largely autonomous. Issue networks, on the other hand, comprise a large number of participants with quite variable degrees of mutual commitment or of dependence on others in their environment; in fact it is almost impossible to say where a network leaves off and its environment begins. Iron triangles and subgovernments suggest a stable set of participants coalesced to control fairly narrow public programs which are in the direct economic interest of each party to the alliance. Issue networks are almost the reverse image in each respect. Participants move in and out of the networks constantly.[29]

Whether we describe them as "iron triangles" or "issue networks," these institutional by-products of a bureaucratized society clearly create new problems for those who think "the people" ought to be in a position to control those who wield power.

The Twilight of Authority

Robert Nisbet, a distinguished sociologist, has written compellingly of the "twilight of authority." In his view, the bureaucratization of our society (characterized by the permanent military state, the permanent welfare state, and the proliferation of iron triangles and issue networks) has been accompanied by an ominous decline in legitimate authority. He cites the widespread decline of credibility in government leadership and government institutions during a period when, as he puts it, the walls of politics appear to be tumbling.

Large-scale government, with its passion for equalitarian uniformity, has prepared our minds for uses of power, for invasions of individual privacy, and for the whole bureaucratization of the spirit that Max Weber so prophetically identified as the disease of modernity.[30]

When established authority lacks credibility, who will oppose the momentum of the bureaucracies? The upward-mobiles? The indifferents? The ambivalents? What can be done to make a bureaucratic system function better? What can be done to bring bureaucracy, iron triangles, and issue networks within the control of the general citizenry or even within the control of elected political leaders?

The Need for Better People

One obvious approach is to attract able people into the bureaucratic organization. If upward-mobiles see the government bureaucracy as an attractive career possibility, it is not impossible to put this strategy into effect. In Great Britain, the administrative class of the civil service enjoys great prestige, and recruitment from the leading universities remains highly competitive. There probably was no way to pursue a political career in the former USSR *except* through the various bureaucracies. With nearly 20 million local, state, and federal public servants in the United States, we are bound to attract some talent, as well as more than a little mediocrity.

James Q. Wilson has posed the basic problem, at least as we experience it in the United States: there simply isn't enough administrative talent to go around. As he puts it, "The supply of able, experienced executives is not increasing nearly as fast as the number of problems being addressed by public policy."[31]

Furthermore, in this country many able and experienced executives work for our large private organizations—especially the industrial and financial corporations. Their administrative talent is only rarely used for public purposes. And those appointed to public positions on the basis of their expertise may not be attuned to the nuances of political change.

The Need for Clearer Objectives

Another approach assumes that a more efficient bureaucracy would be more to our liking. Wilson and others have suggested that, because talent is scarcer than money, we have to be clearer about what it is we are trying to accomplish. Wilson believes that "coping with the bureaucracy problem is inseparable from rethinking the objectives of the programs in question."[32] This is easier said than done in a political context as fragmented as ours. The idea of a political process in which program objectives are rethought systematically and rationally is attractive in theory. However, we are not able to point to a national society today in which such a laudable procedure is carried out.

Efforts to Reorganize

What does happen in the real world of bureaucracy and bureaucratic politics, we suggest, is that very often, when faced with "the bureaucracy problem," political leaders try to *reorganize* the bureaucratic structures.

Starting with FDR, every American president has made an effort in this direction—some more seriously than others. Two recent attempts were launched by Richard M. Nixon and Jimmy Carter.

Nixon's major reorganization effort was directed toward the institutionalized presidency. The one lasting result of this effort is the Office of Management and Budget. OMB, which replaced the old Bureau of the Budget, is a somewhat larger staff agency with a broadened charter; but there is little evidence to suggest that OMB is any more "effective" than its predecessor. President Nixon also entertained the idea of creating a number of superdepartments that would combine existing Cabinet agencies, but this scheme was an early casualty of the Watergate era.

As a candidate in 1976, Jimmy Carter made a point of emphasizing the need to reorganize the federal bureaucracy. This may have been the first time "bureaucratic reorganization" was exploited as a major theme in a presidential campaign. Carter's record in office produced at least two major reorganizations: the creation of the Department of Energy and the Department of Education. The first was accomplished after an intense political struggle, by taking a wide scattering of bureaucratic agencies dealing with this or that aspect of energy and combining them into one department employing 18,000 people and operating on a budget of some $10 billion. The new department, which came into being in August 1977, was headed originally by an experienced Washington superbureaucrat, Dr. James Schlesinger. The reorganization did not, however, solve the nation's energy problem, nor did it provide long tenure for Dr. Schlesinger, who was fired by the president in the summer of 1979.

In addition, President Carter carved a Department of Education out of the former Department of Health, Education, and Welfare (HEW). He also effected a reorganization that combined the activities of the U.S. Information Agency with those of the cultural and educational arm of the State Department. In effect, the new Department of Education transferred some $20 billion of program activity from HEW and placed it in still another new Cabinet-level department. But the existing educational programs continued, and many of the political executives chosen to manage the new department were veterans of the old Office of Education.

These recent events in this country, and Minister Crossman's experience in Britain discussed earlier in this chapter, suggest that reorganization is no panacea. Reorganization often tends merely to mask the powerful force that bureaucratic momentum exerts in keeping programs and bureaus going indefinitely.

The Reagan administration arrived in Washington in 1981 committed to do battle against "the bureaucracy." Under the provisions of the Civil Service Reform Act of 1978 (a Carter-era measure), career bureaucrats had been encouraged to shift from regular government service (GS) grades into a new senior executive service (SES). There were to be special pay provisions for SES executives; and in return, it was agreed that these top bureaucrats could be transferred to new jobs within their agencies once a new administration had been in place for 120 days. The Reagan White House made extensive use of these transfer powers and labored diligently to fill as many positions as possible with persons sympathetic to the administration's agenda. While this seems to have engendered greater bureaucratic responsiveness to the president, it has had costs in terms of top personnel leaving government after being transferred.[33] And the Reagan administration was never able to deliver on the president's campaign pledge to shrink the federal bureaucracy by eliminating the Department of Energy and the Department of Education, and folding their responsibilities back into other departments.

As in all other respects, the Bush administration's approach was less confrontational. (Indeed, it could afford to be since the bureaucratic ground had already been broken for it.) But the style of Bush's Office of Management and Budget, under Richard Darman, indicated the administration's determination both to direct the executive bureaucracy and to fend off congressional efforts at "micromanagement." President Clinton's choice of a well-respected former member of Congress, Leon Panetta, as his Budget Chief, may or may not lead to better relations between the White House and Capitol Hill on issues of fiscal policy.

SUMMARY

We live in an age of bureaucratic organizations based on specialization of functions, elaborate division of labor, and hierarchical structures. These bureaucracies offer uniformity of treatment, accountability, and efficiency; they are also supposed to be responsive to the individual needs of large numbers of people.

Actually, bureaucracies possess informal as well as formal organizations, and familiarity with these informal patterns is crucial to understanding the communications flow within a large organization.

The term *bureaucratic politics* refers to the internal processes by which people within these large organizations pursue their own interests and objectives. It also refers to the fact that public bureaucracies have their own organizational interests, which they promote in the larger arena of governmental decision making. They institute as well as implement public policies. They engage in political conflict.

Bureaucrats have been divided into several categories: climbers, conservers, zealots, advocates, and statesmen.

Because bureaucracies are participants in a complex bargaining process, elected officials at the top frequently find themselves bargaining with permanent members of the bureaucracy who may be resisting—as well as implementing—policy leadership. This is true, for example, in the United Kingdom as well as in the United States.

Individuals adapt differently to living and working in an organizational society. Robert Presthus, a respected authority, divides people into upward-mobiles, ambivalents, and indifferents, depending on the nature of their general adaptation to life and work within large organizations.

In any event, bureaucracy is here to stay as long as we have an industrialized society driven by the imperatives of modern technology— a society in which struggling interests severely challenge our ability to control conflict. It is no longer possible to think seriously about politics without addressing the fact that bureaucracy has become a prime political force in contemporary society.

NOTES

1. See James Q. Wilson, "The Bureaucracy Problem," *Public Interest,* no. 6 (Winter 1967).

2. See W. J. Mommsen, *The Age of Bureaucracy* (New York: Harper and Row, 1974). This book offers perspectives on Weber's political sociology that combine great scholarship with an attempt to make Weber understandable to the intelligent lay person.

3. Anthony Downs, *Inside Bureaucracy* (Boston: Little, Brown, 1966), offers a complete survey of the massive body of technical literature available about the internal "life" of bureaucracy. For an introduction to bureaucracy in relation to politics, see Francis E. Rourke, *Bureaucracy, Power in National Politics: Introductory Readings in American Politics,* 3rd ed. (Boston: Little, Brown, 1978).

4. One of the best and earliest treatments of this informal communications network is put forth in Chester Barnard, *Functions of the Executive* (Cambridge, Mass.: Harvard University Press, 1942). Barnard was a corporate executive who also had experience in public service. Compare F. Gordon Tullock, *The Politics of Bureaucracy* (Washington, D.C.: Public Affairs Press, 1965), pp. 137–41. Tullock finds that officials tend to distort information passing through them *upward* in a bureaucratic hierarchy.

5. See Robert F. Kennedy, *Thirteen Days* (New York: Norton, 1971), pp. 72–73; with an afterword by Richard E. Neustadt and Graham T. Allison.

6. Downs, *Inside Bureaucracy,* p. 88.

7. Ibid., pp. 88–89.

8. Arthur Mass, *Muddy Waters: The Army Engineers and the Nation's Rivers* (Cambridge, Mass.: Harvard University Press, 1951), p. 21.

9. For a full account, see Morton Halperin, with the assistance of Priscilla Clapp and Arnold Kanter, *Bureaucratic Politics and Foreign Policy* (Washington, D.C.: Brookings Institution, 1974).

10. Charles E. Lindblom, "The Science of Muddling Through," *Public Administration Review,* 19 (1959): 79–88. For a further treatment, see his *The Intelligence of Democracy* (New York: Free Press, 1965).

11. Seweryn Bialer, "The Political System," in Robert F. Byrnes, ed., *After Brezhnev* (Bloomington: University of Indiana Press, 1983).

12. Richard Crossman, *The Diaries of a Cabinet Minister* (New York: Holt, 1975), p. 22.

13. Ibid., vol, 3, *1968–1970,* p. 833.

14. John P. Mackintosh, *The British Cabinet,* 2nd ed. (London: Stevens and Sons, 1968), p. 535.

15. Denis Barnes and Eileen Reid, *Governments and Trade Unions: The British Experience, 1964–79* (London: Heinemann Educational Books, 1980).

16. Quoted in Robert E. DeClerico, *The American President,* 2nd ed. (Englewood Cliffs, N.J.: Prentice-Hall, 1983), p. 112.

17. Ibid., pp. 112–13.

18. Arthur M. Schlesinger, Jr., *A Thousand Days* (Boston: Houghton Mifflin, 1964), p. 681.

19. Alpheus Mason, in an interview with William McCleary, *Princeton Alumni Weekly,* January 15, 1979, p. 14.

20. Hugh Heclo, *A Government of Strangers: Executive Politics in Washington* (Washington, D.C.: Brookings Institution, 1977).

21. Richard E. Neustadt, "Politicians and Bureaucrats," in David B. Truman, ed., *The Congress and America's Future* (Englewood Cliffs, N.J.: Prentice-Hall, 1965), p. 119.

22. Robert Presthus, *The Organizational Society,* rev. ed. (New York: St. Martin's, 1978).

23. Ibid., p. 204.

24. Ibid., p. 151.

25. Ibid., p. 183.

26. Ibid., p. 228.

27. Ibid., p. 251.

28. Hugh Heclo, "Issue Networks and the Executive Establishment," in Anthony King, ed., *The New American Political System* (Washington, D.C.: American Enterprise Institute, 1978), p. 100.

29. Ibid., pp. 100–101.

30. Robert Nisbet, *The Twilight of Authority* (New York: Oxford University Press, 1977), p. 227.

31. Wilson, "Bureaucracy Problems," p. 7.

32. Ibid., p. 9.

33. See William M. Lunch, *The Nationalization of American Politics* (Berkeley: University of California Press, 1987), p. 191.

SUGGESTED READINGS

Barnard, C. *The Functions of the Executive*. Cambridge, Mass.: Harvard University Press, 1942. A classic analysis of informal communications networks inside large organizations, by a sophisticated corporation executive.

Barnes, D., and E. Reid. *Government and Trade Unions: The British Experience, 1964–1979*. London: Heinemann Educational Books, 1980. Barnes, a retired mandarin, takes the reader inside British policymaking.

Crossman, R. *The Diaries of a Cabinet Minister*, Vols. 1–3. New York: Holt, 1975, 1976, 1977. A revealing inside account of high-level British politics and cabinet decision making.

Downs, A. *Inside Bureaucracy*. Boston: Little, Brown, 1966. A brilliant distillation of the entire technical literature on the nature of bureaucracy.

Fry, B. R. *Mastering Public Administration: From Max Weber to Dwight Waldo*. Chatham, N.J.: Chatham House, 1989.

Halperin, M. H., with the assistance of Priscilla Clapp and Arnold Kanter. *Bureaucratic Politics and Foreign Policy*. Washington, D.C.: Brookings Institution, 1974. A case study of weapons system decision making by a political scientist who has served inside the Pentagon and the National Security Council.

Hummel, R. P. *The Bureaucratic Experience*. New York: St. Martin's, 1977. A good overview for the undergraduate student.

Mommsen, W. J. *The Age of Bureaucracy*. New York: Harper and Row, 1974. An attempt, largely successful, to make Max Weber intelligible for the nonspecialist.

Nathan, R. *The Administrative Presidency*. New York: Wiley, 1983. Useful especially on the early Reagan administration efforts at bureaucratic reform.

Presthus, R. *The Organizational Society*, rev. ed. New York: St. Martin's, 1978. An impressive study of large organizations and their influence on human behavior.

Seidman, H. *Politics, Position, and Power: The Dynamics of Federal Organization*, 3rd ed. New York: Oxford University Press, 1980. The author, a former high-ranking career official in the Bureau of the Budget who is now an academic, combines practical experience with theoretical insights.

Weber, M. *The Theory of Social and Economic Organization*. Translated and edited by A. M. Henderson and Talcott Parsons. New York: Free Press, 1947.

The basic theoretical statement by the father of scholarly analysis of bureaucracy.

Wilson, J. Q., ed. *The Politics of Regulation*. New York: Basic Books, 1980. An excellent collection of essays on the politics of regulation. Especially revealing is the account of the formation of the Environmental Protection Agency, written by A. Marcus.

10

The Roles of Courts and Judges

The discretion of the judge is the first engine of tyranny.

—Thomas Gibbon

The judiciary of the United States is the subtle corps of sappers and miners constantly working under ground to undermine the foundations of our confederated fabric.

—Thomas Jefferson

Let justice roll on like a river and righteousness like an everlasting stream.

—Amos 5:24

COURTS AND RIGHTS

Shortly before he took leave from the Supreme Court of the United States to travel to Europe and serve as chief U.S. prosecutor at the Nazi war crimes trial, Justice Robert H. Jackson wrote,

The American case is being prepared on the assumption that an inescapable responsibility rests upon this country to conduct an inquiry, preferably in association with others, but alone if necessary, into the culpability of those whom there is probable cause to accuse of atrocities and other crimes. We have many such men in our possession. What shall we do with them? We could, of course, set them at large without a hearing. But it has cost unmeasured thousands of American lives to beat and bind these men. To free them without trial would mock the dead and make cynics of the living. On the other hand, we could execute or otherwise punish them without a hearing. But undiscriminating executions or punishments without definite findings of guilt, fairly arrived at, would violate pledges repeatedly given, and would not set easily on the American conscience or be remembered by our children with pride. The only other course is to determine the innocence or guilt of the accused after a hearing as dispassionate as the times and horrors we deal with will permit, and upon a record that will leave our reasons and motives clear.[1]

219

Up until this point it had been the position of the British government, and of many with the American, Soviet, and French establishments, that summary execution of leading Nazis was the course of wisdom. An attempt to provide the accused with a trial would be fraught with difficulties.[2] Existing international law spoke to the behavior and obligations of nations, not of individuals. One of the major accusations leveled against the prospective defendants was that they had waged "aggressive war," and it could not be plausibly denied that this charge involved essentially a political judgment of a sort foreign to the domestic criminal codes of the Western powers. And though certain acts of the Nazi leaders were undoubtedly violations of existing German law, the war crimes tribunal was not proposing to sit as a German court, observing German procedural law and restricting itself to what was criminal under the code of the Reich. There would be an uncomfortable ex post facto character to the proceedings, no matter how fair the judge might struggle to be.

Nonetheless, the official American position—in favor of a trial despite all the difficulties—carried the day quickly. Perhaps it was easier for the Americans, and especially for Justice Jackson with his Supreme Court experience, to understand that courts can usefully function in part as political institutions while still retaining their character as judicial institutions, operating under rules, and obliged to explain what they do. To treat the matter in a judicial fashion—even if not a *perfectly* judicial fashion— might have an ultimately civilizing effect; summary executions would simply extend the barbarism of war.

THE EVOLUTION OF COURTS

In the highlands of Scotland during the late Middle Ages, the more powerful feudal chiefs (who were also leaders of clans made up of allied and loosely related families) were said to "hold with pit and gallows." That is, within their fiefdoms, they exercised what we would today call "judicial power" over their vassals and clansmen. In the event of crime, the accused might be brought before the lord or chief. That worthy would examine the wretch, make a decision on the spot, and impose sentence (death, mutilation, or some forfeiture of goods). The efficiency of the system (its capacity to deter people from committing crimes and to encourage them to keep the peace) and the justice of the system (accurate identification of the guilty and the innocent) depended entirely on the skills, character, and conscientiousness of the chief. And in any case, the spheres of authority of the chiefs were limited. The king of Scotland, in theory at least, was responsible for judicial oversight of the lords and chiefs. But communications were tenuous, the land was wild, and, as one commentator has observed, "No title to possession, however legal, was worth anything without armed force to back it, and it was in the interests of a chief to have as many followers as he could effectively muster."[3]

The obvious point here is the relationship between very rudimentary and intermittent judicial mechanisms and the violent lawlessness of highland life. But there is a subtler point as well: the judicial function was simply one aspect of the power of the all-purpose leader. Judging was just another aspect of ruling. It was the "king's peace" that was to be enforced, and judges were executive officers. In England where the medieval judicial machinery was much better developed than in the highlands, the executive character of the courts was equally clear. In addition to the king's own courts, Londoners, for instance, had available a set of sheriffs' courts and mayors' courts.[4]

The evolution of judicial independence of executive power (which we casually take for granted in the United States today) was every bit as slow and painful as the development of legislative assemblies with independent power. Historian G. Edward White, describing the role of judges in colonial America, observed that they "generally served in two capacities: as intermediaries between colonial executives and local communities and as leadership figures in the localities."[5] It would be two centuries before the judiciary of India would drive the late Prime Minister Indira Gandhi from power (albeit temporarily) by convicting her of violating election law, and before the U.S. Supreme Court would force President Richard Nixon's resignation by requiring him to surrender the Watergate tapes.

Courts perform a number of important functions. They are mechanisms for settling disputes; they define and apply the law; they adjudicate intragovernmental disputes; they operate to control antisocial behavior; and (in some systems more than others) they make fundamental public-policy decisions. In some contemporary political systems, courts do not operate independently of the executive ruler of the moment. This is true of all totalitarian and some authoritarian systems. In such settings, courts do perform such ordinary judicial functions as settling private disputes and punishing criminal behavior, but they are also called on to enforce political orthodoxy by bearing down on those who criticize the regime. (One of the surest indicators of change from a totalitarian or authoritarian system to an open democratic system is that courts are no longer called upon to perform the role of enforcing political orthodoxy.) We shall briefly examine each of the above functions.

COURTS AS MECHANISMS FOR SETTLING DISPUTES

Private Weaver and Private Ward were soldiers in different companies of the London militia. One day in 1616 the two companies engaged in maneuvers on a field outside the city, one company attacking the other's defensive position. In the course of the maneuver, Ward's musket accidentally discharged and wounded Weaver. There was no question of any criminal action. Clearly, Ward lacked felonious intent in wounding Weaver, but Weaver argued that the absence of a felonious intent did not end the matter. Ward had been careless, said Weaver, in the way he carried his musket; although there may have been no crime, Ward owed him something as a private matter. If Ward had been *negligent* in the discharge of his musket, he would then be liable for damages—monetary compensation for the injury that Weaver sustained.

This was the first English case to draw the distinction between a purely accidental injury for which no one may be said to bear responsibility and an accidental injury resulting from behavior that, although not criminal, fails to meet a minimal standard of care and is therefore negligent.[6]

Any government of a complicated society must provide a mechanism for deciding which farmer owns the field (the *law of property*), what Mr. X owes Mr. Y when Mr. X fails to deliver promised tents in time for the circus to open (the *law of contracts*), and who owes whom (if anyone owes anything) after A's Bentley has wiped out B's Subaru (the *law of torts*).

The necessity of courts to settle essentially private disputes is vividly illustrated in the history of the Soviet Union. In his classic study of the development of courts in the new communist regime after the October Revolution in 1917, John Hazard records that "a sordid dispute over the ownership of a samovar [was] . . . the first matter to come before the new court created in Moscow after the Russian Revolution."[7]

The leaders of the revolution—especially V. I. Lenin—had hoped that in the new socialist order there would be a greatly reduced need for courts and lawyers to settle disputes. Lenin's hopes were soon dashed, and the new regime was forced to develop judicial mechanisms to replace those of the czar, which had been swept away.

The point is not that judicial mechanisms for settling disputes have to be elaborate, but that they must deliver authoritative rulings in a fairly expeditious fashion. John R. Wunder has described American frontier justices of the peace at their work. He points out that the decisions of these justices were not often appealed, and he gives the example of Charles Reame, a justice of the peace in the Indiana and Michigan territories in the early 1820s. Reame was partial to "gifts" of whiskey and was given to honing his hunting knife while holding court.

> Two men appeared before him [Reame], the one as plaintiff, the other as defendant. The Justice listened patiently to the complaint of the one and the defense of the other; then rising, with dignity, he pronounced his decision. "You are both wrong. You Boisvert," to the plaintiff, "you bring me one load of hay; and you, Crely," to the defendant, "you bring me one load of wood; and now the matter is settled." It does not appear that any exceptions were taken to this verdict.[8]

COURTS AS DEFINERS OF LAW

In the United States, we tend to think of rights principally in terms of the federal Constitution. The Bill of Rights and similar provisions in state constitutions have been interpreted by our courts as providing a variety of protections for individuals against the coercive power of government. But judicially created and protected individual rights need not be a matter of constitutional law. Indeed, in the history of our own legal system and in the legal systems of other nations, many kinds of protections are created by courts for individuals and do not involve the interpretation of a basic written charter. An excellent example of such a nonconstitutional individual protection is the development of the insanity defense.

On the afternoon of Friday, January 20, 1843, Edward Drummond—secretary to the British prime minister Sir Robert Peele—was shot from behind as he was returning from an official errand to No. 10 Downing Street. Drummond's assailant was immediately seized by police and disarmed. He proved to be a Scot from Glasgow named Daniel Mc-Naughten.

It appeared after interrogation that McNaughten had mistaken Drummond for the prime minister. And when Drummond died on the morning of January 26, the charge against McNaughten became murder. It developed that McNaughten had for some time shown symptoms of serious mental breakdown. His former landlady in Glasgow reported he had repeatedly told her that devils in human forms were seeking his life, and he had shown her weapons that he declared he would use against his tormentors.

His principal tormentors, apparently, were the leaders of the governing Tory (Conservative) party—Sir Robert Peele's party. In Glasgow, about a year before the Drummond assault, McNaughten had asked the police to protect him against Tory persecution.

At his arraignment at the famous Bow Street Magistrate's Court in London, McNaughten was reported to have complained that the police "follow and persecute me wherever I go, and have entirely destroyed my peace of mind. They followed me to France, into Scotland, and all over England. . . . I cannot sleep at night. . . . I believe they have driven me into a consumption." He ended by declaring it was clear to him that the leadership of the Tory party intended to murder him.

McNaughten was represented at his trial by a distinguished barrister (trial advocate), Mr. Cockburn. The heart of Cockburn's defense of McNaughten was that his mental state made it impossible for him to understand the nature of the act he was committing. That is, McNaughten was incapable of reason and therefore could not be said to have acted with criminal intent in causing the death of Drummond. Then, because intent is an element of the crime of murder, McNaughten could not be found guilty.

The judges took a narrower view. Chief Justice Tyndall charged the jurymen that they should find McNaughten not guilty by reason of insanity if they were convinced the evidence demonstrated beyond reasonable doubt that, at the time of the act, he was unable to distinguish between right and wrong—that he was incapable of understanding that what he was doing was both morally wrong and legally forbidden.[9] The jury returned the verdict of not guilty by reason of insanity; and rather than facing the hangman, McNaughten was committed to a mental institution "at the Queen's pleasure." He died in the Broadmore insane asylum in May 1865.

Many modern critics attack the McNaughten rule (which allows a finding of insanity only when the defendant cannot distinguish between right and wrong) as too narrow. But there is no question that, in both England and the United States (where the McNaughten precedent was generally followed), this judicially created defense has spared the lives of many defendants whose crimes were committed while they were seriously disturbed.

So important has the rights-defining function of courts become in modern times that such recently launched democracies as India,[10] Japan,[11] and pre-unification West Germany[12]—in the course of drafting their constitutions—made determined efforts to fix the responsibility for defining rights and individual protections inescapably in the judiciary. Mexico has even provided a special type of "suit for constitutional protection" *(amparo)* to facilitate the performance of this function by its federal courts.[13]

COURTS AS INTRAGOVERNMENTAL ARBITERS

In Chapter 3 we discussed the meaning of constitutionalism, and we noted that it depended on the effective limitation of the powers of the state in accordance with written or, in some cases, unwritten rules and understandings.

We are all familiar with the way the Supreme Court of the United States exercises its power of judicial review (its power to declare acts of Congress, the president, and the states unconstitutional). Less familiar but equally important is the role courts can play in upholding constitutionalism by policing the relationships between parts of the state—between agencies and departments of government.

Perhaps the most dramatic recent example of a court's successfully resolving a major intragovernmental conflict was the decision of the U.S. Supreme Court in 1974 in the case of *United States v. Nixon*.[14]

Several of Richard M. Nixon's closest White House aides were on trial for obstruction of justice in their attempt to cover up the administration's involvement in the Watergate break-in. Many who followed the case closely were convinced that Nixon himself had been involved.

On June 16, 1973, a former White House employee named Alexander Butterfield testified before the Senate Watergate Committee that Nixon had secretly taped all conversations in the Oval Office during the relevant period. The hunt was on. Archibald Cox, then special Watergate prosecutor (and thus prosecutor in the pending criminal cases), sought subpoenas (judicially enforceable orders) for those tapes that were most likely to include incriminating conversations—conversations that could be important evidence in his case.

But such conversations, if they could be proved to have taken place, would almost certainly lead to Nixon's resignation or to an impeachment trial in the Senate. Nixon fired Cox as special prosecutor in an attempt to get the subpoenas withdrawn; but Cox's successor—prominent Texas lawyer Leon Jaworski—continued to press for the tapes. Jaworski was supported by the judge of the Watergate trials, "Maximum John" Sirica.

The White House—through its special counsel, prominent Boston lawyer James St. Clair—argued that the constitutional doctrine of checks and balances between the branches of the national government guaranteed the privacy of presidential conversations with White House aides. St. Clair asserted that such intimate communication was absolutely protected by the doctrine of "executive privilege."

The case was bound for the Supreme Court, and the justices braced themselves. There was serious division with the Court. Justices William J. Brennan, Jr., and William O. Douglas were eager for a sweeping repudiation of executive privilege, but Chief Justice Warren Earl Burger and Justice Lewis F. Powell wished to affirm it substantially. Everyone could agree, however, on the tapes: in the extraordinary circumstances. of 1974, they had to be surrendered to the trial court.

There were hasty and often heated negotiations, maneuvering, and sentence trading within the court. The chief justice is reported to have sauntered into Justice Thurgood Marshall's office at one point and interrupted a caucus of Potter Stewart, Byron White, and Marshall, who were tearing apart a portion of his draft opinion. Burger withdrew in obvious anger, leaving embarrassed silence behind him. "Jesus," Marshall said, "it's like getting caught with the goods by the cops."[15]

What emerged, however, was a serviceable compromise product. The Court recognized the importance of confidentiality for presidential communication with aides; it affirmed that checks and balances mandated a sphere of executive privilege. But it concluded that the president could not be left absolute judge of what was protected, and that in this instance the need of the courts for important evidence in a criminal trial outweighed the claim of privilege.

To have such an intragovernmental conflict defused by the judiciary can be important to the very survival of a political system. One of the most forceful expositions of this point came from the pen of Justice Mano Tsuyoshi of the Supreme Court of Japan. Justice Mano was writing in a 1953 case in which, for technical reasons, his court had found it necessary to refrain from deciding whether the Japanese cabinet had the power to dissolve the House of Representatives under the postwar constitution. So important was the question that Justice Mano felt called upon to give his answer to it, even though he ruefully agreed with his associates that they were not empowered to authoritatively resolve it.

> Responsibility concerning government, which is the essence of acts of state, must be borne by the several organs of the state that carry out government in accordance with the principles of separation of powers and checks and balances.[16]

Article 7 of the Japanese Constitution provided for dissolution by the emperor on the "advice and approval of the Cabinet." The cabinet could no more act without the emperor than the emperor without the cabinet.

COURTS AS MECHANISMS OF SOCIAL CONTROL

An important function of courts in all political systems—even primitive systems—is to settle questions concerning who is guilty of crime and, by so doing, to encourage obedience to the criminal laws. This has never been a simple matter and is certainly vexatious today. Sir Leon Radzinowicz of Cambridge University is one of the world's foremost criminologists. In a disturbing book entitled *The Growth of Crime*[17] and published in 1977, Sir Leon portrays a world in the grip of a pandemic of crime. Although the causes of this increase are not well understood, Radzinowicz suggests that they have to do with the very nature of modern industrialized society. Radzinowicz argues that no country is immune, and that, although U.S. crime rates appeared to have stabilized in the mid-1970s, this "stability" was at historically high levels.[18]

Rising crime rates in the United States in the 1960s and 1970s—rates that have started upward again as the 1990s began—placed exceptional strains on the American courts as the ultimate enforcers of the criminal law. Three factors seem to have conspired to create something approaching a crisis in the criminal justice system. (The situation is so bad that one wag has remarked that "the thing isn't a system, and it certainly isn't just; it's only criminal.")

First, there was an increase in population and, particularly during the late 1960s and early 1970s, an increase in the number of individuals in their late teens and early twenties—the most crime-prone portion of any population. That is, not only were there more people, but these increased populations committed increasing numbers of crimes.

Second, there was an increase in urbanization and a breakdown of such traditional "small town" agencies of social control as families, churches, and neighborhoods.

Third and finally, at the very time when more and more "business" was being generated for the criminal courts, a process of evolution that had begun in the late nineteenth century had worked itself out to a point where the American criminal trial was a terrifically complicated, expensive, and time-consuming procedure.

As a result of rising numbers of criminal defendants (and increasing complexity and costliness of trials), the American prosecutors, judges, and defense attorneys have been forced to open a "back door" in the criminal justice process to expedite the flow of business. This back door is the system of *plea bargaining,* whereby a defendant is induced to plead guilty to some offense (and can thus be sentenced without the necessity of a trial) in return for a promise of leniency in sentencing or a reduction of the original charge to a less serious offense. So large has this back door become that most of the criminal business in the United States now passes through it. Trial is becoming a rarity; it can be afforded only in the most serious, complicated, and hotly contested cases. Upward of 90 percent of all serious crimes are disposed of by inducing a guilty plea in return for some form of leniency.

Although some students of criminal justice in America have attempted to defend plea bargaining on the grounds of practicality (trials being so costly),[19] two arguments against the practice seem very powerful.

First, there is injustice at the expense of the defendant. The pressures on the defendant to "cop a plea" may result in an innocent person's pleading guilty to something he or she did not do. Another result may be that an individual who has legitimate constitutional grounds to object to the prosecution (for instance, that incriminating evidence was illegally obtained) simply gives up this line of defense in return for a light sentence or a reduction in charge.

Second, there is injustice at the expense of society. Plea bargaining clearly results in large numbers of defendants receiving less severe sentences than they would receive if convicted at trial.[20] It also results in the reduction of serious criminal charges (say, the charge of rape) to lesser and sometimes even comparatively trivial charges (say, simple assault.)

Criminal justice is a double-edged concept. It is as reprehensible for individuals to plead guilty when they are innocent as it is for serious offenders to "plead" to crimes far less serious than those of which they are, in fact, guilty.

The system of plea bargaining has grown up in substantial part because of the complexity of the contemporary American criminal trial and the elaborate and time-consuming structure of postconviction remedies (such as appeal and habeas corpus possibilities) that has grown up around it.

One student of the problem, John H. Langbein, has suggested a somewhat startling analogy to plea bargaining.[21] Langbein points to the practice of the medieval European courts of resorting to torture in order to extract a confession of guilt from a defendant. What, asks Langbein, led the medieval jurists to such torture? They certainly understood its cruelty and the risk that it would produce an unreliable confession. They were *forced* to adopt torture, Langbein suggests, because of the unreasonably high standards of proof that had previously been adopted as the criteria of guilt at a trial.

In medieval Europe, proof of guilt required the testimony of two eyewitnesses. Because such a stringent requirement could be satisfied in only a small percentage of cases, it became necessary to find a way around a trial standard that was a "voluntary' confession. Incredible as it may be to the modern mind, the practice of torture—couched in an elaborate set of procedural "protections"—was used to extract confessions and thereby to achieve a rate of criminal convictions high enough so that the courts could operate and hope to succeed as mechanisms of social control.

In the same way, Langbein argues, we have forced U.S. judges, prosecutors, and defense counsel into finding a way around a criminal trial that has become, in the search for perfect fairness, so expensive and time-consuming and complicated that it can no longer serve the society as a mechanism for determining guilt or innocence.

How to put things right is by no means clear. To reverse the trend for any social institution as important as the Anglo-American criminal trial—to take it back to an earlier stage in its development—is horrendously difficult. Efforts in this direction in Great Britain have been frustrated for more than a decade.[22] On the other hand, to jettison our inherited system and to adopt something radically different (something modeled, perhaps, on the "inquisitorial" systems of continental Europe, which relied heavily on a judicially supervised preliminary investigation) appears even less likely as a basis of reform.[23]

But one thing is certain. This generation is faced with the problem of reshaping the criminal justice processes of the United States. At the heart of that process is the criminal trial. If the courts are to perform adequately their function of social control in America, a new balance between effectiveness and safeguards for the defendants must be struck. We must develop more efficient mechanisms without regressing to an arrangement that stacks the deck in favor of the state and against the individual.

COURTS AS MECHANISMS OF POLITICAL CONTROL

All court systems seek to operate as mechanisms of ordinary social control, discouraging crime and attempting to identify and punish its perpetrators; but there is a perversion of this function with which we are all too familiar. In authoritarian and totalitarian systems, the courts are also used to support political orthodoxy.

Nowhere was this authoritarian judicial role on better display than in the People's Republic of China after the violent crushing of the prodemocracy movement in Tiananmen Square in the spring of 1989.

During the early part of the spring of that year, demonstrators—many of them students—had peacefully established themselves in the square and had issued manifestos demanding reform and democratization of the Chinese political system. Some of their leaders engaged in hunger strikes, and they had erected a handmade statue (roughly modeled on the Statue of Liberty) called the "Goddess of Democracy," which became the symbol of the demonstration.

With world attention focused on the protest and on Tiananmen Square, the leadership of the People's Republic seemed, at first, divided as to its reaction. The Communist party general secretary, Zhao Zhiyang, seemed to favor waiting and attempting to persuade the students to give up their occupation of the square. However, hardliners led by Li Peng won over the aging Deng Xiao Ping and other key members of the top leadership. On June 4, elements of the Twenty-seventh Chinese Army entered the square and dispersed the demonstrators—which resulted in great bloodshed. Zhao Zhiyang lost his job as party secretary and was replaced by a hardliner, Jiang Zemin.

But the military stage of the repression was then followed by a "judicial repression." There were large numbers of arrests by regular police—not only in Beijing, but in other cities around the country where there had been democracy protests. The judiciary—the entire legal system—fell in with the demands of the leadership that the "counterrevolutionaries, hooligans, and thugs" be "severely punished" and that "not an iota of forgiveness" be shown.[24]

Sometimes the people arrested were charged with actual violent behavior—attacking soldiers, or burning or smashing military trucks. However, the arrest warrant issued for Fang Lizhi—a prominent Chinese dissident who was given shelter in the American embassy—charged simply "committing crimes of counterrevolutionary propaganda and instigation." Nor were these numerous arrests and trials a legal bluff. In mid-June the executions began—always within a few days of sentencing, and by the classic technique of a single pistol bullet in the back of the head. *People's Daily,* the voice of the ruling Communist party, reported that "the Supreme People's Court had issued a notice urging that punishment without leniency should be extended to those who are charged in violent protests, who planned the chaos and who organized the counterrevolutionary propaganda."[25] Through the summer and into the fall of 1989 the aggressive use of the police and the judiciary to enforce political orthodoxy continued.

In some authoritarian regimes, there is a degree of sheepishness about punishing political dissent as a crime. Dissidents are falsely characterized as "terrorists" (people who commit acts of violence for political reasons) in order to make their prosecution look better. Totalitarian systems suffer no such inhibition because their ideological assumptions dictate that it is legitimate to punish people for their ideas. No one has stated this more clearly than Mao Tse-tung.

> This experience of several decades . . . tells us to put the people's democratic dictatorship [note the contradiction in terms] into effect. That is, it tells us to deprive reactionaries of the right to speak out and only allow the people to have the right to speak.[26]

COURTS AS POLICYMAKERS

This chapter began with Robert H. Jackson's explanation of why it was important to provide a trial for Nazi war criminals rather then punish them summarily. Listen again to Justice Jackson on the role of the Supreme Court of the United States in policymaking in the particularly delicate area of individual rights and national security.

> The task of this Court to maintain a balance between liberty and authority is never done, because new conditions today upset the equilibriums of yesterday. The seesaw between freedom and power makes up most of the history of governments, which, as Bryce points out, on a long view consists of repeating a painful cycle from anarchy to tyranny and back again. The Court's day-to-day task is to reject as false, claims in the name of civil liberty which, if granted, would paralyze or impair authority to defend the existence of our society and to reject as false, claims in the name of security which would undermine our freedoms and open the way to oppression. These are the competing considerations involved in judging any measures which government may take to suppress or disadvantage its opponents and critics.[27]

There is no clearer recent example of the courts' balancing of these interests than in the issue of the public's "right to know." Let us examine American policymaking in this area, and then contrast it with British policy and practice. The United Kingdom faces the same necessity for adjusting the needs of national security and democratic politics as we face in the United States, but the British do not place so great a reliance on the courts in striking the necessary balances (that is, in making policy). Furthermore, Britain has evolved policies that differ significantly from those in America. Comparing these two countries in terms of the right to know, we can learn not only about the ways in which different systems make different uses of courts in policymaking, but also about the ways in which the substantive content of policy may be affected by subtly differing conceptions of democracy.

The Judicial Dimension in America

Several of the Supreme Court decisions of the late 1960s suggested that, in addition to its protection of individuals against government interference with their speech, the First Amendment of the Constitution embodies some sort of general right to know—a right to have access to information. *New York Times v. Sullivan,*[28] which created the special libel standard for public officials and public figures, really rested on a right-to-know basis. And in the *Red Lion*[29] case, Justice Byron White spoke approvingly of "the right of the public to receive suitable access to social, political, esthetic, moral and other ideas."

Two important decisions from 1979 and 1980 further advanced (even if they did not altogether clarify) the First Amendment right to know.

In the *Gannett*[30] case, the Supreme Court rejected a newspaper publisher's attack on an order barring the public from a pretrial hearing concerning suppression of evidence in a murder case. Justice Potter Stewart's opinion for the Court held that the public had no independent constitutional right to insist on access to such pretrial procedures when the accused, the prosecutor, and the trial judge had all agreed to close the hearing in order to ensure a fair trial. Although the justices focused primarily on the Sixth Amendment provision that, in "all criminal prosecutions, the accused shall enjoy the right to a speedy and public trial," First Amendment concerns were also voiced in most of the opinions.

The *Gannett* decision was widely criticized. A number of influential commentators argued that the Supreme Court majority was wrong: some said access was guaranteed on Sixth Amendment grounds; some said, on First Amendment grounds. Particularly galling to critics was Justice William H. Rehnquist's concurrence, which assumed that the decision in *Gannett* applied to trials as well as to pretrial hearings and suggested that state trial judges had virtually unlimited discretion in closing their courtrooms.

But this was not to be. A year after *Gannett,* the Court's 7–1 decision in the *Richmond Newspapers*[31] case held that, "[a]bsent an overriding interest articulated in findings, the trial of a criminal case must be open to the public." Chief Justice Warren Burger's plurality opinion (joined only by Justices Byron White and John Paul Stevens) stated that the "narrow question" was "whether the right of the public and press to attend criminal trials is guaranteed under the United States Constitution." The chief justice built squarely on the distinction he had emphasized in *Gannett* between pretrial hearings and trials and held that the "right of access to places traditionally open to the public, as criminal trials have long been, may be seen as protected" by the First Amendment.

The significance of this—and it is very significant indeed—is that certain basic judicially created rights of access to government information operate in the United States and that, because of the position we accord to the Supreme Court and to constitutional law in our system, both executive and legislative policymaking in the area of public access to government information must honor the basic constitutional restraints that bear on the matter.

The Legislative Dimension in America

Two federal statutes—the Freedom of Information Act (passed in 1966 and substantially amended in 1974) and the Privacy Act (enacted in 1974)—created major statutory rights of citizen access to information at the federal level, and many states have enacted access laws of their own.

At the heart of the Freedom of Information Act (FOIA) is a commitment to a policy of executive branch disclosure—unless the requested materials fall within one of nine exempted categories of information. But the breadth and ambiguity of these exemptions, along with the cumbersome access procedures established by the act, came to be the despair of journalists, scholars, and civil libertarians.

The first of the exemptions was the most problematic. Subsection (b)(1) allowed for the withholding of information the disclosure of which was deemed by the executive to adversely affect national defense or foreign policy. In 1974, subsection (b)(1) was changed to exempt from disclosure only materials "specifically authorized under criteria established by an Executive Order to be kept secret in the interest of national defense or foreign policy." And it is added that materials must be "properly classified pursuant to such Executive Order."

It seems clear that, by tying the secrecy exemption to the existing security classification system, the FOIA reformers thought they were narrowing the exemption. The qualification that the materials must be properly classified seems, just as clearly, to have been intended to invite courts to review materials to determine which of them met the standard of the existing classification guidelines. The crucial question, on which debate continues today, is whether judges—first—should approach classification decisions with a deferential attitude, assuming that the classifying authority acted properly unless it can clearly be shown that he or she did not, or—second—should feel free to make their own independent judgments on whether the material at issue was properly classified.

The Executive Dimension in America

Finally, the security classification system established within the executive branch of the federal government constitutes another set of rules governing access to sensitive information concerned with national security.

It is worth noting that, until the second decade of this century, American state secrets were kept by gentlemen's agreement supported by a general provision (since repealed) of the so-called Housekeeping Act of 1789, which provided for setting up government files.

In 1911 Congress passed, and President William Howard Taft signed into law, a measure (the Defense Secrets Act) criminalizing certain unauthorized gathering of information related to national defense. This was followed and preempted by the Espionage Act of 1917, which created multiple offenses of obtaining and divulging defense information (ambiguous but narrower than information vital to "national security"). Under most of the provisions of the act, there had to be an intent (variously described in various subsections) to harm the interests of the United States.

During World War I, the Headquarters of the American Expeditionary Force in France developed an internal classification system employing the categories *Secret, Confidential,* and *For Circulation Only.* Between the wars, this system become common throughout the Army and Navy. In 1940 President Franklin D. Roosevelt formalized and extended the classification system beyond the military services in Executive Order No. 8381 of March 22, 1940. This order made reference to the espionage laws—particularly the amendments of January 12, 1938, which empowered the president to define certain defense installations and equipment that it would be unlawful to photograph, map, and observe. But this classification system was neither based on nor authorized by statute. It was an executive creation. Authority to classify material as *Secret, Confidential,* or *Restricted* was conferred on the secretaries of war and navy.

During World War II, practice bounded ahead of the formal rules once again, as the classification *Top Secret* came to be used within the uniformed services. This was the situation in February 1950 when President Harry S. Truman issued Executive Order No. 10,104. Here *Top Secret* was authorized as a designation, but authority to classify continued to be restricted to the secretary of defense and the service secretaries. However, on September 24, 1951, a year into the Korean conflict, President Truman issued Executive Order No. 10,290 to supersede Executive Order No. 10,104. This extended the authority to classify to nonmilitary agencies and broadened the category of the classification from defense information to information requiring protection in the interest of "national security." It was at this point that the classification system took on its contemporary form. Executive Order No. 10,104 also widened the gap between what is classifiable and what is protected against malicious disclosure by the espionage laws.

In 1953 President Dwight D. Eisenhower issued Executive Order No.

10,501 in response to criticisms of Truman's program. Many observers felt that too much material was being classified, that authority to classify was too widely diffused, and that the guidelines for classification were unclear. The Eisenhower order withdrew authority to classify from 28 agencies and restricted that of 17 others. Executive Order No. 10,501 also included provisions for periodic review and declassification. As a guideline for classification, the order referred to "national defense," but this term was interpreted to include "foreign relations."

The classification system was never specifically approved by Congress, although it received tacit approval when its existence was recognized in the Atomic Energy Act of 1946, the National Security Act of 1947, the Internal Security Act of 1950, and (most important) the Freedom of Information Act in 1966.

In 1972, in the wake of the furor over the Pentagon Papers disclosure, President Richard Nixon, on the advice of a Justice Department committee headed by future Chief Justice William Rehnquist, issued a new executive order: No. 11,652. This adopted the national security criterion for classification, but it severely limited authority to classify. Indeed, in the spring of 1975, it was reported that the number of personnel in all agencies authorized to classify material dropped from 59,316 in June 1972 to 15,466 by December 31, 1974. Executive Order No. 11,652 also provided an accelerated declassification schedule; but in its basic architecture, the classification system went unchanged. The disjunction between the classification system and the espionage laws remained. Critics of the system who were on the political left remained unhappy that so much was still being classified, whereas those on the right continued to worry that the system was enforced with only administrative and not penal sanctions.

The Carter administration quickly moved to replace the Nixon classification order with one embodying sharper definitions, and Executive Order No. 12,148 was issued on July 20, 1979. This Carter order also provided that the potential damage to national security had to be "identifiable" and that officials must consider the public's right to know before imposing a security classification on material.

The Reagan administration thought this overly restrictive. In Executive Order No. 12,356 of April 2, 1982, it eliminated the requirement that the public's right to know be considered as an element in classification decisions and dropped the requirement that a potential danger be identifiable—on the argument that, strictly speaking, nothing based on a political judgment about what may happen in the future is precisely identifiable. President George Bush left the Reagan order in place.

Britain, by Contrast

For most of this century, the core of government information policy in the United Kingdom was the Official Secrets Act of 1911 and the system of "D-Notices," initiated administratively in 1912, by which editors and broadcasters agreed (under considerable informal pressure) to accept "advice" to refrain from publication concerning certain defense-related subjects.

Section 1 of the Official Secrets Act was roughly analogous to the American law of espionage. It criminalized transferring official information in a manner that is intended to prejudice "the safety or interests of the State." Moreover, the information had to be of a particular character in order for there to be a crime: it had to concern some prohibited place or material that would be of interest to an enemy of Britain. Broadly speaking, the target of section 1 was spying.

Section 2, however, was very different. It created the criminal offense of *unauthorized* communication of government information, regardless of its character. It also criminalized retaining an official document in one's own possession contrary to duty. Furthermore, it was an offense for a person who had received information in violation of the act to communicate that information to anyone else.

D-Notices (for "Defense Notices") were advisories issued from time to time cautioning against publication of certain information or discussion of certain subjects. There were no legal sanctions for violating D-Notices, which the media accepted voluntarily. The system was supposed to be reserved for the protection of defense information, but this was broadly interpreted. It is clear that, although the D-Notice system was technically voluntary on the part of the press, the big stick of potential prosecution under the Official Secrets Act explained the high degree of compliance.

Throughout the 1970s and 1980s, there was highly vocal criticism of the system and especially of section 2 of the Official Secrets Act. This provision, it was argued, was so broad that civil servants could not tell what they could communicate to persons outside government and what they could not. Several major reviews of the system were conducted,[32] but consensus has failed to develop on an alternative. The Conservative government produced a "White Paper, Reform of Section 2 of the Official Secrets Act" in June 1988. This proposed narrowing section 2 by specifying three categories of information it would be an offense to disclose: (1) information provided in confidence by a foreign government or international organization; (2) information concerning electronic surveillance; and (3) disclosures of matters concerning the intelligence services by current or former members of those services. In 1989 a new Official Secrets Act was enacted by Parliament, leaving section 1 intact and revising section 2 along the lines of the white paper.

Those on the left who oppose the present Conservative government of John Major have expressed the fear that the new narrower language will in fact make prosecutions *easier* than under the old broad language—which British courts were, by the late 1980s, becoming increasingly reluctant to enforce. Critics on the right worry that any further change may propel Britain toward the "American predicament" in which any effective control of official information is perceived as a losing struggle The highly controversial and ultimately unsuccessful 1988 effort of the government to stop publication in Britain of *Spycatcher*—a sensational istic memoir by a former officer of MI-5, Britain's internal security agency—has more Britains debating information policy than ever before A new interest group—"Charter 88"—has been formed to push for a policy of less secrecy. But agreement on further reform is not in sight and *legislative* agreement is key to change in Britain.[33]

The contrast between the United States and the United Kingdom on the right to know is twofold.

First, a legislated policy (the Official Secrets Act as amended in 1989 predominates in Great Britain, with the courts playing a secondary role Professor Kenneth Robertson, a student of both British and American information policy, concludes,

> The courts in Britain have not acted either directly or indirectly as important information producers. They have not sought to act, to create or impose high standards of disclosure. . . .
> In the USA the courts have had the Constitution to rely on as a source of authority to question the operations of government.[34]

Second, the balance between secrecy and disclosure is struck significantly further in the direction of secrecy under the tidy British approach than under the uncoordinated and often unclear American approach Here, all three branches of the national government (and, of course, the state governments) contribute bits and pieces of policy and often struggle among themselves over outcomes. Is the British approach democratic? It really depends on the model of democracy you have in mind. American commentators tend to stress a broad "public right to know" as critical to the vitality of democracy and the integrity of elections. But listen again to Professor Robertson, who is British.

> A political system is democratic insofar as the government is removable as a result of periodic election, and in which the public is entitled to express political views and to organise to that end.
> [This] implies that the important factor in a democracy is the ability of the public to express its opinions. It does not imply that the public have a right to the opinions of any others, whether the government or otherwise. Given this right to express views and organise accordingly, there will necessarily be competition for office and this will force the government, or any other contender for office, to state what it intends to do and to defend its past performance. It then becomes a matter of how the competition for office is organised and how officeholding is organised as to how much information will be released.[35]

We can compare grossly similar political systems to considerable intellectual effect by examining the roles their courts play in policymaking and the differences in public philosophy that impinge on that policymaking.

SUMMARY

Just like executives, legislatures, and bureaucracies, courts perform important governmental functions and are inevitably the focus of political conflict. In this chapter we examined the dispute-settling and policymaking functions of courts. We also examined their functions as arbiters of intragovernmental conflict, as mechanisms of social control, and as enforcers of political orthodoxy. Although some of these functions (such as settling disputes) must be performed in any fairly complicated society, the task of enforcing political orthodoxy need be undertaken only in authoritarian and totalitarian systems.

Furthermore, courts in a particular political system may, at any given time, perform some of their functions well and some badly. This is dramatically apparent in the American context. In acting as intragovernmental arbiters (as in the case of the Nixon tapes), U.S. courts—and especially the Supreme Court—have been generally successful. But judicial performance of the function of maintaining order has been increasingly inefficient (reflected in the growth of plea bargaining). In the area of policymaking (as in the case of the right to know), the record is mixed.

NOTES

1. Robert H. Jackson, "Memorandum for the President," April 29, 1945; quoted in Eugene C. Gerhart, *America's Advocate: Robert H. Jackson* (Indianapolis: Bobbs-Merrill, 1958), p. 319.

2. For a work on the complexities of the Nazi war crimes trials, see Robert E. Conot, *Justice at Nuremberg* (New York: Harper and Row, 1983).

3. R. W. Munros, *Highland Clans* (London: Octopus Books, 1977), p. 22.

4. Helen Cam, *Law-finders and Law-makers in Medieval England* (New York: Barnes and Noble, 1963), pp. 85–94.

5. See G. Edward White, *The American Judicial Tradition* (New York: Oxford University Press, 1976), p. 7.

6. *Weaver v. Ward,* 80 English Reports 284 (1616).

7. John N. Hazard, *Settling Disputes in Soviet Society* (New York: Columbia University Press, 1960), p. 1.

8. Quoted in John R. Wunder, *Inferior Courts, Superior Justice* (Westport, Conn.: Greenwood Press, 1979), p. 36.

9. *M'Naghten's Case,* 8 English Reports 718 (1843).

10. Pratap Kumar Ghosh, *The Constitution of India* (Calcutta: World Press 1966), pp. 233–64.

11. Masami Ito, "The Rule of Law: Constitutional Development," in Arthur T. von Mehren, ed., *Law in Japan* (Cambridge, Mass.: Harvard University Press 1963), pp. 205–38.

12. Roger Hewes Wells, *The States in West German Federalism* (New Haven Conn.: College and University Press, 1961).

13. Richard D. Baker, *Judicial Review in Mexico: A Study of the Amparo Sui* (Austin: University of Texas Press, 1971).

14. *United States v. Nixon*, 418 U.S. 638 (1974).

15. Bob Woodward and Scott Armstrong, *The Brethren: Inside the Supreme Court* (New York: Simon and Schuster, 1979), pp. 336–37.

16. Quoted in John M. Maki, ed., *Court and Constitution in Japan* (Seattle University of Washington Press, 1964), p. 371.

17. Sir Leon Radzinowicz and Jean King, *The Growth of Crime: The Interna tional Experience* (New York: Basic Books, 1977).

18. See Jan M. Chaiken and Marcia R. Chaiken, "Crime Rates and the Active Criminal," in James Q. Wilson, ed., *Crime and Public Policy* (San Francisco: ICS Press, 1983).

19. See Thomas W. Church, Jr., "In Defense of Plea Bargaining," *Law and Society Review* (Winter 1979). But see Steven J. Schulhofer, "Is Plea Bargaining Necessary?" *Harvard Law Review* (March 1984).

20. See the data compiled by Professor Hans Zeisel and presented in Franklin E. Zimring and Richard S. Frase, eds., *The Criminal Justice System: Material on the Administration and Reforms of the Criminal Law* (Boston: Little, Brown 1980), pp. 558–61.

21. John H. Langbein, "Torture and Plea Bargaining," *Public Interest* (Winter 1980): 43–61.

22. Criminal Law Revision Committee, *Eleventh Report: Evidence* (London Her Majesty's Stationery Office, 1972).

23. One of the few American legal scholars to urge reform in this direction is Lloyd L. Weinreb, *Denial of Justice* (New York: Free Press, 1977).

24. *New York Times,* June 30, 1990.

25. *New York Times,* June 20, 1990.

26. Quoted in Jerome A. Cohen, *The Criminal Process in the People's Republic of China, 1949–1963* (Cambridge, Mass.: Harvard University Press, 1968), p. 72 On the changes in the roles of courts and lawyers in the larger process of politica change in the former USSR, see Eugene Huskey, "Between Citizen and State The Soviet Bar *(Advokatura)* under Gorbachev," *Columbia Journal of Transna tional Law,* 28 (November 1990): 95–116.

27. Quoted in Gerhart, *America's Advocate,* p. 296.

28. *New York Times v. Sullivan,* 376 U.S. 255 (1964).

29. *Red Lion Broadcasting Company v. Federal Communications Commission,* 395 U.S. 367 (1969).

30. *Gannett Company v. DePasquale,* 443 U.S. 368 (1979).

31. *Richmond Newspapers v. Virginia,* 448 U.S. 555 (1980).

32. See, for example, Chairman Lord Franks, *Departmental Committee on Section 2 of the Official Secrets Act* (London: Her Majesty's Stationery Office, 1972).

33. See David Morgan, "Media–Government Relations: The Right to Manage Information versus the Right to Know," *Parliamentary Affairs* (October 1991).

34. K. G. Robertson, *Public Secrets: A Study in the Development of Government Secrecy* (New York: St. Martin's, 1982), p. 7.

35. Ibid., pp. 195–96.

SUGGESTED READINGS

Abel, R. ed. *The Politics of Informal Justice.* New York: Academic Press, 1982. An important collection of essays on nonjudicial mechanisms for resolving disputes and maintaining social control.

Abraham, H. J. *The Judicial Process,* 4th ed. New York: Oxford University Press, 1980. A very useful introduction to the court systems of the United States, England, and France.

Bedford, S. *The Faces of Justice.* New York: Simon and Schuster, 1961. Beautifully written short description of court proceedings in England, West Germany, Austria, Switzerland, and France.

McClosky, Herbert, and Alida Brill. *Dimensions of Tolerance: What Americans Believe about Civil Liberties.* New York: Sage, 1983. An interesting and methodologically scrupulous investigation of contemporary American attitudes concerning rights and liberties.

Pyle, C., and R. Pious. *The President, Congress, and the Constitution: Power and Legitimacy in American Politics.* New York: Free Press, 1984. Some may dissent from the author's "minimalist" view of executive power, but this is an excellent set of commentaries and materials on American separation-of-powers questions.

Rubin, H. *The Courts: Fulcrum of the Justice System,* 2nd ed. New York: Random House, 1984. A useful road map of the American judicial system.

Schubert, G., and David J. Danelski, eds. *Comparative Judicial Behavior.* New York: Oxford University Press, 1969. Ground-breaking effort to investigate the processes of judicial decision making in different legal systems and cultures.

Simon, J. F. *The Antagonists: Hugo Black, Felix Frankfurter, and Civil Liberties in Modern America.* New York: Simon and Schuster, 1989. Fascinating account of the intellectual struggles between two giants of American constitutional history who had very different views of the proper role of courts in democratic political systems.

Sowell, T. *Preferential Policies: An International Perspective.* New York: William Morrow, 1990. Confronts the issue of "affirmative action" (which in many instances involves judicially crafted requirements) in a comparative context attempting to discern lessons for the United States in the experience of other countries.

Theberge, L. J., ed. *The Judiciary in a Democratic Society*. Lexington, Mass.: Lexington Books, 1979. A collection of essays on the problems that arise in connection with judicial review in democracies.

Thompson, Kenneth W., ed., *The U.S. Constitution and the Constitutions of Asia* (Lanham, Md.: University Press of America, 1988); and *The U.S. Constitution and Constitutionalism in Africa,* Vols. 4 and 5 of the University of Virginia's Miller Center Bicentennial Series on Constitutionalism (Lanham, Md.: University Press of America, 1990).

Turner, R. *The War Powers Resolution: Its Implementation in Theory and Practice*. Philadelphia: Foreign Policy Research Institute, 1983. A plea to the American courts to redress what the author considers an unconstitutional encroachment by Congress on executive power.

Wilson, J., and Herrnstein, R. *Crime and Human Nature*. New York: Simon and Schuster, 1985. Possibly ground-breaking exploration of the American "crime problem," rich in implications for social and judicial policy.

Zainaldin, J. *Law in Antebellum Society: Legal Change and Economic Expansion*. New York: Knopf, 1983. A study of the ways in which an emergent American liberal individualism resulted in the "privatization of rights."

Part IV

Problems of Political Change

11

International Relations and the Cold War Arms Race

If there were an absence of arms, you would have cause to be alarmed. The presence of arms . . . is reassuring, because it means we are prepared to defend what we believe in.

—Margaret Thatcher

The history of arms control is a history of great visions eventually mugged by reality.

—Kenneth Adelman

As for disarmament, it complements deterrence. Deterrents are made to prevent war; the object of disarmament is to reduce the risks of war. It all converges.

—François Mitterrand

With all of the heinous character of the nuclear weapon, it cannot be disinvented. And if one looks back to the troubled conclusion of World War II, it has been that nuclear weapon that has preserved the peace over those almost 50 years.

—Alexander M. Haig, Jr.

Nuclear weapons and security are not synonymous. Security becomes stronger when those weapons disappear.

—Edward Shevardnadze

Wishful thinking is equally as effective for arms control as it is for birth control.

—Caspar Weinberger

GOALS AND GOAL FORMATION

The relationship between the superpowers—the United States and the then Soviet Union—changed many times during the period from 1917 to

243

1991. Yet, after 1945, an arms race between the two countries consumed more and more resources until, by the end of the 1980s, both sides spent more than 30 percent of their annual budgets for defense. Why? What set of priorities propelled both superpowers into spending nearly 30 percent of their total national budgets for military preparedness during the 1980s? What goals do the principal decision makers have in the 1990s? What do these priorities and goals mean to each of us? How can we understand the complicated questions about disarmament or make difficult choices among the existing and proposed weapons systems? How much "defense" is enough? How can we as citizens understand the entire process of international interaction?

In light of the enormous changes in the former Soviet Union and Eastern Europe, many have acknowledged that the arms race has now been halted and the saved resources can be redirected toward other problems. Yet the process of shifting resources is very much bound up in the context of how goals can be changed within different political systems.

In this chapter, we are concerned with the process of *goal formation,* that is, the set of objectives that a government chooses for itself and for the people it governs. We shall look at the broad categories of goals that a nation can follow, look at the way some of those goals are arrived at, and judge how a country's goals can be measured. We shall also consider the international ramifications of those goals and the ways in which states—even antagonists—seek to work together in the dual process of cooperation and conflict.

In the process, we shall examine what many consider to be the most important issue of our time: the nuclear arms race, the worldwide spread of nuclear devices, and how to stop both. What elements of cooperation and what elements of conflict were present in the Cold War arms race between the United States and the Soviet Union? Can the race now be reversed? How can such competition be measured, and how can the world be made safer, or at least less dangerous? How can the two still most influential and militarily powerful countries in the world come to grips with the goals they have set for themselves and with the impact those goals may have on the entire planet even as the former Soviet Union superpower shrinks into Russia?

Before proceeding to look at the arms race in the context of goals and international relations, we begin by examining the process of goal formation itself—for goal formation is practiced by all governments, whether they control large or small populations or countries, and irrespective of their ideologies.

When we speak of a nation's goals, we are in effect talking about the goals of a relatively small number of people who are in the government, even though we often personify the political system by such statements as "China wants" or "Lebanon needs." This does not mean that the current government cannot speak for some or even most of the population of that country. In fact, the government may in practice pursue a goal or set of goals that is also the goal of its population. However, in point of fact, there are many situations in which the current government pursues international goals that may not be very important or noticeable to the general population.

It follows that international goals of a particular government may or may not be the goals of its population, and we as student/citizens are constantly making judgments about whether these coincide. It is our belief that students and professional scholars alike should look at goals in two ways. First, they ought to evaluate the *ability* of a government or nation to reach its goals. For example, we ought to be able to make some objective assessment as to whether or not Argentina can pay its international debts, or whether India can reduce its birthrate, or whether Syria and Israel can ever sign a peace treaty.

Second, we should also be able to give our opinion—which may in fact be subjective, not objective—as to the *desirability* of a particular country's attaining its goals. To illustrate, if you were looking at the international goals of Germany under Adolf Hitler, you could make an objective assessment that Germany had the strength to conquer most of Western Europe. That is, Germany had the military power and will to attain this goal. At the same time, you could feel strongly that this was not a "good" goal for either Germany or Europe.

We start with the premise that the goals of a country are multiple and subject to change and that they are often simply the goals of the principal government leaders at a given moment. In addition, we see the goals that a country chooses as representing a bridge between the country's domestic political activity and its international activity. This bridge carries traffic both ways: the domestic politics affects other countries in the world, just as the international politics affects the internal affairs of that country.

For example, the United States has followed a policy of support and encouragement for the Republic of Israel. The United States has done so, in part, because successive American administrations since President Harry S. Truman have felt that such a policy was in our best interests and, in part, because these administrations feared loss of political support among the 5 million American Jews. This goal—with its domestic implications—obviously has had and continues to have major repercussions in the Middle East and elsewhere. Moreover, it affects the attainment of other goals, such as obtaining a supply of Arab oil at reasonable prices.

You should not conclude that any country can seek any goal it wishes at any time. The basic international power configuration and the global ethos at a given moment set the limits for some goals. In other words, the distribution of political, economic, and military power throughout the nations of the world may make some policies possible while severely limiting others. For example, if the international system is *bipolar*—that is, with most power confined to two superpowers and their immediate allies—the state in question will not have the same room for maneuvering that it would have if the international system were *diffuse*, that is, with power dispersed among a number of states and groups of states.

Likewise, the prevailing *ethos* (or international sentiment) may structure the choice of goals. For example, the maintenance of the slave trade was a possible goal for a variety of states in the seventeenth century. In fact, Great Britain, the Netherlands, Spain, France, and other countries sought monopolies over the transportation of slaves as an intrinsic part of their warfare goals, and many treaties of the period specifically included sections giving that power to one state or another. Clearly, any state avowing such a goal today would find itself declared an international outcast. Likewise, the physical occupation and control of overseas territory was a goal widely held among European states in the nineteenth century. Far from being a derogatory term, "colonialism" was seen by those states as a desirable goal—not just for them, but for the territories they occupied as well. The changing international ethos following World War II, however, made colonialism and overseas occupation difficult to defend, let alone pursue.

Thus the goals that governments may follow will change over time, just like the governments themselves and the people who administer them. Yet there appear to be patterns of policies that endure over time, and the literature of international relations is shot full with analyses of the goals of nation-states. Hans Morgenthau stresses the goal of power,[1] while Raymond Aron offers the recurring patterns of "power, glory and idea."[2] K. J. Holsti is concerned with core values, middle-range goals, and long-range goals;[3] A. F. K. Organski emphasizes "power, wealth, culture, welfare, and peace."[4] Organski also lists sets of opposites that cut across these basic values: absolute versus divergent goals, national versus humanitarian goals, long-range versus specific goals, actual versus stated goals, and a seeking of the status quo versus the pursuit of change.[5] For their part, Robert Dahl and Charles E. Lindblom accent such values as "democracy, equality, freedom and security."[6]

As these writers have indicated, there seem to be patterns of goals pursued by the various countries around the world—not just at the present, but back in time as well. Before looking at the arms race in particular (with its interesting mixture of goals), we shall examine 11 major goals that are pursued year after year not just by the United States and the former Soviet Union and other major powers, but by other states throughout time and space. The following list is neither exhaustive nor all inclusive, but it should give the reader a sense of the complexity of international relations and the extent to which these reoccurring patterns influence the way the world behaves.

Survival

The first goal is *survival*—the commitment of a nation's leadership (and usually of the people as well) to the continued existence of the nation as an entity. All governments follow this goal, whatever other goals they may seek and to whatever extent the following of those goals may jeopardize the survival of their state (such as through a defeat in war and subsequent amalgamation into another unit). The United States and the Soviet Union, for example, both declared in the 1950s, 1960s, 1970s, and 1980s that the enormous yearly expenditures on arms were necessary to ensure their survival—as a country. That premise was questioned in both countries. It is important to distinguish between the survival of a regime and the survival of the state itself. This distinction has important ramifications for intrastate, as well as interstate, behavior. That is, once a state is formed, it is reluctant to "give away" or let go portions of its territory or its population. Canada tries to hold onto Quebec. Spain does not want the Basques to separate, and Iraq refuses to let the Kurdish people establish their own state.

The existence of this core value—so widely held—is a very real impediment to the establishment of new federations or unions in which a state would submerge its identity in another larger entity. It is widely believed, for example, that the various African peoples would possess more economic and political clout if the nations of Africa were joined together in a continent-wide union. Although most African leaders pay lip service to the concept of Pan-Africanism (or the union of African states), very little has come of the movement precisely because the African states, once established, have not wanted to give up their sovereignty and independent status.

Freedom

As used here, *freedom* means *freedom from the control of others*. States seek freedom to pursue their own ends without interference from other states. Because the world has become far more interdependent during the twentieth century, freedom has become a relative term involving lesser or greater room for political and economic maneuverability. Gone are the days when nations like the United States could be more or less self-sufficient and therefore free from most types of foreign interference (except major wars).

For much of our history, it did not matter who ruled the countries around the Persian Gulf. Now, the United States takes a very concerned look at the area and tries to judge which regime or which local outcome would be to the benefit or detriment of our world position.

Nevertheless, countries continue to seek the goal of freedom, at least in the sense of wanting to have greater room to maneuver (as in the case of finding alternative sources of energy or substitutes for coffee). Thus, freedom is often a function of a nation's power and wealth; a small weak country may find it difficult to be as relatively free from influence and coercion as a rich powerful country. When countries around the world complain of "neocolonialism," they are often simply complaining about their relative lack of power, and hence their relative lack of freedom.

Stability

Countries may also adopt the goal of *stability,* whereby they seek to preserve the existing internal political, social, and economic order, even though they may involve themselves in the affairs of other states. For example, the monarchy of France in the eighteenth century sought to keep its social structure intact, only to have it overwhelmed by the French Revolution. Today, the government of Saudi Arabia—although a vital force in the international community, and a country bent on economic development—nevertheless wishes to keep its deeply religious society intact. The Saudi government makes a special effort to keep 'harmful" outside influences to a minimum. Its leaders are very concerned that the social and political dislocations that resulted in the 1979 Islamic revolution in Iran do not occur in their country.

Given the dynamics of international politics, in order to achieve true stability over a long period of time it would be necessary to prevent *all* outside influences from coming into the society in question. Such a feat is extremely difficult to accomplish under any circumstances. Perhaps the best a state can hope for is that changes altering the status quo will be gradual rather than sudden, and peaceful rather than violent.

Economic Development

Economic development is a term widely used to describe an increase in the gross national product and the per capita income of a country. Governments often seek to increase their economic capabilities in order to enhance their relative position in the world order. At the same time, they may seek to obtain raw materials or markets in other countries in order to bring benefits to their citizens in the form of jobs and job security. Economic development also involves governmental support for investment in production capacity.

Economic development is likely to have a major impact on a society. It often involves the movement from a subsistence to a cash economy, and because it involves industrial development, it usually leads to the migration of people from rural areas to urban ones. Clearly, economic development has a number of international ramifications as well. Countries seeking raw materials and markets are brought into simultaneous cooperation and competition with other countries. Countries often seek foreign capital to develop their own resources. Wealthy nations may seek locations to invest their excess capital.

For example, Swaziland in Southern Africa contained large deposits of high-grade iron ore. During the 1960s, the Swazis wished to develop this resource, but lacked the necessary capital to do so. At the same time, Japan—dependent on foreign sources for its raw materials—was willing to invest millions of dollars to develop the iron ore mines and to build a railroad to transport the ore to the port of Lorenco Marques (now Maputo), located in Mozambique. In exchange for the capital for development, the Japanese received long-term contracts for the ore that was eventually produced.

Political Development

Political development is a term that achieved wide usage in the 1960s and 1970s, resulting in a blurring of its precise meaning. As used here in the analysis of national goals, political development is taken to mean *a willingness on the part of a government to change, to grow, and to be flexible in creating new political structures and processes that can meet changes in the domestic and international environments.*

In terms of international relations, political development as a goal often means a willingness to enter into a federation or union with other states. This was a goal for Egypt, for example, in the 1960s, as it was for various German states in the latter decades of the nineteenth century. In fact, the states we refer to as Italy and Germany were created in part by various smaller units that had the goal of political development during this period. For a variety of reasons, federations have not generally proven too viable during our era; witness the failure of the United Arab Republic (Egypt, Syria, and Yemen) and the breakup of the Malaysian Federation (Malaya, Singapore, and North Borneo) and the East African Community (Uganda, Tanzania, and Kenya). Would you agree that this goal also helps explain our own American experience?

Although true federations have not proven to be enduring, other forms of international organizations—such as common markets—have turned out to be quite successful. The European Economic Community, for example, has grown over the years until today it includes most of Western Europe.

Social Welfare

A government may also seek to pursue a policy of increasing the physical and psychological well-being of its citizens. It may devote its energies and commit its resources to health care, social security, unemployment compensation, and educational opportunities. The result of such *social welfare* efforts may be that the population of the country becomes healthy and more prosperous. This general improvement of the society, and the motivation behind it, may thus have subsequent international implications if the government makes a similar effort to assist other countries less fortunate than itself.

By the time Ronald Reagan took office in 1981, the American political system had—under various presidents and parties—dramatically shifted the amount of the federal budget spent on such items as Social Security checks to the elderly, welfare checks for the poor, pensions for retired soldiers and civilian workers, and health care until they totaled nearly 50 cents out of every dollar spent. Clearly, the goal of social welfare was the single most important goal of the United States, as measured by its yearly commitment of dollars. Even after Reagan's first term—despite all of his highly publicized "cuts"—this percentage of the total budget remained the same; he had managed to cut the rate of increase of those program expenditures, but not the actual amount of the total. Under President George Bush, these expenditures rose even faster.

Democratic Decision Making

Although *democratic decision making* is often referred to as a characteristic of a particular political system, it may also represent an attempt to make the system "polyarchal," to use Robert Dahl's term—that is, to have leaders chosen by nonleaders. National leaders may choose to accent political forms and processes to ensure that the system remains or becomes polyarchal. Elections may or may not be held. Elections may or may not be meaningful. But if the leaders of a particular political system choose to set this as a goal, then scarce resources—time, money, and personnel—will have to be allocated for this purpose.

Since a majority of the 155 states in the world call themselves "democratic," the term has become virtually meaningless unless it is further qualified. Therefore, for the purposes of this study, we have chosen the term *polyarchal*. Although there may well be endless debate about the methods of achieving polyarchal politics, the choice of leaders by nonleaders is clearly different from other processes such as hierarchical politics in which nonleaders do not have any say in the choice of leaders.

In addition to the element of leadership selection and alteration, democratic decision making involves the idea of "choice" over national policy. This is not to say that every public choice is made by every citizen, but rather that there are patterns of citizen participation in the decision-making process and ultimately in the selection of national goals.

Command Decision Making

Other states are run on the assumption that political power ought to remain in the hands of an elite; that is, nonleaders are told what to do by leaders, and have no say in the choice of leaders. Clearly, this goal differs from that of democratic decision making. China, North Korea, and Cuba have accented such *command decision making* in recent years. But in the early 1990s it became apparent that decision by command is sometimes counterproductive. Witness the demise of the Soviet Union and East Germany.

International Prestige

A country may look inward to itself, concentrating its energies on its domestic situation. Or it may seek influence in the affairs of others by concluding military or economic pacts with additional states. In some cases, a country may seek to enhance its international standing without a specific military or economic payoff in mind. A government seeking *international prestige* and importance will even allocate scarce resources toward that end.

Two historical examples come to mind. The first would be the regime of President Sukarno (1949–65) in which the government of Indonesia sought international recognition by attending and dominating a series of international conferences. In a somewhat similar manner, the government of Ghana under Kwame Nkrumah (1956–69) spent considerable time and money in an attempt to achieve international prestige. Despite its small size and relative weakness, Ghana spent tens of millions of dollars in hosting Pan-African gatherings, in order to gain support for those who favored Ghana's role and its leader, Nkrumah.

International Influence

As David Baldwin has indicated, if country A gets country B to do something that B would have done anyway, then this is not influence or intervention in B's affairs. It is simply a "confluence of interests."[7] On the other hand, if A gets B to do something that B would not have done, then this *is* influence.

In the international setting, states may seek to influence the behavior of others. This may simply mean the buying of more goods from the state in question. Or it may mean diplomatic support in an international forum. Or it may mean a military alliance, a change in foreign policy direction, or even a change in government ideology.

Most states seek to exert some kind of *international influence*. Libya tries to get Egypt to make war on Israel. Israel helps to bring General Idi Amin to power in Uganda because his predecessor sought to stop the flow of Israeli arms to rebels in the Sudan. The Soviet Union tried to get the country of Somalia to let it station warships in the harbor of Berbera. The United States tries to get Saudi Arabia to keep down the price of oil, or to produce more oil, or to give financial support to Egypt. All of these situations are examples of states seeking international influence.

International Conquest

States may also set a goal of *international conquest*. A government can decide that it needs to physically occupy another country. Thus, Japan decided in 1931 to occupy China and in 1941 to occupy Formosa, the Dutch East Indies, the Philippines, and Indochina, and to expand its holdings in China. Or, in another example, North Vietnam set for itself the goal of conquering South Vietnam and Iraq took over Kuwait in 1990.

Of course, states are not always successful in their pursuit of international conquest. North Korea has been unsuccessful in its goal of occupying South Korea, despite a war. In 1977 and 1978, the government of Somalia sent troops into the Ogaden region of Ethiopia in an attempt to aid Somalia guerrillas and to physically occupy the region. This invasion was eventually turned back by Ethiopian and Cuban troops.

Since World War II, there have been few cases of successful physical occupation or conquest. Most wars that have resulted in the successful alteration of a country's international standing have been wars of decolonization (such as Algeria's or Guinea-Bissau's fight for independence) or wars of secession (such as Bangladesh's secession from Pakistan with the help of India).

THE JUDGMENT OF GOALS

The list of goals outlined above could be expanded or contracted, but it includes those that are widely articulated and frequently pursued. Decision makers in a variety of countries have stressed these goals in speeches, constitutions, policy statement, diplomatic correspondence, and other documents. It should be clear, however, that espousing a goal in a speech does not guarantee that the country will actually follow it. It is also quite clear from the list that some of these goals conflict with others, particularly at a specific moment. They cannot all be pursued simultaneously or with equal vigor.

Political and economic development may well threaten stability. Welfare costs cannot be invested in armaments. Survival may be in competition with democratic or command decision making. Political development may be in opposition to freedom or independence, particularly if federation or union is being considered. International conquest may lead to reprisals and a loss of freedom—even the destruction of the country in question.

In order to separate a country's actual goals from its stated goals or to decide which goals are more important than others, certain criteria may be applied. What are the allocations of resources that a government makes in order to pursue a particular goal? How much time, capital, and personnel are allocated to each goal? There may be allocations that can be used for more than one goal. For example, the capital allocated to arms production may be designed to ensure international survival, internal stability, or international conquest.

THE COLD WAR ARMS RACE

With both the United States and the former Soviet Union spending nearly 30 percent of their entire national budget for defense during the 1970s and 1980s, many citizens questioned the necessity of spending so much, especially since the momentous events of 1989–92. Both sides, by their budgetary allocations, made "survival"—as defined by them—their primary goal. Since both sides had the capacity to destroy each other many times over, could the levels of spending be deemed necessary?

In this section, we look at the allocation of scarce resources—whether time, money, or personnel—to the arms race and ask questions about this mutual interaction that lay at the heart of Soviet–American relations. Not only is this an important topic since it puts into sharp focus the budgetary priorities of the United States and the former Soviet Union and their concomitant goal formations, but also it may well speak to what is probably the most important issue of our day: the survival of humankind.

Writing almost 20 years ago, Raymond Aron pinpointed the intricate and complex nature of the relationship between the United States and the then Soviet Union when he referred to them as "warring brothers,"[8] who are

inevitably enemies by position and by the incompatibility of their ideologies, the United States and the Soviet Union have a common interest not in ruling together over the world (of which they would be quite incapable), but in not destroying each other.[9]

Both the United States and the Soviet Union entered the Atomic Age with recent and painful historical trauma. The United States—attacked at Pearl Harbor by the Japanese—suddenly found itself plunged into a world war that was the most destructive in its history, with the exception of the Civil War. The USSR—caught off guard by the German invasion of 1941—suffered more than 20 million soldiers and civilians killed in the ensuing conflict. Both resolved never to be caught unprepared again. Both saw in nuclear weapons a way to deter would-be aggressors, and both vowed never to let another get enough of a military superiority to think that such an attack would prove successful.

In the 20 years after Aron wrote these words, however, the two superpowers escalated the nuclear arms race over and over again. Each military step forward did not result in either side feeling safe vis-à-vis the other, but rather led to some additional countermeasure or similar buildup until both sides were, in relation to one another, in approximately the same place.

At the time of the Cuban Missile Crisis in October 1962—which was probably the closest the two superpowers ever came, in 40 years, to actually using nuclear weapons against each other—the United States had approximately 400 nuclear missiles that it could launch against the USSR. Not including the intermediate-range ballistic missiles that they put into Cuba in 1962 and subsequently withdrew, the USSR had 100 ballistic missiles. Both sides' missiles each carried a single nuclear warhead.

Today, the United States and the countries of the former Soviet Union possess a truly bewildering array of missiles and warheads. In fact, both sides have so many different weapons, and in such different configurations, that it is difficult to count them all. Certainly it is difficult to get both sides to count them all the same way. As Tables 11-1–11-3 illustrate, there is a variety of ways of counting each side's nuclear arsenal. We begin this section with an attempt to put those arsenals in common perspective.

One way to compare the U.S. and former Soviet arsenals is to count *strategic launchers,* the long-range weapons that can carry their warheads directly to the other side. Some of these are intercontinental ballistic missiles (ICBMs) based on land. In 1988, the USSR had approximately 6,530 of these while the United States had 2,450.

Others of these strategic launchers are submarine-launched ballistic missiles (SLBMs). Russia, the Ukraine, and Kazakhstan have 3,642 of these; the United States has 5,024. If one were also to include and count air-launched cruise missiles, the United States would have 1,600 of these to the Soviet Union's 640. (See Table 11-1 for details.)

This is not the whole story, however. At the time of the Cuban Missile Crisis, the strategic launchers generally carried a single warhead, al-

Table 11-1. Number of Strategic Launchers, 1988

System	United States	USSR
ICBMs	2,450	6,530
SLBMs	5,024	3,642
Air-launched Cruise Missiles	1,600	640
Total	9,074	10,812

Note: Although the United States has more long-range bombers, when medium-range bombers are included, the Soviet total goes to 958 in comparison to the Americans' 328. Soviet Tu-16 Badgers (440), 210 Tu-22m Backfires (210), and Tu-22s/Blinders (165) are all medium-range bombers, but the United States feels that the Backfires and Blinders have long-range capabilities.

though the aircraft could carry more than one nuclear bomb. But since then, first the United States and then the Soviet Union changed from single warheads to multiple warheads. The multiple independently target-able reentry vehicles (MIRVs) meant that each side could launch a single missile but, when it began to return to earth, it would release three or more different warheads, all of which could hit different targets.

Still, experts say that it is not enough to look at just the number of strategic launchers that each side has. Some launchers are capable of carrying a larger *payload* than others. Payload refers to the weight of the weapons and penetration aids carried by a delivery vehicle, be it a plane or a missile. Not only is there a difference between the sizes of the nuclear arsenals of both sides, there is a different configuration within those arsenals.

For several decades, the United States tended to concentrate on smaller, more accurate missiles while the Soviet Union developed much larger but less accurate missiles. In the 1980s, however, Soviet technology improved markedly, and some American defense planners voiced partic-ular concern over the much larger total Soviet missile payload.

The United States has a land-based missile payload of 2,250 tons, while the states of the former Soviet Union have a total of 9,630 tons. Likewise, they enjoy a big advantage when one counts submarine-launched pay-loads: 2,120 to 1,135. Some experts have countered by pointing out that the United States has a huge advantage in terms of the total payload of long-range bombers: 21,000 tons to 5,000 tons. American officials point out, however, that the American advantage in long-range bomber payload is offset by both the former Soviet land-based missile advantage and by the fact that the Soviets enjoyed a big lead in the payload of its interme-diate-range bombers: 27,000 tons to 16,000 tons.

Most current American concern revolves not around the total payload of each country's total arsenals, but around the lead of the former Soviet republics in *throw-weight,* or the weight a missile can lift off the ground and carry to a target, not including its own weight or the weight of its engine and fuel. Generally speaking, the more throw-weight a missile has, the more warheads it can carry or the greater the tonnage of the payload it can deliver. Current estimates put the combined ex-Soviet throw-weight at 11.2 million pounds and the U.S. throw-weight at 4 million pounds.

Just how the two postwar superpowers got into this situation lies beyond the scope of this chapter. The central fact for our purpose is that there is a substantial difference in the total payloads and throw-weights of each side, as well as the way those capacities are distributed through-out the nuclear arsenals of both sides. There is also the ancillary question of how many millions of pounds of throw-weight will ever be enough for both sides to feel secure.

When we leave aside the question of launchers and payload and look at just the number of nuclear devices, the numbers that both sides possess become greater. If we take the warheads for missiles, the nuclear bombs for aircraft, all short-, medium-, and long-range warheads of every type, nuclear warheads for artillery shells and tanks, and other weapons such as nuclear mines and depth charges, we find a combined total of over 60,000 nuclear devices for the United States and the former USSR. (See Table 11-2.) This figure should be compared with that of 1946, when the superpowers had a total of 9 nuclear weapons between them, all of them in the hands of the United States.

The combined total includes approximately 30,000—or half the total—in low-level "tactical" battlefield nuclear weapons. The United States currently has 25 tactical models: 8 long-range such as the Trident and Minuteman missiles; 9 short-range such as the Pershing II; 5 types of bombs; air-defense missiles; and 2 types of land mines. The Department of Energy currently produces 2,000 warheads per year.

These combined totals reported here do not include the nuclear weapons of other nations that have joined the nuclear club: Britain in 1952 following the United States in 1945 and the Soviet Union in 1949; France, 1960; China, 1964; and India, 1974; plus other suspected members such as Israel and South Africa.

Obviously, though, the U.S.–USSR arms race took place against the backdrop of what other states were doing. The former Soviet Union argued, for example, that the French and British nuclear forces had to be taken into account when counting nuclear weapons in Europe, and that those of China were relevant when counting totals necessary for Russia's overall defense.

Ironically, both superpowers opposed the spread of nuclear weapons technology, while maintaining that they themselves had to have the weapons to keep the peace. Argentina, Italy, Japan, Iraq, Pakistan, Sweden, and Switzerland are even now on the threshold of being able to build nuclear weapons; and in the next decade, Australia, Belgium, Brazil, South Korea, Norway, Spain, and Taiwan will also have the capability. One hundred fourteen countries have signed the 1969 Treaty of Nonproliferation of Nuclear Weapons (NPT), but among the 50 that have not signed it are such important players as France, China, India, Israel, South Africa, Brazil, and Pakistan.

A fourth way experts compare the nuclear arsenals of the United States and the former Soviet Union is by *deliverable nuclear warheads,* or the number of warheads that each side could deliver on the other's targets.

Table 11-2. Number of Nuclear Weapons, 1988

	United States	USSR
Total warheads, weapons	26,000	34,000
Combined Total	60,000	

Here again, there is rough parity overall, but significant differences in terms of each country's total configuration. In 1988, the Soviets could deliver 5,500 nuclear warheads from their land-based ICBMs; the United States, 2,152. The United States could deliver 4,750 warheads from its submarine-launched ballistic missiles, compared to 1,900 for the Soviets. The United States also has a 2,500:600 advantage in terms of nuclear warheads deliverable by long-range bombers. (See Table 11-3 for totals.)

What do all these figures mean? How can we translate these numbers into images we can understand? However one counts these weapons, however one compares the twin arsenals of the United States and former Soviet Union, one cannot help but be somewhat overwhelmed by the sheer size of them. How can we comprehend what they mean in the aggregate? How can we make the numbers intellectually manageable so as to address the issues they raise?

The explosive power of these nuclear weapons is very hard to grasp. We talk of a weapon's *yield,* or the energy released when it explodes. We measure the yield of a nuclear weapon in terms of the thousands (kilotons) or millions (megatons) of tons of TNT required to create the same release of energy. In terms of destruction, we can compare the explosive power of today's nuclear weapons with those that were dropped on the Japanese cities of Hiroshima and Nagasaki during World War II, each having the equivalent of 20,000 pounds of TNT.

If only one-third of the current U.S. strategic nuclear forces hit their target in the next war, this would be the equivalent of 4,400 megatons of explosive power, or roughly equal to 100,000 Hiroshima-type explosions. One-third of the ex-Soviet strategic forces hitting the United States would result in a significantly greater range of destruction because of their larger yield per missile.

The World Health Organization projects that a nuclear war of this magnitude would kill at least 1.5 *billion* people and seriously injure another 1.1 billion (out of a planetwide total of 4.5 billion). The entire world system as we know it would collapse with starvation, epidemics, and the breakdown of the social and political order on an unprecedented basis. In fact, some scientists have argued that a nuclear exchange involving 5,000 megatons of nuclear explosions would result in catastrophic effects on the whole planet itself.[10]

The initial explosions would kill more than a billion people and would

Table 11-3. Number of Deliverable Nuclear Warheads, 1988

System	United States	USSR
ICBMs	2,152	5,500
SCBMs	4,750	1,900
Long-range Bombers	2,500	600
Total	9,402	8,000

result in unimaginable firestorms that would release toxins into the atmosphere on an unprecedented level. Radiation from the fallout would be far more severe and would continue longer than previously thought. The particles thrust into the atmosphere would result in the descent of darkness—dust clouds thick enough to disrupt photosynthesis and to reduce worldwide temperature to −15°C. This nuclear "winter" would last for at least several years and might indeed eliminate life as we know it from the planet.

Reasonable people may differ on how they accept such projections of destruction. Indeed, reasonable scientists clearly differ on how to measure such destruction and on what degree of disruption would be caused by a nuclear exchange. But there is an air of unreality to these discussions, for who in his or her right mind wants to find out what the actual results of a nuclear exchange would be. What curiosity—and what cause—would be worth a 100 million people dead? A billion?

Or take the number of nuclear warheads in existence. Assume that about half of the total held by both sides are for use on the battlefield. Assume that, of their strategic arsenals, both sides in the initial exchange would hold back half for subsequent "war-fighting" purposes. Assume that only 85–90 percent of those weapons sent toward their targets actually reach them. Imagine such a heavy strike hitting the United States.

This heavy strike on the United States would mean the nuclear equivalent of 6.6 billion tons of TNT (or 13 trillion pounds of TNT). Such an attack would dwarf the relatively tiny attack depicted in the movie made for television, *The Day After*. How can we imagine so much TNT? Imagine that explosive power as being in the form of TNT in cases, each case about 2 feet in length. This much TNT would equate to a "road" of cases 600 feet wide and 100 million miles long—or from Earth to the sun and beyond! Or to put it another way, if the boxes of TNT were piled up, they would amount to 2.7 cubic *miles* in volume—or the equivalent of 4,300 pyramids the size of the Great Pyramid in Egypt!

Then remember that this amount of explosive material would not include what the United States would, at the same time, be dropping on the former USSR or the amount that would go off in the nuclear exchanges that would take place in Europe.

Obviously, no one in his or her right mind would want to use these weapons, then, given their potential to destroy the human species. But if the weapons have been made in order not to be used, what is their purpose? At the heart of the nuclear arsenals of the United States and the former USSR (and, by extension, at the heart of the arms race that continues to exist even as you are reading this) is the notion of *deterrence*. The possession of nuclear weapons is designed to prevent—by the threat of force—the use of other kinds of military force as well as the use of nuclear weapons by one's opponent. Deterrence is hence a relationship between the opponents, based on the fact that one will not do something if it means the other will use nuclear weapons. In the Alice in Wonderland logic of nuclear weaponry, we have them in order not to use them.

While we can measure the potential deterrence by counting the weapons that each side can deliver on the other under any circumstance, it is far more difficult to ascertain a measurement of the will and the means to do so. This is the notion of *credibility*. Is the threat to use nuclear weapons in a given situation credible? Would the United States actually have used nuclear weapons in the event the Soviets invaded West Germany in the 1980s? Would the Soviets actually have used nuclear weapons if the United States had moved to "liberate" Poland in the 1980s? And if either side decided to use those weapons, could they accomplish their mission? That is, would those weapons survive defensive countermeasures and arrive on their designated targets?

Further, *when* each side would use their nuclear weapons is a matter not only of great concern, but also of judgment. Would either side use them in a *first-strike* capacity, that is, the first offensive move of a general nuclear war? Would either side attempt to knock out all of the other side's nuclear weapons so as to be free from retaliation? A first strike implies an intention to knock out the opponent's ability to retaliate.

Much of the credibility of both sides' nuclear arsenals is based on their *second-strike capabilities,* that is, their ability to absorb a nuclear attack and still have enough retaliatory power left to destroy the attacker. This is another area where a country's perceived capacities are as important as the numbers of missiles and bombers it has. Could those weapons systems survive in order to retaliate? Does the opponent mean to use its weapons systems first?

Which side is "ahead" in first-strike capability or second-strike capability, then, depends on one's viewpoint. Just as people argue about what weapons count, so too they argue about what weapons systems are required for what purposes. There is also the question of who is ahead at any particular moment, in this spiral of competition. In the era of the escalating arms race, both superpowers insisted they were going ahead with "modernization" or "updating" in response to the advances of the other side. In short, both sides always blame the other for escalating the race.

In looking at perceptions on both sides, it is interesting to note the differences between their ways of looking at nuclear weapons and the possible use of them. From the end of World War II until the early 1960s, the U.S. military and civilian planners talked about a strategy of use called "massive retaliation" in which it was stated that, if the Soviets did something such as send bombers or missiles against the United States or invade Western Europe, then the United States would massively retaliate against them—send very large numbers of missiles and bombers to utterly destroy the Soviet Union.

U.S. administrations from John F. Kennedy on took the position that this doctrine was too simpleminded and that it limited American options. Instead, they argued, the United States should have a policy of *flexible response,* meaning that we would not use all of our nuclear weapons at once.[11] We might fight the Soviets in a conventional war in Europe and, if it looked like we were losing that, use tactical nuclear weapons in Europe—but not unleash the whole strategic nuclear arsenal of the United States.

The United States could thus fight a *limited nuclear war,* and up the nuclear ante only as necessary, holding back the massive strategic forces until the last minute.[12] Flexible response even involved complicated scenarios in which one side would attack the other's military centers but not its civilian targets, hold back nuclear portions of the arsenal, and threaten to hit the cities again, only as a last resort. This targeting of strategic military weapons was called the doctrine of *counterforce* to distinguish it from the doctrine of *countervalue,* in which the strategic forces would be used against cities and other nonmilitary targets.

As the Soviets increased their offensive capabilities, however, it became clear by the early 1970s that both sides already had the capability of destroying each other several (or later, many) times over. Neither side, it was argued, would go to all-out nuclear war, because its adversary could destroy it no matter what it did or how it tried to fight the war. This joint annihilation prospect was termed *mutual assured destruction* (MAD). Whether such a strategy is MAD or simply mad is still being debated. But in any case the argument ran that, even with MAD lurking in the background, it was possible to fight nuclear wars of a limited nature, have a flexible response, and escalate up a nuclear ladder. This American perception about the *controllable* nature of a nuclear war, and the need for flexibility in terms of how it would be fought, continued in the Reagan administration with its insistence on maintaining the U.S. "war-fighting" ability—that is, its ability to fight and "prevail" (since nobody would "win" in this context) in a nuclear situation, to be able to wage a nuclear war not for a few hours or days, but for weeks and months.

Reagan's new U.S. doctrine suggested that, after the initial nuclear exchange, the United States must be prepared to fight and prevail. How would this be accomplished when each side will have absorbed 8,000 nuclear blasts, each one of them ten to a hundred times as powerful as those that hit Hiroshima? Indeed, the notion of "managing" nuclear war seems hard to grasp. But at its core is the notion that the United States must "prevail" even under conditions of prolonged nuclear war. This is a direct outgrowth of the decades-old strategy.

There was at least one fundamental difficulty with this entire development, however, and that was the lack of similar perceptions on the side of the Soviets.[13] All of the notions of limited nuclear war, flexible response, and controlled escalation using nuclear weapons had no parallel in Soviet military doctrine. The former Soviets always argued that a nuclear war, once begun, inexorably leads to a massive strategic exchange. Once the nuclear genie is let out of the bottle, they argued, it cannot be put back in—and since a massive strategic exchange is therefore inevitable, it follows that they should seek superiority in arms, and a massive use of strategic weapons as soon as possible following the outbreak of conflict.[14]

Some commentators have taken this line of thinking to mean that the Soviets sought not sufficiency in weapons, but superiority—not retaliation power, but offensive action, a preemptive first strike to wipe out the enemy's capability of using nuclear weapons against them first.[15] Others have argued that, while there is a good deal of evidence the Soviets (and former Soviets) believe that an outbreak of nuclear war cannot be contained, they are not inclined to launch such a preemptive strike.[16] But Soviet military philosophy clearly stated that deterrence is best achieved by an ability to fight and win a nuclear war. The best way to wage nuclear war is to anticipate and preempt the first strike of your opponent. A Soviet strategist put it this way:

> Mass nuclear missile strikes at the armed forces of the opponent and at his key economic and political objectives can determine the victory of one side and the defeat of the other at the very beginning of the war. Therefore, a correct estimate of the elements of the supremacy over the opponent and the ability to use them before the opponent does are the key to victory in such a war.[17]

SUMMARY: ENDING THE ARMS RACE

During the entire course of the arms race—that enormously expensive competition between the superpowers—there was a parallel effort accenting arms control and arms reduction, or at least reducing *some* of the slope of the arms race. In 1963 the United States and the Soviet Union accepted a Test Ban Treaty that limited aboveground and atmospheric testing of atomic weapons, and established a telephone hot line between the two countries; the Threshold Test Ban Treaty followed in 1974, and the Peaceful Nuclear Explosions Treaty in 1976. There was also the Strategic Arms Limitation Talks (SALT I and SALT II) and the Strategic Arms Reduction Talks (START, which the Russians call "SALT III"), which have sought to limit U.S./USSR arms along a broad spectrum of weapons and weapons systems.

Surely, all of this is old history. Surely, no one seriously thinks the arms race can—let alone should—continue in the 1990s, especially with the breakup of the Soviet Union. Indeed, right before he left office in

Box 11-1. The START Treaty: New Limits for Strategic Forces				
	Current Forces		Understart	
	United States	USSR	United States	USSR
Intercontinental ballistic missiles	2,450	6,530	1,444	3,060
Submarine-launched ballistic missiles	5,024	3,642	3,456	1,840
Short-range attack missiles	3,000	400	3,440	2,000
Air-launched cruise missiles	1,600	640	1,840	1,350
Submarine-launched ballistic missiles in overhaul	—	—	576**	528**
Submarine-launched cruise missiles	350	0	880†	880†

Notes:
**Missiles in overhaul had been counted toward totals in the past.
†U.S. proposed limits is 758 or fewer.
Source: *Arms Control Association.*

early 1993, George Bush reached an agreement with Russian President Boris Yeltsin to reduce nuclear weapons to the levels attained in 1962.

But consider this set of factors as they affect goal formation. First, both the military and intelligence communities in both countries have an enormous stake in continuing the arms race—at least in some form. Second, if the START talks are to proceed and the number of weapons both sides possess actually reduced, there will be mounting pressure to modernize those weapons and weapons systems that each side is able to keep under the new agreements. Third—especially in the case of Russia—with the collapse of the Warsaw Pact and the movement of the effective defensive border of the former states of the Soviet Union much closer together (with the concomitant reduction in conventional forces), there will be increased interest on the part of the former Soviet military to retain their nuclear position vis-à-vis the United States.

Fourth, while the 1990s seem to be witnessing a decrease in tensions between the United States and the former Soviet Union, there continue to be threats to both from other countries, and a portion of the arms race will continue to be justified by what Iraq or China or Iran or some other country is doing. Fifth, political instability within the states of the former Soviet Union may make it difficult to control the military in any dramatic destruction of nuclear stockpiles, just as the American military can be counted on to resist more than token reductions in the arms race. As a result of the breakup of the Soviet Union, the Ukraine has now become the possessor of the third largest nuclear arsenal in the world. How to deal with the new realities of political fragmentation as they impinge on nuclear weapons?

Thus, citizens in the United States may be frustrated to find that, while the Cold War is officially over, the arms race goes on. Perhaps not at the same frantic pace as in the past 40 years, but going on nevertheless. There is a great deal of bureaucratic momentum in the arms race, and a long tradition of citizen acceptance of the enormous costs involved in having "survival" as a goal. Goal formation may turn out to be a far more complicated process than one might have assumed before looking at the arms race.

NOTES

1. Hans J. Morgenthau, *Politics among Nations* (New York: Knopf, 1960), pp. 38–86.

2. Raymond Aron, *Peace and War: A Theory of International Relations* (Garden City, N.Y.: Doubleday, 1966), pp. 71–94.

3. K. J. Holsti, *International Politics* (Englewood Cliffs, N.J.: Prentice-Hall, 1967), pp. 124–54.

4. A. F. K. Organski, *World Politics* (New York: Knopf, 1961), pp. 55–77.

5. More recently, Organski has developed some interesting methods for measuring the ability of a state to recover after a major defeat in war resulting from the espousal of an unwise goal. See A. F. K. Organski and Jack Kugler, "The Costs of Major Wars: The Phoenix Factor," *American Political Science Review*, 71, no. 4 (December 1977): 1347–66.

6. Robert A. Dahl and Charles E. Lindblom, *Politics, Economics, and Welfare* (New York: Harper and Row, 1963), p. 22.

7. David Baldwin, "Foreign Aid, Intervention, and Influence," *World Politics* (April 1969): 425–47.

8. Aron, *Peace and War*, p. xi.

9. Ibid.

10. There is no agreement among scientists on this point.

11. Maxwell Taylor, *The Uncertain Trumpet* (New York: Harper and Row, 1959).

12. Henry Kissinger, *Nuclear Weapons and Foreign Policy* (New York: Harper and Row, 1957).

13. These scenarios also assume a degree of objective dispassionate patience on the part of the principal actors during a nuclear exchange. In reality, how would the Russians or the Americans "know" what was coming or wasn't coming next? With time speeded up by events, they would probably not err on the side of

caution, in any case. Stephen M. Meye, "Soviet Theatre Nuclear Forces," Adelphi Papers No. 187, Institute of Strategic Studies, London, 1984.

14. How this Soviet philosophy would have meshed with the suggestion of McGeorge Bundy and others that the United States should react to any nuclear attack with a "substantially smaller one" is not clear.

15. See Richard Pipes, "Why the Soviet Union Thinks It Could Fight and Win a Nuclear War," *Commentary,* 64, no. 4 (July 1977): 21–34.

16. Admiral Stansfield Turner, head of the CIA under President Jimmy Carter, was a primary exponent of this viewpoint: "Nothing I have seen persuades me that the Soviet leaders' intention in building their nuclear war machine is to use it offensively"; *New York Times Magazine,* March 13, 1983, p. 95.

17. Desmond Ball, "Can Nuclear War Be Controlled?" Adelphi Papers No. 169, Institute of Strategic Studies, London, 1981, p. 31.

SUGGESTED READINGS

Beckman, Peter R. *The Nuclear Predicament: An Introduction.* Englewood Cliffs, N.J.: Prentice-Hall, 1989. A detailed introduction that follows the arms race from Hiroshima to the era of Star Wars and studies how we can try to solve our nuclear predicament.

Betts, Richard K. *Nuclear Blackmail and Nuclear Balance.* Washington, D.C.: Brookings Institution, 1987.

Bialer, Seweryn, and Michael Mandelbaum. *The Global Rivals.* New York: Knopf, 1988. Provides a useful overview of the dimensions of Soviet–American rivalry and the ways in which that rivalry took on a life of its own.

Kurtz, Lester R. *The Nuclear Cage.* Englewood Cliffs, N.J.: Prentice-Hall, 1988.

Lincoln, W. Bruce. *Red Victory.* New York: Simon and Schuster, 1989. A book that provides astonishingly important insights into the Soviet government and its formation and helps the reader to understand the true origins of the arms race.

May, Michael M. *Strategic Arms Reduction.* Washington, D.C.: Brookings Institution, 1988.

McNamara, Robert S. *Blundering into Disaster.* New York: Pantheon Books, 1987. An interesting and provocative change in policy, from one of the architects of flexible response.

Nye, Joseph S., Jr., Graham T. Allison, and Albert Carnesale, eds. *Fateful Visions.* Cambridge, Mass.: Ballinger Publishing, 1988.

12

Superpower Relations

There are on earth today two great people who . . . seem to be advancing toward the same end. They are the Russians and the Anglo-Americans. . . . Their points of departure are different, their paths are divergent; nevertheless, each seems summoned by a secret design of providence to hold in his hands, some day, the destinies of half the world.

—ALEXIS DE TOCQUEVILLE, 1830

We will bury you!

—NIKITA KHRUSHCHEV, 1960

The Soviet Union is the focus of evil in the modern world.

—RONALD REAGAN, 1981

We are going to do a terrible thing to you—we are going to deprive you of an enemy.

—GEORGI ARBATOV, SOVIET POLICY CONSULTANT, 1989

World War II is over. Since then our friends became our enemies, our enemies became our friends, and now it's all changing again. Life goes on and so must we.

—SOVIET CITIZEN, 1990

The Russian state, having chosen democracy and freedom, will never be an empire, or an elder brother or a younger brother. It will be an equal among equals.

—BORIS YELTSIN, PRESIDENT OF RUSSIA, AFTER FAILED 1991 COUP ATTEMPT OF HARDLINE COMMUNISTS AGAINST MIKHAIL GORBACHEV

THE POLITICS OF NATIONS

In Chapter 1 we saw that *power* in political systems is the capacity to compel people to behave in a certain way by persuasion, fear, or respect for authority, with *politics* directing that behavior toward policy objectives. In pluralistic societies, it is understood that conflict is the essence of politics, as different individuals and groups mobilize resources to persuade, cajole, or manipulate others to accept policy objectives. This conflict is acceptable because it is all carried out within established "rules of the game": commonly accepted boundaries of political and social power, as reinforced by national law and a court system and police force.

In international politics, by contrast, there is less of an agreement on commonly accepted rules of the game, given that the more than 150 actors have different histories, cultures, languages, interests, and expectations. The interplay of a group of sovereign states—each with its own set of aims, strategies, and resources—makes the stakes of power, politics, and conflict much higher.

In the anarchic system of international relations, power and international politics are backed by armies and the threat of massive destruction directed toward entire nations and control over vast territories. Conflict could result in not simply disagreements, changes in policy, or dismissal from political office, but in horrendous atrocities, physical destruction, and control over the course of the lives of entire nations.

Power in international relations has many different dimensions:

- military capacity and preparedness
- coercion through nonmilitary means, such as secret police and intelligence service organizations
- imperialism (imposing one's political/economic/social system on another nation, whether through coercion or persuasion)
- internal and external economic strength, including the use of economic incentives and sanctions
- diplomacy (persuading other nations' leaders to follow one's policy objectives) in either bilateral, multilateral, or international forums
- values, international mores, international public opinion

Different combinations of these forms of power will always be directed by international actors toward the pursuit of two broadly defined objectives: (1) ensuring the security of a nation; and (2) pursuing the policy objectives of a nation's leaders in the international arena. Oftentimes, different perceptions of their own and others' security needs, as well as conflicting policy objectives, can result in war or a tenuous and unstable peace—one based merely on the absence of war.

It is in this context that we examine one of the most important problems in international relations: the relationship between the two nations that—by virtue of their military strength, natural resources, productive capacity, and sense of mission—consolidated and manipulated enormous power in international relations after World War II. These nations are the United States and the former Soviet Union.

For 40 years, international relations were dominated, in varying degrees, by these two "superpowers." Such superpower domination was a unique phenomenon in history—a result of two catastrophic world wars that destroyed a European balance of power where several nations formed alliances to prevent any one nation from becoming too powerful. During World War II, the United States and the USSR were allies in fighting Nazi expansionism. After the war, these two powers became adversaries on every front, from the geostrategic to the ideological. Their geostrategic interests were at odds in every region of the world, especially in Europe; and they had diametrically opposed political values and economic systems. These differences led to the development of a "Cold War" that began in 1947—a war waged on every level except direct military confrontation. It was a war of words, a war of military buildup, a war of influence, a war of ideas. As Louis J. Halle eloquently states,

We may compare the cold war . . . to an earthquake, which occurs in a particular locality but sends its tremors all around the globe. The epicenter was along a line that ran from Lubeck, below the Danish islands, to the head of the Adriatic. . . . In the years to come the radio waves of the whole world would carry the noise of controversy, covert operations and propaganda would be conducted on all the continents, but the main confrontation would be along this line. . . . [N]o one concerned with drawing it, on either side, had thought of it as a line that, for at least a generation to come, would divide from each other two great warring camps.[1]

THE POSTWAR WORLD: DIFFERING VIEWS

At the end of World War II in 1945, the victorious Allies (the United States, the USSR, Great Britain, and France) collaborated to prevent the reemergence of a militaristic Germany and to forge a new European order out of the ashes of war. In a series of Allied conferences, the "Great Powers" met to decide the fate of Europe. The negotiations of the Potsdam, Teheran, and Yalta conferences held between 1943 and 1945 illustrated the vastly divergent views of international and domestic politics held by the participants.

Winston Churchill, the charismatic prime minister of Great Britain throughout World War II, viewed international relations in terms of a balance of power: states should form alliances to promote their common interests and to prevent any one power from becoming too strong. Franklin Delano Roosevelt, president of the United States from 1933 until his death in 1945, carried on the idealist tradition of American international politics that began with Woodrow Wilson,[2] hoping to create an international order of peace on the basis of the newly organized United Nations. He hoped to avoid the jockeying for power among states and alliances fostered by the balance-of-power approach to international relations, by bringing all nations together in a multilateral forum of international policymaking. Roosevelt sought to avoid conflict and instability by urging all nations, including the Soviet Union, to establish common interests and pursue them through international organizations. For this reason, Roosevelt tended to appease Joseph Stalin's demands for influence in Eastern Europe in return for Soviet membership in the United Nations. Though Churchill and Roosevelt employed different strategies in the arena of international relations, they both supported the self-determination of nations. The game of international relations, they agreed, is separate from internal politics and should be played by sovereign states.

Stalin, on the other hand, viewed international relations with great mistrust and was convinced that his war-weary Marxist-Leninist state had to protect itself against all foreign aggressors, both real and imagined. Stalin thus had two goals at the end of World War II that collided with the West's demand for self-determination of nations: (1) to construct a buffer territory around the perimeter of the Soviet Union to protect the heart of the empire from Western aggression,[3] and (2) to assert the legitimacy of the USSR as leader of a worldwide Marxist-Leninist movement. For both of these tasks, Stalin needed loyal communist regimes in the border states of Poland, Hungary, Czechoslovakia, Bulgaria, Romania, and Yugoslavia.[4] The external security of the USSR, he argued, could not be guaranteed without the allegiance of the political regimes of the Eastern European states. Therefore, Stalin was not willing to allow independent Eastern European countries to join in a neutral confederation, as Churchill proposed, or to allow them to determine freely their domestic and strategic interests, which would most likely lead them into an all-European fold, with its cultural, social, economic, and political ties with the West.

While the Western powers made a perfunctory demand for "free and unfettered elections" at the Yalta Conference in February 1945 (and Stalin accepted their demand), they were not prepared to take any action when the Soviet Union—through means of subversion (the secret police), military coercion, and political manipulation—occupied eastern European territory and installed puppet communist regimes in Poland, Hungary, Czechoslovakia, Bulgaria, and Romania. To the victors of the brutal, bloody, and inhumane world war, international peace was worth the price of self-determination in Eastern Europe.

From 1945 to 1947, the superpowers attempted to maintain some semblance of their wartime partnership by cooperating in the rebuilding f Europe. At the Potsdam Conference in July and August 1945, the USSR joined the United States and Great Britain in dividing defeated Germany into four administrative zones—one designated to each Allied power—under the supervision of the Allied Control Council, a common governing authority for defeated Germany. In this forum, Allied represen-atives met to discuss policies for the rebuilding of the German state. The former capital of the German Reich—Berlin—was situated in the Soviet-controlled portion of Germany, but all four powers had control over the city. Increasingly, the Soviets demanded control over all of Berlin; and when the Western partners persistently refused to comply, the Soviets ceased cooperating with the Allies in the Allied Control Council. As tensions increased, the Soviets blockaded Western access to Berlin and consolidated their control over their portion of Germany by making unilateral decisions. By May 1949, as a reconstituted western Germany developed under the leadership of Konrad Adenauer, a sovereign East German state (called the GDR, the German Democratic Republic) was created under the tutelage of the USSR. The division of Europe was, at that point, institutionalized. Winston Churchill summed up the results of postwar Great Power action and reaction in a speech given at Fulton, Missouri, in 1946: "Across Europe, from Stettin in the Baltic to Trieste in the Adriatic, an Iron Curtain has descended across the Continent."[5]

For a decade after this, hostile relations deepened between the super-powers. The division in Europe increasingly solidified as the United States responded to the perceived threat of Soviet hostility by funneling aid to Western Europe through the Marshall Plan[6] and became the senior partner in the North Atlantic Treaty Organization (NATO), a defense organization created in 1949 to protect Europe from the threat of com-munist aggression. U.S. leadership of NATO became a central component of the *Atlantic alliance*. "Alliance" refers to a group of countries that willingly *coordinate* their joint foreign and defense policies according to a commonly accepted set of interests. Stalin consolidated his power in Eastern Europe and responded to Western policies by creating the Warsaw Treaty Organization (WTO, or the "Warsaw Pact'), a joint defense organization of the USSR and Eastern European countries (ex-cept Yugoslavia) that was created in 1955. This, along with the Council of Mutual Economic Assistance (CMEA, or "Comecon")—a joint eco-nomic community—constituted the *Eastern bloc*. "Bloc" refers to the USSR's *control* over the internal politics of the Eastern European states as well as over their foreign policies. The seriousness with which the USSR took the division of *spheres of influence* in Europe and the ensuing hostility between East and West was symbolized by the building of the Berlin Wall in 1962, dividing the German nation by a mass of stone, barbed wire, and armed soldiers.

U.S. POLICIES TOWARD THE SOVIET UNION

Different policy orientations toward superpower relations emerged in the United States and USSR, as the two struggled to forge a relationship that would prevent war without sacrificing ideals or national interests. This was to be a problematic endeavor, given that their ideals and national interests were so diametrically opposed. As the division of Europe crystallized, policymakers in the United States worried about continued Soviet expansionism through military and ideological means. A famous article in the journal *Foreign Affairs,* written by seasoned diplomat George Kennan, induced American strategists in the Truman administration to pursue a policy of *containment* of Soviet aggression.[7] This required "containing Soviet power within its existing boundaries until internal changes within the Soviet leadership produced an abandonment of aggressive intentions."[8]

For some, containment was overly passive. The threat of communist aggression required the more active response of *rollback,* a policy whereby the United States, as leader of the "free world," would push the Soviet aggressor from those states it had conquered after World War II—most notably those in Eastern Europe.

For others such as Walter Lippmann,[9] both containment and rollback were based on false assumptions about the motivations of Soviet behavior. Lippmann argued that the Soviets sought to expand their sphere of influence only to protect legitimate national-security concerns. On that basis, he advocated *superpower disengagement* to diffuse the tense situation in Europe. If the United States would pull its troops out of Europe and dismantle NATO, according to this theory, the Soviets would do the same because they would not feel threatened. The way to deter Soviet aggression was to eliminate its causes, which stemmed not from internal or external tendencies toward expansionism, but from legitimate geostrategic concerns and fear of invasion.

In the end, rollback proved overly risky in sparking direct superpower confrontation; disengagement was too much of a gamble in light of USSR military capabilities and its deployment of troops in Europe. Containment was tested first in the Korean War in 1950—when the United States, under UN mandate, sent in troops to respond to an attack on South Korea by the North Koreans aided by the USSR and China—and later in the Vietnam War in the 1960s and 1970s. Containment, as both of these wars illustrated, was based on the superpower significance of all regional conflicts: the USSR encouraged and aided communist revolutionary movements through subversion and military aid, and the United States responded with massive military buildups. The wars were costly and bitter and, in the long run, only exacerbated superpower tensions without resolving the regional conflict.

Over the course of the Cold War, U.S. foreign policy was shaped in large part by two conflicting approaches to the Soviet Union. One approach assumed that the Soviet Union was driven by an aggressive Marxist-Leninist ideology that oppressed the Soviet population and promoted an expansionist foreign policy. According to this view, the United States could influence Soviet domestic and foreign politics through a *linkage policy,* by tying a conciliatory U.S. foreign policy to a liberalization of the Soviet political system. If the Soviet leadership relaxed its oppressive control over its own population by allowing increased Jewish emigration, for example, the United States would promote Soviet international interests, such as granting the Soviet Union "most-favored-nation" status in international trade. Soviet internal repression or foreign policy aggression would be matched with aggression by the United States. The Soviet Union should not be accepted as an equal actor in international relations unless and until it abided by standards of international human rights in its domestic politics and backed away from its militaristic approach to international relations.

While the second approach was also critical of Soviet internal politics, it sought to separate domestic politics from the dynamic of international relations. The United States had to accept the USSR as a sovereign and powerful international actor, given its military might and influence throughout the world. Aggressive policies would both endanger the superpower relationship and exacerbate tensions in international relations. To avoid this, the United States had to accept the USSR as a powerful state with legitimate geostrategic, economic, political, and national security concerns. Only by limiting the expectations it had with respect to changing Soviet domestic and foreign policies could the United States reduce tensions by searching for mutual interests with the Soviet Union and recognizing the spheres of influence claimed by each power. Some proponents of this view claimed that the United States had no right to demand any changes in Soviet domestic politics. Others argued that altering Soviet domestic policies was indeed the goal, but changes had to be brought about by integrating the USSR into the world political and economic community and exposing it to the values and human rights policies of the West.

The different approaches led to questions about the superpower relationship that were never satisfactorily answered during the Cold War years. Should political values and human rights play a role in determining U.S. foreign policy? Is, in fact, there a set of universal values that every country should be expected to abide by? If so, who determines what those values are, and how is a foreign policy sculpted to best encourage adherence to those values? On the other hand, is "pragmatism" the highest value in international relations, given that the stakes of the superpower relationship are so high? For example, in accepting Soviet hegemony in Eastern Europe and fashioning a workable relationship between the United States and the USSR, U.S. policymakers implicitly accepted that the pragmatic relationship between the United States and USSR—based on their respective spheres of influence—was more important than self-determination in Eastern European countries. This may have been unavoidable in the era of nuclear weapons.

> Paradox confuses our perception of the problem of peaceful coexistence: if peace is pursued to the exclusion of any other goal, other values will be compromised and perhaps lost; but if unconstrained rivalry leads to nuclear conflict, these values, along with everything else, will be destroyed in the resulting holocaust.[10]

SOVIET POLICIES TOWARD THE UNITED STATES

After Stalin's death in 1953, Nikita Khrushchev assumed leadership of the Communist Party of the Soviet Union (CPSU) and attempted to dismantle the most brutal internal and external controls of the Stalinist years without fundamentally changing the Soviet system. At the twentieth party congress in 1956, Khrushchev denounced the "excesses" of Stalinism and announced a loosening of control both inside the USSR and in the Soviet-dominated Eastern bloc. In doing so, he created for himself the *Khrushchev dilemma*: how to decentralize power to give Soviet citizens and Soviet client states more autonomy without relinquishing complete control. In the end, Khrushchev never solved this dilemma. After uprisings in East Germany and Poland in the early 1950s, a revolution in Hungary in 1956, and dissent from Soviet bureaucrats whose positions he was threatening with reform, Khrushchev was forced to renege on his reforms and revert to more centralizing policies.

His policy toward the United States and approach toward international relations was blustery and bold. The USSR during the 1950s and 1960s was intent on being recognized as a superpower on a level with the United States, though it had not at that time developed the military capacity and worldwide influence to claim that position. To flex the Soviet Union's muscle on the international stage and speed worldwide recognition of its status as superpower, Khrushchev played with the dangerous policy of *brinkmanship,* most notably in placing nuclear missiles in Cuba, 90 miles off the coast of the United States.

The proliferation of nuclear weapons and the placing of nuclear missiles in Cuba that could reach the U.S. mainland—precipitating the 1962 "Cuban Missile Crisis"—brought the United States and the USSR as close to the brink of nuclear war as ever, and illustrates the meaning of "brinkmanship":

> [The] danger of uncontrolled escalation of commitments. The process of proceeding stepwise to the brink of thermonuclear war. In this process . . . ,

Box 12-1. The Lithuanian Dilemma

After five years of Mikhail Gorbachev's policies of glasnost' *(openness) and* peres-troika *(a restructuring based on decentralization of decision making), the Baltic Soviet Republic of Lithuania declared its independence from the USSR on March 11, 1990. One of the 15 republics that constituted the USSR, the Lithuanian parliament voted to secede and to establish itself as the independent Republic of Lithuania. Following are the dilemmas presented by this decision to Lithuanian, Soviet, and American leaders. Which choices would you have made?*

Lithuania. *Lithuania, along with Estonia and Latvia, was forcibly incorporated into the USSR in 1940 as a result of the 1939 Secret Protocol of the Molotov–Ribbentrop Pact between Stalin's USSR and Nazi Germany. That pact—and, along with it, Lithuania's incorporation—has been recognized as illegal according to the tenets of international law by all parties involved. In 1990 after the first free elections to the Lithuanian parliament in 50 years (made possible by Gorbachev's reforms), the first non-Communist Lithuanian president and premier decided to take the opportunity to secede from the USSR. They realized that Lithuania's economy was heavily depen-dent on the Soviet economy and that this declared secession could cause much instability; but they thought that, if they didn't secede at this point, they could lose their only chance.*

The Soviet Union. *This presented Gorbachev with a dilemma. If he refused to grant Lithuania independence, he would appear hypocritical since one of the components of his "new political thinking" was the self-determination of nations, which was granted to all Eastern European countries. How could he deny independence to one of his own republics, especially since the constitution granted the republics the right to secede?*

On the other hand, if he let Lithuania secede, he could have been faced with a civil war as all the republics chose to follow the same path, or threatened with a coup by hardline conservatives and the military who blamed Gorbachev for the breakup of the Soviet state.

In the end, he called for a compromise: Lithuania could eventually secede, but only by first going through a long legal secession process that depended on a vote by the Soviet parliament.

The United States. *As the Lithuanian leaders called on Washington to recognize the new Republic of Lithuania, American leaders were faced with their own dilemma. If they did not recognize Lithuania, they risked criticism that superpower relations were more important than the fate of a 2.9 million–strong nation that freely determined its own independence. This would make it seem as if small nations were expendable if they threatened superpower interaction.*

On the other hand, if the United States recognized Lithuania and sent it economic aid, it risked undermining the tenuous trust that had been established between the USSR and the United States since Gorbachev came to power. U.S. recognition might lead to the overthrow of the reformist Gorbachev team, bringing to power more militaristic leaders who would have threatened U.S. security.

After months of a stalemate, economic sanctions, and a cautious U.S. response that fell short of condoning Lithuanian independence, Lithuanian leaders agreed to postpone the date of secession without retracting the declaration of secession.

each side attempts to convince the other that its commitment is irrevocable and that it is the other party's responsibility to defuse the situation.[11]

The crisis was defused after the United States blockaded further Soviet shipments of weapons headed to Cuba and, days later, Khrushchev backed down. This, along with domestic dissent, promoted rival Soviet leaders to depose Khrushchev in 1964. (One of the positive outcomes of the crisis was the installation of a U.S.–USSR "telephone hot line"—a means for direct communication between the superpower leaders in the event of a crisis.) The Cuban Missile Crisis was Khrushchev's attempt to give a most dramatic sign to the West that the USSR had the nuclear capability to threaten the security of the Western world. The futile scheme also illustrated that such provocation was not worth the attendant risks; from then on, the superpowers carried out their competition in the less threatening (to them) forums of regional conflicts, ideological warfare of words, and the struggle for influence in Europe and the Third World.

Khrushchev's successor, Leonid Brezhnev (in power 1964–82), consistently and methodically built up the power of Soviet nuclear and conventional forces. During his rule, Soviet influence in the Third World expanded considerably. By the end of the 1960s, the Soviet Union was indeed recognized as a military (though not economic) superpower comparable to the United States in military potential and Third World prestige. Brezhnev's goal was to attain strategic nuclear parity with the United States; and that he did, increasing the number and firepower of Soviet land-based missiles (ICBMs), and modernizing other strategic and conventional forces.

During the Brezhnev period, leaders in the Soviet Union had their own debates about how to deal with the United States. The *traditionalists* asserted that capitalism was inherently imperialistic and hostile toward the socialist states, thereby necessitating a strong military presence in Europe and the Third World. Influence from the West—especially the antisocialist United States—would be harmful to Soviet domestic goals. It would be in the Soviet Union's best interest to strive for autarky—complete independence from outside influence—in economic and technological development.

The Soviet *modernizers,* on the other hand, saw Soviet security more in economic and technological terms than in military terms. They argued that the USSR needed to establish trade ties with the West to strengthen a sagging economy and upgrade its obsolete technology. Reducing international tensions with the United States would enhance the internal development of the USSR and make it a stronger power in the long run. The USSR could import Western technology, they claimed, without importing its values. The Soviet Union should thus move toward economic integration with the West while maintaining its defenses against potential Western military aggression. Like American analysts, Soviet foreign policy experts were thinking about the relationship between domestic and foreign policies. Would economic and technological interdependence lead to a surrender of political independence? Is national security tied more with a healthy domestic economy or with military power?

DETENTE

After the tension-ridden two decades following World War II in which the superpowers built up their nuclear arsenals and battled for influence in Europe, Asia, the Middle East, and Africa, both U.S. and Soviet leaders realized that the time bomb of potential aggression had to be defused. Known as "realpolitik," this view dominated U.S. policy making under the careful guidance of Henry Kissinger and his policy of *détente*.

Détente was based on the assumption that the United States and the USSR—despite their fundamental differences—had to devise a relationship based on a minimum agenda of common interests. Each side would pursue its own political, ideological, and regional goals while cooperating in areas of mutual concern. In short, détente sought ways to guarantee *peaceful coexistence* between the two hostile powers of the United States and the USSR.

> However competitive they may be at some levels of their relationship, both major nuclear powers must base their policies on the premise that neither can expect to impose its will on the other without running an intolerable risk. . . . Where the age-old antagonism between freedom and tyranny is concerned, we are not neutral. But other imperatives impose limits on our ability to produce internal changes in foreign countries.[12]

Unless one understands the dual basis on which the U.S.–Soviet relationship was built from the Cold War until the ascent of Mikhail Gorbachev, the confusing vacillation of increased cooperation and acerbic confrontation between the United States and the USSR can muddle an interpretation of the relationship.

For example, in the late 1960s it appeared as if the superpowers were seriously building a policy of mutual cooperation. The USSR called for a Conference on Security and Cooperation in Europe (CSCE) that would bring together all of the nations of Europe along with the United States, Canada, and the USSR to discuss international security issues. In 1967 and early 1968, the Soviets enthusiastically agreed to participate in nuclear arms control negotiations with the United States so as mutually to limit numbers of weapons and avoid nuclear conflict through the SALT (strategic arms limitation talks) accords.

In 1972, Richard Nixon, then president of the United States, and Leonid Brezhnev, as general secretary of the Communist party, signed a Basic Principles Agreement designed to establish a cooperative relationship between the two superpowers. Following are several provisions of the Basic Agreement:

1. There is no alternative to peaceful coexistence due to nuclear weapons. Ideological differences will not prevent bilateral ties.
2. Both avoid military confrontations and agree to prevent nuclear war. Settle differences by peaceful means. No unilateral advantage.
3. Seek to promote conditions so that all countries can live in peace and security and not subject to outside interference in their internal affairs.
4. Facilitate commercial and economic ties.
5. Arms limitations and establishment of international security system are two principles of the UN.
6. Deepen cultural ties and familiarization with cultural values.[13]

This cooperation proved to be illusory, however, when it came to defining actual superpower relations in the international arena. In 1968, Warsaw Pact troops—at the behest of the USSR—invaded the small country of Czechoslovakia, which had tried to introduce reforms and civil liberties under the communist regime so as to create what it called "socialism with a human face." This invasion was justified by what came to be known as the *Brezhnev Doctrine,* or doctrine of limited sovereignty, whereby the USSR claimed the right to intervene militarily in any of its socialist client states where the "gains of the revolution" were threatened. Superpower tensions continued when, in 1973, the Soviets and the United States airlifted military supplies to their opposing allies in the Middle East War. In the late 1970s, the superpowers provided arms to opposite sides in the Ethiopian–Somalian conflict in the Horn of Africa.

The West continued to denounce Soviet foreign policy without countering it. While abhorrence of the Soviet invasion of Czechoslovakia was expressed throughout the West, the Western alliance limited itself to verbal criticism, taking no punitive action against the Soviets. The United States participated in the CSCE conference in 1974, attempting to commit the USSR to abide by an international code of human rights in its own country and in its client states of Eastern Europe. In return for (unfulfilled) Soviet promises, the United States tacitly acknowledged the Soviet sphere of influence in Eastern Europe by recognizing the inviolability of existing borders. The superpowers continued to support opposing clients in the Middle East and Africa, yet attempted to defuse the crises by adopting more moderate strategies.

What can explain this paradoxical relationship between the United States and the USSR? Two reasons, related to each other, are most important. The first is that both superpowers had a dual agenda: (1) to avoid direct confrontation and the possibility of a nuclear conflict, and (2) to propagate their own values and interests in their spheres of influence. Thus it was in the interests of both superpowers to forge peaceful and cooperative arrangements in order to strive mutually toward a stable international order that would avoid direct confrontation and nuclear escalation (which neither wanted nor saw in its interest). Once this "peace by absence of war" was established, the superpowers felt free to maintain their own diametrically opposed agenda in the international arena: the Soviet Union supporting communist insurgencies or communist regimes in the Third World, and the United States supporting anti-communist regimes (even if the alternative was not very democratic); the Soviet Union maintaining its iron grip on the Eastern European nations and fostering anti-American sentiment in Europe, and the United States sanctioning the Soviet Union for its activities in Eastern Europe, while trying to strengthen the NATO alliance—sometimes over the objections of its Western European partners.

This dual-track policy resulted in a stable international order based on the common goal of avoiding nuclear confrontation. That is, both sides recognized the others' sphere of influence in Europe, each accepted the other as a military superpower, and each had relatively comparable conventional and nuclear arsenals that were sufficient to deter direct superpower confrontation or a nuclear war in Europe. However, the dual-track policy also resulted in an underlying instability resulting from opposing values and conflicting regional interests. The ideological battles, the confusion and instability that resulted from shifting U.S. and Soviet allegiances and military support in the Third World and regional conflicts, and the ideological and military threats that made peace dependent on the fear of ultimate destruction meant a constant tension between the superpowers that cast a great pallor—given superpower dominance—over all of international relations.

The beginning of the 1980s illustrated the shaky foundation on which détente had been built. In December 1979, the Soviets invaded bordering Afghanistan to protect its fledgling Marxist regime against a non-Marxist coup. The invasion was condemned worldwide and soon became known as the "Soviets' Vietnam." In 1981, the Polish communist regime declared martial law in the shadow of possible Soviet military intervention when the democratic movement Solidarity threatened to undermine Soviet-backed Communist party rule. The Brezhnev regime limited the number of Soviet Jews allowed to emigrate and continued its internal repression against dissidents and independent groups.

America's new president, Ronald Reagan, illustrated the depth of Cold War roots when he called the Soviet Union "the focus of evil in the modern world," and introduced military buildups to protect the security of the West in the face of an aggressive Soviet state. Tensions between the superpowers steadily built as the new administration developed the contours of the *Reagan Doctrine,* a "foreign policy aimed at countering Soviet expansion, with specific applications in Central America, Africa, and Asia."[14] Under this policy, the Afghan resistance movement, the Contras (or "freedom fighters," in Reagan's terminology) in Nicaragua, and the Angolan guerillas fighting Soviet- and Cuban-funded troops, each received millions of dollars in military and humanitarian aid. No infusion of funds, however—and no ideological war of words—could reduce the tensions that were building up in regional conflicts and in the direct U.S.–Soviet relationship.

It was clear that there could be no fundamental change in the superpower relationship unless and until both the Soviet Union and the United States redefined their understanding of security and changed the assumptions on which their post–World War II relationship had been built. After 40 years of distrust, animosity, threats, and the specter of nuclear warfare, just such dramatic changes did indeed occur as the Soviet Union retreated from empire to focus on internal problems, and the United States responded by adjusting its perceptions and its policies.

GORBACHEV: THE GREAT CHANGE

Although international trends had been lessening the influence of the two superpowers on world politics, the major impetus for the unprecedented changes in world politics at the end of the twentieth century came from the USSR. Faced with mounting economic problems, a crumbling infrastructure, and festering internal dissent, Mikhail Gorbachev—general secretary of the Communist party and president of the USSR—watched over the disintegration of the Soviet bloc in Eastern Europe and the breakup of the vast Soviet empire.

In 1989 Gorbachev's foreign policy resulted in a momentous, exhilarating, and completely unexpected emancipation of the Eastern bloc countries from the 40-year yoke of Soviet domination. One by one—either through negotiations, massive peaceful demonstrations, mass exodus, or a violent retaliation against Communist party leaders—the countries of Poland, Hungary, Czechoslovakia, East Germany, Romania, and Bulgaria fought for their long-delayed self-determination and established independent, noncommunist, or reformed-communist regimes. And the Soviet Union, in a grand attempt to illustrate the substance of its new foreign policy initiatives, withdrew its troops and even declared some of its past actions illegal according to the tenets of international law. What sparked the change? The components of Gorbachev's "new political thinking" in foreign policy and its domestic roots are examined in Boxes 12-2 and 12-3.

Box 12-2. New Political Thinking: Gorbachev's Foreign Policy Agenda

1. *The Soviet Union's national security should be based more on economic strength, technological capabilities, and internal stability than military might and dominance over other countries.*
2. *International security should be based not on a zero-sum game (the more Soviet security, the less U.S. security; and vice versa), but on the basis of* mutual security, *whereby all countries gain by the reduction of conventional and nuclear arms, peaceful resolution of conflicts, and international stability.*
3. *International relations should move from a bipolar to a multipolar foundation. This means that superpower relations should not dominate the international agenda, independent nations should freely pursue their aims based on self-determination, and regional conflicts should be addressed on their own terms, not in light of superpower rivalry.*
4. *Europe should not be a battleground for competing armies and ideologies. A* common European home—*including the USSR—would be based on common all-European interests such as economic cooperation, resolution of nationality conflicts, and a predominantly European defense community, (like the CSCE).*
5. *Political negotiation—not military competition—should be the basis of a new international system of peace and security.*

THE NEW SPECIAL RELATIONSHIP

By the end of the 1980s, the Soviet Union was an empire in retreat—a massive superpower that could no longer bear the internal costs of a sweeping militarily backed presence throughout the world. The Soviet leadership recognized that the USSR was operating from a position of serious weakness. It had overcommitted itself in terms of its military might and the instruments needed to maintain its superpower status. In so doing, it neglected its internal development and was in danger of economic collapse. In order to avoid an internal catastrophe, it had to lessen its coercive role in international relations and turn inward—devoting to the domestic economy the resources that had previously been funneled to the military and weapons technology. Gorbachev's foreign policy agenda began as a broad set of goals that would allow the USSR to retreat gracefully from its overextended position in international relations by promoting international cooperation and economic integration. The linchpin of this policy was a new superpower relationship.

In a *Pravda* interview, Gorbachev made this statement about the United States: "In conditions of the new epoch, history gives us a chance to trust each other and cooperate fruitfully." Initially, U.S. policymakers

---

Box 12-3. Domestic Incentives for Gorbachev's New Political Thinking

1. The USSR no longer had the economic capacity to maintain its military commitments around the globe. The domestic economy suffered at the expense of military buildup—resulting in a well-fed, fine-tuned, and technologically advanced military with a starved, threadbare, and primitive domestic economy. By 1986, the domestic economy could no longer stand the strain.

2. To foster internal development, the USSR desperately needed Western technology and economic capital and investment; all of these were circumscribed, in varying degrees, given the West's mistrust of and animosity toward the Soviet Union. Only by constructing a foreign policy that was not predicated on the assumption of an unavoidable competition between socialism and capitalism could the USSR hope to develop ties with Europe and the United States.

3. Social problems such as alcoholism, crime, corruption, falling living standards, and decreasing worker productivity were dramatically increasing. In order to shore up the reserves necessary to solve them, the Gorbachev leadership recognized the need to reduce military expenditures and to promote a peaceful international order that would allow the USSR to focus on its internal problems.

4. The ideology of Marxism-Leninism became increasingly irrelevant as a form of socialization and political rule. As ideology lost its meaning to the Soviet domestic audience, it also lost its power to drive an aggressive and expansionist foreign policy.

---

were divided over the most prudent response to the Soviet initiative for increased superpower cooperation. Some warned that Gorbachev's so-called new political thinking was a calculated move to weaken the United States while the USSR retrenched by building a stronger domestic economy to support future military buildups. The United States would only undermine its own position vis-à-vis the Soviet Union if it relaxed its policies in response to Gorbachev. Others recognized that Gorbachev's new foreign policy was designed to strengthen Soviet internal politics, but urged the United States to take advantage of Soviet initiatives to lessen tensions in world politics. The United States could use Soviet weakness to negotiate mutual reductions in military spending, further arms-control measures, and reduce antagonistic superpower involvement in regional conflicts. Still others heralded Gorbachev's foreign policy as a new era in international politics ushered in by a charismatic Soviet leader who espoused values of international peace, cooperation, and stability. They urged U.S. policymakers to match Soviet initiatives with visible and dramatic military reductions, the elimination of trade barriers, and the integration of the USSR into international political and economic systems.

The Bush administration chose the middle road—encouraging Soviet reforms, but acting with great caution before altering the pattern of U.S. foreign policy. The objective was to ensure that Soviet reforms were irreversible before the United States made any significant changes that could weaken its own position if the Soviet leadership changed course. This policy of pragmatism left the United States sitting in the wings of the international relations theater, waiting for the USSR to make unilateral concessions to prove its resolve to decrease world tension and watching for signs of change in Soviet domestic politics. Three years into the Gorbachev era, changes in Soviet domestic and foreign politics convinced U.S. policymakers that the stage was ready for a reformulation of the superpower relationship. By the end of the 1980s, the United States and Soviet Union entered a new period of guarded cooperation in forging a new course of military, economic, and political relations.

In 1989, both sides committed to a significant reduction of both conventional forces in Europe and nuclear weapons stockpiles on their own territories. Permanent on-site verification procedures for ensuring adherence to nuclear arms–control agreements were established—with the United States and the USSR each sending its own representatives to the other's country for surprise spot checks of weapon sites. The golden arches of the McDonald's fast-food restaurant chain hoisted above Pushkin Square in Moscow in 1990 represented the new era in U.S.–Soviet economic relations. Previously impossible because of U.S. political restrictions and Soviet denunciation of capitalism, joint ventures became the hallmark of economic integration between the two former rivals. The United States eventually dropped its resistance to Soviet membership in international economic organizations such as the General Agreement on Tariffs and Trade (GATT) and the World Bank, incorporating the USSR for the first time into the world economic system. On a political level, the end of the superpower rivalry led to a change in the nature of U.S.–USSR-dominated regional conflicts. The Persian Gulf crisis of 1990–91 illustrated the capacity for U.S.–USSR cooperation in regional politics through multilateral diplomacy and the United Nations. The Bush administration—seeking to portray the Iraqi invasion of Kuwait as an international crisis—sought the Soviet Union's cooperation in condemning Iraqi aggression, and Soviet participation in UN efforts to maintain world peace. One of the fallouts of the end of the Cold War has been an increased role for international organizations such as the United Nations, which can finally assume its original role as a mediator of peace rather than a broker of superpower conflicts.

In addition to strengthening international forums of superpower cooperation, U.S.–Soviet relations have been radically affected by the new ease of citizen exchanges, cooperation in education, the arts, and cultural affairs, and increased travel between the two countries.[15] Whereas we mostly think of international relations as dominated by diplomats, foreign policy leaders, and heads of state, we should not overlook the importance of *mass perception* in international affairs. Mutual isolation, Soviet xenophobia (fear of foreign influence), and ideological masks created not so much a hostility between the American and Soviet populations as an ignorance of each others' characteristics, culture, and habits. When Soviet students (not KGB operatives as they would have been in the 1960s or 1970s) began to sit in American classrooms, American business managers started giving lectures to budding Soviet entrepreneurs in Moscow, and American onlookers shouted "Gorby, we love you!" at a U.S.–Soviet summit in Washington, it was clear that at least the perception of the "evil empire" or the "capitalist aggressors" had receded into the background of a Cold War past.

This new era of superpower cooperation would indeed prove to be very short-lived—not because Soviet leaders reverted to repression, but because the tidal wave of change within Eastern Europe and the Soviet Union itself swept away not only the remnants of an aggressive Soviet foreign policy, but also the entire Soviet bloc and Soviet empire. In 1990, Soviet influence in the former bloc was completely eroded as Germany united on the ruins of its Berlin Wall, freely elected democratic governments came to power throughout Eastern Europe, and the Warsaw Pact with its economic cousin, the CMEA, died a quiet death. That same year the foundations of the Soviet empire began to rot as the Communist party gave up its hegemony inside the country by sanctioning a multiparty political system, popular fronts demanded independence in all the Soviet constituent republics, and new democratic leaders fought tooth and nail to remove the Communist bureaucracy from the heights of power. Only a year later, in August 1991, the tumultuous upheavals culminated in a coup attempt by Communist hardliners anxious to turn back the tide of change. Their failure not only changed the course of Soviet politics (see Chapter 14), but fundamentally altered established patterns of international relations as the Soviet Union literally disappeared from the map.

THE BREAKUP OF THE SOVIET EMPIRE—REGIONAL IMPACT

Arising from the ashes of the Soviet empire, the former Soviet republics became independent states, struggling to construct stable political systems and viable national economies. Russia, the Ukraine, Belarus, Estonia, Latvia, Lithuania, Moldova, Armenia, Azerbaijan, Georgia, Turkmenia, Uzbekistan, Kazakhstan, Tadzhikistan, and Kirghizia suddenly became new actors in the arena of international relations. Their presence immediately began to alter the established pattern of regional and international politics. The peoples and states in the region of the former Soviet empire faced three new urgent problems: (1) regional security, (2) territorial disputes, and (3) nationalities policy.

The Soviet central state had controlled all the resources of its vast territory, maintained a cohesive and disciplined army, and prevented interethnic rivalry within its borders. Once the strong arm of Soviet power was severed, there was an explosion of conflict among the peoples living in the former Soviet territories, as issues that were forceably subdued by Soviet rule now rose to the surface in the new atmosphere of political freedom and national independence. With no central state, what would prevent chaos and unending conflicts over territory, resources, and political power? What would be the basis of regional security on former Soviet territory after the breakup of the Soviet empire?

The leaders of the new independent states recognized the need for a regional organization to coordinate military, nuclear arms, and economic policies. Russia—with its vast land mass, rich natural resources, and control over 80 percent of the nuclear arsenal of the former Soviet Union—is clearly the dominant power in the region. Nonetheless, Russia also depends on the newly independent states surrounding it. Without the former Soviet republics on its perimeter, there is little access from the vast Russian lands to warm-water ports. In the past, Russians have obtained food from their traditional breadbasket—the Ukraine—and raw materials from the former Asian republics. Finally, with tens of thousands of its citizens living in the newly independent states of the former Soviet Union, Russia has an interest in protecting their rights.

Eleven of the former 15 Soviet republics—now independent states—formed the *Commonwealth of Independent States* (CIS) in January 1992 to promote regional security in the wake of the disintegration of the Soviet empire. Georgia refused to join (though it sends observers to CIS summits), as did the Baltic countries, which formed their own regional organization: the *Baltic Assembly*.

The CIS attempts to coordinate military, economic, and ecological policies among its 11 member states. The most crucial concern of its members was to transfer the vast Soviet army to the command of CIS officials and establish joint political control over former Soviet nuclear arsenals on the territory of Russia, the Ukraine, Belarus, and Kazakhstan. The CIS has its own commander in chief of the armed forces—former Soviet Defense Minister Evgenii Shaposhnikov—and a coordinated strategy to dismantle nuclear weapons complexes on its territory. Despite these positive steps, the CIS is built on a very shaky foundation. Its member countries are extremely jealous of their newly won independence and rarely delegate power to CIS command structures, mostly out of fear that Russia—heir to much of the former Soviet Union's assets—will dominate its activities. Russia accuses the Ukraine of ignoring CIS decisions, while the Ukraine claims that Russia is controlling former Soviet resources that should be distributed to all CIS states.

The status of the military has proven to be the biggest problem for the CIS. Can former Soviet soldiers be expected to take an oath of loyalty to the CIS—a regional organization that was created in great haste—or will they identify more with their native lands? This question is especially relevant to the Black Sea Fleet, stationed off the shores of what is now the Ukraine. It is composed largely of Russian and Ukrainian soldiers. Formerly one of the most important units of the Soviet military, the Black Sea Fleet is now subject to competing jurisdictional claims by the CIS, Ukraine, and Russia. The Ukraine claims territorial rights to the fleet; Russia argues that it has funded the fleet in the past. Each considers the fleet to be an essential part of its national security. Given these irreconcilable differences, the CIS renounced jurisdiction over this component of the former Soviet military. Resolution of the conflict is now subject to a political agreement between Russia and Ukraine. Because of the inability of the CIS to resolve regional conflicts or command the loyalty of former Soviet soldiers, Russia created a separate army in May 1992 with President Boris Yeltsin as commander in chief. The other former Soviet republics will no doubt soon follow suit.

Also in May 1992, six CIS states including Russia signed a collective security agreement. Both the Ukraine and Belarus—two important independent Slavic states on Russia's border—refused to sign the agreement. The conflicting jurisdiction over military forces and holes in the patchwork of collective security have rendered the CIS weak and, some of its members warn, temporary. While the organization has held together the disintegrating forces sweeping the region of the former Soviet empire, the problem of long-term regional security is far from solved. Constantly tugging away at the cohesiveness of security are daily disputes over state borders and territory.

One need only look at a map to understand the territorial problems and foreign policy changes generated by the reconfiguration of national borders after the fall of the Soviet empire. The importance of geography in international politics has never been so clear. Whereas once the Soviet Union controlled the vast tract of land from the Baltics to Vladivostok, now jurisdiction over territory and resources is subject to bitter debates among the new states that have formed on former Soviet territory.

Ukraine, for example, claims ownership of the Crimea—the strategic peninsula in the Black Sea—while the Russians in the Crimea voted for incorporation into Russia, which once ruled the land. The Baltic states are demanding immediate Russian troop withdrawal from their territory, but the Russians claim ownership of the military bases constructed there under Soviet rule. The Russians living in the Dniester region of independent Moldova—part of Romania before incorporated into the Soviet empire—claim that their land is part of Russia. They have asked the Russian army to come to their aid in their armed struggle against the popularly elected Moldovan government.

These territorial battles are based largely on nationality conflicts and ethnic tensions. Most of the new independent states are comprised of a hodgepodge of the dozens of ethnic groups that populate the region. After the common fight for independence against the central Soviet state was won, different ethnic groups began to fight against each other to consolidate power on their land. Many of the ethnic disputes that shadow post-Soviet independence have deep roots in centuries-old history; some were created by the Soviet nationalities policy. The case of Latvia illustrates the complexities involved in creating just and democratic nationalities policies.

After 1939, when the Soviets took possession of Latvia as part of a deal with Nazi Germany, they forcibly expelled many native Latvians from their Baltic homeland and sent them to camps in Siberia. The Soviets intended to repopulate Latvia with Russians to facilitate the incorporation of the country into the Russian-dominated Soviet empire. Over the years, many Russians settled in Latvia permanently, getting jobs, marrying native Latvians, and raising families. By the end of the 1980s, 40 percent of all Latvia was inhabited by ethnic Russians; in the capital city Riga, the figure was almost 50 percent.

When Latvia attained independence in 1991, one of the major goals was to ensure that the Latvian culture—largely destroyed or subverted under Soviet rule—be reinvigorated and that ethnic Latvians rule over their own land. Not only had rightful rule over their country been forcibly ended by the Soviets (who have since admitted the action was illegal), but the Latvian language, tradition, and national culture were undermined by domination of the Russians. To even the playing field and address past wrongs, the first postcommunist Latvian government pushed for restrictive citizenship rights that would give full privileges to native Latvians but circumscribe some rights—including full voting rights and the right to hold public office—to Russians who have no roots in the country. The Russians in Latvia and in Russia are furious at this nationalities policy, claiming that it is undemocratic and a violation of international covenants on human rights. They argue that constitutional rights cannot be denied to any group based on its nationality or ethnic origins. The Latvians argue that it is impossible to apply established democratic standards to the citizenship issue because the Russians used undemocratic and forceful means to change the ethnic composition of the country.

Clearly, none of the former Soviet Union's territorial or nationality conflicts are straightforward or easily solved. Once abstract concepts of citizenship, independence, and national sovereignty carry with them the weight of Soviet history and the anticipation of an uncertain future. The absence of cohesive regional security organizations, constant conflicts over territory and borders, and bitter disputes among ethnic groups will continue to foster regional insecurity in the once stable region of the mighty Soviet empire.

THE BREAKUP OF THE SOVIET EMPIRE—INTERNATIONAL IMPACT

Regional instability will have a spillover effect in international relations as new independent states jockey for power and start to position themselves in the international system. The most compelling issue to emerge from the regional unrest sparked by the dismantling of the Soviet bloc and disintegration of the Soviet empire is the relationship between a nation and a state—two concepts that Americans often confuse. Specifically, when should a *nation*—a group of people who share a common ethnic, religious, territorial, or historical background—command its own *state,* or political control over the territory on which the nation lives? The momentum of independence from Soviet domination did not stop at the borders of the multinational states that were created on the territory of the former Soviet Union. Nations within traditional state borders took to the streets, the national parliaments, and sometimes the battlefield to fight for their own states. The result affects international as well as regional politics.

Yugoslavia has been a bloody example of the cruelty of nationality conflicts as Serbs battle Croats, Bosnians, Montenegrins, and others on former Yugoslav territory. The immediate cause is a conflict over control of land, the military, and political power; but the roots of the war go back to historical animosities among peoples of different ethnic, religious, and political backgrounds. Wanton destruction of innocent people and centuries-old buildings in historic cities is carried out in the name of nationalism. These nationality disputes undermine attempts by international organizations to pursue multilateral policies based on the mutual interests of all nations. They also raise questions about responsibility for international peacekeeping. Should the United States—having established its military influence in the 1991 Gulf War—commit troops to the former Yugoslav area to prevent further aggression? Will the European community—closer in proximity and history to the battlefield—take the lead in mediating an end to the conflict? Will the United Nations mobilize its own forces to put down the military conflict on the territory of the former Yugoslavia? United Nations–sponsored ceasefire talks and humanitarian aid airlifts have been thwarted by national military units in the area. The means by which the conflict is resolved—by a single powerful country, a group of European nations, or an international organization—will tell us much about the future shape of politics in the post-Soviet international arena.

Perhaps the most significant impact of the disintegration of the Soviet empire is the consequent change in superpower relations and the reconfiguration of the international system from a bipolar to a multipolar power structure. With the demise of the USSR and the emergence of an independent Russia on most of the former Soviet territory, the issue of

U.S.–Russian relations has come to the forefront of international affairs. At the beginning of this chapter is a quote by Alexis de Tocqueville, who wrote in the early nineteenth century that America and Russia would always be antagonists in the international arena because of their sprawling territories, conflicting international and regional interests, and different national values. That was, however, more than a century ago, before the advent of nuclear weapons, international organizations, and a commitment by Russian leaders to a democratic political system. Can the United States and Russia establish relations that usher in a new era of peaceful international politics?

When the first postcommunist government came to power in Russia under President Boris Yeltsin in August 1991, the main issue on the agenda was Western aid. The Western countries debated whether they should bail Russia out of its economic crisis as an investment in democracy. In the United States, this question was especially delicate in a midrecession election year when political leaders were hesitant to commit millions of dollars to a former enemy. U.S. taxpayers generally expected a "peace dividend" for America as the elimination of the Soviet threat prompted reductions in the defense budget. They argued that more dollars should be spent on social programs and the national infrastructure than on aid to the Russians. The Russians, for their part, refused to be treated as a fallen power on its knees, and argued that Western aid was necessary for international security and should not be seen as a form of charity to a desperate people.

Western leaders, including those in the United States, decided that aid, loans, and credits were essential to ease the demoralization caused in the lands of the former Soviet empire by food shortages, a protracted economic crisis, skyrocketing inflation, and disruptive change—all potential causes of an authoritarian backlash by Russian nationalists. Assistance would be a small price to pay for stability in Russia. In the spring of 1992, Western nations agreed on an aid package of $24 billion. In July 1992, the U.S. Senate overwhelmingly approved an economic aid package of $470 million to Russia and surrounding states, marking what one observer called a "milestone in the transformation of relations between the two major protagonists of the Cold War era."[16]

In a similar display of cooperation, the United States and Russia have signed arms-control agreements that will significantly reduce the numbers of both missiles and warheads and establish permanent verification teams stationed on each other's territory. With the breakup of the Soviet Union, however, the United States must negotiate not only with Russia but also with the three other former Soviet republics—now independent states—that house nuclear arsenals: Ukraine, Belarus, and Kazakhstan. A frightening potential problem caused by this dispersion of political control is the sale of nuclear weapons and nuclear power components to third-world countries in violation of international agreements. The desperate need for hard currency in the former Soviet lands may prompt individuals and states to sell their nuclear arsenals to countries in the Middle East, Africa, or Asia. So while the nuclear weapons issue has been largely diffused as a source of the U.S.–Russian conflict, the potential for unregulated nuclear proliferation may increase as the search for economic security replaces the race for military superiority.

In forging new patterns of international relations, much will depend on the role Russia chooses for itself in the international arena. A year after the emergence of Russia in international politics as an independent state, political forces inside the country are vigorously debating its status among the family of nations and states. By mid-1992, three different approaches to Russian foreign policy emerged from within the country.

The *Atlanticists* envision Russia as a productive and cooperative player in the political and economic institutions of the Atlantic community—the United States, Canada, and Europe. Through membership in the International Monetary Fund (IMF), the General Agreement on Tariffs and Trade (GATT), and the World Bank, Russia will first recover its economic stability and then become a contributing member of the thriving Western economy. By opening up its markets to Western businesses, Russia can promote economic and political integration, benefit from established free-market practices, and improve its economic performance. Russia should also turn westward for its models of representative democracy and seek to be accepted as a member of the community of Western democracies pursuing international peace and stability. While Russia should retain its unique national culture and separate identity, the predominant goal is to become an equal player in the Atlantic community where nationalism and the unilateral search for power are secondary to the search for mutual security and common economic gain.

The *Eurasianists,* on the other hand, argue that a turn westward will reduce Russia to secondary status as it tries to enter established patterns of trade and diplomacy from a considerably weakened position. By bowing to the economic might of the Atlantic powers, Russia will become only a "raw-material appendage" of the West—providing Western economies with valuable resources, but never being accepted as an equal partner in trade or political negotiations. Russia should resist the West's attempt to influence its domestic politics through economic leverage, as evidenced in IMF demands for political and economic reforms in exchange for its Russian aid and credit package. The proud history of Russia's role as a world power can be maintained only if Russia turns east and strives to assume leadership in Asia. Better to be a dominant power among the less developed countries of the East than a second cousin to the established powers of the West.

Finally, the *empire-builders* argue that Russia can turn neither West nor East until it has reestablished its rightful role as leader of a great empire. The political forces inside the country that espouse this role are represented both by Communist hardliners and extreme nationalists. The disintegration of the Russian-dominated empire in 1989–91 was a historical sacrilege that must be put to rights by the reestablishment of a Slavic empire—whether it be within nineteenth-century Russian or twentieth-century Soviet borders. The separation of the Slavic peoples into the independent states of Russia, the Ukraine, and Belarus was a sin against nationhood and must be rectified before Russia can assume its role as a world leader. Russia should continue to be a multinational state from the Baltic Sea to the shores of Vladivostok on the basis of its territorial expanse, cultural influence, and rich resources. The empire-builders want to turn inward to reconsolidate imperial power as a foundation for establishing a more predominant role in international relations.

All three approaches share the common assumption that Russia has entered the international arena as a "great power," even though it has been temporarily disarmed by economic crisis and internal disintegration. If and how Russia proves to play the role of a great power will tell us much about the criteria for great-power status in post–Cold War world politics: control of territory, military might, economic prowess, or internal stability based on democratic government.

SUMMARY

During the years of superpower rivalry, the United States and the Soviet Union dominated international relations by their control over vast military forces and leadership of their respective spheres of influence. The potential for conflict between the two superpowers was so great with the advent of nuclear weapons that they struggled to forge channels of cooperation even as they pursued opposing geostrategic, regional, ideological, and economic goals. The result was a 50-year Cold War—mutual attempts by the two great powers to undermine each other's power and influence while avoiding direct military confrontation.

The tension involved in this unstable peace was alleviated by Mikhail Gorbachev's foreign policy of "new political thinking," a strategy designed to reorient Soviet power in international relations from confrontation and coercion to cooperation. Neither the Soviet bloc in Eastern Europe nor the multinational Soviet empire survived the tension between Soviet central control and the momentum of independence. The consequent disintegration of the Soviet Union led to an explosion of ethnic disputes, territorial conflicts, battles for political power, and the creation of new states—all of which has had a momentous impact on international relations.

The disappearance of superpower rivalry as the cornerstone of world politics has illustrated the conflict between stability and national self-determination in the international arena. While the bipolar system dominated by the United States and the Soviet Union during the Cold War resulted in peace, it was an uncertain peace that denied independence to the nations and states in the orbit of Soviet control. Though the multipolar system that emerged after the disintegration of the Soviet empire is based on free and independent nation-states, it has produced the potential for constant international conflict, as new nations fight over territory, power, and resources. Despite this tension between order and freedom, the atmosphere at the end of the twentieth century is one that is heady with opportunities and hope for a stable and deep-rooted peace. It is a hope that may prove illusory, given the nature of power in the international arena; but it is nevertheless a hope that has been absent for the past 50 years.

NOTES

1. Louis J. Halle, *The Cold War as History* (New York: Harper and Row, 1967), pp. 160–61.

2. President Wilson was the chief architect of the League of Nations in 1919 after World War I, only to see U.S. participation rejected by an isolationist Congress. The League, which the USSR joined in 1933, proved to be ineffective in preventing international power conflicts.

3. Russia was invaded by Napoleon Bonaparte in 1812; the Soviet Union by Hitler in 1941, resulting in millions of casualties and massive destruction.

4. Yugoslavia, under the leadership of Josip Broz Tito, remained communist but managed to escape from Soviet tutelage.

5. *New York Times,* March 6, 1946, p. 4, as quoted in Steven J. Rosen and Walter S. Jones, *The Logic of International Relations,* 2nd ed. (Cambridge, Mass.: Winthrop Publishers, 1977), pp. 44–45.

6. The USSR did not allow its Eastern European satellites to accept the West's offer of financial assistance. For example, Czechoslovakia originally accepted Marshall Plan aid, only to find out on Western radio broadcasts that the USSR had refused it for them.

7. X (George Kennan), "The Sources of Soviet Conduct," *Foreign Affairs* (July 1947): 566–82.

8. Rosen and Jones, *Logic,* p. 46.

9. Walter Lippmann, *The Communist World and Ours* (Boston: Little, Brown, 1959).

10. Henry A. Kissinger, *American Foreign Policy,* 3rd ed. (New York: W. W. Norton, 1977), p. 144.

11. Rosen and Jones, *Logic,* p. 248.

12. Kissinger, *American Foreign Policy,* pp. 144–47.

13. "Basic Principles of Relations between the Union of Soviet Socialist Republics and the United States of America," *Pravda* and *Izvestia,* May 30, 1972,

p. 1, reprinted in Gordon Livermore, ed. *Soviet Foreign Policy Today, 1986–1989,* 3rd ed. (Columbus, Ohio: Current Digest of the Soviet Press, 1989), pp. 42–43.

14. Raymond W. Copson, "Contra Aid and the Reagan Doctrine: An Overview," *Congressional Research Service Review,* 8, no. 3 (March 1987): 1.

15. "Soviet Exchanges with U.S. Booming," *New York Times,* May 28, 1990, p. 7.

16. Helen Dewar, "Senate Approves Russian Aid Package," *Washington Post,* July 3, 1992, 1.

SUGGESTED READINGS

Bialer, Seweryn. *The Soviet Paradox: External Expansion, Internal Decline.* New York: Knopf, 1986. Details the development of problems and paradoxes that emerged in Soviet society and throughout the Eastern bloc since World War II, illustrating the costs to the Soviet Union in maintaining its pre-Gorbachev foreign policy goals.

Bialer, Seweryn, and Michael Mandelbaum, eds. *Gorbachev's Russia and American Foreign Policy.* Boulder, Colo.: Westview Press, 1988. A collection of timely articles by Soviet specialists on internal changes in the USSR under Gorbachev and the implications for U.S.–Soviet relations.

Gati, Charles. *The Bloc That Failed: Soviet–East European Relations in Transition.* Bloomington: Indiana University Press, 1990. Examines the strengths and weaknesses of the pre-Gorbachev Soviet–Eastern European relationship and the attempt by Gorbachev (which subsequently proved unsuccessful) to manage the tension between greater freedom for Eastern Europe and the maintenance of the "socialist bloc."

Gromyko, Anatoly, and Martin Hellman, eds. *Breakthrough/Proriv: Emerging New Thinking.* New York: Walker, 1988. Essays by Soviet and American scholars on changing concepts of international security, forging superpower cooperation, and mutual prevention of the outbreak of confrontations.

Hoffman, Erik P., and Frederic J. Fleron, Jr. *The Conduct of Soviet Foreign Policy,* expanded 2nd ed. New York: Aldine Publishing, 1980. Collection of essays that focus on the domestic motivations of Soviet foreign policy and their implications for intern relations.

Mastny, Vojtech. *Russia's Road to the Cold War: Diplomacy, Warfare, and the Politics of Communism, 1941–1945.* New York: Columbia University Press, 1979. Explains the Russian point of view in the events that led up to World War II and the consequent development of Soviet–U.S. tensions in the postwar period.

Sherr, Alan B. *The Other Side of Arms Control: Soviet Objectives in the Gorbachev Era.* Boston: Unwin Hyman, 1988. Detailed account of Soviet objectives in pursuing nuclear arms control and verification agreements in the

Gorbachev period, with a clear and detailed explanation of Gorbachev's foreign policy, economic, and military objectives at the end of the twentieth century.

Ulam, Adam B. *Expansion and Coexistence: Soviet Foreign Policy 1917–1973,* 2nd ed. New York: Holt, Rinehart, and Winston, 1974. Classic work on Soviet foreign policy from World War I until Vietnam. Provides a rich and fact-filled account of Soviet aims and strategies that artfully combines meticulous detail with broader theoretical analysis.

13

Stability and Change

All progress is precarious, and the solution of one problem brings us
face to face with another problem.

—Martin Luther King, Jr.

All great changes are irksome to the human mind, especially those
which are attended with great dangers and uncertain effects.

—John Adams

A party of order or stability, and a party of progress or reform, are
both necessary elements of healthy state and political life.

—John Stuart Mill

All is change; all yields its place and goes.

—Euripides

THE FORCES OF CHANGE

As events in the former "Eastern bloc" and the Soviet Union of 1989
and 1990 demonstrate, political systems—even those 40 or 50 years old—
are susceptible to dramatic change, often in relatively short periods of
time. How can political systems, considered strong and powerful, be
overtaken by events? What aspects of change can produce dramatic
alterations in the political systems of a given country? What economic
and social forces can overcome the efforts of political systems to remain
in control of their populations? What aspects of the nature of change can
be utilized by political systems in order to maintain themselves, and
which are likely to undermine those systems?

Few observers of the political situation in the late 1980s in Eastern
Europe and the Soviet Union predicted the amazing and far-reaching
changes that swept over these areas. Fewer still were able to project the
pace of events or even the time of their onset. Within a matter of months,
cataclysmic changes swept through Poland, Czechoslovakia, Hungary,
Bulgaria, East Germany, and Romania. In the Soviet Union, unrest

accelerated or intensified as events in Eastern Europe raced to a hereto-
fore unthinkable conclusion: the swift end of communist domination in
those countries. The year 1993 saw the further breakup of the countries
of Czechoslovakia and Yugoslavia.

We are often conditioned to expect change and revolution in the less
developed countries of the world, especially among the newly emergent
countries of Africa and Asia; but we are often taken by surprise when
such events occur in "developed" or "modern" countries. Yet many of
the same forces are actually at work in the most developed countries,
even though the pace of the change is more likely to be evolutionary than
revolutionary. And a historian looking at Europe after the dramatic
changes in 1848 might see many similarities with the kind of changes
occurring in those polities of the former Eastern bloc today.

How can we make sense of these changes? How can we appreciate the
types of influence vectors that lead to political changes? How can we
come to grips with the fundamental natures of stability and change? What
are the forces of change and stability that can be analyzed and understood? Which can be contained and modified by governmental action? In
order to examine these questions, we turn to the nature of society.

In this chapter, we examine the dynamic nature of society to see how
different peoples and different governments face economic and political
change while trying to preserve stability. Increasingly, we all live in a
global village, with outside forces impinging constantly on our daily lives.
No state and no ruler can totally insulate his or her people from the forces
of change that affect their lives. With Cable News Network (CNN) and
other television programs catching the nature of political and social
change on a minute-by-minute basis, we can all be made aware of changes
even as they happen.

Because both the internal and external environments of any political
system are constantly changing, the political system itself must be able
to adapt. It faces new demands from its people. It also faces new realities
in the international community, whether they be the price of raw materials such as copper or iron or a new government in some neighboring
country. The political system must also deal with the changing nature of
its own society.

It was Talcott Parsons who pioneered the study of societies from the
point of view of the role of individuals and the patterns or relationships
between individuals and their societies.[1] Among other contributions,
Parsons noted that a key difference between "traditional" and "modern"
societies has to do with the relationship between an individual and the
degree of status that he or she enjoys. For Parsons, individuals in
traditional societies are born into certain social classes and, as a consequence, enjoy certain privileges. These ascriptive aspects differ greatly
from the achievement orientation of modern society, in which people
typically attain status on the basis of what they have accomplished as
individuals.

Now, for most Americans (except perhaps those of high social and economic status), the idea of being born into a class and not being able to work one's way out of it no matter what one does is unsettling. We like to think that we can go out, attain an education, make some money, accomplish a set of goals, and thereby improve our station in life. On the other hand, traditional society often offers a sense of order and tranquility that derives from knowing that one has a place and is secure in that position.

Although it is difficult for us to imagine what it would be like to live in a truly traditional society, we should be aware that certain aspects of such societies have sometimes been glorified. We may be told, for example, that the thirteenth and fourteenth centuries in Europe were the happiest of all because people knew their place in society and because they almost universally accepted the Christian faith, with its belief in life after death and its guarantee of a place in eternity.

This picture of traditional European society is one sided, to say the least.[2] War, pestilence, famine, and the Black Death swept across the continent during this same period, carrying off as much as 30 percent of the population. If one's place in eternity was a matter of importance for the average person of the day, imagine the stress placed on such an individual when asked to choose between first two, then three popes, each claiming that he represented the only true way to eternal life. At the same time, belief in witchcraft, devils, and spirits was common in every-day life. Mental illness was also rather common. Life was brief and often brutal. In short, the totally traditional society of the past was not necessarily the pastoral landscape sometimes depicted in art and literature.

Living as we do in the United States during the 1990s, we find our attention fixed on drugs, crime, and the other stresses of modern life. Bombarded as we are by advertisements for all manner of medicines to help us cope with the problems of daily existence, we often forget or find it hard to identify with the stresses in less modern societies where the search for food and other necessities of life require an almost endless effort.

Nor can we as Americans appreciate the importance of individual freedom in our daily lives. Most of us take that for granted. To the students in China or the populations of Eastern Europe, however, the ideas of "freedom" or "democracy" or "liberty" and the striving for them become stress ridden if not life threatening as well. We talked about the implications of terminology and concepts in Chapter 3, and have alluded to these stressful aspects in other chapters.

STAGES OF SOCIETAL DEVELOPMENT

Here we wish to focus more closely on what a *traditional* society is like and then trace how it develops into a *transitional* society and finally becomes *modern*.

Traditional Society

A *traditional society* is most consistently characterized by strong kinship attachments. The family, the extended family (including cousins, aunts, and uncles), and the clan are the social units that mean the most. Individuals belong to the society through membership in certain families. Individuals also belong to certain classes as a result of being born into certain families. Birth determines status because the society as a whole is quite static. Indeed, it is often rigidly stratified according to class or caste. *Social mobility,* or the ability of individuals to move from one class to another, is quite limited.

In traditional society, custom remains all important. Youth does not set any trends. No one particularly cares what young people would like to wear, what music they would like to hear, or indeed what they want to be when they grow up. It is expected that they will become what their mothers and fathers already are. There is a strong sense of religion, whether it be Christian, Islam, Hindu, or tribal. Much of what happens to one's life is ascribed to the will of the gods. Society as a whole looks to worlds beyond this one, either in terms of a future heaven or hell or in terms of one's ancestors and of the yet unborn—all viewed on a continuum with present-day society.[3]

To many Americans these are difficult concepts to grasp—let alone identify with—but in many parts of the world, religion continues to play an overriding role in everyday life. Consider, for example, the concept of martyrdom. In the world of fundamentalist Islam, should one die promoting the faith in fighting against infidels, one goes directly to paradise. Few Americans would accept the notion that anything in the next life is worth losing this one; but as the Iraq–Iran War demonstrated, many tens of thousands of people were willing to freely give up their lives in the name of religion, bolstered by the firm belief that what they were doing in this life would dramatically improve their lot in the next.[4]

The economic life of the community in a traditional society is closely tied to subsistence agriculture or animal herding. In fact, many societies in this stage depend on simple food gathering and hunting. A major feature of traditional society is the importance of land. Often, land ownership is monopolized by a single class or ethnic group. An individual simply does not go out and "buy" land, either because there is no way to accumulate the cash necessary to buy it or because society discourages landownership if one belongs to a certain class (or even if one is not the eldest son in a family that already owns land).

There is generally a low level of technology. The physical infrastructures that we associate with an industrial economy—roads, bridges, harbors, and railroads—are frequently lacking. The cash sector of the economy is small or nonexistent. Most families and villages grow their own food, engaging in barter for other required items. If labor is organized, it is by class, caste, or guild. Individuals do not suddenly decide that they want to be carpenters or masons. Long periods of training and acceptance are required. Population increases slowly because the high birth rates of this country are almost matched by high death rates (see Figure 13-1). Life expectancy may not exceed 30 years, and half of the children may die before they are ten. Illiteracy is high (perhaps 90 percent), and the number of people living in cities is low (often under 10 percent).

In recent years, we have seen that the introduction of medical technology from outside the traditional society (such as brought via bilateral aid or the World Health Organization) can save many lives that would otherwise have been lost. At the same time that it is saving lives, however, the new technology is putting a significant strain on the entire fabric of society: increased birth rates and decreased death rates can produce a population explosion that outruns the ability of the society to cope with it.

In the United States today, we have a very low net population increase per year. In fact, we are now worried about the possible implications of the "greying" of America as the workforce matures and there are likely to be greater labor needs than previously thought, entering the twenty-first century.

But across the world, the population explosion continues unabated: 250,000 people are added to the world's population daily. This means that a population the size of the former USSR is added to the world every four years. In many countries such as Mexico, Nigeria, Morocco, or Indonesia, fully 50 percent of the population is under 15 years of age, and these rapidly growing populations place enormous strains on virtually all aspects of daily life.

Figure 13-1. Stages of Development as Seen in Birth and Death Rates

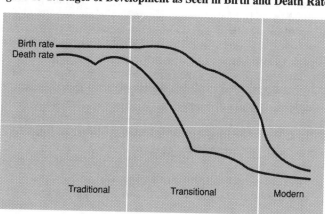

Within the political system of a traditional society, the central government is weak. Most people look first to their local leaders. There are few national political institutions; basic decisions are usually made by a small number of elites. Participation in decision making is limited. The legitimacy of the political system is based on traditional values. (The people who rule are *expected* to rule. It is their birthright.) There is usually a small professional army and bureaucracy, and the capability of the central government to change the status quo is quite limited. In fact, in many traditional societies the political authority spends most of its time trying to stay in power. On the other hand, political systems based within traditional societies may remain in power for long periods of time if there are no major intrusions from outside and if the rulers make little effort to alter the nature of society. Stability often persists in traditional political systems until the moment that social change begins to overwhelm them.

Transitional Society

If stability is the hallmark of traditional societies, change characterizes transitional ones. *Transitional societies* are societies in flux, with changing demographic, economic, and political patterns. Perhaps most important are changes in fundamental attitudes and values that accompany the transition. Richard Critchfield has done a marvelous job in capturing the ebb and flow of new forces as they alter life in transitional societies, painting a most optimistic portrait of change as it has occurred around the globe.[5]

The political center asserts its authority as it tries to contain or reduce the influence of regional forces. Groupings based on ascription continue to be important, but other formations—associational in character—also develop. Labor unions are often formed, for example; and they have no ethnic or family basis. Political parties may be formed, either by the government or in spite of it.

Extensive changes also take place in the economic systems, as people begin to swtich from agricultural pursuits to nonagricultural ones. They leave their farms and homesteads, seeking employment in the cash sector. As industrialization becomes widespread, major improvements in the physical infrastructures of the country take place: railroads and ports are built; airfields and roads are constructed. As per capita income rises, so does the gross national product. Most important is the process of capital accumulation. Whether investment is carried out by individual entrepreneurs in capitalist societies or by government agencies in socialist ones, it rises from 5 percent to 10 percent a year in traditional societies and as high as 25 percent a year in transitional ones.

As A. F. K. Organski has pointed out, the approach to economic development chosen in a given society is crucial in determining the eventual nature of the society.[6] Organski sees three fundamental political approaches to the problem of capital formation and economic change in transitional societies: (1) the bourgeois or capitalist approach, in which individuals and companies provide the major reinvestment thrust; (2) the Stalinist or repressive approach, in which the government forces the society to reinvest; and (3) the syncretic approach, in which a combination of industrial and agricultural elites seeks to slow down the process of industrialization in order to restabilize society.

Whatever form it takes, the process of economic development in transitional societies is usually slow, and it is often bloody. The only way to accumulate enough capital to industrialize is to get it from somebody, whether through 14-hour workdays or forced collectivization. Furthermore, capital reinvested in productive capacity is not available to meet consumer demands, so individuals and their short-term interests may be sacrificed for the "greater" good of the state. Thus, the Enclosure Acts in eighteenth-century England, the collectivization of the peasants in twentieth-century Russia, and even the American Civil War in the nineteenth century can all be seen as results of the modernization process.

Yet, during the transitional stage, the capabilities of the central government—its ability to tap its human and natural resources—improve dramatically. Increasing numbers of people come under its jurisdiction. Industrialization and economic development increase its productive base, enabling it to support an expanded bureaucracy and army. Literacy climbs and communication improves. More and more people move to the cities. At the same time, citizens show more awareness of government and place greater demands on it. Some writers feel that high political participation by those who benefit inadequately from a growing economy tends to result in greater economic equality and a more stable situation overall.[7]

Samuel Huntington and Joan Nelson, however, argue that the process of modernization—in bringing about an increase in political participation—may actually threaten the existing political authority.[8] With greater access to information and with raised expectations, groups within the society may soon demand more rewards than the system is able to deliver as pressures develop for increased welfare, medical care, and educational opportunity. Furthermore, as the 1979 revolution in Iran clearly underscored, in a transitional society the traditional authorities may be revitalized enough to challenge the existing regime, which is unable to keep the changing demands in balance.

A transitional society has a profound effect on individuals as well. Instead of remaining totally oriented toward the traditions of the past, individuals must now develop new ways of dealing with the changes they are confronting on all sides. They must develop what David Riesman has called a "psychological gyroscope"[9] to help them adjust. Whether we term the process "detribalization," "Westernization," "emancipation," or "defeudalization," the individual's entire frame of reference may shift from the past to the present as old values are challenged and overridden. This change may produce a "freer" and more open society, but it may also lead to unrest and concern. It may even produce a reversion to traditional beliefs, as it has in the Middle East, where the forces of Islam are reasserting themselves against the forces of modernity.

In this regard, Michael Novak argues persuasively that indigenous cultural factors—rather than exogenous forces (such as international imperialism)—are more important, in the long run, in determining the rate and success of the modernization process.[10]

No matter what reverberations are felt in the political system, the nature of everyday life changes as well. Instead of responding to the demands of nature and the rhythm of seasons, individuals find themselves responding to the demands of machines and industry. New health aids, greater awareness of disease patterns, and better nutrition lead inevitably to substantial declines in the death rate and a corresponding increase in life expectancy. Yet, for a period of time (often a generation or more), high birth rates also continue, thereby leading to the population explosion indicated in Figure 13.1. More people stay alive longer and have more children, more of whom survive to adulthood; and these people in turn have more children. Thus, a country such as Mexico may end up with a major portion of its population under the age of 20 and a population growing faster than either the economy or food production. The attractions of urban life mask the accompanying squalor and unemployment. All in all, transitional societies reflect troubling times as well as times of great opportunity. It takes a wise and prudent government to harmonize the forces of change and stability in such a way as to make the modernization process less disruptive.

Modern Society

Having considered the dynamics of change in traditional and transitional societies, we will briefly examine the comparable aspects of *modern societies*. However, we should point out right at the beginning that most "modern" societies contain elements of transitional and traditional societies as well. It is the broad distinctions, therefore, that you should keep in mind.

A modern society is characterized by high levels of literacy, industrialization, and urbanization. Typically, more than 90 percent of the population is able to read and write. Over 50 percent of the workforce is engaged in nonagricultural pursuits, and over half the population lives in urban areas. Communications are extensive; there are often more radios and television sets than people.

Demographic patterns also change as the birth rate declines and the death rate—after its precipitous drop during the transitional stage—levels off. Families become more mobile, and breadwinners change jobs frequently. Smaller families become the norm. With advantages in medical technology, the average life span increases to 70 years or longer. Cancer, heart disease, and strokes replace malaria, tuberculosis, and pneumonia as the major killers.

Society as a whole is dominated by associational groups. Although birth into a very rich or very poor family may clearly help or hinder a person's social progress, merit increasingly makes social mobility possible. Society is characterized by a decline in religious activity, and the general ethos becomes more secular. The central government is large, its bureaucratic agencies reaching out into all aspects of life. Bureaucratic government—whether on the national, state/provincial, or local level—is the order of the day. Individuals find that society has changed; there is often more "social" security in the form of health care, educational opportunity, unemployment compensation, and the like. At the same time, a sense of alienation increases as traditional values are cast aside and the socializing forces of the family and church decline in importance.

A paradox also arises: individuals have more personal freedom in that they are not required to conform to the traditions of the past, yet certain aspects of mass society impose new form of conformity. For example, in the United States, McDonald's hamburgers are the same wherever they are sold, and Holiday Inn's universal slogan proclaims, "The best surprise is no surprise." Diversity and individualism may be sacrificed in favor of monotonous conformity. In the face of huge corporations, big government, big labor unions, and other associational groups, all too often the individual may feel frustrated, powerless, and alone.

Moreover, in the modern societies created as the result of the imposition of communism in Eastern Europe by the Soviet Union following World War II, we see the additional factor of individualism being subordinated not just to modern life, but to a strict ideology as well. Just as the desire for independence masked tribal rivalries and ethnic competition in the new states of Africa and Asia, so too the ideology of communism papered over ethnic and nationalist conflicts in those societies, including the former Soviet Union.

POLITICAL LEADERSHIP AND THE FORCES OF CHANGE

The foregoing analysis of the three stages of societal development is the customary view of those professionals whose business it is to analyze the forces of change and stability. To Americans of the 1990s, however, legitimate questions arise about possible further stages of societal change. What about zero population growth? What happens to an industrial society that has been founded on the availability of cheap energy when that energy becomes expensive and difficult to come by? At what point do occupational patterns shift and people begin returning to the land? Is there enough land to return to?

As the United States works its way through the 1990s, it is clear that it is a far different world than its leadership faced in the 1960s or 1970s or 1980s. With the fading of the Cold War and the emergence of Japan as an economic powerhouse, with the seemingly unmanageable U.S. federal budget deficit, and with many American products and policies on the defensive all across the world, what will be required of U.S. political leadership?

The answers to these and similar questions lie beyond the scope of this chapter, but you should keep the questions in mind as you read the sections that follow. In them we shall be examining the quality of political leadership as it struggles with the problems presented by the past. We shall be looking at the ways in which different leaders respond to changing circumstances as well as the different challenges of stability and change as they are perceived in different cultures. However, as we ponder these issues we should be aware that, even as leaders grapple with change, the pace of change may be accelerating.

We often refer to political leadership in a way that suggests we prefer "strong" leaders—people who know what needs to be done and who set about doing it. Yet we may forget to examine the existing level of political development within the political system at the time of the leader's ascension to power. We frequently fail to realize that a leader may make the "right" decisions, but that the state of the political system may make it impossible to carry out those decisions. Valerie Bunce has argued that not only leadership itself but also changes in leadership make an important difference in political life, regardless of the type of political system.[11] Furthermore, as James MacGregor Burns has pointed out, leadership also involves "followership." There is clearly a dynamic relationship between the leader and those who support his or her leadership,[12] and the nature of this relationship is not well understood, even by experts.

In studying political development and the relative strength of different political systems, we face serious problems of measurement. How do we measure political development? How can we say that one political system is more developed than another? True, we can often measure social or economic differences with some precision. The per capita income in Somalia is less than $100 a year, whereas in Sweden it exceeds $20,000. Thus we have no difficulty in saying that Sweden's *economy* is more developed than Somalia's. However, judging political systems and dividing them into categories such as "primitive," "developing," or "developed" proves far more difficult. We have to use words such as "flexibility" and "rationality"—words that cannot be quantified in the same way as rates of literacy or urbanization. In short, it is far more difficult to judge *political* systems than societies or economies.

Before we try to establish some criteria for judging political systems (and also the relationship of those systems to the societies they govern), we must realize that all governments—whether those of Native American hunting bands or the People's Republic of China—attempt to perform essentially the same functions. The government of Kuwait and that of Ireland do the same basic things for their citizens—within their respective limits. Because governments differ in size, scale, and goals, we should not make the mistake of assuming that they are intrinsically different in what they do. All governments depend on support (whether of individuals, classes, groups, organizations, or masses), and all have to deal with demands placed on them (again, whether by individuals, classes, groups, organizations, or masses).

All political systems—no matter how small-scale or "primitive"—provide basic legal and societal order, process demands, elicit support, make decisions that are enforced, and set goals. Although the simplicity and sporadic nature of the decision-making process in traditional societies may confuse observers, the differences between systems are often more of degree than of kind.

Many traditional political systems do, in fact, exhibit some traits associated with significant levels of development, even if one uses conventional criteria as yardsticks of measurement. For example, small hunting-band societies (such as the Eskimos of North America, the Bambuti pygmies of the Ituri forest, and the Kung bushmen of the Kalahari Desert in Africa) exhibit "democratic" and "rational" decision-making procedures, even though they are small-scale, low-technology societies. The leader of the band may or may not be the son of a previous headman. Collective decisions are made by the group as a whole, although individuals generally initiate their own activities.

As we shall suggest, however, political development usually entails a variety of characteristics; and if a system exemplifies only one characteristic of high development, that fact does not make up for a lack of the others.[13] It is important to remember that the degree of development depends ultimately on a cluster of characteristics, all of which are important and none of which is sufficient.

The four characteristics that we are about to examine are interrelated. They tend to be mutually reinforcing in terms of the political system. Also, the internal dynamics of different societies require differing balances of these characteristics. For example, the country of Zaire contains people from more than 100 different tribal backgrounds. Clearly, the government of Zaire must emphasize national unity and work for effective "linkage" between itself and these diverse groups if it is to survive. The government of Sweden, on the other hand, faces a society that is homogeneous, wherein virtually all citizens share a common language and ethnic background and even a common set of historical experiences. Its need to promote effective linkage is of a quite different order.

Effective Linkage

The first of the characteristics of political development is *effective linkage*. In the case of Zaire, there is clearly a great need for effective linkage because the history of that country reflects a series of rebellions and disaffections with the efforts of government. The breakup of Pakistan into two states (the second subsequently named Bangladesh in 1971) is a good example of a system's failure to develop sufficiently effective linkage to hold the country together. And linkage is the goal as the new government in Nicaragua tries to establish control over, and support from, the Indian tribes on its northern frontier.

In the former Soviet Union, moreover, after 70 years of communist rule, we have seen the limited extent to which whole groups of people—the Latvians, the Estonians, the Lithuanians, the Uzbeks, the Armenians—were actually "linked" to the system and, in fact, preferred independence to remaining within the Soviet state.

Stated simply, effective linkage is the set of physical and psychological bonds that link the central political authority to the society (or societies) that it governs. In a developed political system, the primacy of the center (your government) is acknowledged by the overwhelming majority of its citizens. This means that they acknowledge the right of the government to make laws and to enforce them; in addition, it means that there is a set of national symbols that is generally accepted as having meaning for the citizens. In short, these citizens believe in the nation and accept the political system's right to govern them. Many times it is necessary for the political leadership to go out and create those symbols and inculcate those meanings.

Widened Political Participation

There has been a running debate in political science circles for several decades over just what *political participation* is—and, more controversially, what "meaningful" participation is. Yet, political participation remains an important criterion of political development in the sense that a political system's ability to utilize fully its human resources may depend on citizen participation.

We are not for a moment suggesting that political participation must take place in a particular form. The framework for participation—whether democratic or totalitarian, whether single-party or multiparty—may be less important than increased role playing by the citizens of the polity. In other words, if a government can get, let us say, 75 percent of the population to voting booths and get them to vote on a given day, this tells us something about the ability of the government to marshal its human resources—even if that 75 percent can cast their ballots only for a single slate of candidates who were handpicked by the government.

Now we might say that there is greater, or "more meaningful," or even "better" participation if those people are given a choice at the polls. But the sheer act of voting represents at least a rudimentary level of political development different from that of not voting at all, partly because participation through voting indicates that the political elite is attached—however tenuously—to representative institutions. Widened political participation is generally accompanied by a broadening of recruitment patterns and the inclusion of a wider spectrum of socioeconomic groups on the basis of achievement rather than ascription.

However, any system operating on the assumption that forced participation in an election where there is no choice of candidates (even if they are of the same party) is as meaningful as if the people's selection were made openly and freely is likely to make many mistakes in adopting politics based on that assumption.

As indicated earlier, however, scholars such as Samuel Huntington have suggested that too rapid or too widespread participation may overwhelm the political system; indeed, there is a fine line between encouraging participation and letting it get out of control. In addition, one cannot automatically say whether a certain participation level indicates the health or illness of a political system. For example, only slightly more than 50 percent of the American electorate votes in our presidential elections. Some have argued that this low turnout is bad for the Republic—that it reflects the fact people think they are not getting much of a choice. On the other hand, it could certainly be argued that one reason why many Americans don't vote is that they are relatively satisfied with the system and are convinced whoever wins is not going to jeopardize the existing society or political system. It could mean, also, many believe that, no matter who wins, not much will be done to improve their lot.

Conversely, in situations where extremely high levels of participation are observed, one can sometimes see the weakness—not the strength—of the political system. For example, during the final months of the Weimar Republic in Germany—as socialists, Nazis, and communists struggled to determine the future of the country—a series of national elections took place in which participation was high (over 95 percent). People voted because they dared not stay home. It was too important. The future of the entire system was at stake. In short, as a criterion of political development, formal citizen participation in and of itself may tell us little about a system.

Increased Capabilities

Another useful category of analysis in comparing different political systems looks to the capabilities of central decision makers to implement their goals and carry out their programs. In fact, *increased capabilities* constitute a major ingredient in the cluster of variables we encounter when we analyze political development.

"Capabilities analysis" grew out of the efforts made by Gabriel Almond and James Coleman[14] to apply to political systems the structural/functional approach of sociologist Talcott Parsons. By focusing on the ability of a political system to attain its goals, they attempted to measure the performance of the political system in organizing and utilizing its human and natural resources.

Some of the important capabilities to be considered in any analysis of a functioning political system are the regulative, extractive, distributive, rejuvenational, and symbolic capabilities. These capabilities are outlined in Box 13-1.

As a result of increased capabilities, the political system develops institutions that become permanent ongoing structures, rather than intermittent stop-and-go ones. Institutions are established that not only outlive individuals and even specific governments, but also achieve a permanent status with renewed membership as well as a continuing process for political recruitment.

The increased organizational network represented by this institutional development is an essential ingredient of an advanced political system, for it is this "set" of institutions that enables the system to cushion itself from destructive effects of the forces of change. They provide a kind of political insulation that permits the absorption of new individuals, groups, and pressures without letting them impinge directly on the political center.

This discussion of increased capabilities and corresponding institutional development may sound rather theoretical. But as a ruler, you will discover its practical importance almost immediately. If your government is to survive and sustain itself, it must have a set of institutional buffers so that a single group of dissatisfied students, a striking labor union, or a clique of restless army officers cannot bring the entire system down. Most coups take place in countries where the political system either has not created these institutional buffers or has allowed them to atrophy through disuse.

Flexibility

One of the most important ingredients in a developed political system is its institutional *flexibility*. By that we mean the ability of the political system to deal with change, to meet new situations, to formulate new goals, and to process new demands and supports.

As a new ruler, you are well aware of the importance of political leadership in providing enough flexibility to take existing political systems and transform them. Fidel Castro of Cuba, Peter the Great of Russia, and Kemal Ataturk of Turkey are all examples of individuals who made

Box 13-1. Capabilities Analysis

Regulative Capability. This term *refers to the ability of a political system to control the actions of its populace and to influence its membership to behave in certain ways. It includes the army, police, and people's militia as well as the formal legal framework of laws, courts, and prisons.* The regulative capability *also involves the ways in which the leaders of the political system regulate society by the use of economic measures, the dissemination of information, and political actions.*

Extractive Capability. The extractive capability *of a political system is its ability to tap its human and natural resources. It involves the production, collection, and utilization of those resources and includes such elements as the number and quality of natural resources (either its own or those to which it has access), the size and "health" of the population (its life expectancy and its educational and medical assets), and the bureaucratic apparatus available to get at the resources. One can assess extractive capability by looking at such factors as the percentage of taxes collected versus the percentage of taxes levied, the educational system, the relative balance of the economy, the level of industrialization, and the system's ability to feed the population.*[1]

Distributive Capability. The distributive capability *of a system is its ability to reward its members through the allocation of goods, services, and status. The distributive function may be handled directly in a command economy or via government inputs into the pricing mechanism in a market or mixed economy. In analyzing this capability, we need to know not only how large a pool of goods and services is available for distribution, but also the manner of distribution. A poor country may dole out its rewards in a fair or an unfair manner. A rich country may be dominated by a small group of people who obtain the lion's share of the wealth, or it may feature an equitable distribution of the wealth.*

Rejuvenational Capability. Because the internal and external environments of a political system are *constantly changing, adjustments in the system's various capabilities and in the system as a whole must be made regularly. The ability of the political system to reinforce itself, to maintain its institutional structures, and to replenish its personnel is its* rejuvenational capability.

In Chapter 4, we examined the process of political socialization, which is an important feature *of rejuvenational capability. So, too, is the critical area of information usage. A political system needs to absorb and utilize new information—not simply information used in technology and production processes, but all aspects of human knowledge. This inflow of information and its utilization are of such importance that Karl Deutsch, in developing his communications theory, connects the self-destruction of a political system with "the process of self-closure," or the shutting off of outside information.*[2] *The ways in which a political system uses information are of vital importance in determining its ability to change and to "grow."*

Symbolic Capability. The symbolic capability *of a political system includes the overall image that it projects and is a reflection of the other capabilities together with the goals that the system is perceived to be following and perceptions about the nature of its decision making. It undergirds* the legitimacy *of the system, or its right to rule the population.*

In some countries, we can measure the people's commitment to the system by taking polls and *doing attitudinal surveys. In others, we often have to rely on more indirect or even negative indexes, such as the number of political prisoners, exiles, and refugees and the volume of propaganda the government feels it necessary to indulge in. Often this propaganda takes the form of exaggerating foreign threats in order to bolster internal solidarity.*

Notes:

1. For an examination of the relationship between internal and international development, see P. T. Bauer, Reality and Rhetoric: Studies in the Economics of Development *(Cambridge, Mass.: Harvard University Press, 1984).*

2. Karl W. Deutsch, The Nerves of Government *(Glencoe, Ill.: Free Press, 1963).*

dramatic changes in the lives of their people. But you are also aware that, unless the force, vigor, and fluidity of the charismatic leader can be institutionalized, the chances for substantial and sustained political development are slim.

How can flexibility be institutionalized? In India, an efficient and effective bureaucracy was created.

The important thing to remember about flexibility is that only those systems adaptable—and adapting—to change are likely to survive for long. And yet, creative flexibility requires that some elements of stability be maintained even as the system is modifying itself to meet the demands of change.

Thus, when trying to compare political systems and using these criteria, we see that a developed political system will exhibit effective integration or linkage, widened leader participation, institutional differentiation, and a rational and flexible style in its decision making. These attributes have a generalized cumulative effect on the heightening of the capabilities of the political system. A developed political system will therefore be more effective and more likely to achieve a favorable pattern of problem solving, both internally and externally.

POLITICAL DEVOLUTION

In outlining the aspects of political development and the characteristics that a political system ought to exhibit if it is to have a good chance of blending stability and change, we have not accented the obvious corollary: systems do not simply develop; they decay, as well. Although, in the literature, there is much more written on political development than on political decay, some important works nevertheless suggest that we know a good deal about *political devolution* (or political decay), too.[15] There is also a huge amount of material on revolutionary change,[16] which, after all, is the flip side of the devolution coin—the overthrow of a political system as seen by those who are overthrowing it. Just as economic growth can be retarded or reversed, so can political development degenerate and the political system in question devolve. In fact, rapid economic or social progress may cause the buildup of pressures and the evolution of interest groups that do not accept the existing political framework. An ethos of distrust and hatred may prevent the orderly flow of information and its rational assessment and use. If there are not sufficient and properly functioning institutions of a local and regional nature—to regulate communal conflict, to mute shrill demands of the national government, and to act as baffles for dysfunctional forces—the system will be threatened. Overloading the system may cause devolution.

In a sense, *total* reversal of political development seldom occurs (although there are examples of this phenomenon, such as the Holy Roman Empire). In a particular system, many institutions may cease to function properly, or important symbols may lose their efficacy; but these institutions or symbols continue to exist, although the capabilities of the political system decay. The central authority may no longer be able to regulate society, let alone develop it. Many of its symbols may become outdated and unable to elicit support. Its ability to rejuvenate itself may be drastically curtailed. Its political elite may fix on a series of irrational goals and destroy the system in an attempt to achieve them. In short, the system suffers a decline in political efficiency, decreased institutionalization, irrational decision making, reduced participation, and structural changes in societal and political activity. Underdeveloped or developing political systems are not the only victims of these malfunctions. Modern states also go through periods of transition in which the forces of modernization ebb and flow.

SUMMARY

In this chapter, we have tried to point out the various dimensions of the modernization process and indicated the extent to which social, economic, and political change are intertwined. We have also underscored the extent to which change and stability both provide challenges even to effectively functioning political systems.

In analyzing the aspects that signal political development, we also pointed out the extent to which these accomplishments and characteristics are reversible. Political systems can devolve as well as evolve, and political decay may occur as well as political development.

Perhaps the most important aspect to be remembered is the extent to which political leadership turns out to be a key variable in the development or devolution process. Political leadership can make the difference between a political system that becomes more effective in dealing with its problems and one that becomes less effective in dealing with them.

NOTES

1. Talcott Parsons, *The Social System* (Glencoe, Ill.: Free Press, 1951); and Talcott Parsons and Edward Shils, *Toward a General Theory of Action* (Cambridge, Mass.: Harvard University Press, 1951).

2. Barbara Tuchman, *A Distant Mirror* (New York: Knopf, 1978). See Michael Wood, *In Search of the Dark Ages* (New York: Facts on File, 1987).

3. See the very illuminating work by E. LeRoy Ladurie, *Montaillou: The Promised Land of Error* (New York: Random House, 1979).

4. For an interesting analysis of the relationship between various types of

government and the role of religion, see Terrance Carroll, "Secularization and the Stages of Modernity," *World Politics*, 36, no. 3 (April 1984): 362–82.

5. Richard Critchfield, *Villages* (Garden City, N.Y.: Doubleday, 1983).

6. A. F. K. Organski, *The Stages of Political Development* (New York: Knopf, 1965).

7. Ikuo Kabashima, "Supportive Participation with Economic Growth," *World Politics*, 36, no. 3 (April 1984): 304–38.

8. Samuel Huntington and Joan Nelson, *No Easy Choice: Political Participation in Developing Countries* (Cambridge, Mass.: Harvard University Press, 1976).

9. David Riesman, *The Lonely Crowd* (New Haven, Conn.: Yale University Press, 1961).

10. Michael Novak, "Why Latin America Is Poor," *Atlantic*, 249, no. 3 (March 1982): 66–75.

11. Valerie Bunce, *Do New Leaders Make a Difference? Executive Succession and Public Policy under Capitalism and Socialism* (Princeton, N.J.: Princeton University Press, 1981).

12. James MacGregor Burns, *Leadership* (New York: Harper and Row, 1979). Antonia Fraser has also probed the nature of leadership in her *The Warrior Queens* (New York: Knopf, 1989).

13. See Harry Eckstein, "The Idea of Political Development: From Dignity to Efficiency," *World Politics*, 34, no. 4 (July 1982): 451–86. See also David Apter, *The Politics of Modernization* (Chicago: University of Chicago Press, 1965); C. E. Black, *The Dynamics of Modernization* (New York: Harper and Row, 1966); Irving Horowitz, *Three Worlds of Development* (New York: Oxford University Press, 1966); Samuel Huntington, *Political Order in Changing Societies* (New Haven, Conn.: Yale University Press, 1968); Marion J. Levy, *Modernization and the Structure of Societies* (Princeton, N.J.: Princeton University Press, 1966); Organski, *Stages of Political Development;* and W. W. Rostow, *Politics and Stages of Growth* (Cambridge, Mass.: Harvard University Press, 1971).

14. Gabriel Almond and James Coleman, eds., *The Politics of Developing Areas* (Princeton, N.J.: Princeton University Press, 1960); and Gabriel Almond and G. Bingham Powell, *Comparative Politics: A Developmental Approach* (Boston: Little, Brown, 1966).

15. Edward Gibbon, *The Decline and Fall of the Roman Empire* (New York: Macmillan, 1899); Hannah Arendt, *The Origins of Totalitarianism* (New York: Harcourt, Brace, 1951); Samuel P. Huntington, "Political Order and Political Decay, " in Huntington, *Political Order in Changing Societies* (New Haven, Conn.: Yale University Press, 1968); and Juan J. Linz and Alfred Stepan, *The Breakdown of Democratic Regimes* (Baltimore: Johns Hopkins University Press, 1978).

16. See Burnett Bolloton, *The Spanish Revolution* (Chapel Hill: University of North Carolina Press, 1989). See also Hannah Arendt, *On Revolution* (New York: Viking, 1963); Crane Brinton, *The Anatomy of a Revolution* (New York: Vintage

Books, 1956); Regis DeBray, *Revolution in the Revolution? Armed Struggle and Political Struggle* (New York: Grove Press, 1967); Geoffrey Fairbairn, *Revolutionary Guerrilla Warfare* (Baltimore: Penguin, 1974); V. Nguyen Giap, *People's War, People's Army* (New York: Praeger, 1967); Che Guevara, *Episodes of the Revolutionary War* (New York: International Publishers, 1967); Yank Levy, *Guerrilla Warfare* (Baltimore: Penguin, 1942); Barrington Moore, Jr., *Social Origins of Dictatorship and Democracy* (Boston: Beacon, 1966); and Franco Venturi, *Roots of Revolution* (New York: Grosset and Dunlap, 1966).

SUGGESTED READINGS

Almond, Gabriel A., and G. Bingham Powell, Jr. *Comparative Politics Today: A World View,* 4th ed. Glenview, Ill.: Scott Foresman/Little, Brown, College Division, 1988. An engaging look at the process of comparative politics, based on the updated structural/functional approach.

Andrain, Charles F. *Political Change in the Third World.* Boston: Allen and Unwin, 1988. A look at political change models and how politics have changed in the Third World countries of Vietnam, Cuba, Chile, Nigeria, and Iran.

Cammack, Paul A. *Third World Politics: A Comparative Introduction.* Baltimore: Johns Hopkins University Press, 1988. A detailed study of the political history in Third World countries along with a look at the factors that have shaped politics today in these countries, such as the military, women in politics, revolution, and society.

Kohli, Atul, ed. *The State and Development in the Third World.* Princeton, N.J.: Princeton University Press, 1986. Specific case studies of Third World countries and their political and cultural development.

Lincoln, W. Bruce. *Red Victory.* New York: Simon and Schuster, 1989. The most important book one can read to understand the Russian Civil War and the implementation of communism by Lenin, Trotsky, and Stalin. Gives extremely important insights into the processes of politics in the former Soviet Union.

Stewart, William. *Understanding Politics.* Novato, Calif.: Chandler and Sharp, 1988. A basic introductory look at politics and some of the forces that influence politics. This book also examines radical liberalism, democratic socialism, and other various political systems.

Theen, Rolf H. W. *Comparative Politics: An Introduction to Six Countries.* Englewood Cliffs, N.J.: Prentice-Hall, 1986. An interesting look at the political systems of six different countries. Each country's political history, political framework, and political system's performance is studied and then compared and contrasted against the other countries' systems.

Tucker, Robert C. *Politics as Leadership*. Columbia: University of Missouri Press, 1981. An insightful look at politics and how to use politics in order to establish leadership.

Weiner, Myron. *Understanding Political Development*. Boston: Little, Brown, 1987. A must for understanding and analyzing political development. Political participation, religion, and society are areas examined to explain political change.

14

Change in a Communist Political System: The USSR

The leading and guiding force of Soviet society and the nucleus of its political system, of all state and public organizations, is the Communist Party of the Soviet Union.

—ARTICLE 6 OF THE 1977 USSR CONSTITUTION

In the time since April 1985, we have felt . . . the truth that no party has an eternal monopoly on power and that vanguard status is not bestowed by the Constitution.

—N. I. RYZHKOV, CHAIRMAN OF THE USSR COUNCIL OF MINISTERS

Restructuring processes are continuing to develop, freeing the powerful energy of the people. The most important result of restructuring so far . . . is the emancipation of society, thanks to which millions of Soviet people have gained civic dignity and are taking the management of the state into their own hands.

—MIKHAIL S. GORBACHEV

We somehow try to show everyone that the people are for restructuring that in less than five years has plunged the country into the abyss of crisis and has brought it to a point at which we have come face to face with a rampage of anarchy, the degradation of the economy, the grimace of general ruin and a decline in morals. Wasn't it a mistake to proclaim the total democratization of society and forget about the other side of the coin—bringing discipline and order to the country?

—V. I. BROVIKOV, SOVIET AMBASSADOR TO POLAND

The peoples of Russia are becoming masters of their destiny. . . . We are absolutely confident that our countrymen will not permit the sanctioning of the tyranny annd lawlessness of the putschists, who have lost all shame and conscience.

—PRESIDENT BORIS YELTSIN, DEFENDING THE RUSSIAN WHITE HOUSE ON THE FIRST DAY OF THE AUGUST 1991 COUP ATTEMPT

The rapid unfolding of the historical drama of the 1989 revolutions that culminated in the end of communism in Eastern Europe and the Soviet Union reveals the potential impact of change on outwardly stable political systems. In this chapter, we examine those changes that began as an attempt to reform the communist political system of the Soviet Union and ended with the birth of democracy in Russia. In many ways, changes in the communist system were similar to those that regularly occur throughout the lifetime of other political systems: leadership succession, demographic shifts, economic development or decline, value transformation, institutional reform. The dramatic events of the 1980s and 1990s, however, have illustrated the uniqueness of change in communist political systems. It was the power of political change that allowed history to be witness to what Zbigniew Brzezinski called the "birth and death of communism in the twentieth century."[1]

THE NATURE OF CHANGE IN POLITICAL SYSTEMS

Change is a constant feature of politics. In political science, patterns of change can help us understand, for example, the impact of societal development on political systems, the relationship between economic development and political rule, and the effect of popular values on policies and leadership. Political change can be approached in many ways. Students of *political development,* for instance, try to discern patterns in the transition from tradition to modernity, as political systems respond to social and economic pressures for increasing efficiency, equality, and democracy. *Political modernization* focuses on changes in political systems as they adapt to requirements of a rapidly evolving international economic system. Some scholars examine the changes that lead to the *breakdown of liberalism and democracy into totalitarianism,* while others look at how change leads to an orderly *transition from authoritarianism to democracy.* A Marxist, as we saw in Chapter 2, examines change as *progressive stages of historical development.*

THE CASE OF THE SOVIET UNION

The Soviet Union was established by a group of revolutionaries, led by V. I. Lenin, who ascribed to the Marxist theory of change, which asserts that societies pass through successive stages of economic development. Politics, according to this theory, is not an autonomous sphere of activity, but develops as an outgrowth of economic power relations. Thus, each stage of social development—from feudalism to capitalism to socialism, and finally communism—is characterized by a political system based on control of economic resources. Capitalism, according to Karl Marx, improved economic productivity by rationalizing the production process. However, the political system it produced is unjust because the bourgeoisie—those who own material resources and run the economy—also control political power, exploiting the working class. Only a workers' revolution could right the political wrong of capitalism by giving workers control over the means of economic production and, with it, political power. In socialism—the next stage after capitalism—a workers' state would control the equitable distribution of economic resources until all the vestiges of an exploitative capitalism were eliminated. In communism, there would be no need for a state or any political system based on coercion or exploitation.

Lenin's Bolsheviks (forerunners to the Communists) spearheaded the 1917 Russian Revolution with the idea that Russia must skip that capitalist stage of development and immediately become a socialist workers' state. The Bolsheviks—who later created the Communist Party of the Soviet Union (CPSU)—represented the workers in every sphere of life, from the state to the factories to the universities. The CPSU organized its rule in party cells that were placed in all public forms of social organization. The party established state power through a hierarchy of councils ("soviets") that ruled in the smallest villages all the way up to the state. By 1924, after Russia annexed territories on the perimeter of its borders, the country became known as the Union of Soviet Socialist Republics (USSR, or Soviet Union), that is, a union of republics based on political rule by socialist councils. By 1940, after Stalin attained the three Baltic countries in a mutual security pact with Nazi Germany, the Soviet Union was composed of 15 "republics" (some of them formerly independent countries), of which Russia was the largest.

Social, political, and economic development in the USSR was supposed to be based on continual revolutionary change. The CPSU was the vanguard of change, acting temporarily in the name of the working class to create the material basis for an affluent society and the political basis for worker rule. Eventually the need for the CPSU to control and distribute economic resources and direct the political system would disappear as worker control over the economy and state administration ushered in the new age of communism.

Lenin's successor, Joseph Stalin, catapulted a backward country of peasants into the modern age during his years of rule from 1928 to 1953, at great cost to the Soviet population. By the end of World War II, Stalin had made the USSR a great military and industrial power through methods of oppression, deceit, and terror. As the spoils of war, he controlled the internal and foreign policies of the countries of Eastern Europe, where replicas of the Stalinist political system were established. After Stalin died in 1953, the structures of the political system he devised remained in place, while the mass terror he used to perpetuate them ended. Whereas in democracies the political system adapts to changes in society, under Stalinism the political system was supposed to shape social development, to prepare workers for eventual self-rule.

At the time that Mikhail Gorbachev became general secretary of the CPSU—then the highest political office in the land—in 1985, the Stalinist system was still in place.[2] The characteristics of the Stalinist political structure that outlived Stalin in the USSR and Eastern Europe are as follows:

• domination by a single, highly organized political party that controls the state and tolerates no independent political opposition.

• control of all political, economic, and social processes by the party—from the highest levels of the state to the lowest levels of community and workplace.

• a centralized economy based on coercive planning (the factories are told what and how much to produce). This results in high levels of industrialization, but is characterized by constant shortages, a lack of consumer goods, and environmental devastation.

• an ideology of Marxism-Leninism that is used to socialize the population into accepting the goals of the political system as articulated by the leaders of the Communist party. It represents the official core values of the political system—the basis on which the leaders legitimize their rule.

• an atomized society—one dominated by the party/state and having no autonomy from political control. If a social or interest group is to meet freely and without any fear of punishment, it must be recognized by and subject to the control of the party and state.

• the dominance of economic rights over political rights. Citizens are guaranteed the right to housing, employment, and adequate food and material goods.[3] These rights are considered more important than the political rights of freedom of speech, assembly, or civil liberties.

• a vast bureaucracy that prevents creative policymaking and stifles political initiative and citizen access to political leaders.

• constitutions that create de jure democratic political systems—usually parliamentary in structure, with a premier, a government, and a national legislature—but that are de facto controlled by the Communist party, which enjoys a formal (constitutional) monopoly of power.

One of the ironies of Soviet history is that its social system—supposed to be based on revolutionary change—became one of the most bureaucratic, conservative, and oppressive political systems in the world.[4] The engine of change sputtered and died as the Soviet system became mired in a long period of what the Russians call *zastoi*—stagnation.

THE PERIOD OF STAGNATION AND PRESSURES FOR CHANGE

Why, starting in 1989, did the Stalinist system burst apart at the seams in Eastern Europe and the Soviet Union? Why—after decades of strong control by the Communist parties over politics, the economy, and society—did the populations take to the streets, demanding change and control over their own lives, while trying to dismantle or destroy the vestiges of an entrenched political order? It is tempting to answer that question with one word: Gorbachev. It is true that the dynamism and vision of Mikhail Gorbachev, the reformer who became general secretary of the Soviet Communist party in 1985, gave the go-ahead for the pent-up waves of change that swept over Eastern Europe. Upon closer examination, however, it becomes apparent that Gorbachev is more like the straw that broke the camel's back of communist control. Pressures for change had been building up in these change-resistant systems for decades. The refusal of the party leaders to admit the need for fundamental change made these pressures even stronger. Like gas in a closed chamber—with no chance for release, with no pressure valve to allow for incremental changes—when the container was opened by a charismatic leader, there was an explosion that resulted in a breakdown of the whole system.

Economic Centralization

In the Soviet centralized economy, or the "command-administrative economic system," the party-state replaced the market as the mechanism of exchange and distributor of economic goods. The market, so the reasoning went, produces gross inequalities in wealth and perpetuates a wide gap between social classes. Economic equality would be attained only if the Communist party-state established all the prices (so that, for example, everyone could afford the staples of bread, milk, and meat), determined what factories produced which products, set mandatory production quotas for each factory and farm, and guaranteed full employment.

In a market economy, the production, availability, and prices of goods depend on consumer demand and producer competition; in a command economy, the party-state tried to shape consumer preferences by controlling economic production and eliminating the uncertainties caused by competition. Decades of stagnation indicated that the party-state failed to replace the market as an effective instrument of economic productivity. By the time Gorbachev came to power in 1985, the Soviet economy had proven disastrously inefficient in promoting the production of consumer goods, agricultural output, and technological progress.

The production of consumer goods, like everything else in the command economy, was determined by the state plan. The plan set quotas for each product every factory produced, allocated materials for the production of goods, and set the price on the products before they reached the consumer. Quotas were often unrealistically high, and quality of the production materials consistently low. This combination resulted in an emphasis on quantity over quality and a proliferation of shoddy goods. Because there was only one supplier of materials—the state—factories would hoard state supplies, causing shortages throughout the economy. Workers were rewarded for fulfilling the plan, not producing products of high quality. A thriving black market emerged for an exchange of production materials, replacement parts, and consumer items that people had pilfered from the workplace or obtained from abroad.

The lack of a work ethic and limited opportunities for advancement resulted in poor worker productivity. While the party-state's mandatory employment policy ensured every Soviet citizen a job, it produced worker complacency, inefficiency, and a bloated workforce. It was almost impossible for a manager to fire even the most unproductive and disinterested worker, whose job and wages were guaranteed by the state.

The collectivization of agriculture produced the same inefficiencies in the rural economy. All land was collectivized—owned or controlled by the state—and all farms were run by state managers. The lack of private farmland meant that those who worked the land were beholden to the state and not driven by private initiative. Mismanagement, corruption, and a crumbling infrastructure led to constant shortages of agricultural goods. Almost one-third of the farm produce sent to the cities rotted on the way because of poor roads, broken-down equipment, and inefficient workers. Urban dwellers suffered shortages of fruits and vegetables as well as consumer products. A farmer expressed his frustration at consistent food shortages in this land of plenty: "We have such a vast expanse of good land in this country. When you fly across it, you're just surprised at how much land we have. Yet we don't have any food. . . . This is our tragedy."[5]

In addition to chronic shortages of consumer and agricultural goods, the Soviet economy suffered from the inability to produce rapid technological advances. The surge in technological achievements by the advanced industrialized economies, especially in the field of computers and electronics, was based on the decentralization of economic processes, individual incentive and innovation, and the ability of a market economy to adapt new forms of technology to a flexible production process. To compensate for the command economy's inability to produce high technology, the USSR resorted to "reverse engineering," whereby scientists illegally or legally acquired high-technology items from abroad, dismantled them, and then put them back together using their own parts. By the time the process was completed, this technology was usually five or ten years behind the advances made in the interim.

All of these economic deficiencies weakened the basis of communist rule as well as the status of the Soviet Union as a world superpower. U.S. President Ronald Reagan stung the Soviet leadership in the early 1980s by calling the USSR a "first-rate military nation with a Third World economy." Soviet planners were quick to realize that they needed butter as well as guns to run a superpower.

Political Stultification

When we think of politics as "who gets what—when, where, and how," we usually think of an interplay of power among politicians, interest groups, political parties, and voters. In the Soviet Union, politics for the average citizen was reduced to administrative fiat. Policies were decided at the top levels of the CPSU leadership and passed down through the levels of the CPSU hierarchy and over to the various levels of the state—including the popularly elected legislative councils, or soviets. Over the course of 70 years, the Communist party, the political system, and the Marxist-Leninist ideology thus became insulated from the needs of a changing society.

In liberal democracies, the function of political parties is to *represent* a diversity of social interests, *aggregate* those interests in a political platform, and *compete* for the chance to govern society after winning free elections. In the Soviet Union, the function of the CPSU was quite different. Because there was only one set of legitimate interests in society—that of the working class—the only legitimate political party was that which represented worker interests: the CPSU. The Communist party *shaped* as well as represented interests, *mobilized* society to encourage the formation of interests rather than aggregated independent interests, and governed not as result of political competition but by virtue of its *historical role* as the vanguard of the working class. The destiny of the political party did not depend on its social base; rather, the destiny of society depended on the will of party leaders.

Outwardly, the Soviet political system exhibited signs of popular participation and representative rule. Ninety-nine percent of Soviet citizens voted every four years for the election of "people's deputies" to legislative councils—from the city soviets to the All-Union Supreme Soviet, the supreme body of state power according to the 1977 constitution. The soviets deliberated policies, passed legislation, and responded to the call of citizens' groups for innovative policies in the fields of international peace or economic productivity. In reality, however, the political system was controlled by the highest levels of the CPSU organization. Candidates for people's deputy were chosen through the *nomenklatura* system, whereby the CPSU hierarchy maintained a list of people loyal to the party who were chosen as candidates in the legislative elections. *Mandatory voting* produced a high voter turnout to legitimize CPSU rule. *Single-candidate elections* (only one name appearing on the voter's ballot) virtually ensured that the CPSU's candidate would handily win the seat. The soviets at every level merely *rubber-stamped* the policies ironed out by the CPSU leadership. Policies were implemented by the CPSU *apparat,* a sprawling bureaucracy that oversaw adherence to party decisions in every city, factory, university, and housing complex. The only legal social and political organizations were those initiated or controlled by the CPSU. With no infusion of independent interests, no battles waged in the halls of a legislature jealous of its independence from state leaders, and no pluralism to give it life, Soviet politics became confined to the inner sanctums of Communist party rule, themselves increasingly isolated from the world outside.

Social Degradation

The social problems that began to beset the USSR by the 1980s had become just as significant for the immobilization of the Soviet system as economic and political stagnation. But what kind of social problems would exist in a country where everyone is provided housing, subsidized food prices, a job, free medical care, and free education? Wouldn't we expect there to be fewer problems in a country where individuals are provided for by the state? Not always. Usually the state—not subject to competition or the threat of bankruptcy—is not the most efficient provider of goods and services. Widespread state welfare programs, while providing a social net for society's poor, at the same time stifle individual initiative and a search for creative social policies. Both of these problems plagued the Soviet welfare state. Not only was the state inefficient as well as deficient in providing its citizens with adequate levels of material welfare, but this inefficient cradle-to-grave welfare system stifled individual and social initiative to the point where Soviet citizens felt helpless in trying to improve their own lives, let alone reform the Soviet system.

Some trends that have developed since World War II are telling in this respect. The Soviet state provided all citizens with jobs; but very often these jobs were boring, redundant, and not commensurate with the worker's level of education. There was little opportunity to advance, change careers, or improve an individual's standard of living. Everyone was provided with an apartment; but the apartments were run-down, cramped, and overcrowded. Three generations usually lived in a three-room apartment with little privacy. The state subsidized food prices, but people had to stand in line for hours every day just to get the necessary ingredients for dinner. The result was greater frustration, exasperation, and demoralization of a large part of the Soviet population. This was reflected in the statistics on the health of society. An excessive alcoholism rate plagued the population; petty crime and drug abuse were on the rise. Abortion rates among Soviet women were some of the highest in the world because of the lack of contraceptives and the dim prospects of family life. The USSR was the only industrial country in which the child mortality rate increased over the years, and an inadequate public health system proved unable to respond to the needs of the Soviet people. In addition to the obvious cost of all these social ills borne by the population and the economy, the CPSU's refusal to publicly acknowledge the problems was maddening. Because crime, drug abuse, and alcoholism were not *supposed* to exist in a socialist society, statistics were not publicly available and the CPSU ignored these annoying discrepancies from the socialist ideal.

If social problems highlighted the inability of the CPSU to provide for the material and spiritual welfare of Soviet citizens, social modernization increasingly rendered the CPSU inadequate in representing the new interests of the society over which it ruled. The single-party political system had not adequately adapted to the needs of a rapidly changing society. Increasing *urbanization,* widespread higher *education,* higher standards of *professionalism* in the natural and social sciences, a work environment based on *mental creativity* more than *physical labor,* and exposure to new sources of *information* shaped Soviet society by making it more complex, curious, sophisticated, and cynical. The more urban a population, the more likely it is to form groups to protect its interests in a crowded and competitive environment. A highly educated people is less likely to believe simple political formulas or politicians' promises for a grand and glorious future. The more professional a group of experts, the greater their emphasis on facts—at the expense of an irrelevant ideology. A workforce based on the use of mental creativity requires individual autonomy and organizational decentralization. Increasing information subjects political ideology to the test of alternative world views and visions of the future. For the past three decades, Soviet society had developed a complex array of interests, ideas, and needs that could not be met within the confines of the communist political system. The CPSU remained a monolithic organization that tried to shape social development according to old methods of organizational centralization and ideological indoctrination. It lost the ability to respond to changes in society and thus lost touch with its social base. As a result, a deep fault line ran between the entrenched party-state and the rapidly developing Soviet society. There were no mechanisms such as political parties, interest groups, or a representative legislature to make sure that social and political development kept pace with each other. With such a deep rift, by the time Gorbachev came to power in 1985, Soviet society—outwardly apathetic and complacent—was an earthquake waiting to happen.

THE GORBACHEV ERA I: REFORM FROM ABOVE

By the late 1970s and early 1980s, Soviet political reformers and progressive social scientists realized the potential time-bomb of economic, political, and social stagnation. The Soviet party-state could no longer afford to support a decrepit economy; a suffocating bureaucracy stifled creative political reforms; and Soviet society had been cowed into such submission by a repressive state that widespread apathy and demoralization threatened to halt further social development. The only hope was drastic change, and the only direction from which change could come was the highest ranks of the CPSU. The early 1980s thus saw a struggle for power between reformers and conservatives in the top echelons of the CPSU. Finally, after much resistance, the reformers got their say in the person of Mikhail Sergeevich Gorbachev, the seventh—and the last—political ruler of the USSR.

Gorbachev, as general secretary of the CPSU, set out to spearhead an all-encompassing reform from above that would revitalize the socialist system and make it work the way it was intended. The program of change that was introduced to the country by the CPSU reformers at the Twenty-seventh All-Union CPSU Congress[6] in 1986 was designed to *improve* the existing system, not *overthrow* it. Soviet reformers, with Gorbachev at the lead, introduced a widespread program of change to revitalize the Soviet system by making it more responsive to the demands of a modern economy, a diversity of political interests, and the material and spiritual needs of a complex society.

Economic Decentralization

The most immediate goal was improvement of the economic system—the foundation for a stable political system and healthy society. Hoping to make the planned economy more efficient, the Gorbachev leadership introduced the policy of *uskorenie*—"acceleration" of economic processes to improve the production process and get more high-quality goods out to consumers. To make the centralized economy more efficient, the acceleration process was designed to increase the productivity of workers by improving conditions in the workplace, rationalize the distribution process by weeding out waste and corruption, and improve the performance of factories by introducing incentives and profit sharing.

When acceleration failed to revitalize the economy, Gorbachev went further in his blueprint for economic change and introduced *perestroika*—a "restructuring" of the economic system. Some of the basic components of economic perestroika were decentralization of economic decision making, more autonomy to enterprises and workers in carrying out economic activities, an increase in the production of consumer goods and services, less administration (a loosening of the plan), and more market (production and prices based on supply and demand).

It was harder than anyone expected, however, to enliven the petrified forest of centralized control engendered by the command-administrative economic system. Perestroika's goal of introducing a "regulated market economy" ran up against many roadblocks. Government ministries were jealous of their control over factories and enterprises and sabotaged the decentralization process at every turn. Party and state bureaucrats were loathe to relinquish the perks that accompanied their control over economic activities. Unprofitable factories were still largely shielded from

bankruptcy by a party-state that feared the effects of economic dislocation, massive unemployment, and uncontrolled prices. Workers had not
developed the work ethic necessary to promote high productivity and
high-quality goods. Soviet citizens, who had heard about the evils of
capitalism their entire lives, feared that the move to a market might
increase economic productivity but eliminate the social benefits and
economic rights guaranteed to them by a paternalistic state.

After two years of sputtering economic reform, Gorbachev acknowledged that a decentralization of the economy could not take place without
concomitant political decentralization and a revitalization of social life
free of constant control. The history of comparative politics shows that,
once groups attain some measure of economic power, they demand
political power and representation. Economic change also produces social
change as new groups dominate social life and reconfigure power relations. Since the only way for Gorbachev to improve the Soviet economy
was to give Soviet individuals and groups more economic power and
control, he realized that he also had to restructure Soviet politics and
society. He started with his own party.

Political Rejuvenation

Article 6 of the 1977 Soviet constitution claimed that the CPSU was
"the leading and guiding force of Soviet society"—an inspiration to the
working class, and the finest example of hard work and sacrifice. After 70
years of overseeing every aspect of Soviet life, however, the CPSU
organization had devolved into a morass of entangled bureaucratic regulations. The mechanism by which the CPSU was supposed to make policy
was called "democratic centralism." This meant that local party organizations—at the workplace, in the university, in villages, towns, and
cities—would freely discuss the needs of their constituencies and make
policy recommendations to regional, republic, and all-union (USSR) party
organizations. CPSU leaders would then make the policies and would
direct local party organizations to implement them, with no further
discussion or questioning. Over the years, the centralist side of the
equation completely overshadowed the democratic. Top party leaders
made policies that were funneled down the chain of command in the party
and the state. No significant creative input or discussion from below was
tolerated. This made for a stagnant and alienated party organization:
because everyone acted on orders from above, local party and state
organizations couldn't respond to the immediate needs of their constituencies. Local party leaders and people's deputies were not accountable
to their constituents because their authority to rule came from the higher
ranks of CPSU leaders, not from the voting public. Soviet citizens
increasingly found the Communist party irrelevant to their everyday lives,
even though every aspect of their lives was dominated by the party.

Gorbachev's first political reform was thus the *democratization of the Communist party*. Only by revitalizing the democratic component of party life could the CPSU live up to its charge of leading the Soviet people toward a better life. Gorbachev never set out to introduce a multiparty system; in 1987 he called that idea "rubbish." The CPSU was still the only legitimate political party in the Soviet Union. Gorbachev's intent was to introduce radical reforms into party life by placing his reformist colleagues in leading CPSU positions and undermining the heavy hand of the party bureaucracy.

Gorbachev managed to place political reformers in high CPSU positions in the Politburo—a small committee of party leaders who ran the country—and the CPSU Central Committee, the larger deliberative arm of the party. He could not, however, completely rid the CPSU of conservative leaders who feared that Gorbachev's reforms would undermine the authority of the CPSU. These conservatives—or party "hardliners"—tried to slow down or even sabotage the reform process. In 1987 a letter written by schoolteacher Nina Andreeva, appearing in a prominent conservative newspaper, lambasted Gorbachev's reform program as a betrayal of Marxist-Leninist ideals and a subversion of everything that had made the Soviet Union a great power. It was widely believed that Andreeva's letter was sponsored by CPSU hardliners who wanted to illustrate widespread public opposition to Gorbachev's reforms. Clearly, the conservative faction of the CPSU was still a force capable of undermining Gorbachev's reforms.

To offset the power of the conservative CPSU leadership, Gorbachev tried to create a coalition of sorts between reformist CPSU leaders and rank-and-file party members, to root out those middle layers of the entrenched bureaucracy that were impeding reforms. Gorbachev hoped to encourage local party organizations to engage in wide-ranging discussions about how to solve local problems and get workers, students, and residents actively involved in initiating creative policies. The top CPSU leadership, led by Gorbachev, would support these initiatives as they were presented to the middle layers of the CPSU bureaucracy at the regional and territorial levels. It proved impossible, however, to budge the party bureaucrats from their comfortable positions of power. Few observers had realized the extent to which the tentacles of party power reached into the fabric of society. Chairmen of party committees controlled every detail of life in their districts, from the supply of production materials to de facto control over the fate of the accused in legal trials. Many party chairmen ran their constituencies like little fiefdoms—pockets of power dominated by party lords accountable to no one for their policies. They owed their positions to the single-party status quo. It was in their interest to resist—not promote—Gorbachev's changes.

Because the CPSU proved so resistant to change and so incapable of democratizing itself, Gorbachev introduced the second phase of his political reforms: a *transfer of political authority from the CPSU to the state*. The idea was to lessen, increasingly, the influence of the Communist party in politics by enhancing the role of the soviets—from the local level to the all-union legislature. If CPSU bureaucrats would not make themselves accountable for their policies, Gorbachev would force them to be accountable to a constituency of voters through free elections for people's deputies to the soviets. With this in mind, he announced the creation of the Congress of People's Deputies—a new legislative body superimposed on the old soviet system at the all-union level—elected in March 1989 by the freest elections ever held in the history of the Soviet Union.

"All power to the soviets!" had been the official rallying cry of the Bolsheviks during the Russian Revolution of 1917; since then, the councils had been the official institutions of policymaking in the Soviet system. While the soviets were supposed to have remained independent from the Communist party, they were in fact always dominated by it. Part of Gorbachev's political reform was to give real power to the soviets by changing the flow of authority from the top down (CPSU-dominated, nomenklatura, single-candidate elections) to the bottom up (multicandidate elections; independence from the CPSU; infusion of significant legislative power).

Prior to 1989, the Supreme Soviet—a bicameral legislature (Council of the Union, and Council of the Nationalities)—looked, on paper, much like Western parliaments and was elected in an all-union vote every four years. Supreme Soviet deputies voted on policies, ratified appointments to government positions (the Council of Ministers), and guided the political course of the Soviet Union. All of these processes, however, were controlled by the CPSU; there was never a single dissenting vote in the Supreme Soviet on a CPSU-introduced policy or government minister. Gorbachev wanted the Congress of People's Deputies to be a *working legislature*—not just a rubber stamp on Communist party policies, but an active legislature that would make and ratify the laws of the land.

In March 1989, nationwide multicandidate elections to the Congress of People's Deputies were held. The elections generated much enthusiasm among Soviet voters who, for the first time, had a chance to choose their representatives in bodies of state power. Even though at the time of the elections the CPSU was still the only legal political party, the profusion of Communist radical reformers and independents running for seats in the new legislature infused new energy into the political process.

CPSU functionaries, who previously controlled the soviets, now had to win a people's deputy seat by running for election. They were stunned by the results. Voters consistently refused to vote for party bosses in their bids for soviet seats. Even if their name was the only one on the ballot (which it was in many cases), voters crossed it off—in effect voting for no one. Since candidates needed at least 50 percent of the votes to win, this forced a new election with different candidates. The four most powerful party bosses of the city of Saint Petersburg (then Leningrad) ran for seats and lost by embarrassing margins. In newspaper accounts the following day, the four were clearly flabbergasted that they had lost their positions and power at the hands of simple voters. It was precisely the lesson that Gorbachev wanted them to learn: party leaders would have to start pleasing the voters if they wanted to retain the privilege of holding public office.

The Congress of People's Deputies proved to be a mixed bag of democracy and authoritarianism, partly because Gorbachev had a dual agenda. He wanted to revitalize the political process by reinvigorating a working legislature; at the same time, he wanted the legislature to function within the context of a single-party system under his watchful eye. The new congress would debate specific policies, but an enlightened CPSU leadership would still steer the general course of social develop-ment. The two years of congress activity reflected this dichotomy. On the one hand, it was a lively forum for an exchange of political views and the scene of vitriolic attacks by deputies on the CPSU leadership. The first session was spent in testing the waters of political debate and strategy and learning the basics of legislative politics: "Our first day in the first grade of the school of democracy," said one deputy. On the other hand, the independence of the new legislature was clearly undermined by the continuing influence of the Communist party. Fully one-third—or 750 of the 2,250 seats in congress—were reserved for deputies elected from within the ranks of CPSU-sponsored social organizations, including 100 from the Communist party itself. This weighted CPSU influence inside the congress and prevented the establishment of a "one person, one vote" legislative system. Gorbachev clearly dominated the agenda-setting functions of the congress, leading some opposition democrats to complain that the new legislature was merely an appendage of his rule. To add fuel to the fire of this criticism, the Congress of People's Deputies elected Gorbachev president of the Soviet Union in March 1990, granting to him the highest state authority in the country—a post that ran parallel with his leadership of the Communist party.

The Boris Yeltsin story is another lesson in accountability. Yeltsin publicly criticized the pace of Gorbachev's reforms and insulted the hardline members of the CPSU. As a result of his bold behavior, he was dismissed from the Politburo in 1987. He thus lost one of the top positions in the Communist party because his superiors felt that his public com-ments and activities threatened party control and legitimacy. He was given a governmental position in the construction ministry where, it was felt, he wouldn't make trouble for the party regulars. He decided to run for deputy in the Congress of People's Deputies from District 1—the Moscow City region.

Yeltsin ran a very active and exuberant campaign, with people turning out by the thousands to support him and cheer him on. He won the seat by an overwhelming majority, was elected to the policymaking Supreme Soviet by his fellow deputies in the Congress of People's Deputies (after a controversy over first *not* being elected), and led an opposition group ("the Interregional Deputies' Group") that attempted to speed up the pace of the reforms. Though he lost his party position, he was able to obtain a leading role in the new legislative system through popular elections—another radical shift in the flow of authority. Before Gorbachev, it would have been impossible for Yeltsin to assume any leadership function after the disgrace of being dismissed from the Politburo. Under the new conditions, Yeltsin assumed such a role not by virtue of party authority, but—more significantly—through direct elections where he was accountable to his constituents, not the party hierarchy.

Social Rejuvenation

Gorbachev and reformers like him knew that economic and political reforms would not by themselves provide the dynamism necessary to reinvigorate the Soviet system. They thus set out to activate what they called the *human factor*—active participation by the Soviet masses in the creation of policy and the implementation of reforms. A healthy economy requires interested, able, and devoted workers; a vibrant political system depends on knowledgeable voters and civic-minded individuals and groups.

Gorbachev needed to lift the heavy veil of apathy from the eyes of the Soviet population so as to generate interest in the reforms and mold active citizens where once there were only passive subjects. The first step on that road was the elimination of people's fear—a fear that had been cultivated by the police state for decades. Criticism of the regime, participation in an unofficial social group, or discussion of alternatives to Communist policies had all been considered treason before Gorbachev came to power. The Committee on State Security (KGB) was the eyes and ears of the regime, penetrating society and punishing those who dared to question CPSU rule. To eliminate this entrenched fear, Gorbachev introduced *glasnost'*—openness or publicity—to encourage an open atmosphere of discussion, debate, and constructive criticism in Soviet society. No one was prepared for the response.

The result was breathtaking. Storms of public criticism raged from within the depths of society. People criticized every imaginable aspect of Soviet life; thousands of people offered opinions that merely five years earlier would have landed them in jail, cost them their jobs, or led to serious reprimands. Movies about the oppression of Stalinism, the bleakness of modern Soviet life, and people's alienation from the system appeared for the first time. Newspapers were filled with letters complaining about officials, long lines, Communist party privileges, and social conditions. As Gorbachev went on walking tours of Soviet factories, he was barraged with complaints by workers about working conditions, inadequate pay, and shortages of consumer items. Glasnost' was a cathartic experience for the Soviet people, who finally had a chance to release their frustrations to a leader genuinely concerned about their problems.

Gorbachev hoped to use glasnost' as support for his reform program and as a public tool against the party and state bureaucracies. People were not satisfied, however, with the airing of public opinion. They soon began to organize in groups of all different sizes and kinds: discussion clubs, rock bands, cultural societies, nationalist organizations, workers' movements, political clubs. By 1989 there were 60,000 *informal groups*—social organizations not sponsored by or affiliated with the CPSU. No one suspected that so many diverse interests prevailed in Soviet society and that people were willing or able to organize to pursue those interests in a public forum. Once again Gorbachev adapted his reform program to accommodate the forces unleashed by social change, by promoting *socialist pluralism*—the sanction of organized interests in society directed under the guiding eye of reformist CPSU leaders.

Gorbachev, like many Soviet leaders, feared the potential chaos of unstructured mass participation in a society traditionally dominated by an iron hand of authoritarian rule. Noted Soviet scholar Seweryn Bialer observes that the greatest concern of Soviet leaders throughout the history of the USSR was the maintenance of *order* in society.[7] While Gorbachev differed from his predecessors in advocating mass participation in reforms, he too was concerned with maintaining social order. As a devoted socialist in the Marxist-Leninist tradition, Gorbachev wanted to direct mass participation through channels of constructive socialist change. An organized pluralism of interests could flourish in society as long as it promoted the attainment of socialist goals.

Hoping to harness the energy released by the formation of thousands of informal groups in the service of socialism, Gorbachev encouraged the new social groups to work with party and state reformers in umbrella organizations such as the "Popular Front in Support of Perestroika." He hoped to co-opt new social organizations within the existing one-party system, using them to revitalize the system but not allowing them to detract from its power. Soviet society, however, had millions of minds of its own; newly independent individuals and groups—intoxicated with the oxygen of freedom—refused to stay within the boundaries of Gorbachev's socialist pluralism. The Pandora's box of social change was finally opened; social activists sought vengeance on the party that had kept it closed for so long.

THE GORBACHEV ERA II: REVOLUTION FROM BELOW

Political scientist Samuel Huntington points out that, if a political system does not produce adequate institutional channels through which increased participation can be directed, the prevailing social order breaks down as new social activists seek other ways to press their claims against the state. Soviet social participation during the final years of the Gorbachev era supports Huntington's argument. The explosion of new activism unleashed by Gorbachev's reforms from above could not be contained within the institutional channels of the CPSU, the CPSU-dominated Congress of People's Deputies, or even the federal structure of the Soviet Union itself. The result—an undirected, uncoordinated, and incomplete revolution from below—finally tore the country apart.

In the highly charged, heavily politicized atmosphere of this popular revolution, politics assumed primacy over economics, at least temporarily. Activists seemed more interested in democracy than the stability necessary for economic productivity; the constituent republics demanded political independence even though this would threaten their economic security. The dynamics of the Soviet popular revolution were complex and convoluted; here we examine three of the political forces that took shape from within Soviet society as a result of these dynamics: *political pluralism, civil society,* and *nationalism.*

Political Pluralism

The thousands of people who took to the streets in 1990 and 1991— organizers of new social groups, recently elected people's deputies, and political activists—refused to confine their activities or ideas to the institutions of the Communist party. The logical next step to recognizing a wide variety of interests in society was the institutionalization of those interests in political parties. Gorbachev's "socialist pluralism" increasingly became a contradiction in terms. How could pluralism—the interplay of a diverse range of interests—be reconciled with the imposition of one prevailing ideology? Real political pluralism, it seemed, could be realized only by the acceptance of independent political organizations that represent particular social interests. This recognition led Gorbachev finally to sanction a *multiparty political system* in the Soviet Union. In March 1990, Article 6—the one proclaiming the CPSU the sole legitimate political party in the USSR—was struck from the Soviet constitution. Immediately, a proliferation of political parties emerged, espousing a wide range of political views: monarchist, anarchist, nationalist, communist, Bolshevik, socialist, socialist democratic, Christian democratic, liberal, democratic, entrepreneurial. This initial attempt to institutionalize political pluralism through the creation of new political parties was a fundamental turning point in the course of revolutionary change in the USSR. Gorbachev had been compelled—by the forces of social change— to back away from his insistence on the maintenance of one-party rule. Once unleashed, these forces demanded their own political representation based on ideas, interests, and organizations emanating from below.

Civil Society

The profusion of independent activism in social groups and political parties represented the emergence of a *civil society* in the Soviet Union. Civil society is the self-organization of society whereby individuals and groups seek to pursue their private and public interests independently from the state. Civil society can be *apolitical,* as when individuals seek to pursue economic interests in the market or groups organize to pursue social goals, or *political,* as when interest groups in the United States lobby Congress to change a policy or when political parties try to win presidential or legislative elections. In classical political science, it has long been thought that an independent civil society is essential to safeguard the freedom of individuals from the potential power of state domination. A civil society both protects individuals from the state and acts as the source of stable state power.

In the Soviet Union a civil society never existed, for reasons of both ideology and power. Marxist-Leninists eschewed Western civil society as dominated by the bourgeoisie, who use their economic power to oppress working-class interests and control the reins of political power. Soviet leaders never allowed independent social organization, because of its potential to undermine the authority of the Communist regime. The emergence of a civil society under Gorbachev was a unique phenomenon: the birth of an independent society amid the crumbling ruins of a totalitarian regime. A big question mark hung over this birth. Did the Soviet population have the capacity to organize itself after years of an iron-hand rule? To a political scientist, this question is one of *political culture.* Political culture is the orientation of a certain people toward political processes and state rule. A democratic political culture requires the ability to organize for common political goals, tolerance of other opinions and interests, the willingness to compromise and consensus as to the rules of the political game. After years of subjugation and repression, would these qualities emerge from the depths of Soviet society?

Partially. In the last year of Soviet rule, the eclectic, conflicting, and argumentative democratic opposition agreed on one thing: the power of the Communist party had to be undermined at every available opportunity. In the context of the disintegrating Communist regime, democratic forces in Soviet society exhibited the prerequisites of the political culture necessary to support an independent civil society. The most important evidence was the independent political organization engineered by the democratic opposition in the local and republic elections of March 1990.

Registration of candidates for the March 1990 elections had been scheduled before the legalization of a multiparty system; thus, the new political parties could not officially run candidates in the elections. Nevertheless, independent social groups and political organizations mobilized to support all "democratic" candidates—those renouncing hardine communism and extreme Russian nationalism. First of all, many of he independent social groups joined together in voting clubs, such as the Moscow Association of Voters and the Interregional Voters Group, to support the democrats in the election. Then, many of the voters' organiations created a large electoral bloc called "Democratic Russia," which an an electoral campaign for the democratic candidates. Democratic Russia—given its disadvantages in competing with the long-established, well-funded, and very powerful Communist party—scored a great success n the spring elections. Largely through its efforts, democratic candidates won majorities in the two most important city soviets of Moscow and Saint Petersburg and about one-third in the more conservative Russian arliament.

For the first time in Soviet history, political representatives in bodies f state power derived their authority from an independent society that ad organized its forces to compete in elections. These democratic epresentatives still faced an uphill battle, since the Communist party etained a firm grip on state power. Nevertheless, the elections were an unprecedented victory for the Soviet people who, in putting themselves n an equal footing with the Communist party-state, had cemented the oundation for active civil society.

Nationalism

The strongest and least expected of the social forces unleashed by Gorbachev's reform program was a sweeping, uncompromising, and emotional *nationalism*. Once the waves of nationalism began rolling across the USSR, no state policy, no army, no evolutionary program of change could hold them back. In the end, it was nationalism that changed he course of history and led to the end of the Soviet empire.

Nationalism is the common identity shared by a certain group of people who live on a given territory. That identity stems from shared experience the form of ethnic background, historical memory, language, culture, eligion, or allegiance to a political system. The form that nationalism ssumes—multicultural, chauvinistic, tolerant, or violent—depends on he characteristics of the group and the circumstances in which they xpress their nationalism.

In the Soviet Union, the nationalism that emerged during the Gorbachev period resulted from the nationalities policy promulgated by the revious Communist regimes. Soviet leaders—adhering to the Marxist ssumption that *class* was more important than *nation* as the foundation or a peoples' identity—promoted *socialist internationalism* among the more than 100 ethnic groups and 15 republics that constituted the USSR. he intention was to replace the national cultures, historical memory, hnic identity, and traditions of all the ethnic groups with one new Soviet ulture—a culture based on the socialist ideals of the "new Soviet man"

who would lead all nations toward the future of communism. Russia wa
the core republic—the largest and most populated, as well as the birth
place of the 1917 Bolshevik Revolution. The Russian language was thu
the lingua franca uniting the various peoples of the Soviet Union. Sovie
leaders, however, were careful to ensure that Russian nationalism did no
undermine socialist goals. The legacy of czarist rule, the Orthodo
religion, and the Russian literary tradition and culture were all swep
under the rug of socialist internationalism.

To the people in the non-Russian republics, central control had resulte
in a mixture of Russian and Soviet imperialism. Russians flooded into th
republics after World War II, and the Russian language was the officia
state language, spoken at work and in school. Soviet holidays, cultura
ceremonies, and state atheism swept away historical monuments and th
public celebration of national holidays and religious devotion. Even th
reference to all the peoples of the Soviet Union as "Soviet citizens" wa
meant to erase peoples' identity as Latvians, Georgians, Azerbaijanis, o
Kazakhs.

When Gorbachev led the drive to activate the human factor of mas
participation, no one had any idea how driven by their national identit
the new social activists would be. Given the opportunity to express thei
opinions, fully organize, and pursue independent activities, the people
of the republics set out to rediscover the roots of their ethnic identity an
national culture. At first, activism revolved around culture and history
Activists demanded the reinstatement of the native language as the officia
language of the republic; groups organized to refurbish historical monu
ments and reopen churches the Soviets had closed; city administration
began to change street names from those of Soviet to national heroes. B
1989, the excitement of rediscovery was electric as festivals celebrate
national folk songs and traditional costume, national flags replaced Sovie
republic flags atop historical buildings, and national newspapers ad
dressed republic issues. In the Baltic countries, which had been indepen
dent in the interwar period, nationalism emerged as a unifying an
peaceful force, as the small nations of Estonia, Latvia, and Lithuani
dusted off their national heritages. In other republics, nationalism prove
exclusive and violent, as ethnic or religious groups took up arms to figh
for territory and influence.

The demand for cultural autonomy soon developed into pressures fo
political independence, as republic leaders fought for self-rule against th
Soviet central state. National-based popular fronts quickly emerged i
the republics, as independent political activists threw in their lot wit
former native Communist party leaders to seek the common goal c
political independence from the Soviet center. Communist leaders in th
republics, as a rule, identified more strongly with their national heritag
than with the all-union Communist party. This nationalist allegianc

acilitated a relatively broad-based mass movement against the Soviet
Communist regime.

Increased political autonomy developed its own momentum toward
elf-determination and the formation of independent states. Those repub-
ics that had been independent before becoming part of the Soviet empire
lenounced their incorporation as illegal by the standards of international
aw. The fever of independence spread to the other peoples of the USSR,
vho argued that the only way to escape the web of Communist control
hroughout their land was to break completely free and create indepen-
lent states on the basis of national rule. Drawing on the heritage of
Woodrow Wilson and appealing to the international community, the
ations of the Soviet Union sought to become *states* (see Chapter 12).
When nationalist leaders won—by wide margins—the March 1990 elec-
ions to republic parliaments, the three Baltic countries and Armenia
leclared independence; the rest of the republics were not far behind.

The case of Russia was in some ways unique. The specific features of
Russian nationalism were not so clear as in the non-Russian republics,
ince many Russians confuse characteristics of traditional Russian nation-
lism with Soviet patriotism. This began with Stalin, who (though himself
. Georgian by birth) used traditional Russian symbols of military might,
eligious orthodoxy, and territorial defense to mobilize the Soviet popu-
ation into war against Nazi Germany in World War II. Since the Com-
nunist party emerged in Russia, some Russians identified much more
vith their communist heritage, which many saw as an important contri-
•ution to Russian history. Finally, the Russians—as the core of the Soviet
mpire—did not have the common anti-imperialist sentiment that united
diverse range of social groups in the other republics.

The identity of Russians as a group of people with a set of shared
xperiences is thus not as clearly defined as in the Baltics, Transcaucasus,
Moldova, or the Asian republics. For the Russians, then, nationalism did
ot act as the social glue that united the opposition against the Communist
enter. There was no grand coalition between the democratic opposition
nd the Communist leadership on the basis of a shared Russian identity.
Most of the Russian democrats advocate a tolerant and nonexpansionist
ationalism, viewing the communist period as an aberration and drawing
n constructive Russian traditions. Much of the former Russian Commu-
ist leadership mixes Russian and Soviet nationalism, advocating a re-
uilding of empire that would encompass the borders of the former
ussian or Soviet empires. The extreme nationalists—anti-Semitic and
ulturally superior in tone—renounce the Soviet communist past but, like
he Communists, promote a new Russian empire on the basis of Russian
ominance in the region.

While these conflicting strains of nationalism precluded a mass Russian
pposition movement, in 1990 and 1991 the Russian Republic as a whole
raveled the path of independence and increasingly asserted its autonomy

against the all-union leadership of Mikhail Gorbachev. Russian politica‹ independence began with the election of Boris Yeltsin in June 1991 as th‹ first popularly elected president in the history of Russia. Assuming ‹ leading role in the Russian parliament, the charismatic and popula‹ Yeltsin easily won a presidential campaign run by the electoral blo‹ Democratic Russia. With an independent political base as president i‹ the most powerful Union Republic, with the support of the Russia‹ voters, and with command over the vast resources of the Russian terri‹ tory, Yeltsin was set to challenge Gorbachev, president of the USSR, i‹ the battle for political power. It was to be a battle not of two men, but o‹ the new Russia against the old Soviet empire.

A FAILED COUP AND THE END OF EMPIRE

Few events in the history of the world are as dramatic as the demise o‹ a large and powerful empire. Like the fall of empires before it, th‹ disintegration of the Soviet Union resulted in a boiling cauldron o‹ territorial conflicts, mass emigration, and bloody struggles for power i‹ newly emancipated republics. The Soviet empire, composed of 15 con‹ stituent republics with 285 million people, encompassed one-sixth of th‹ Earth's landmass. Its military power and influence extended throughou‹ the globe. It dominated half of Europe, controlled half of the world'‹ nuclear arsenal, and commanded one of the most powerful conventiona‹ armed forces in history. And yet in the space of a few years, the Sovie‹ empire crumbled at the hands of its own peoples. Military might, force‹ and coercion were no match for demands of freedom, independence, an‹ national autonomy.

By transferring the basis of Soviet rule from coercion to consent‹ Gorbachev created his own "Khrushchev dilemma" (see Chapter 12). A‹ the core of this dilemma was how to grant the peoples of the USSR th‹ autonomy over their internal affairs necessary for their allegiance, whil‹ maintaining orderly control over new social forces. Like Khrushche‹ before him, Gorbachev failed to resolve the irreconcilable dilemma be‹ tween independence and unpopular central control. In 1989 this dilemm‹ resulted in the demise of the Soviet bloc, as the countries of Easter‹ Europe broke free from both domestic and foreign Soviet tutelage. I‹ 1991 the same paradox tore asunder the Soviet empire, as its people‹ resisted one last attempt by Soviet hardliners to hold the USSR togethe‹ through the force of arms.

Throughout 1990 and 1991, Gorbachev struggled to strike a balanc‹ between allowing self-rule for the 15 republics of the USSR and maintain‹ ing centralized Soviet control over major military, political, and economi‹ decisions. The last leader of the Soviet Union found himself caugh‹ between the forces of independence and the forces of reaction. Gorba‹

chev's attempt to stand the middle ground left almost everyone dissatisfied, nervous, and frustrated at the uncertain power relations inside the Soviet Union.

The pressures for independence in the republics—especially after the March 1990 elections—developed a momentum that was too strong to stop by either threat of force or coercion. Bowing to the inevitability of change, Gorbachev had cobbled together a formula for a reconstituted Soviet Union, giving more independence to all of the republics. The *New Union Treaty*, based on a federated union, specifically delineated powers between the republics and the central state. The republics received extensive control over their own land and natural resources, as well as extensive political autonomy. The central state was delegated power to command an all-union army, devise a common military strategy, and direct a coordinated economic trade policy. The highest executive authority in the union was to be a president popularly elected by the peoples of the constituent republics. Nine of the 15 republics agreed to this accord; six had declared complete independence and refused to be subject to the authority of any central Soviet state. The New Union Treaty—also called the "9 + 1 Treaty"—was to be signed on Tuesday, August 20, 1991. The day before the signing ceremony, a stunned world awoke to the news that Soviet leader Gorbachev had disappeared and an "Extraordinary Commission on the State of Emergency"—a group of hardline Communists—had taken control of Moscow.

"The pride and honor of the Soviet people," the coup leaders declared, "must be restored in full. . . . [O]ur multi-cultural people have lived for centuries, proud of their Motherland. We have never been ashamed of our patriotic feelings and we hold it natural and rightful to raise the present and future generations of citizens of this great power in this spirit." The eight members of the Extraordinary Commission appealed to the peoples of the Soviet Union to restore order, discipline, and patriotism in the lands of the Soviet empire. The coup leaders were from the Soviet military, the KGB, and the interior ministry—precisely those officials who would lose their power if the New Union Treaty had been signed as scheduled. Their attempt to turn back the tide of independence was futile and inept. Even the armored tanks they sent in to take over the parliament building—the "Russian White House"—could not overcome the waves of popular resistance to strong-arm Soviet rule. The coup leaders found that they commanded no allegiance from the majority of the population; the tanks and security forces had no power over the authority of public opinion, as thousands of Russians rushed to the side of Yeltsin when he defiantly guarded the parliament building.

The surrender of the coup leaders, three days after their ill-fated attempt to patch up the threadbare USSR, initiated the precise course of events that they had tried to stop. The perpetrators of the attempted coup wanted to prevent the signing of the New Union Treaty because it undermined the power of the central Soviet state. The failed coup led to demands for independence by all of the republics—demands that would soon not just weaken, but finally destroy, the Soviet empire.

Before the attempted coup, Gorbachev had to answer to hardline forces that had influence inside the military and KGB. No one knew exactly how much power they had or to what extent the military and security forces would support their attempt to hold together the USSR at any cost. This uncertainty prompted independence leaders in the republics to accept a balance between republic autonomy and Soviet central control. After the failed coup attempt, the hardline forces were immobilized. Their leaders were arrested, their influence severely weakened. As a result, in the months following August 1991 there was a burst of independence declarations by all of the former Soviet republics. The Baltics, Ukraine, Belarus, and the central Asian republics all declared independence and sought recognition from the world community for their new status as independent states.

When a shaken Gorbachev (still, at that time, the president of the USSR) returned from his captivity in the Crimea, he and Russian President Boris Yeltsin—whose authority had skyrocketed—tried desperately to forge a postcoup Union Treaty. This treaty, hastily drawn up the month after the coup attempt, would have retained the bare bones of a union government, led by a collective executive composed of representatives from all the signatory republics and giving them even more control over their internal affairs. Why would Gorbachev and Yeltsin try to save even a drastically weakened Soviet Union after the coup? Gorbachev wanted to retain his power base, and both he and Yeltsin realized that total independence for all of the republics might lead to chaos. If all the republics declared independence from a central unifying power, who would inherit the Soviet army? Who would control the vast nuclear arsenals compiled by the USSR? Who would regulate the economy that had been structured on the basis of a single union?

But the restive republics—seeing what might be their last chance to break completely free from the weakened institutions of central Soviet power—demanded complete and total independence. On December 17, 1991, Gorbachev and Yeltsin jointly announced that on January 1, 1992, the Soviet Union would cease to exist. Two weeks later, Mikhail Gorbachev resigned his post as president and the red flag of the USSR was quietly lowered from the Kremlin for the last time on a cold and dark Moscow night.

A NEW RUSSIAN DEMOCRACY?

With the dawn of democracy in Russia, President Yeltsin and the Russian population face a daunting array of problems as they struggle to build a stable society on the ruins of communism. Democracy, after all, is not an abstract concept or a moral platitude. As a political process, democracy must be carefully constructed to allow for a balance between mass participation and an efficient and orderly state. Three particular problems of constructing democracy in postcommunist Russia emerge: (1) the vestiges of communism; (2) the tension between new executive and legislative power; and (3) the relationship between a market economy and political democracy.

The first problem, then, stems from the fact that Russia is not a blank slate as it travels the path of democracy. The democratic process is being superimposed on a political system and society greatly influenced by the impact of Communist rule. Ex-Communist bureaucrats still staff most administrative positions because the revolutionary democrats—forced into inactivity during the communist years—lack the experience necessary to run a modern state. Ex-Communist factory managers continue to control economic activity, leading some to characterize the transition to a market economy as *nomenklatura privatization*. Some scholars, like Soviet specialist Peter Reddaway, argue that "Russia's deeply Sovietized political culture is . . . highly unsuited to free markets, entrepreneurism, privatization and the rule of law."[8] To counter the influence of the communist system and prevent a resurgence of Communist power in the face of current economic problems, President Yeltsin tried to make the Communist party illegal and confiscate all its property. This led Communists to complain loudly that their rights had been violated. In a democracy, they argue, every political group should have an equal opportunity to develop a social base and take part in the political process. This leads to a political conundrum. Does a democratic state have the right to use undemocratic methods in extreme situations to guarantee social stability?

A second problem is the relationship between the executive branch under President Yeltsin and the legislative branch, including a Russian parliament elected before the August 1991 coup attempt and divided between ex-Communist conservatives, Russian nationalists, and democrats of all colors. While a balance of power between the two branches is the ultimate goal, in the troubled conditions of a new democracy the relationship is not so clear. State leaders, including Yeltsin, argue that a strong executive is essential to counter Russia's political instability and economic crisis. The president and his administration must be given extraordinary powers to end political conflict and introduce radical economic reforms if Russia is to survive the postcommunist period. The political conflict generated by squabbles in the legislature impedes the democratic reform process. The executive branch must be entrusted to use its extensive powers in the name of democracy until the reforms produce the stability necessary for a constructive participatory democracy.

The democrats in the legislature counter that Yeltsin's approach is authoritarian and reminiscent of Communist strong-arm methods of rule from above. The only way to counter the authoritarian tendencies of the state is to give parliament extensive powers over legislation and the executive branch. Even though the legislature is divided into small splintered political factions that may produce unstable governments, the price of instability must be paid if democracy is to grow roots in the depth of Russian political and social life. The debate over executive versus legislative powers raises another important problem in political science. Which value prevails in conditions of extreme instability: democracy, or order?

The third problem is that the complicated relationship between economics and politics has dominated Russia's transition to democracy. In the realm of domestic economics, the impact of free-market "shock therapy" may have very destabilizing political consequences. Skyrocketing prices, high inflation, private property, and a visible gap between wealthy and poor may lead Russians—steeped in a history of social egalitarianism—to associate democracy with an intolerable level of economic inequality. This could give extreme nationalists the opportunity to overthrow the democratic regime as foreign and unjust in light of traditional Russian ideals. The Russian situation also highlights the tremendous impact of the international economic system on domestic politics of economically unstable countries. Russia desperately needs loans, aid, and debt relief from the International Monetary Fund and World Bank to pull itself out of its economic crisis. These institutions will grant economic aid only if Russia agrees to introduce the shock therapy of radical economic reforms. Shock therapy requires the use of strong executive political powers to tighten the money supply, reduce the deficit, hold down wages, and reduce state subsidies of food and consumer goods. Democrats, socialists, workers, trade unions, and the average citizen will resist such policies, as they are forced to tighten an already suffocating economic belt. The political tensions raised by domestic and international economic policies produce another dilemma in democracy building. Can the consolidation of a market economy, with its sometimes authoritarian and inegalitarian methods, take place simultaneously with the introduction of political democracy?

SUMMARY

The dilemmas that confront Russia are the product of an unprecedented change in the course of political history from Soviet totalitarianism to Russian democracy. Seeking to introduce evolutionary reforms from above to revitalize Soviet economics, politics, and society, Mikhail Gorbachev was forced to adapt his reform program to revolutionary changes from below. Gorbachev's middle course between the forces of democracy and the forces of reaction produced contradictions impossible to resolve in the confines of the Soviet Union. The result was the death of an empire and the birth—painful but full of promises for the future—of democracy in postcommunist Russia.

NOTES

1. See Zbigniew Brzezinski, *The Grand Failure: The Birth and Death of Communism in the Twentieth Century* (New York: Charles Scribner's Sons, 1989).

2. By a "Stalinist system," we mean those political, economic, and social institutions initiated during Stalin's reign beginning in 1928 and surviving his death in 1953. It is important to note, however, that the Soviet Union after 1953 was vastly different from that of the Stalin period. The use of terror as an instrument of politics ceased, the political process—though still dominated by the single Communist party—became more bureaucratized and predictable. For a Soviet dissident's account of the Stalin period, see Roy Medvedev, *Let History Judge: The Origins and Consequences of Stalinism* (New York: Knopf, 1973).

3. After 1985, the Communist Party of the Soviet Union admitted that its organization had proved incapable of fulfilling its responsibility to provide the Soviet population with adequate material (and spiritual) goods. The party-state guarantee of full employment meant that the entire economy was inefficient, resulting in low production and poor quality of goods. The waiting time for a cramped apartment was between 8 and 20 years; for a car, usually 7 years. While people had adequate bread and potatoes, there was always a shortage of fruit and no variety of foodstuffs or consumer items.

4. By this we mean that the political system resisted adapting to inputs from its own society or from the external environment. In the latter case, for example, the information and computer revolution that rocked the world in the second half of the twentieth century led to a wider dissemination of information and the profusion of personal computers in the West. Since the Communist party insisted on maintaining its monopoly on information and control over all communication processes, it continued to limit access to information and limited the distribution of computers.

5. "Russia's Radical Farm Privatization Plan Meeting Resistance," *Washington Post,* January 25, 1992, p. A16.

6. The CPSU congress should not be confused with a governmental legislative body. The party congress was the most important gathering of CPSU members (about 5,000 out of a total 19 million members), which was held once every five years. Before 1989 it was the CPSU congress—and not any legislative body—that guided economic, political, and social policies for the USSR.

7. See Seweryn Bialer, *Stalin's Successors* (Cambridge, U.K.: Cambridge University Press, 1980), pp. 145–46.

8. Peter Reddaway, "Next From Russia: 'Shock Therapy' Collapse," *Washington Post,* July 12, 1992, p. C7.

SUGGESTED READINGS

Brumberg, Abraham. *Chronicle of a Revolution: A Western–Soviet Inquiry into Perestroika.* New York: Pantheon, 1990. Essays by Soviet and Western scholars on the attempt by Soviet leaders from Khrushchev to Gorbachev to provide alternatives to the Stalinist system, focusing on the emergence of democracy and pluralism in the late 1980s.

Brzezinski, Zbigniew. *The Grand Failure: The Birth and Death of Communism in the Twentieth Century.* New York: Charles Scribner's Sons, 1989. A thought-provoking account of the social and technological pressures that resulted in "communism's irreversible historical decline," by the Polish-born former national security advisor to U.S. President Jimmy Carter.

Colton, Timothy J. *The Dilemma of Reform in the Soviet Union,* rev. and expanded ed. New York: Council on Foreign Relations, 1986. An interesting and systematic exploration of the systemic pressures for reform in the Soviet Union.

Doder, Dusko. *Shadows and Whispers: Power Politics inside the Kremlin from Brezhnev to Gorbachev.* New York: Penguin Books, 1988. A fast-moving journalistic account of the intrigue and politicking that abounded at the top levels of the Communist party, peppered with the author's personal experiences with the Soviet bureaucracy as former Moscow bureau chief for the *Washington Post.*

Hosking, Geoffrey. *The Awakening of the Soviet Union,* 2nd ed. Cambridge, Mass.: Harvard University Press, 1991. Examines the political emancipation of society in the Soviet Union. Analyzes Russian social organizations and civil society from a historical perspective.

Laqueur, Walter. *The Long Road to Freedom: Russia and Glasnost.* New York: Charles Scribner's Sons, 1989. A detailed exploration of glasnost' and change in the context of Soviet history, politics, society, and culture. Highlights the difficulties of significant and long-term reforms in light of Soviet historical experience.

Mandel, Ernest. *Beyond Perestroika: The Future of Gorbachev's USSR.* London: Verso Press, 1988. A critique of Gorbachev's reform policies from the left of the political spectrum, arguing that perestroika hurts the Soviet worker and that radical socioeconomic reform is unfeasible.

15

Conclusion: Seeing Politics Whole

> The end of history will be a very sad time. The struggle for recognition, the willingness to risk one's life for a purely abstract goal, the worldwide ideological struggle that called for daring, courage, imagination, and idealism, will be replaced by economic calculation, the endless solving of technical problems, environmental concerns, and the satisfaction of sophisticated consumer demands.

> —Francis Fukuyama

> Liberalism is not the end of politics in the world at large any more than it is the end of politics at home. A liberal international order may be less violent, may look less like the state of nature. But just because power takes on new forms, it will not cease to exist or cease to define a hierarchy of those who count and those who do not. As a result, the strong will (still) do what they can; the weak will (still) do what they must.

> —Stephen Sestanovich

In Chapter 1 we noted the widely discussed 1989 article by Francis Fukuyama called "The End of History,"[1] which led to a book in 1992.[2] We dissented, mildly, from Fukuyama's argument that, because authoritarian regimes were in an irreversible decline, general levels of political and armed conflict in the world would abate. And even though he softened and qualified his argument somewhat in his book, we remain skeptical. The Soviet empire—to take the obvious example—has collapsed, but it has certainly not left peace and liberal democracy in its wake. Perhaps these will come, but they have not yet. Now, at the conclusion of our book, it is worth returning to ask what can be said, in general, about the direction of change in the politics of the world as we approach the twenty-first century. Is there *anything* to *any* of the great master theories of political change that can help us understand where we are going?

In his essay, Fukuyama followed the general model of analysis advanced by the great nineteenth-century German philosopher of history Georg Wilhelm Freidrich Hegel (1770–1831). Hegel was an "idealist"; that is, he saw history as driven and shaped by the clash of ideals in a logical process known as the *dialectic*. One concept (the thesis) inevitably generates its opposite (the antithesis), and the interaction produces a new concept (the synthesis). This new concept, or ideal, animates unfolding reality, constituting itself as the new thesis—and provoking a new anti-thesis. In Hegel's view, this ideological unfolding was progressive, with history moving ineluctably to the final expression of an absolute ideal. In his time, Hegel regarded the Prussian state in which he lived as the most advanced (the most intellectually and historically advanced) government, and Napoleon Bonaparte as the highest expression of the evolving world soul. Despite what may seem to us today as simple chauvinism and perhaps a somewhat sinister hero worship, Hegel's thought became a powerful model for late-nineteenth-century and twentieth-century theo-ries of historical progress.

But while Fukuyama and other neo-Hegelians believe history is pro-gressive, others believe that politics within and among nations is a process of inherent never-ending conflict. There are only periods and places where things are relatively worse or relatively better; the better continu-ally struggles against the worse and is, in turn, continually being under-mined by it. In this view, what is happening in Eastern Europe, for instance, has less to do with democracy than with the reemergence of national societies, ethnic identities, and religious loyalties that had been "driven underground" during four decades of communist domination.[3] Here there is no progressive march of history; rather, politics is seen as a continuous struggle to preserve hard-won decency in political systems from the ever present dangers of decay and dissolution, and to nudge inhumane systems in desirable directions—or, in the extreme case, to do battle to contain or destroy them. It is interesting to reflect, in this regard, on the fact that Fukuyama's essay appeared before Iraq's invasion of Kuwait, with all that has flowed from it.

Another sort or type of master theory that has been much discussed recently involves the rise and fall of dominant powers on the world stage. Such an argument was made most dramatically several years ago by Yale University historian Paul Kennedy in a best-selling book called *The Rise and Fall of the Great Powers*.[4] For Kennedy the master pattern of modern world politics is one of imperial overextension. Great Britain, he argued, had overreached at the height of its power in the late nineteenth century; its once dominant industrial base was incapable of supporting the global military and administrative apparatus it had put in place. All this was asserted by Kennedy to constitute a clear lesson for the United States. With a now shaky and obsolescing industrial base and a far-flung network of expensive military commitments, America, Kennedy argued, is slip-ping fast as a world power—especially with respect to those competitors with more modern industrial infrastructures and far fewer military and overseas obligations such as, ironically, Japan and Germany.

But Kennedy's thesis did not long remain unchallenged; perhaps the most carefully worked out response came from Joseph Nye, a political scientist at Harvard. In a book titled *Bound to Lead: The Changing Nature of American Power*,[5] Nye argued that the elements that make for national and international power are changing. No longer are raw materials or heavy industry or even raw military might the sole keys to power; increasingly, human resources and information technology (so-called soft factors) are building blocks of power. Far from seeing American power as being in a decline (as Kennedy had maintained), Nye suggests that, while no longer cast in the dominant role in which it had found itself at the conclusion of World War II, the nation's power has remained essentially uneroded over the past 20 years. While the United States faces an array of vexing problems at home, there is no evidence of "decline." Professor Nye speculates, though, that there may indeed be a decline in the importance of its military power. In the immediate wake of the collapse of Soviet power, this might have appeared plausible. But within months of the publication of Professor Nye's book, American military power had allowed the nation to frustrate Saddam Hussein's bid to take over control of a major portion of the world's oil supply, assuming the leadership of the most impressive international coalition formed since World War II in order to contain Iraq's aggression.

So the dangers of theorizing on a grand scale are legion, and perhaps a better wisdom for students of politics in this era of rapid change was offered by Professor Lucian Pye in his 1989 presidential address to the American Political Science Association.

> In the last decades the exponential growth in all of the variables that energize the modernization process has stimulated a lot of imaginative speculation. Some have sought to encapsulate what has been taking place by theorizing about a knowledge, or information, revolution. The study of advanced industrial societies has been pushed to the point of theories about postindustrial societies. More specifically, there has been speculation about the "end of communism." Clearly, the long historical trend that favored the strengthening of centralized state power has seemingly come to an end, and the trend now favors the pluralism of decentralized authority.[6]

But the problems of sustaining the politics of pluralism are far from trivial, as the events in eastern Europe and the former Soviet Union make clear. Rather than the debating of grand theories or the speculating about historical determinisms, it may be these more mundane but infinitely important problems that constitute the real agenda of political analysis for your generation.

NOTES

1. Francis Fukuyama, "The End of History," *National Interest* (Summer 1989): 3–35.

2. See Francis Fukuyama, *The End of History and the Last Man* (New York: Free Press, 1992).

3. Paul Gottfried, "Ouis Judicabit?" *Chronicles* (February 1990): 16.

4. Paul M. Kennedy, *The Rise and Fall of the Great Powers: Economic Change and Military Conflict* (New York: Random House, 1987).

5. Joseph Nye, *Bound to Lead: The Changing Nature of American Power* (New York: Basic Books, 1990).

6. Lucian W. Pye, "Political Science and the Crisis of Authoritarianism," *American Political Science Review* (March 1990): 8.

Index

Abortion, 68, 84–87
Adams, Henry, 146
Adams, John, 293
Adelman, Kenneth, 243
Adenauer, Konrad, 269
Advocates, 194
Afghanistan, 277
Alexander the Great, 28–29
Almond, Gabriel, 134, 306
Ambivalents, 210
The American Voter, 134
Amin, Idi, 251
Anarchism, 21–22
Ancient Law (Maine), 44
Andreeva, Nina, 324
Antiballistic missile system, 197
Antony, Marc, 29
Apportionment, 125–26
Aquinas, Thomas, 51
Arbatov, Georgi, 265
Ardagh, John, 104
Arendt, Hannah, 48–49
Argentina, 8, 160, 161
Argumenty i Fakty, 80–81
Aristocracy, 27
Aristotle, 24, 27–29; political systems, 45–46; Polybius and, 46–47
Armenia, 6
Arms race, 274; Cold War and, 253–63; control of, 243–47; first-strike capability, 259; global destruction, 257–58; Gorbachev and, 279; reduction of, 261–63; strategic launchers, 254–56; survival and, 247. *See also* Nuclear weapons
Armstrong, William, 202, 204
Army Corps of Engineers, U.S., 196–97
Aron, Raymond, 246, 253
Atatürk, Kemal, 306–308
Atlanticists, 288
At-large elections, 127
Atomic Energy Act of 1946, 234

Augustine, 31
Authoritarian systems, 5, 48, 94, 123–24
Authoritarianism, 27
Authority, effective linkage and, 304; Middle Ages, 30–33; Nisbet on, 211–12; state and, 19–20, 33–34; Weber on, 21
Azerbaijan, 6, 9–10, 74

Bagehot, Walter, 67, 170
Bailer, Seweryn, 328
Bakunin, Mikhail, 21
Baldwin, David, 251
Ball, Terence, 61
Ballot measures, 131–33
Baltic Assembly, 283
Barnes, Denis, 202–205
Beer, Samuel, 172
Belarus, 284, 287, 289; national character, 75
Benn, Tony, 128
Berelson, Bernard, 136–37
Berlin Wall, 4, 5, 282
Bernstein, Eduard, 38
Bevan, Aneurin, 171
Blumstein, James, 127
Bolsheviks, 20, 98, 315, 325
Bonaparte, Napoleon, 102, 342
Bound to Lead: The Changing Nature of American Power (Nye), 342–43
Bourgeoisie, 26, 36–38
Brandeis, Louis, 206
Brandt, Willy, 39
Bray, Linda, 7, 10
Brennan, William J., Jr., 225
Brezhnev, Leonid, 274, 276–77
Bridges, Edward, 204
Broder, David S., 123
Brovikov, V. I., 313
Brown, George, 173
Brown, Pat, 154
Brzezinski, Zbigniew, 48, 314

Budgets, Great Britain, 180–81; United States, 181–82

Bulgaria, 7

Bunce, Valerie, 302

Bureaucracy, 148; as organization, 191–96; efficiency of, 212–13; Great Britain, 198–205; growth of, 178, 208–214; mass media and, 149–50; overview, 189–90; political style and, 204–208; presidency and, 158; reorganization of, 213–14; Roosevelt on, 194; Soviet Union Communist party, 324; types, 193–95

Bureaucratic politics, 192–98, 214–15

Burger, Warren, 231

Burma. *See* Myanmar

Burns, James MacGregor, 145, 302

Bush, George, 130, 151, 155, 174; bureaucracy and, 214; social welfare spending, 250; Soviet Union and, 281

Butler, Samuel, 67

Butterfield, Alexander, 225

Byrd, Robert, 175

Caesar, Augustus, 29

Callaghan, James, 96, 100, 205

Calvin, John, 34

Cambodia, 71

Campaigns, 128–31. *See also* Elections

Campbell, Angus, 134

Capabilities analysis, 306–307

Capitalism, 314–15

Capitalists, 36–38

Carrington, Peter, 161

Carter, Jimmy, 151, 154, 155; Army Corps of Engineers and, 196; bureaucracy and, 205, 213; security classification system and, 234

Castle, Barbara, 202–204

Castro, Fidel, 306–308

Ceausescu, Nikolai, 5, 9

Central Intelligence Agency (CIA), 75, 84; Noriega and, 8

Cephalogy, 133

Chamfort, 67

Change, forces of, 293–95; political leadership and, 301–308; traditional society, 296–98; transitional society and, 298–300

Charlemagne, 31

China, as totalitarian government, 49; Communist party, 49, 229–30; courts, 229–30; political socialization and, 73; Tiananmen Square, 229–30

Chirac, Jacques, 104, 108–109

Christianity, 30–31, 33

Church and state, separation of, 34–35

Church of Rome, 30

Churchill, Winston, 99, 144, 162; international relations and, 267–69; on House of Commons, 170

Cicero, Marcus Tullius, 29–30, 32

City of God (Augustine), 31

City-states, 24–25, 27–29

Civil Government (Locke), 169

Civil service, 207

Civil Service Reform Act of 1978, 214

Civil society, Soviet Union, 329, 330–31

Climbers, 193

Clinton, Bill, 79, 130, 214

Cold War, 267, 270–71, 275, 287, 302

Coleman, James, 306

Collective bargaining, 98–99

Colombia, 8, 9

Common law, 51

Common Sense (Paine), 58

Commonwealth of Independent States, 283–84

Communal society, 56

Communism, death of, 39

Communist Manifesto (1848), 37, 38

Communist party, 5; China, 49, 229–30; France, 106–107, 109–110; Romania, 9; Soviet Union, 7, 50, 52, 74, 95, 111–18, 272, 315–36; United Kingdom, 96

Conference on Security and Cooperation in Europe, 275, 276, 279

Conflict, leadership and, 143–45; nuclear power and, 11–12; politics and, 4–5, 8, 10–12; types of, 8–10

Congress of People's Deputies, Soviet Union, 325–27, 329

Congress, U.S., 167–69, 190; as na-

tional legislature, 151–53; committees, 176–77; contrasted with Parliament, 171–72, 174; executive and, 181–82; overview, 173–74; representation, 182–83; staff, 175–76 Congressional Budget Office, 181
Congressional Government (Wilson), 145
Conservatism, contemporary, 60–61
Conservative party, British, 96, 99–101, 103, 160, 162, 172
Conservers, 193, 253–63
Constitutionalism, 50–52
Constitutions, 52; Soviet Union, 52; United States, 92, 124, 126, 131, 151
Converse, Philip, 134
Corinth, 24
Council of Mutual Economic Assistance, 269, 282
Courts, as dispute settlers, 221–22; as intragovernmental arbiters, 224–26; as law definers, 223–24; as policymakers, 230–36; as political control mechanisms, 228–30; as social control mechanisms, 226–28; China, 229–30; evolution of, 220–21; functions, 221; rights and, 219–20; security and, 236. *See also* Judiciary
Cox, Archibald, 225
Crime, courts and, 226–28
Crossman, R. H. S., 199–205, 213
Crozier, Brian, 49
Cuban Missile Crisis of 1962, 254–55, 273–74
Czechoslovakia, 7, 276

Dagger, Richard, 61
Dahl, Robert A., 54, 55, 57, 246, 250
Daedalus, 7
Darman, Richard G., 189, 214
Darwin, Charles, 44
de Gaulle, Charles, 91, 95, 105–108, 111
de Gortari, Carlos Salinas, 95
Decision making, command, 250–51; democratic, 250; goals, 252–53
Defense Department, U.S., 190, 197
Democracy, 27, 29, 52–53, 94; as government form, 5, 45–46; Dahl on, 54; definition, 149; Greece, 24–28; laws and, 51; liberty and, 57; one-party system and, 95; opinions and, 236; political democracy, 94; Russia, 336–38
Democratic socialism, 38; United Kingdom, 98–99
Deng Xiao Ping, 229
d'Estaing, Giscard, 107
Détente, 275–78
Deutsch, Karl, 70, 307
Devolution, political, 308–309
Dialectical materialism, 38
Dictatorship, 28. *See also* Authoritarian systems
The Discourses (Machiavelli), 32
Disraeli, Benjamin, 97, 98
Divine right of kings, 33
Dole, Robert, 123, 175, 177, 184
Douglas, William O., 225
Downs, Anthony, 193–95
Drug trade, 6, 8, 9
Drummond, Edward, 223
Duverger, Maurice, 126

East Germany, 6
Eastern Europe, 4, 5; change in, 293–94; ethnic conflicts and, 7; socialism and, 39
Easton, David, 23
Economic development, 299; as national goal, 248–49
Economist, 159–61, 162, 180
Education Department, U.S., 213–14
Egalitarianism, 58
Eisenhower, Dwight D., 156, 158; iron triangle and, 211; security classification system and, 233–34
Elections, at-large, 127; ballot measures, 131–33; campaigns, 128–31; leadership and, 150–51; legal aspects, 124–26; overview, 124; party systems and, 126–28; Soviet Union, 335; voting, 133–37
Empire-builders, 288–89
Employment and Productivity Department, United Kingdom, 202–204
The Empty Polling Booth (Hadley), 135

Energy Department, U.S., 213–14
Engels, Friedrich, 37
England, rulers, 32–33; sectarian warfare and, 33. *See also* Great Britain; United Kingdom
Environmental groups, 117
Equality, 58; liberty and, 57
Espionage Act of 1917, 233
Estonia, 7
Eurasianists, 288
Euripides, 293
European Common Market, 161
European Economic Community, 161
Executive, conditions conducive to, 145–50; constraints on, 150–54; overview, 143–44; privilege, 225; transactional, 145; transformational, 145. *See also* Leadership

Fabian Society, 98
Falkland Islands, 160, 161
Family, role of, 43–44
Fang Lizhi, 229
Federalist (Madison), 92, 123, 143
Fenno, Richard, 173–75
Feudalism, 31–32, 38
Figgis, John Niville, 43
Fiorina, Morris P., 134–35
Fleming, Thomas, 19
Ford, Gerald, 174
Foreign Affairs, 270
Fourier, Charles, 36
France, Assembly for the Republic, 106–110; Communist party, 106–107, 109–110; elections, 109, 110; Fifth Republic, 105–107, 108; Fourth Republic, 105; interest groups, 102–111; labor unions, 104; National Assembly, 105–108, 110; National Front, 106, 109–111; political parties, 102–111; rulers, 32–33; Socialist Party, 106, 107; Third Republic, 105; Union of Democracy, 106–107, 109–110
Franco, Francisco, 48, 49, 50
Free market policies, 61
Freedom, 59; national survival and, 247–48

Freedom of Information Act of 1966, 232, 234
Freedom of speech, 131
French Revolution, 58
Friedrich, Carl, 48
Fukuyama, Francis, 5, 124, 341–42

Gandhi, Indira, 153, 221
Gandhi, Mahatma, 144, 162
Gannett Co. v. DePasquale (1979), 231–32
General Accounting Office, U.S., 182
General Agreement on Tariffs and Trade (GATT), 281, 288
Germany, German Social Democratic party, 39; national character, 72–73
Gerrymandering, 126, 127
Gibbon, Thomas, 219
Ginsberg, Ruth Bader, 67
Glasnost', 327–28
Goldwater, Barry, 154
Gorbachev, Mikhail, 5, 6–7, 265, 313; as leader, 145, 162–63; Communist party and, 115–17; Lithuania and, 273; on strikes, 91; political conflicts and, 9–10; polls and, 78–79, 80–83; reforms, 50; role in change in Soviet Union, 316–17, 321–32, 334–38; Soviet national character and, 74–75; Soviet Union breakup and, 278–82, 289; Soviet workers and, 113–15
Great Britain, bureaucracy and, 198–205; Conservative party, 96, 99–101, 103, 160, 162, 172; global politics and, 178–79; Labour party, 96, 98–101, 103, 163, 173; legislature, 168–69. *See also* Parliament, British; United Kingdom
Greece, as authoritarian government, 48; political theories of, 24–29, 39
Greenstein, Fred I., 189
The Growth of Crime (Radzinowicz), 226
Gysi, Gregor, 6

Hadley, Arthur T., 135, 137
Haig, Alexander M., Jr., 243
Halle, Louis J., 267
Halperin, Morton, 197
Hamilton, Alexander, 123, 143

Hazard, John, 222
Health and Human Services Department, U.S., 190, 195
Health and Social Security Department, United Kingdom, 201–203
Heath, Edward, 160, 205
Heclo, Hugh, 207, 211
Hegel, Georg Wilhelm Freidrich, 341–42
Hegemonic systems, 54
Heseltine, Michael, 160
Hitler, Adolf, 73, 99; as leader, 144–45, 162; goals of, 245
Hobbes, Thomas, 33–35, 19
Holsti, K. J., 246
Hook, Sidney, 144–45
Horowitz, Donald, 127
House of Commons. *See* Parliament, British
Housekeeping Act of 1789, 233
Howe, Geoffrey, 160
Hume, David, 35
Hungary, 7
Huntington, Samuel, 299, 305, 328–29
Hussein, Saddam, 343

Impeachment, 182, 225
Imperial bureaucracy, 206–208
Independent national legislatures, 151–53
Individual, interest groups and, 92; labor unions and, 97–98; liberty and, 57, 58; national character and, 74–75
Industrial Revolution, 36–39, 97; power centralization and, 146–48
Industrialization, 60, 103, 190, 192
Information utilization, 70–71
Institution, 44
Institutional Revolutionary Party, Mexico, 95
Interest groups, 10; attitude sharing, 93; definition, 92–93; economic, 92; elections and, 125; France, 102–111; Netherlands, 47–48; PACs, 130; political parties and, 93–96; Soviet Union, 111–18; United Kingdom, 96–102; United States, 48
Internal Security Act of 1950, 234

International Monetary Fund (IMF), 288, 338
International relations, bipolar, 246; conquests, 252; influence, 251; politics of, 266–67; prestige, 251
Iran, 6–7; change capability and, 72
Iraq, 48
Iron triangles, 157–58, 210–11
Iroquois League, 44–45
Issue networks, 157–58, 210–11
Italy, 53

Jackson, Robert H., 219–20, 230
Jancks, Christopher, 58
Jarrett, Clifford, 202–204
Jaworski, Leon, 225
Jefferson, Thomas, 151, 155–56, 219; influence of Locke, 169
Jiang Zemin, 229
Johnson, Andrew, 182
Johnson, Lyndon B., 151, 153, 154, 174; ABM system and, 197–98; rhetoric and, 12
Judiciary, 219; as restraint on executive, 153–54; United States, 231–32. *See also* Courts
Justice, 59–60

Das Kapital (Marx), 37, 38
Karpov, A. S., 76
Kazin, Alfred, 146
Kennan, George, 270
Kennedy, Edward, 183
Kennedy, John F., 145, 151, 174; arms race and, 260; bureaucracy and, 193, 206
Kennedy, Paul, 342–43
Kenya, 95
Key, V. O., Jr., 75, 129, 134
Khrushchev, Nikita, 265, 272–74, 334
King, Martin Luther, Jr., 293
Kinnock, Neil, 101
Kissinger, Henry, 275
Korean War (1950–1953), 270
Kornhauser, William, 55–56

Labor unions, France, 104; Great Britain, 97–98, 112; Soviet Union, 112–15, 118; workers' rights and, 98

Labour party, British, 96, 98–101, 103, 161, 173
Langbein, John H., 228
Laos, 71
Laski, Harold, 57, 170–71
Latin America, 6; information utilization in, 71
Latvia, 7, 117, 285
Laws, Aristotle and, 27–28, 29; aspects of, 51; Cicero, 29; definition, 44; election, 124–26; legislatures and, 169; Montesquieu, 35; Plato, 27. *See also* Courts
Laws (Cicero), 29
Laws (Plato), 27
Lawson, Nigel, 160
Leadership, constraints on, 150–54; examination of, 155–57; executive, 145–55; politics and change, 301–308; public and, 146; transactional, 145; transformational, 145
Leadership (Burns), 145
Legislature, as restraint on executive, 151–53; functions of, 168–70; role of, 178–79, 184; study of, 167
Lenin, V. I., 20, 37, 38; as leader, 144–45, 162; courts and, 222; Marx and, 314–15; on working class, 111–12
Li Peng, 229
Liberal party, British, 96, 101
Liberalism, 32–36, 341; contemporary, 60–61; Marxism and, 36–39
Libertarian Party, 61
Liberty, 57; freedom and, 59; individual and, 58
Ligachev, Yegor, 116
Lincoln, Abraham, 67
Lindblom, Charles E., 198, 246
Lindsay, A. D., 149
Linkage mechanisms, 271, 303–304; interest groups and political parties, 93–96; Soviet Union, 118–19, 304; United Kingdom, 96–102; working class, 99
Lippmann, Walter, 133–34, 270
Lithuania, 7, 9–10, 117, 273
Locke, John, 35, 60, 152, 169
London Observer, 159, 162

Lukyanov, Anatoliy, 80
Luther, Martin, 34
Lutz, William, 12–13

Macaulay, Thomas Babbington, 143
MacDonald, Ramsay, 98–99
Machiavelli, Niccolò, 31–32, 152, 156
MacIver, Robert, 43–44
McKinley, William, 145–47
Mackintosh, John, 204
McNamara, Robert, 71, 197
McNaughten, Daniel, 223–24
Madison, James, 92
Maine, Henry, 44
Major, John, 101; security classification system and, 234–35
Mano Tsuyoshi, 226
Mansfield, Harvey C., Jr., 152, 167
Mao Tse-tung, 37, 144, 162, 230
Marshall Plan, 269
Marshall, Thurgood, 225
Marx, Karl, 36–38; democratic socialism and, 98; equality and, 58; on working class, 111–12; theory of economic development, 314–15
Marxism, 36–39, 56; equality and, 61
Mason, Alpheus, 206–207
Mass, Arthur, 196
Mass media. *See* Media
Mass societies, 54–57
Mayhew, David, 175
Media, 149–50; elections and, 130–31, 133; international change and, 294; presidency and, 155–57; Reagan and, 154–55
Medical technology, 297
Menem, Carlos Saul, 8
Mexico, drug trade and, 9; Italy and, 53; one-party political system, 95
Middle Ages, 30–32; wealth and, 38
Militarism, 72–73
Mill, John Stuart, 293
Miller, Warren, 134
Mintusov, Igor, 83
Mitchell, George, 175
Mitterrand, François, 107–111, 243; bureaucracy and, 207
Modern society, 300–301
Modrow, Hans, 6

Moi, Daniel Arap, 95
Monarchy, 27, 47; as government form, 45–46; divine right of, 33; leadership and, 152; Scotland, 45
Montesquieu, Baron de, 35
Morgenthau, Hans, 72–73, 246
Morgenthau, Henry, 194
Moseley, George, 199–200
Muddy Waters (Mass), 196
Mugabe, Robert, 56
Multiparty political system, 53, 95, 126; France, 102–111, 105–107; Soviet Union, 329, 330–31
Muskie, Edmund S., 177–78
Mussolini, Benito, 50
Myanmar, 124

National Abortion Rights League, 86
National Assembly, France, 103, 105, 107–108, 110–11
National character, 72–75
National Right to Life Committee, 86
National Security Act of 1974, 234
National will, 73
Nationalism, Russia, 10; Soviet Union, 117, 329, 331–34
Nationality, 69
Natural law, 29–30, 51
Nelson, Joan, 299
Neocorporatism, 104, 118
Neorealist democracy, 53
Netherlands, 47–48
Neustadt, Richard E., 15–16n, 156–57, 208
New Union Treaty, Soviet Union, 335
New York Times, 8, 231
New York Times v. Sullivan (1964), 231
Nicaragua, 9
Nie, Norman, 134
Nisbet, Robert, 211–12
Nixon, Richard M., 151, 153, 174; bureaucracy and, 205–206, 213; Congress and, 182; courts and, 221, 224–25; security classification system and, 234; Soviet Union and, 276
Nkrumah, Kwame, 251
Nomination of candidates, 129
Nonvoters. *See* Voting
Noriega, Manuel, 6, 7–8, 10

North Atlantic Treaty Organization (NATO), 5, 269, 270, 277
North, Oliver, 189
North Vietnam, 71
Novak, Michael, 300
Nuclear weapons, 11–12; international relations and, 287–88. *See also* Arms race
Nunn, Sam, 181
Nye, Joseph, 342–43

Ochlocracy, 28, 46
Office of Management and Budget, U.S., 181, 190, 213
Official Secrets Act of 1911, 234–36
Oligarchy, 25–26, 28, 47; as government form, 45–46
On the Origin of Species (Darwin), 44
One-party political system, 95; Soviet Union, 115, 117
Opinions, democracies, 236; leadership and, 150
Opposition, 54–56
Organization. *See* Bureaucracy
Organski, A. F. K., 246, 298–99
The Origins of Totalitarianism (Arendt), 49
Ornstein, Norman, 174
Orwell, George, 91
Owen, Robert, 36

Paine, Thomas, 58
Panama, 10; invasion of, 7–8; political conflicts, 9; U.S. military intervention in, 6
Panetta, Leon, 214
Parliament, British, 96, 170–73, 174, 184; executive and, 179–81; representation, 182–83
Parsons, Talcott, 294, 306
Peabody, Robert, 175
Peace, 13
Peaceful Nuclear Explosions Treaty of 1976, 261
Peele, Robert, 223
People's Daily, 229
Perestroika, 6, 322–23, 328; poll on, 83
Pericles, 25
Peru, 9

Peter the Great, 306–308
Petrocik, John, 134
Pierce, Franklin, 147
Pinochet, Augusto, 43
Plaid Cymru (Welsh), 96
Plato, 24–28; political systems, 45–46
Plea bargaining, 227–28
Pluralism, 343
Pluralist systems, 7, 47–48, 56
Poindexter, John, 189
Policy, 3–4
Policymakers, 3, 190–91, 230–36
Political action committees (PACs), 130
The Political Consequences of Electoral Laws (Rae), 124–25
Political culture, 74
Political development, as national goal, 249
Political devolution, 308–309
Political equality, 35, 58
Political liberty, 48
Political participation, 304–305
Political parties; bureaucracy and, 200–201; campaigns and, 128–31; elections and, 126–28; France, 102–111, 105–108; Great Britain, 96–102, 160, 161, 162, 171–72, 173, 184; interest groups and, 93–96; leadership and, 150–51; Soviet Union, 111–18
Political process, 77
Political recruitment, 70
Political rhetoric, 129–30
Political socialization, 69–70, 72; national character and, 73
Political systems, capabilities analysis and, 306–307; change and, 301–308, 314; constitutional government, 50–52; definition, 22, 43; democracy, 52–53; diversity and, 77; government form of, 45–46; information utilization and, 70–71; intragovernment conflict and, 225–26; mass societies, 54–57; multiparty, 105–107, 329, 330–31; one-party, 95, 115, 117; polyarchy, 54; primitive, 43–45; regime type, 47–50; Soviet Union, 314–40; Sweden, 72; Switzerland, 72; two-party system, 94–95
Politics, bureaucracy and, 192–98;

conflicts and, 4–5, 10–12; courts and, 228–30; decay of, 308–309; definition, 4, 5, 91–92; equality and, 36; France, 102–111; global, 178–79; Great Britain, 201; international, 266–67; media and, 12–13; power and, 177–78; public opinion and, 77–78; Soviet Union, 319–20; study of, 13–14; United States, 145–46; United States and Soviet Union relations, 270–72; voting and, 137
The Politics of Mass Society (Kornhauser), 55
Polling, abortion, 84–87; Great Britain, 162; public opinion and, 78–87. *See also* Voting
Polyarchy, 54, 55, 250
Polyarchy: Participation and Opposition (Dahl), 55
Polybius, 46–47
Pompidou, Georges, 107
Pontius Pilate, 190
Population, 297
Pork-barrel projects, 196–97
Power, definition, 3–4
Pravda, 279–80
Presidency, bureaucracy and, 205–206; examination of, 155–57. *See also names of individual presidents*
Presthus, Robert, 208–210, 215
The Prince (Machiavelli), 32
Privacy Act of 1974, 232
Proletariat, 36, 37, 38, 192
Proportional representation system, 125–26; France, 106–107
Protestant Reformation, 33, 34
Proudhon, Pierre-Joseph, 21
Public Opinion, 133
Public opinion, 75–87; definition, 75; formation, 72; polls and, 78–87
Public policy, 23, 177, 199
Pye, Lucian, 343

Radzinowicz, Leon, 226
Rae, Douglas W., 124–26, 128
Raphael, Adam, 159
Reagan, Ronald, 123, 265; aides, 189; arms race and, 260; as leader, 145, 151, 153–55, 157–58, 162–63; Con-

gress and, 182; reorganization of bureaucracy, 214; rhetoric and, 12; security classification system and, 234; social welfare spending and, 250; Soviet Union and, 277–78, 318

Reame, Charles, 222

Recruitment of candidates, 128

Red Lion Broadcasting Co. v. FCC (1969), 231

Reddaway, Peter, 337

Referendum, 131–33

Regan, Donald, 189

Rehnquist, William H., 231, 234

Rejuvenational capability, change and, 72; definition, 69; information utilization and, 70–71; political recruitment and, 70; political socialization and, 69–70

Representation, in legislature, 182–83

Republic (Cicero), 29

Republic (Plato), 26–27

Responsible Electorate (Key), 134

Retrospective Voting in American National Elections (Fiorina), 135

Rickover, Hyman G., 197

Riddelsdell, Mildred, 203

Riesman, David, 299

Rigby, T. H., 50

The Rights of Man (Paine), 58

The Rise and Fall of the Great Powers (Kennedy), 342–43

Robertson, Kenneth, 236

Rocard, Michel, 109–110

Roe v. Wade (1973), 86

Romania, 5, 9, 78

Romans, 28–30, 39

Roosevelt, Franklin D., as leader, 144–45, 149, 151, 153, 157, 162; bureaucracy and, 194, 206; Congress and, 178; international relations an, 267–68; reorganization of bureaucracy, 213; security classification system and, 233

Roosevelt, Theodore, as leader, 146–47, 152–53; Congress and, 178

Root, Elihu, 147

Rose, Richard, 96, 173, 201

Rostenkowski, Dan, 177

Rousseau, Jean-Jacques, 35

RU-486, 85

Russia, 5, 289; as leading successor of Soviet Union, 283–85; as totalitarian government, 49; change capability and, 72; democracy and, 336–38; fall of Soviet Union and, 117–18; international relations, 286–89; national character, 73, 75; nationalism and, 333–34; relations with United States, 286–88; rulers, 32–33; sectarian warfare and, 33; Ukraine and, 283–84. *See also* Soviet Union

Ryzhkov, N. I., 313

Sabato, Larry J., 130

Sabine, George A., 29, 37

St. Clair, James, 225

Sampson, Anthony, 171

Sandinistas, 9

Schlesinger, Arthur M., Jr., 206

Schlesinger, James, 213

Schroeder, Patricia, 8

Scotland, judiciary, 220

Scottish Nationalists, 96

Security classification system, 232–34; United Kingdom, 234–36

Separation of powers, 35, 152, 153, 181–82; Russia, 337–38

Serbia, 50

Sestanovich, Stephen, 341

Seward, William H., 147

Shaposhnikov, Evgenii, 283

Shevardnadze, Edward, 243

Shultz, George, 205–206

Sirica, John, 225

Smith, Adam, 35, 60

Social Democrats, British, 96

Social mobility, 296

Social regulation, 44

Social welfare, as national goal, 249–50; bureaucracy and, 148; Bush and, 250; liberalism and, 60–61

Socialism, 39

Socialist International, 39, 331–32

Socialist pluralism, 328–29

Society, individual and, 34; modern, 300–301; traditional, 296–98; transitional, 298–300

Socrates, 25, 26

Solidarity, 277
Solovyev, A., 76
South Vietnam, 71
Sovereignty, 19
Soviet Union, 4–5; arms race, 244, 247, 253–63; as study in change, 314–40; breakup of, 6–7, 278–89; bureaucracy and, 207–208; Bush and, 281; change in, 293–94; Communist party, 7, 50, 52, 74, 95, 111–18, 272, 316–36; Congress of People's Deputies, 325–27, 329; constitution, 52; coup of 1991, 334–36; détente, 275–78; economy, 317–18; former Soviet republics, 7, 331–36; interest groups, 111–18; labor unions, 112–15, 118; linkage and, 118–19, 304; Lithuania and, 273; national character, 74–75; Nixon and, 276; one-party system and, 95; political conflicts and, 9–10; political system, 111–18, 314–40; politics, 319–20; polls and, 78–79, 80–83; public opinion in, 76; Reagan and, 277–78; relations with United States, 267–90; social problems, 320–21; Supreme Soviet, 47, 325, 327; trade unions, 112–15, 118; working class, 111–12. See also Cold War
Spain, as authoritarian government, 48, 49; rulers, 32–33; sectarian warfare and, 33
Sparta, 24–25
Spin doctors, 12
The Spirit of the Laws (Montesquieu), 35
Spycatcher, 236
Stability, as internal goal, 248
Stafford, Lord, 143
Stalin, Joseph, 37, 50, 73; as leader, 144–45, 162; change in Soviet Union and, 315–16; international relations and, 268–69; on trade unions, 112; Russia and, 333
Stalingrad, Battle of, 73
Starkov, Vladislav, 80
State, authority and, 33–34; definition, 19–20; individual and, 36; legality of, 21; Locke and, 35–36. See also

Church and state, separation of; City-states
Statesmen, 194
Stevens, John Paul, 231
Stewart, Potter, 225, 231
Stokes, Donald, 134
Stone, Harlan, 206–207
Strategic Arms Reduction Talks, 261–62
Strikes, Great Britain, 160; Soviet Union, 113–14
Sukarno, Achmed, 251
Sun Yat-sen, 144
Supreme Court, Japan, 226
Supreme Court, U.S., 221, 224–25
Supreme Soviet, 47, 325, 327
Surveys. See Polling
Sweden, political system, 72; United States and, 53–54
Switzerland, political system, 72
Syria, 48

Taft, William Howard, 233
Taming the Prince: The Ambivalence of Modern Executive Power (Mansfield), 152
Technology, in traditional society, 296–97
Tennessee-Tombigbee Waterway, 196–97
Test Ban Treaty of 1963, 261
Thatcher, Margaret, 96, 97, 99–101, 243; as leader, 145, 158–63; as member of Parliament, 184; party leadership and, 172; political recruitment and, 128
Thebes, 24
Thernstrom, Abigail M., 127
Tocqueville, Alexis de, 43, 265, 287
Totalitarian systems, 48–50, 94, 123–24; mass society and, 55
Totalitarianism, 56
Trade unions. See Labor unions
Traditional democracy, 53
Transactional leadership, 145, 163
Transformational leadership, 145
Trotsky, Leon, 20
Truman, David B., 91, 92–93
Truman, Harry S., 156; Israel and,

245; security classification system and, 233

Twilight of authority, 211

Two Treatises on Civil Government (Locke), 35

Two-party political system, 94–95

Tyrrell, R. Emmett, 3

Ukraine, 7, 9–10, 117, 287, 289; national character, 75; Russia and, 283–84

Ulyanov, Vladimir Ilyich. *See* Lenin, V. I.

Unemployment, Great Britain, 161

United Kingdom, Alliance, 96, 101; Communist party, 96; democratic socialism, 98–99; interest groups, 96–102; labor unions, 97–98, 112; political parties, 96–102, 160, 161, 162; security classification system, 234–36; two-party system, 94–95; working class, 103–105, 128, 183. *See also* Parliament, British

United States, arms race, 247, 253–63; change capability and, 72; Constitution of, 231–32; détente, 275–78; global politics and, 178–79; interest groups, 48; Lithuania and, 273; relations with Russia, 286–88; relations with Soviet Union, 267–90; security classification system, 232–34; Sweden and, 53–54; two-party system, 94–95. *See also* Cold War

United States v. Nixon (1974), 224

Upward-mobiles, 209–210, 212

Uskorenie, 322

Utopian theories, 36

Verba, Sidney, 134

Vidal, Jean-Louis, 110

Vietnam War (1961–1975), 71, 270

Voting, 133–37

Voting Rights Act of 1965, 126, 127

Warfare, leadership and, 148

Warsaw Treaty Organization, 5, 67, 269, 282

Wealth, 38–39

The Web of Government (MacIver), 43–44

Weber, Max, 20–21, 189, 212; on bureaucracy, 192

Webster v. Reproductive Health Services (1989), 87

Weinberger, Caspar, 243

Welfare. *See* Social welfare

What Is to Be Done? (Lenin), 38

White, Byron, 225, 231

White, G. Edward, 221

Whitehall, United Kingdom, 201

Wilson, Harold, 173, 202, 205

Wilson, James Q., 212

Wilson, Pete, 123

Wilson, Woodrow, 145–47, 152–53; international relations and, 268; nationalism and, 333

Working class, bureaucracy and, 209; France, 103–105; linkage mechanisms, 99; Soviet Union, 111–12; United Kingdom, 103–105, 128, 183. *See also* Labor unions

World War I (1914–1918), 147

World War II (1939–1945), 73, 103, 147–48, 333; postwar period, 5, 267–69, 332, 343

Wunder, John R., 222

Yeats, W. B., 3

Yeltsin, Boris, 116–18, 145, 265, 284, 313; coup of 1991 and, 336; rise of, 326–27; Russian democracy and, 336–37; Western aid and, 287

Yugoslavia, 286

Zakharova, T., 76

Zealots, 194

Zhao Zhiyang, 229

Zhulyev, V. D., 76

Zimbabwe, 56

About the Authors

JOHN CHAUNCEY DONOVAN, DeAlva Stanwood Alexander Professor of Government at Bowdoin College, died on October 3, 1984, shortly after completing work on this book. He received his B.A. from Bates College in 1942, and served on a destroyer in the South Pacific during World War II. He returned to graduate study as part of that remarkable postwar generation in the Harvard Government Department—which has provided so much of the leadership of the discipline of political science over the past four decades. He received his M.A. in 1948, and his Ph.D. in 1949. During the early 1950s, John Donovan was part (along with Edmund S. Muskie) of a quiet revolution in Maine politics that saw the Democratic party emerge as a competitive force for the first time in this century. He was state Democratic chairman in 1957–58, and managed Governor Muskie's successful senatorial campaign in 1958. He went to Washington in 1959 as Senator Muskie's administrative assistant. In 1960, in his only personal bid for elective office, he was an unsuccessful congressional candidate in Maine's second district. In 1962 he was named special and executive assistant to Secretary of Labor Williard Wirtz, and became U.S. Manpower administrator in March 1964. He was present in the creation of much that became known as "the War on Poverty"; and while he became increasingly uncomfortable within the Johnson administration, especially after the early Vietnam escalations, he was at the president's shoulder for the signing of the Economic Opportunity Act of 1964—his proudest moment in public life. In February 1965 John Donovan resigned from government to accept the Alexander chair at Bowdoin. His widely acclaimed book on the War on Poverty, *The Politics of Poverty,* was published in 1967; and this was followed by *The Policy Makers* in 1970, *The Cold Warriors* in 1974, and (with Richard E. Morgan and Christian P. Potholm) two textbooks: *American Politics: Direction of Change, Dynamics of Choice* (1979, 1982) and the first edition of *People, Power, and Politics* (1981).

RICHARD E. MORGAN is William Nelson Cromwell Professor of Constitutional Law and Government at Bowdoin College. He received his B.A. from Bowdoin in 1959, and his M.A. in 1961 and Ph.D. in 1967 from Columbia. He has taught at Columbia and Harvard as well as Bowdoin. His primary professional interest is with the history, law, and politics of the First Amendment. He was director of a Twentieth Century Fund study of political surveillance in America, chairman of the Special Com-

357

mission on Legislative Compensation in Maine, and presently chairs the Maine Advisory Committee to the U.S. Commission on Civil Rights. His books include *The Politics of Religious Conflict* in 1968, *The Supreme Court and Religion* in 1971, *Domestic Intelligence: Monitoring Dissent in America* in 1980, and *Disabling America: The Rights Industry in Our Time* in 1984. He is also the author of *The Law and Politics of Civil Liberties,* a textbook.

CHRISTIAN P. POTHOLM received his B.A. degree from Bowdoin College in 1962. He attended Fletcher School of Law and Diplomacy where he was awarded an M.A. degree in 1964 and a M.A.L.D. degree in 1965. Professor Potholm has traveled to and researched such countries as Great Britain, Portugal, and Greece, and has traveled extensively on the continent of Africa. In 1967 he was awarded a Ph.D. for his thesis, "Political Development in Swaziland." Besides *People, Power, and Politics,* his major works include *Four African Political Systems* (1970), *The Theory and Practice of African Politics,* and *Strategy and Conflict: The Search for Historical Malleability.* He has been listed in *International Authors and Writers Who's Who, Contemporary Authors,* and the *International Scholars Directory.* Christian Potholm has taught at such institutions as Dartmouth, Vassar, and Tufts. He is currently a professor and chairman of the Department of Government and Legal Studies at Bowdoin College in Brunswick, Maine. He resides in South Harpswell with his wife and two children. He is also a registered Maine guide.

MARCIA A. WEIGLE is assistant professor in the Department of Government and Legal Studies at Bowdoin College, where she specializes in Soviet/Russian, East European, and comparative politics. She has also been a member of the Department of Government at Notre Dame. She received her Ph.D. from the University of Notre Dame in 1988 after completing her dissertation on "Technology and Society: Ideological Implications of Information and Computer Technologies in the Soviet Union." She has traveled extensively in Russia, Belarus, the Baltics, and Eastern Europe where she conducted interviews with leaders of new social movements in 1989. She has published several articles on civil society and political parties in Russia and Eastern Europe. In 1991–92 she was a National Fellow at the Hoover Institution, Stanford University, where she conducted archival research for a manuscript on the emergence of civil society in Gorbachev's Russia.